"This series promises to be spiritually and doctrinally info[...] solid biblical exegesis. The method and content of this work w[...] [...]pful to teachers of the faith at different levels and will provide a reliable guide to people seeking to deepen their knowledge and thereby nourish their faith. I strongly recommend the Catholic Commentary on Sacred Scripture."

—**Cormac Cardinal Murphy-O'Connor**, Archbishop of Westminster

"In preparing for the international Synod of Bishops on 'The Word of God in the Life and Mission of the Church,' Pope Benedict XVI reminded the Church that a prayerful study of the Scriptures is at the heart of the Church's renewal. The Catholic Commentary on Sacred Scripture promises to directly serve that purpose. Drawing on sound biblical scholarship, the commentaries present the reader with the rich harvest of that study, reflecting on the message of the biblical text and engaging the life of faith from a Catholic perspective."

—**Donald Senior, CP**, president, Catholic Theological Union

"A landmark achievement in theological interpretation of Scripture in and for the Church. Everything about this series is inviting and edifying, from the format, photos, background notes, and cross-references (to Scripture and the Catechism) to the rich exposition of the text, quotations from the Church's living tradition, and reflections for contemporary life. It is a wonderful gift to the Catholic Church and a model for the rest of us. Highly recommended for all!"

—**Michael J. Gorman**, St. Mary's Seminary and University, Baltimore

"The Catholic Commentary on Sacred Scripture is an ideal tool for living our faith more deeply. This extraordinary resource combines superior scholarship and a vivid, accessible style that will serve the interested layperson and the serious scholar equally well. It should be on the shelf of every committed Catholic believer. I highly recommend it."

—**Charles J. Chaput, OFM Cap**, Archbishop of Denver

"When the Scripture is read in the liturgy, it is heard as a living voice. But when expounded in a commentary, it is too often read as a document from the past. This fine series unites the ancient and the contemporary by offering insight into the biblical text—verse by verse—as well as spiritual application to the lives of Christians today."

—**Robert Louis Wilken**, University of Virginia

"This great project of a seventeen-volume commentary on the New Testament represents a much-needed approach, based on good scholarship but not overloaded with it. The frequent references to the *Catechism of the Catholic Church* help us to read Holy Scripture with a vivid sense of the living tradition of the Church."

—**Christoph Cardinal Schönborn**, Archbishop of Vienna

✝ Catholic Commentary on Sacred Scripture

SERIES EDITORS
Peter S. Williamson
Mary Healy

ASSOCIATE EDITOR
Kevin Perrotta

CONSULTING EDITORS
Scott Hahn, Franciscan University of Steubenville
†Daniel J. Harrington, SJ, Weston Jesuit School of Theology
William S. Kurz, SJ, Marquette University
†Francis Martin, Dominican House of Studies
Frank J. Matera, Catholic University of America
George Montague, SM, St. Mary's University
Terrence Prendergast, SJ, Archbishop of Ottawa

First Corinthians

George T. Montague, SM

Baker Academic
a division of Baker Publishing Group
Grand Rapids, Michigan

Published by Baker Academic
a division of Baker Publishing Group
P.O. Box 6287, Grand Rapids, MI 49516-6287
www.bakeracademic.com

Printed in the United States of America

Library of Congress Cataloging-in-Publication Data

Montague, George T.
    First Corinthians / George T. Montague.
       p.   cm. — (Catholic commentary on sacred Scripture)
    Includes bibliographical references and index.
    ISBN 978-0-8010-3632-3 (pbk.)
     1. Bible. N.T. Corinthians, 1st—Commentaries. I. Title
  BS2675.53.M66 2011
  227′32077—dc23
                                             2011023836

Imprimatur: Most Rev. Gustavo García-Siller, MSpS, Archbishop of San Antonio
Nihil obstat: Rev. John A. Leies, SM, STD, *Censor deputatus*

Contents

Illustrations

Editors' Preface

The Church has always venerated the divine Scriptures just as she venerates the body of the Lord. . . . All the preaching of the Church should be nourished and governed by Sacred Scripture. For in the sacred books, the Father who is in heaven meets His children with great love and speaks with them; and the power and goodness in the word of God is so great that it stands as the support and energy of the Church, the strength of faith for her sons and daughters, the food of the soul, a pure and perennial fountain of spiritual life.

Second Vatican Council, *Dei Verbum* 21

Were not our hearts burning [within us] while he spoke to us on the way and opened the scriptures to us?

Luke 24:32

The Catholic Commentary on Sacred Scripture aims to serve the ministry of the Word of God in the life and mission of the Church. Since Vatican Council II, there has been an increasing hunger among Catholics to study Scripture in depth and in a way that reveals its relationship to liturgy, evangelization, catechesis, theology, and personal and communal life. This series responds to that desire by providing accessible yet substantive commentary on each book of the New Testament, drawn from the best of contemporary biblical scholarship as well as the rich treasury of the Church's tradition. These volumes seek to offer scholarship illumined by faith, in the conviction that the ultimate aim of biblical interpretation is to discover what God has revealed and is still speaking through the sacred text. Central to our approach are the principles taught by Vatican II: first, the use of historical and literary methods to discern what the biblical authors intended to express; second, prayerful theological reflection to understand the sacred text "in accord with the same Spirit by whom it was written"—that is, in light of the content and unity of the whole Scripture, the living tradition of the Church, and the analogy of faith (*Dei Verbum* 12).

The Catholic Commentary on Sacred Scripture is written for those engaged in or training for pastoral ministry and others interested in studying Scripture to understand their faith more deeply, to nourish their spiritual life, or to share the good news with others. With this in mind, the authors focus on the meaning of the text for faith and life rather than on the technical questions that occupy scholars, and they explain the Bible in ordinary language that does not require translation for preaching and catechesis. Although this series is written from the perspective of Catholic faith, its authors draw on the interpretation of Protestant and Orthodox scholars and hope these volumes will serve Christians of other traditions as well.

A variety of features are designed to make the commentary as useful as possible. Each volume includes the biblical text of the New American Bible (NAB), the translation approved for liturgical use in the United States. In order to serve readers who use other translations, the most important differences between the NAB and other widely used translations (RSV, NRSV, JB, NJB, and NIV) are noted and explained. Each unit of the biblical text is followed by a list of references to relevant Scripture passages, Catechism sections, and uses in the Roman Lectionary. The exegesis that follows aims to explain in a clear and engaging way the meaning of the text in its original historical context as well as its perennial meaning for Christians. Reflection and Application sections help readers apply Scripture to Christian life today by responding to questions that the text raises, offering spiritual interpretations drawn from Christian tradition or providing suggestions for the use of the biblical text in catechesis, preaching, or other forms of pastoral ministry.

Interspersed throughout the commentary are Biblical Background sidebars that present historical, literary, or theological information, and Living Tradition sidebars that offer pertinent material from the postbiblical Christian tradition, including quotations from Church documents and from the writings of saints and Church Fathers. The Biblical Background sidebars are indicated by a photo of urns that were excavated in Jerusalem, signifying the importance of historical study in understanding the sacred text. The Living Tradition sidebars are indicated by an image of Eadwine, a twelfth-century monk and scribe, signifying the growth in the Church's understanding that comes by the grace of the Holy Spirit as believers study and ponder the word of God in their hearts (see *Dei Verbum* 8).

Maps and a Glossary are located in the back of each volume for easy reference. The glossary explains key terms from the biblical text as well as theological or exegetical terms, which are marked in the commentary with a cross (†). A list of Suggested Resources, an Index of Pastoral Topics, and an Index of Sidebars are included to enhance the usefulness of these volumes. Further resources, including questions for reflection or discussion, can be found at the series website, www.CatholicScriptureCommentary.com.

It is our desire and prayer that these volumes be of service so that more and more "the word of the Lord may speed forward and be glorified" (2 Thess 3:1) in the Church and throughout the world.

Peter S. Williamson
Mary Healy
Kevin Perrotta

Note to Readers

The New American Bible differs slightly from most English translations in its verse numbering of the Psalms and certain other parts of the Old Testament. For instance, Ps 51:4 in the NAB is Ps 51:2 in other translations; Mal 3:19 in the NAB is Mal 4:1 in other translations. Readers who use different translations are advised to keep this in mind when looking up Old Testament cross-references given in the commentary.

Abbreviations

†	indicates that the definition of a term appears in the Glossary
§	indicates section number in a church document
ABD	*Anchor Bible Dictionary*, edited by D. N. Freedman, 6 vols. (New York: Doubleday, 1992)
ACCS 7	Ancient Christian Commentary on Scripture: New Testament 7, *1–2 Corinthians*, edited by Gerald Bray (Downers Grove, IL: InterVarsity, 1999)
BECNT	Baker Exegetical Commentary on the New Testament
Catechism	*Catechism of the Catholic Church*, 2nd ed. (New York: Doubleday, 2003)
CCSL	Corpus Christianorum: Series Latina (Turnhout: Brepols, 1953–)
CCSS	Catholic Commentary on Sacred Scripture (Grand Rapids: Baker Academic, 2008–)
ET	English translation
FC	Fathers of the Church: A New Translation (Washington, DC: Catholic University of America Press, 1947–)
JB	Jerusalem Bible
JTS	*Journal of Theological Studies*
KJV	King James Version
Lectionary	*The Lectionary for Mass* (1998/2002 USA ed., Washington, DC: Confraternity of Christian Doctrine)
LXX	Septuagint (see Glossary)
NAB	New American Bible (Revised Edition, 2011)
NIV	New International Version
NJB	New Jerusalem Bible
NRSV	New Revised Standard Version
PG	Patrologia graeca, edited by J.-P. Migne, 162 vols. (Paris, 1857–86)
PL	Patrologia latina, edited by J.-P. Migne, 217 vols. (Paris, 1844–64)
RSV	Revised Standard Version
SC	Sources chrétiennes (Paris: Cerf, 1943–)

Books of the Old Testament

Gen	Genesis	Josh	Joshua	1 Kings	1 Kings
Exod	Exodus	Judg	Judges	2 Kings	2 Kings
Lev	Leviticus	Ruth	Ruth	1 Chron	1 Chronicles
Num	Numbers	1 Sam	1 Samuel	2 Chron	2 Chronicles
Deut	Deuteronomy	2 Sam	2 Samuel	Ezra	Ezra

Neh	Nehemiah	Wis	Wisdom	Obad	Obadiah
Tob	Tobit	Sir	Sirach	Jon	Jonah
Jdt	Judith	Isa	Isaiah	Mic	Micah
Esther	Esther	Jer	Jeremiah	Nah	Nahum
1 Macc	1 Maccabees	Lam	Lamentations	Hab	Habakkuk
2 Macc	2 Maccabees	Bar	Baruch	Zeph	Zephaniah
Job	Job	Ezek	Ezekiel	Hag	Haggai
Ps	Psalms	Dan	Daniel	Zech	Zechariah
Prov	Proverbs	Hosea	Hosea	Mal	Malachi
Eccles	Ecclesiastes	Joel	Joel		
Song	Song of Songs	Amos	Amos		

Books of the New Testament

Matt	Matthew	1 Tim	1 Timothy
Mark	Mark	2 Tim	2 Timothy
Luke	Luke	Titus	Titus
John	John	Philem	Philemon
Acts	Acts of the Apostles	Heb	Hebrews
Rom	Romans	James	James
1 Cor	1 Corinthians	1 Pet	1 Peter
2 Cor	2 Corinthians	2 Pet	2 Peter
Gal	Galatians	1 John	1 John
Eph	Ephesians	2 John	2 John
Phil	Philippians	3 John	3 John
Col	Colossians	Jude	Jude
1 Thess	1 Thessalonians	Rev	Revelation
2 Thess	2 Thessalonians		

Introduction to 1 Corinthians

Imagine that in a dream one night you find yourself in a parish where there are several drunks at Sunday Mass; where some members are claiming that there is no resurrection of the dead and that Jesus is not really present in the Eucharist; the parishioners are divided into cliques and factions; the president of the Altar Society is not talking to the head catechist; there is public unchallenged adultery and many marriages are in disarray; a group is dabbling in New Age spirituality; the liberals, the charismatics, and the traditionalists are all trumpeting their version of the church; and Masses are abbreviated for the sake of Sunday football—one of the many signs the parish has compromised heavily with the surrounding secular culture.

A nightmare? Not exactly. You were just experiencing a modern version of the community in Corinth. For this very reason, though, we have a lot to learn from these Corinthians, our enthusiastic but immature ancestors in the faith. The issues Paul faced with them are ones that, in one form or another, the church still struggles with today. Though Paul may not have thought so, we can be grateful that the Corinthians had so many problems because from the Apostle's treatment of them, we can glean wisdom in dealing with ours.

The Author

Readers who know of Paul's life will recall his dramatic conversion from being a strict Pharisee and persecutor of the Christians in Palestine to being apostle of the Gentiles; his struggle to get the authorities in Jerusalem to accept the noncircumcision of Gentiles; his mission to Asia Minor and then to Macedonia and Achaia (today's Greece); and his founding of churches at the

15

price of beatings, imprisonment, and shipwreck. They know also of his martyrdom in Rome under Nero. This is the Paul who planted the Christian faith in Corinth around AD 50 and later wrote this letter from Ephesus, addressing his recent converts.

That Paul is the author of this letter has never been in debate. There is some doubt whether 1 Cor 14:33b–36, forbidding women to speak in the assembly, is from a later hand, since it appears to conflict with what Paul says elsewhere about the active role of women in the community's worship (11:5, 13). If it is a later insertion, it was done quite early, since it appears in all the Greek manuscripts, though some have it at the end of the chapter. In any case, even with its difficulties, these verses were accepted into the canon of the inspired Scriptures, with their relevance to the Church today left to experts to propose and the Church to decide. Though called First Corinthians, this letter is not actually the first one Paul wrote, since he refers to an earlier letter in 5:9, which has been either lost or incorporated into what we know as 2 Corinthians.

Corinth: A Cauldron of Cultures

What kind of environment did Paul find when he first came to Corinth? Located at the end of a neck of land attaching the Peloponnese peninsula to mainland Greece and having a port facing east (Cenchreae) and another with access to the west (Lechaion), Corinth was geographically predestined to be a corridor of commerce and a potpourri of cultures (see map, p. 309).[1] Ships could be hauled across the isthmus on chariots on the four-mile paved railroad-like *diolkos*, whose grooves can still be seen on a surviving strip. This saved mariners sailing from Athens to the Adriatic 185 sea miles, and to Naples or Rome 95 sea miles.[2] It also spared them sailing around Cape Maleae, proverbially treacherous for seafaring. Ships with cargo too heavy for the diolkos would unload at one port and either haul the empty boat over the diolkos or load the cargo into a different boat at the other port. For various reasons, much cargo passed through Corinth itself. Being able to excise duty on the shipping, and celebrated for its shipbuilding and its production of bronze, ceramics, and textiles, Corinth was a wealthy city. It was also one of the ancient world's largest. Its six-mile encircling wall locked into the Acrocorinth, a rocky hill rising to a height of 1,887 feet like an impregnable fortress.

1. For a thorough introduction to Corinth from a historical and archaeological point of view, see Jerome Murphy-O'Connor, *St. Paul's Corinth* (Wilmington, DE: Michael Glazier, 2002).
2. Francis Ambrière, *Greece* (Paris: Hachette, 1964), 391.

Fig. 1. The Acrocorinth seen from the Temple of Octavia, a veiw Paul would have had in Corinth.

Corinth had a reputation of being one of the most sensual cities of the ancient world.[3] The temple of the Greek goddess Aphrodite stood atop the Acrocorinth, and prostitutes had their reserved seats in the theater. The term "Corinthian girl" meant prostitute, and *korinthiazesthai* ("to Corinthianize, live like a Corinthian") meant to fornicate or promote the trade. If Aelius Aristides' remark is true, "[Corinth] chains all men with pleasure and all men are equally inflamed by it . . . so that it is clearly the city of Aphrodite."[4] Still, it was an expensive venture to go there, as reflected by the proverb "Not every man has the means to go to Corinth," a saying known in Rome and applied by Strabo to the cost of fornication. The Isthmian games, held every two years, flourished nearby, and Paul may have arrived in time to witness them, or at least the crowds that flocked to the events. They would supply Paul with a wealth of athletic images, such as that of the imperishable crown awaiting Christians compared to the wreath of celery that the victors in the games received (1 Cor 9:25–27).

The culture of Corinth was such that it considered human lives—or at least certain human lives—expendable. Aside from abortion and the abandonment

3. According to the ancient geographer Strabo (*Geography* 8.6.20), in classical times a thousand "sacred prostitutes" practiced in Corinth. No other Greek cities had "sacred prostitutes," so it is unlikely that Corinth did, and scholars today even doubt whether prostitution was any more common there than in other large Greek cities. But there must have been some foundation for its renown as a center for fornication and sexual immorality.

4. *Orations* 46.25; quoted by Murphy-O'Connor, *St. Paul's Corinth*, 116.

Fig. 2. This lintel, inscribed "Synagogue of the Hebrews," marked the entrance to the synagogue that was the successor of the one in which Paul preached in Corinth.

of babies (dropped off in a temple or left exposed), which was common in Roman times, of all the Greek cities in Paul's day, Corinth was virtually alone in its enthusiastic adoption of the homicidal games of the Roman amphitheater. This may have been due to the Roman influence in its history. Originally a native Greek city, it was devastated by the Roman general Lucius Mummius in 146 BC, then was rebuilt in 44 BC by Julius Caesar, who established it as a colony of freed slaves. When Paul arrived between AD 49 and 51, he found a population of Romans, Greeks, and Near Easterners of every provenance, including a number of Jews—all attracted by the commercial advantages of the city. The city was composed of a small number of wealthy merchants, a large number of poor workmen, and a great number of slaves—an additional sign of the wealth of the city.

It was a city of gods and goddesses. Besides the Jewish synagogue, of which a later lintel has been discovered reading "Synagogue of the Hebrews," there were temples to Apollo, Asclepius, Athena, Demeter, Dionysus, Kore, Palaimon, Zeus, Cybele, Isis, Serapis, Melkart, Sisyphus, and Aphrodite. The cults of Jupiter Capitolinus and of Artemis, the Great Mother, flourished, as did certain of the mystery religions, that of Isis surely, and probably that of Dionysus.

Such was the Corinth that Paul entered in the middle of the first century AD. Fresh from disappointment at the failure of his approach to the "wise" of

---

Achaia

BIBLICAL
BACKGROUND

After years of conflict the Romans destroyed Corinth in 146 BC, but Julius Caesar rebuilt it in 44 BC as a Roman colony of freedmen, and in 27 BC Corinth was made the capital of the Roman province of Achaia, which included roughly the southern half of what is Greece today. It is indicative of its wealth that Corinth, not Athens, was the capital of Achaia.

Athens, who scoffed at Paul's preaching of the resurrection (Acts 17:16–34), Paul began proclaiming that the wisdom and power of God were to be found in the cross (1 Cor 1:23–24).[5] Despite initial difficulties, leading to his break from the synagogue, his ministry of a year and a half there flourished, so that in 2 Cor 1:1 he could greet not only the Christians in Corinth but also "all the holy ones throughout Achaia."[6] From here he wrote his First Letter to the Thessalonians and possibly the second.[7]

The Writing of 1 Corinthians

Paul certainly wrote this letter from Ephesus (1 Cor 16:8). According to Acts, at the end of his initial year-and-a-half ministry in Corinth, Paul sailed for Ephesus, where he stayed only a brief time before moving on to Caesarea, Jerusalem, and then via Antioch to his third missionary journey through Asia Minor (Acts 18:11, 22–23). When in the course of this third journey he arrived again at Ephesus, Apollos, an eloquent preacher from Alexandria who had ministered in Ephesus, had already been sent by that community to Corinth. There Apollos "gave great assistance" to the faithful (Acts 18:24–28), watering where Paul had planted (1 Cor 3:6). During this time, AD 53–54, two events prompted Paul to write our 1 Corinthians. First, a report arrived from "Chloe's people" (1 Cor 1:11) that the community was splitting into factions, each claiming allegiance to

---

5. I do not mean to imply here or elsewhere that Paul did not also preach the resurrection when he began in Corinth. He had obviously done so in Thessalonica (1 Thess 1:10), and 1 Corinthians will conclude with a long discussion about the resurrection. It was simply a matter of which dimension of the †paschal mystery, in his judgment, needed to be stressed at the beginning with the Corinthians, as he does at the beginning of the letter.

6. "By the time of Nero's accession [AD 54], Christianity had a permanent hold in Achaia, already boasting at least twenty churches" (J. A. Pattengale, "Achaia," ABD 1:53).

7. Scholars question whether 2 Thessalonians was authored by Paul or a later disciple.

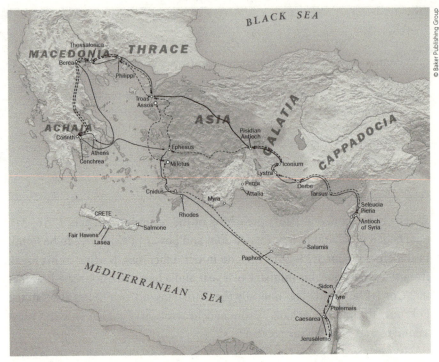

Fig. 3. Paul's missionary journey to Corinth.

one or another minister. The report, or others like it, told of a number of other disorders as well, such as one might expect from persons freshly converted out of paganism. Second, in a prior letter (see 5:9) Paul had warned the faithful, among other things, to avoid "fornication," that is, falling back into pagan sexual practices. The community now responded with a series of doctrinal and moral questions in a letter carried to Paul most probably by Stephanas, Fortunatus, and Achaicus, leaders in the community (16:17).

Structure and Literary Features

Although Paul treats many topics in this letter, he has organized his material in a very clear manner, which makes it easy to follow his thought. Aside from the address at the beginning and the lengthy conclusion in chapter 16, the letter falls into four major parts, as follows:

    I. Address (1:1–9)
    II. Disorders in the Community (1:10–6:20)
       A. Divisions over Personalities (1:10–4:21)
       B. Moral Disorders (5:1–6:20)

Writing as Script

Paul follows the conventions of letter writing in his day. But it is unlikely that he himself *wrote* any of his letters. His letters to the churches were oral both at their origin in dictation and at the point of delivery by a public reading. In many cases, as in Paul's discourse on the cross as power and wisdom (1 Cor 1:18–2:5), we can almost hear him preaching. And that is what he intends his listeners (not readers!) to hear as a single reader proclaims the message to the community to which the letter is addressed. It was ultimately not the written letter that represented Paul but the living voice of his representative. That is why even today Paul's Letters are suited for proclamation at the liturgy. The written word is just a script for proclamation.

Our literate culture has not prepared us to be good listeners. Why should we bother to pay close attention to an oral proclamation if we can read it in our missalette or our Bible? If we forget what the reading was about, we can easily read it later. Not so for the people in Paul's day. The only missalette they had was in their head. And that is where they recorded what they heard. Our literate culture has also taught us to lose our memories. A young technocrat next to me on a flight astounded me when he said: "I don't have to remember anything. Anything I want to know or remember is right here." He pointed to the latest cybertoy in his hand. This reliance on "where we can find it" outside ourselves makes moderns suspect that the words of Jesus in the Gospels were crafted by his followers much later, for who could remember all that he said? The suspicion is ill-founded. Our spiritual ancestors had recorders in their heads and could play them at will![8]

---

8. I lived in an oral culture in Nepal, and often I would give our cook a litany of items he should bring from the grocery. He never took notes, but he remembered everything. I would not dare go to the

Why is this important for us who will be reading the text of Paul? Instead of zipping through the text (this applies especially to those of us who took speed-reading lessons), we need to re-create the sound either by reading it aloud or at least imagining someone proclaiming Paul's preached letter to his addressees. And probably we need to make extra effort when listening to his word being proclaimed in the liturgy.

Literary Techniques

Whether we are listening or reading, it helps to be attentive to some of the literary techniques Paul uses. He uses *wordplays*, as when he plays on the difference between the "wisdom of word" (empty †rhetoric) and the "word of the cross," and on human wisdom and power versus God's foolishness and weakness, which is the true wisdom and power (1 Cor 1:17–25). Or the play on "all things are for me but not all things help me" (my rendering of the Greek wordplay in 6:12, which is not obvious in the NAB). Or between "using" and "using up" in 7:31. Or the double meaning of "followed them" in 10:4. Or the plays on the words "discerning" and "judging," both forms of the Greek *krinō*, in 11:31–33.

Another technique Paul uses is the †*diatribe*, a common rhetorical device in the ancient world in which one argues with an imaginary opponent, as Paul does in 15:36–37 and elsewhere in his letters. You will also encounter *lists of vices* (5:10–11; 6:9–10) and *virtues* (13:1–13; see also 2 Cor 6:6–7; Eph 6:14–17; Col 3:12–14); in Paul sometimes one list immediately follows another (Gal 5:19–23). Paul also cites *proverbs* or wisdom sayings, either his own or ones borrowed from the biblical or Gentile culture of his day: "A little yeast leavens all the dough" (5:6; Gal 5:9). "Bad company corrupts good morals" (1 Cor 15:33). And he knows the power of *metaphor*: "You are God's field, God's building" (3:9). "Your body is a temple of the holy Spirit" (6:19).

Paul delights in asking his listeners *rhetorical questions*: "Do you not know that you are the temple of God, and that the Spirit of God dwells in you?" (3:16). "Do you not know that the holy ones will judge the world?" (6:2). "Do you not know that we will judge angels? Then why not everyday matters?" (6:3). "Can it be that there is not one among you wise enough to be able to settle a case between brothers?" (6:5). "Do you not know that the unjust will not inherit the kingdom of God?" (6:9). "Do you not know that your bodies are members

---

grocery without the list in my pocket. For a concrete example of how memory works in an oral culture, see Kenneth E. Bailey, "Informal Controlled Oral Tradition and the Synoptic Gospels," *Themelios* 20, no. 2 (1995): 4–11.

of Christ? Shall I then take Christ's members and make them the members of a prostitute?" (6:15; see also 6:16, 19; 7:16; 14:6–9, 16). The rhetorical question is both a compliment (the speaker presumes the hearer knows) and a challenge (but you seem to have forgotten).

Early in 1 Corinthians, Paul makes it clear that rhetoric for rhetoric's sake is foolishness, but he does not hesitate to use rhetoric to proclaim Christ, whose message deserves the best in beauty and power.

Theological Themes

From the reports and the questions he received, Paul sensed how serious the situation in Corinth was. Aside from the factions, many were appealing to their new "knowledge" that idols are nothing to justify continuing their pagan practice of sacrificial meals (see commentary on 1 Cor 8); an incestuous man was being welcomed publicly in the community; Christians were taking fellow Christians to pagan lawcourts; sexual immorality was being tolerated in the name of the freedom of the gospel; and a spirit of divisiveness was appearing even in the celebration of the Eucharist, where different groups were eating their meals apart, some even getting drunk while the poorer were left hungry. Even their prayer meetings, for all their enthusiasm, were becoming chaotic. Some of the questions posed by the community were less dramatic: what is the value of marriage, given the imminence of the Lord's return? Do our bodies really share in eternal life, and if so, how?

The community's many problems anticipate many of the throes the Church goes through today, and Paul's responses sowed the seeds of a rich theological development in such areas as the centrality of the cross and the resurrection; the role of the Holy Spirit in revealing the †mystery of Christ, in sanctifying the faithful, and in endowing them with †charisms; baptism and the Eucharist; the Church as the body of Christ and temple of the Holy Spirit; tradition; Christian liberty; marriage; virginity; and †conscience and moral responsibility. No other letter touches on so many different topics that have relevance to the Church today.

The problems dogging the community were not only internal. Also, the Corinthians' relation with Paul was rocky, especially when the Apostle was not around. From 2 Corinthians we can gather that among the members were some who questioned his authority, especially after they had experienced the later ministry of Apollos and Peter, and perhaps of others whom Paul dubs "super-apostles." Part of the difficulty was a negligence in dealing with errant members, and thus there was either inadequate authority in the community or opposition to existing authority. The Letters of Paul had great importance for establishing order and harmony in this rowdy community. Reconciliation eventually won out—a sign of hope that in our Church today it can happen as well.

1 Corinthians: Part of a Whole

In one sense the Bible is a library. There are seventy-three books in the Catholic canon, forty-six of the Old Testament and twenty-seven of the New. Just as in libraries today, some books belong to one literary type, some to another. The collection was compiled over hundreds of years and reflects different historical situations. Often the author or authors of one book did not personally know the author or authors of another. Nevertheless, Christians firmly believe that each book was inspired by the Holy Spirit. And that means that no one book can claim to be complete without the others, and thus each book is like an instrument in a great symphony orchestra. Paul's collection is like a set of instruments within the larger orchestra. Hence, we will look first at the place of 1 Corinthians among Paul's Letters, and then at where these fit in the whole of the canon.

1 Corinthians within Paul's Letters

For our purposes we will consider all the letters traditionally attributed to Paul (excluding Hebrews) as the "Pauline corpus," even though scholars debate whether some of the letters or parts of the letters were the work of his disciples. As we have noted above, in that collection 1 Corinthians makes a major contribution in theological themes. But for more information on the tension between Paul and the Corinthian community, we would turn to 2 Corinthians, which also tells us many details about Paul's apostolic sufferings (11:23–33) and his mystical experience (12:1–5) that we would not know otherwise. First Corinthians does not take up the question of the role of faith in justification, which is the major concern of Galatians and Romans. For Martin Luther, this was the most important theme of the whole Bible, and he believed that anything that gave a qualification to that doctrine, as James does in speaking about the importance of works, should not really be in the canon. But that was not and is not the Catholic view. Romans also has a long and beautiful chapter (8) on the Holy Spirit, which the Fathers of the Church considered the heart of the letter. We also find in Romans three chapters (9–11) on the question of the role of the Jews in God's plan of salvation. First and Second Thessalonians are concerned primarily with the second coming of Christ, which has only a minor role in 1 Corinthians. Philippians is a cordial letter containing the famous hymn about Christ's not claiming divine privileges but emptying himself, taking on "the form of a slave," dying on the cross, and being raised to glory by the Father (Phil 2:5–11). A similar hymn in Col 1:15–20 portrays Christ's role in creation itself and in the new creation of the resurrection. Ephesians is a lengthy, hymnlike letter extolling the wonder of the Church in God's plan. The latter two letters, called †Captivity Epistles, build on Paul's teaching on the Church as the body of Christ, which we find in 1 Corinthians. Ephesians also fills out Paul's sketch on marriage in 1 Cor 7 by showing how it is a symbol of Christ's union with the Church. The other letters harmonize with or develop themes introduced in our letter. But there are passages both within 1 Corinthians and in Paul's other letters that are in tension with other Pauline passages, as we will see in 1 Cor 11:5, 13 and 14:34–35, about women speaking in the assembly. Hence the value of a commentary to explain how these differences can be reconciled.

First and Second Timothy and Titus, although possibly penned by a disciple of Paul in later circumstances, belong to the Pauline canon, for they apply his thought to pastoral situations via the form of address to individual shepherds appointed by Paul. They are important for showing how the ministry of Paul that we see in 1 Corinthians will be carried on after his death—what we call the apostolic succession, a key to what we declare in the creed: "I believe in one, holy, Catholic, and *apostolic* Church."

The Pauline Canon within the Wider Canon

Christians read Paul in the light of the whole biblical canon, from Genesis through Revelation. He is a major contributor, for only one New Testament author (Luke) writes at greater length. His is also the first writing we have about Jesus, since 1 Thessalonians probably predates the Gospel of Mark by more than fifteen years. Yet already at that time Paul has a deep theological understanding of the gospel message. For example, the triad of faith, hope, and love, which later tradition calls the theological virtues, are already firmly established in his consciousness. Yet his reflections are in the form of letters, not narratives about Jesus, as the Gospels are. So although Paul's Letters precede in time, the Gospels precede in honor, not only because they tell us what happened before Paul, but also because they tell the story of the Person who so fascinated Paul and inspired his life and ministry. Rightly so, then, are they placed before the Pauline Letters in the canon.

The Greek Old Testament, the †Septuagint, was Paul's Bible, and we cannot understand the Apostle or his writing apart from it. He quotes from it frequently. Among other New Testament writings, as mentioned above, the Letter of James contextualizes Paul's teaching on justification by faith, insisting that faith must be expressed in works. There is an element of †apocalyptic end-time imagery in Paul (1 Thess 4:15–18) but not to the extent to which it is developed in the book of Revelation or in the Gospels (Matt 24:1–31; Mark 13:1–27; Luke 21:5–28). The Acts of the Apostles tells us of events in Paul's life that are not mentioned in his letters, although there is some overlap here and there.

1 Corinthians for Today

Since you will read this letter through the lens of your own life experience, you will probably see applications that others might not. Sometimes Paul's statements will confirm and console you; at other times they challenge you to think outside the box of your own experience. Such is the richness of God's Word. The discussion questions available online will stimulate your reflection and give you the delight of discovering treasures you never dreamed were there. In the commentary I frequently offer a "Reflection and Application" section as one way to draw out the significance of the passage for our lives today, but this is only to stimulate your own reflection on the passage.

Here is why I find 1 Corinthians "a lamp for my feet, a light for my path" (Ps 119:105). The opening chapters tell me that my church, like that of the Corinthians, is a gathering of saints and sinners, people who are consecrated by the blood of Christ but desecrated by self-centered concerns that hinder the building of a loving, unified community: cliques and turf wars, personal preferences becoming demands, just like these folks in Corinth. I repent of my sins against the unity of the Church. If we would only keep our eyes on the cross, what a difference that would make (1 Cor 1). Maybe when we come to meetings we would fall on our knees and seek God's wisdom first before we promote our own agenda. For there is a spiritual wisdom available to those who are spiritually mature (chap. 2).

But no, we find fault with our priest or †minister, not looking beyond them to see Christ, who has chosen to come to us in the flesh of human, and sometimes all-too-human, instruments. That is part of the sacramental nature, the visible, flesh-and-blood nature, of the Church (chaps. 3–4). And yes, there are scandals in the Church, sometimes even in the clergy. We have heroines like Mother Teresa of Calcutta but also Catholic politicians who don't defend the life of the unborn. Do I belong to this Church? Indeed I do, because the frontier between good and evil passes through my heart too. And if some say I'm a hypocrite, I'll say yes, but nowhere else could I become a saint, and I'm trying (chap. 5). I'm challenged to think of my body and the bodies of everyone I meet not as food for lust but as members of Christ's own body, each one a temple of the Holy Spirit. I try to do that with my students, especially those who in their dress mistake the classroom for a swimming pool (chap. 6).

As a priest I daily witness the disastrous effects of the sexual revolution and pornography on family life, and I long for the day when Paul's wisdom on family life might rule the day. I rejoice that more and more young men and women like myself (no longer young) are finding how life-receiving and life-giving is the gift of oneself in celibate consecration to the Lord (chap. 7). Our idols today are not those of Corinth but the worldly values, the "sensual lust, enticement for the eyes, and a pretentious life" (1 John 2:16) that invite me to compromise my commitment to Jesus and to insist on my rights even when doing so would hurt others. I hope one day to have Paul's thirst for the unity of the Church and the common good of all in the community, "not seeking my own benefit but that of the many, that they may be saved" (10:33; chaps. 8–10).

Like the Israelites in the desert and the Christians in Corinth, I take too much for granted the incredible gifts the Lord has given, especially my baptism, the Eucharist, and the gift of the Holy Spirit (10:1–5), and I repent of the times I have celebrated Mass distractedly or forgotten that the Eucharist means also embracing those who have hurt me and seeking reconciliation (chap. 11). And what about those spiritual gifts, the charisms? They call me out of my cocoon to praise God and to become a channel of his love to others. I praise God that I have received an outpouring of the Holy Spirit—but I leak and need constant renewal. Above all I need God's love to serve others with the gifts he has given me (chaps. 12–14). Finally, Paul's masterful treatment of the resurrection of Jesus as a guarantee of my own and that of my loved ones fills me with assurance and joy. It whets my appetite for the not-yet fulfillment and makes me want to live every day in the power of the Holy Spirit (chap. 15).

Such are some of the treasurers I find in 1 Corinthians. There are many more for you to find.

Living Tradition

This commentary is built on the assumption, made clear in Vatican II's *Dei Verbum* (*Constitution on Divine Revelation*), that Scripture is the consigning to writing of sacred tradition, which, while being unique and unrepeatable in the apostolic writings, continues into our day through the teachings of the Fathers and Doctors of the Church, the liturgy, the lives of the saints, and the Church's magisterium. With that in mind, I make frequent references to that "living tradition" both within the commentary and in sidebars. In a concise phrase *Dei Verbum* says, *Traditio proficit, . . . crescit perceptio*: "Tradition develops, . . . insight grows" (§8). I believe this commentary, like others in the Catholic Commentary on Sacred Scripture, is immensely enriched by our two thousand years of development and insight.[9]

---

9. The frequent quotations from St. John Chrysostom are taken from the *Saint Chrysostom: Homilies on the Epistles of Paul to the Corinthians*, vol. 12 of *Nicene and Post-Nicene Fathers*, First Series, ed. Philip Schaff (1889; repr., Grand Rapids: Eerdmans, 1979), checked against the Greek and occasionally revised into more contemporary English style; http://www.newadvent.org/fathers/2201.htm.

Cliques and the Cross

1 Corinthians 1

Once Paul has greeted his readers and given the customary prayer of thanksgiving for the blessings they have received, he plunges immediately into the first major problem he has to address, that of factions in the community. It leads him to a lyrical preaching of the cross (1:17–2:5), one of the most powerful passages of the entire New Testament.

Address and Greeting (1:1–3)

¹**Paul, called to be an apostle of Christ Jesus by the will of God, and Sosthenes our brother, ²to the church of God that is in Corinth, to you who have been sanctified in Christ Jesus, called to be holy, with all those everywhere who call upon the name of our Lord Jesus Christ, their Lord and ours. ³Grace to you and peace from God our Father and the Lord Jesus Christ.**

OT: Ps 99:6; Joel 3:5
NT: Acts 2:21; 9:14; 18:1–21; Rom 1:1; 1 Cor 10:32
Catechism: all called to holiness, 542–43, 2013–14; holiness of the Church, 825; union with Christ, 1694
Lectionary: Votive Mass of the Most Holy Name of Jesus

Paul follows the conventions of Greek letter writing by beginning his letter with an address, a greeting, and a thanksgiving. He adroitly uses each part of this template to hint at three of the major concerns of the letter—holiness, unity, and the †charisms. But first he titles himself **apostle of Christ Jesus**, thus emphasizing the authority with which he writes. (Contrast 1 and 2 Thessalonians, where he uses no title at all, and Phil 1:1, where he calls himself "servant.") Although Paul will use this authority when necessary (as in the case of the incestuous man in 1 Cor 5:13), he will prefer to leave it implicit, while he exhorts his readers by reminding them of the great graces of their calling. In fact he himself is apostle only because he was **called** by Christ and thus sent not by his own eagerness or choice but **by the will of God**. "Apostle" means one who is sent, like an ambassador authorized to speak for the sender. Although the title is used occasionally for other †ministers (Acts 14:14; Rom 16:7), in applying it to himself Paul is equating his authority with that of the Twelve, who not only were chosen by Christ but also saw the risen Lord and thus were doubly equipped to be his witnesses ("Am I not an apostle? Have I not seen Jesus our Lord?" 1 Cor 9:1).

Paul calls **Sosthenes**, the cosender of the letter, **brother**, the term early Christians used for one another and Paul also used for his collaborators (2 Cor 2:13). Early Christians understood themselves to be an extended family, after the example of Jesus, who called his disciples his brothers, sisters, and even mother (Matt 12:49–50). Sosthenes is possibly the same one mentioned in Acts 18:17 as a leader of the synagogue in Corinth whom other Jews roughed up in front of the governor Gallio. Why they beat Sosthenes instead of Paul is not clear. Perhaps he had angered them by converting to the new faith proclaimed by Paul or by merely showing himself sympathetic to him. Local supporters of an unpopular outsider are often more vulnerable than the outsider himself, because they show a threatening crack in the domestic defense against foreign invasion.

In mentioning a cosender of the letter, Paul follows the practice of other letters.[1] Paul is not a Lone Ranger but a team player.

2   The addressee is not an individual but a community, **the church of God . . . in Corinth**. Though the letter was apparently delivered by Timothy (1 Cor 4:17), who probably read it to the community, offering his own comments to explain when necessary, the absence of a leader-addressee indicates that Paul still feels so close to the community he founded that he can address them directly, though we may assume there were local leaders (16:15–16; 1 Thess 5:12–13). He is himself the authority without equal but also one who has an unparalleled affection for his spiritual children (1 Cor 4:15). By this time, if the number of converts has grown beyond the capacity of one house, which is likely, there would be more than one house church in Corinth (1:11), each no doubt having

---

1. As in 2 Cor 1:1; Phil 1:1; Col 1:1; 1 Thess 1:1; 2 Thess 1:1; Philem 1.

All Are Called

The universal call to holiness is stressed by the Second Vatican Council: "All the faithful, whatever their condition or state, are called by the Lord, each in his own way, to that perfect holiness whereby the Father himself is perfect" (*Lumen Gentium* [*Dogmatic Constitution on the Church*], §11). "If therefore everyone in the Church does not proceed by the same path, nevertheless all are called to sanctity and have received an equal privilege of faith through the justice of God (cf. 2 Pet 1:1)" (§32).

some kind of coordinator. Yet it is significant that he does not speak of churches in the plural but only of a singular church in Corinth—a precursor of dioceses with multiple parishes. If "church" here refers to the sum of house churches, it is easy to see how it could be applied to the one Church universal, as it so clearly is in the letter to the Ephesians. Thus in the desert narrative of the Old Testament, the "assembly of the Lord" includes all the tribes gathered as one. There the Israelites were the people the Lord called out of Egypt to be his own. So God has called the Christians out of the world to a saving union with Christ (1 Cor 1:9). Calling the community the "church of God" links the Corinthian church with the Jewish Christian churches of God in Judea (1 Thess 2:14), as well as those of Galatia, Asia, and Macedonia. Already in this title "church," Paul is inviting them to think beyond their personal interests.

Paul then strikes a major chord when he says that they have been **sanctified in Christ Jesus, called to be holy**. Sanctified means consecrated: set apart for a divine purpose, as a chalice or church might be consecrated today. Though remaining in the world, Christians do not belong to the world (John 15:19; 17:14). We are saints, not in the sense of being consummately holy as are those heroes of holiness who are canonized today. Rather, the radical consecration is that of our baptism. We belong to Jesus Christ. This is the union that sanctifies us, and it has its source in God's call, a gratuitous, unmerited act of love on God's part. The Greek translated "sanctified . . . called to be holy" can also mean "saints because called" by the Lord. In Paul's mind the radical consecration, which he considers a real change in being, calls for a corresponding behavior. "Action follows being," as the philosophers would say. At this point Paul stresses the gift and dignity of the Christian state, which would hopefully evoke gratitude in the Corinthians and provide the basis for Paul's later specific ethical challenges. Chrysostom points out that the idea of "call" is central to this address, signifying that the gospel was not Paul's idea but came from God, as did the call of the Corinthians, who in turn "call" on the Lord.[2]

Paul invites his listeners (the letter would be read publicly) to think beyond their borders. They are part of a much larger community of believers **everywhere who call upon the name of our Lord Jesus Christ, their Lord and ours**. To call upon the divine name is a frequent Old Testament expression for adoring God (Ps 99:6; Joel 3:5). Used here with reference to Christ, it means that divine honor is given him. Thus today those who call on the name of Christ would not include those who deny his divinity, such as Jehovah's Witnesses and Muslims, who reverence him only as a prophet. As the invoking of the name of Yahweh expressed the unity of the people in the Old Testament, so does the name of Christ express the unity of Christians wherever they are. Paul is laying the groundwork for his later condemnation of the maverick attitudes and behaviors of the Corinthians. The word of God did not originate with them; there are many others whom it has already reached (1 Cor 14:36). The customs of the other churches create a law of sorts (11:16).

3   The greeting is in the form of a blessing. Paul takes the customary Greek greeting *chara* or *chaire* ("joy, rejoice") and tweaks it into *charis*, **grace**. This word recalls God's merciful love shown in Jesus Christ and bestowed on Christians through the Holy Spirit. **Peace** is the customary Jewish greeting *shalom*, meaning the fullness of life, well-being, and prosperity. In Paul it means the interior gift that flows from the indwelling Spirit and from charity (Gal 5:22), the spirit of harmony and well-being in the soul reconciled with the Father in the Son. In this initial blessing, Paul combines a tweaked Gentile greeting with a Jewish one, fitting the ethnic mix of the community.

Reflection and Application (1:1–3)

The very beginning of this letter jolts us into an awareness of who we really are. We are a consecrated people. We are set apart by a call from God himself to be holy: consecrated to God and his service. But this is not a private Jesus-and-me arrangement. We are part of a holy people, a holy community, linked with every Christian community throughout the world—from Boston to Bangkok, from London to Lusaka, from San Francisco to Samoa. We are joined with people of every language and every color in the world. And we belong to the community of the past and the future and what we today call the communion of saints. One of the most powerful experiences I have had is attending an

2. Chrysostom, *Homilies on 1 Corinthians* 1.1.

international conference where brothers and sisters of dozens of languages united in one great tide of worship and praise. That is the real meaning of "Catholic": universal. The Second Vatican Council wrestled with the tension between honoring local cultures in the liturgy, on the one hand, and the need for basic uniformity, on the other, so that I can know that the Eucharist I celebrate in San Antonio is the same as what is being celebrated in Africa. Note how in these three opening verses we find the four marks of the Church as one, holy, Catholic, and apostolic (Catechism, 811–70).

Most Catholics still think today of "saints" as those who have either been canonized or are worthy of canonization, those separated from the rest of us sinners by their exalted holiness. Unfortunately, a by-product of such a conception is the all-too-easy, albeit unconscious, release of any serious expectation of our becoming really holy. Many laypeople tend to think of holiness as the call of priests or the religious but not the call of the laity. Such is not the case. "All Christians in any state or walk of life are called to the fullness of Christian life and to the perfection of charity" (*Lumen Gentium*, 40; see also Catechism, 2013–14).

In these first three verses we have also met Paul's "become what you are" theology, which will run through the entire letter. Holiness is not so much a goal we are called to reach as it is a consecration we are called to live out.

Thanksgiving (1:4–9)

---

⁴**I give thanks to my God always on your account for the grace of God bestowed on you in Christ Jesus, ⁵that in him you were enriched in every way, with all discourse and all knowledge, ⁶as the testimony to Christ was confirmed among you, ⁷so that you are not lacking in any spiritual gift as you wait for the revelation of our Lord Jesus Christ. ⁸He will keep you firm to the end, irreproachable on the day of our Lord Jesus [Christ]. ⁹God is faithful, and by him you were called to fellowship with his Son, Jesus Christ our Lord.**

NT: Rom 1:8; 12:6; 1 Cor 12:1–14:40; Phil 1:3–4, 6; 3:20–21
Catechism: prayer of thanksgiving, 2637–38; Church as communion, 787–96, 959
Lectionary: First Sunday of Advent (Year B); Votive Mass of Thanksgiving

The typical format of Greek letters calls for a thanksgiving at this point, but for Paul this is far from a formality. No one more than Paul is aware of the **grace of God** in his own life and in that of his communities (the word "grace" appears eighty-nine times in the Pauline Letters, seven times in 1 Corinthians). Though

Greek letter writers would often thank the gods for keeping the addressee in good health or for some other material boon, Paul always thanks God for some spiritual blessing experienced by his readers, or, in the case of 1 Tim 1:12–17, for the grace of his own conversion. In an earlier letter to the Thessalonians, he thanked God for their faith, love, and hope (1 Thess 1:3). But in the case of the Corinthians, Paul makes no reference to their faith and love, and hope is only implied in their looking forward to the coming of Christ. Why is this? No doubt because Paul finds their faith poorly formed and their love singularly deficient, as we will see in the rest of the letter. Nevertheless, he thanks God for the charismatic graces, which the Corinthians so highly prize, and thus Paul hopes to prepare their hearts to hear what else he will have to say.

5   They have been **enriched in every way**. The image of riches or being enriched by the grace of God is a favorite of Paul, especially in Romans and the †Captivity Epistles.[3] **With all discourse**, or "in all your speaking" (NIV), appropriately translates the literal Greek "in every word," since the Corinthians' assemblies are quite noisy, with some not waiting to speak until others have finished (14:29–33). What kinds of speech would be covered by this generality? Certainly words of praise, thanksgiving, adoration as an upward movement toward God, but especially speech *from* God, such as prophecy or preaching or **knowledge**. The latter apparently refers to an insight into the †mystery of Christ (13:2), perhaps also to the knowledge that some of them claim about idols (8:1–6). Inasmuch as the knowledge here is a prophetic gift, it might include a fact known only by a direct illumination by the Holy Spirit (like Jesus' knowing that the Samaritan woman has had five husbands; John 4:18).[4] Paul here assesses these gifts positively, though later he will say that without love they mean nothing (13:1–13) and "knowledge puffs up, but love builds up" (8:1 NRSV).

6–7   The reason for Paul's positive assessment is given in verse 6. These gifts show that **the testimony to Christ was confirmed among you**. The "testimony *of* Christ" (Greek) has at least two levels of meaning. At a foundational level it refers to the testimony that Jesus gave to God's love by dying on the cross and rising from the dead (the Greek word for "testimony" here is *martyrion*, from which our word "martyr" is derived). But here it also refers more specifically to the "testimony *to* Christ" that Paul bore in his initial preaching of that message to the Corinthians, which was followed by confirming signs (1 Cor 2:4; Mark

---

3. See Rom 2:4; 9:23; 11:33; Eph 1:7, 18; 2:7; 3:8, 16; Col 1:27; 2:2.

4. See also Mark 11:2; 14:13; John 1:48. Examples of this kind of charismatic knowledge are frequent in the Old Testament: Nathan knows about David's sin (2 Sam 12:1–12); Samuel knows that Saul's asses have been found and tells Saul what will happen to him on his journey (1 Sam 10:2–6); Daniel knows and relates King Nebuchadnezzar's dream (Dan 2:28–35).

16:17–20; Gal 3:1–5). The outburst of praise and inspired speech, and probably other signs that followed their conversion and acceptance of Christ, was a surprising visitation of the Holy Spirit, which empowered them in ways they never before experienced. Thus they **are not lacking in any spiritual gift**. The two references to the abundance of gifts (vv. 5 and 7) frame the "testimony of Christ" in verse 6, showing the important relation between the gifts and faith in the message about Jesus Christ. That relation was twofold: they experienced the gifts because they believed in the message, and the gifts gave visible manifestation of the nature of the message—amazing new life. The word "gift" here is *charisma*, referring not to the grace that saves but to the †charisms. (The NAB adds the word "spiritual" in the translation, lest the reader think merely of the Corinthians' natural talents.) After capturing the goodwill of his readers, Paul will soon show how the abundance of these gifts contrasts sharply with the absence of charity in the community. By adding **as you wait for the revelation of our Lord Jesus Christ**, Paul subtly hints that the Corinthians have not arrived at their perfection. The abundance of spiritual gifts in the community does not mean that the day of the Lord is already here (2 Thess 2:2)—a kind of excessively realized †eschatology. On the contrary, the consummation of the kingdom is still to come, and there is much to be done for their own spiritual growth in the meantime. But it will be more the work of the Lord than their own efforts.

He will keep you firm to the end, irreproachable on the day of our Lord Jesus [Christ]. The translation "He will keep you firm" could suggest that the grace is merely one of perseverance, but the Greek verb can also be translated, "He will strengthen you," which suggests that they have weaknesses that the risen Lord will progressively replace with his strength. Paul's positive belief in this happy outcome rests in the fact that **God is faithful**, a belief Paul already held as a Jew and mentions elsewhere (10:13; 1 Thess 5:24; 2 Thess 3:3). The concluding mention of "God" forms a frame with the earlier mention in verse 4, providing an †inclusio typical of Jewish †rhetorical style.

8–9

Just as Paul's mission was based on a call given him by God (1:1), so too the new state of Christians is due to the initiating grace of God, by whom **you were called to fellowship with his Son, Jesus Christ our Lord**. It is striking that in these six verses (vv. 4–9) Jesus is mentioned five times. Obviously it is the Person of Jesus who dominates every consideration of Paul. "Fellowship" is the Greek *koinōnia*, which is sometimes rendered as "union," "communion," or "community." The climax of Paul's thanksgiving is that, through Paul's ministry and their faith, God has called the Christians in Corinth to be one with his Son, which gives them the right to be called God's sons and daughters. At the same time *koinōnia* evokes community with other brothers and sisters, so that it has a horizontal as well as a vertical dimension. Thus the spiritual gifts that so excite the Corinthians derive from their union with Jesus Christ and are ordered to building the community made by faith in him, thus demanding a sensitivity to the common good. In the rest of the letter Paul will draw these consequences. But in this thanksgiving Paul is content to show that they all flow from the unspeakable grace and the holy state with which, through no merit of their own, the Corinthians have been gifted.

Reflection and Application (1:4–9)

Before praying for needs, whether our own or those of others, here we learn from Paul to begin with thanksgiving for gifts that we have already received, whether these be natural gifts or gifts of grace. What do we think of a friend who comes to us only when he or she wants something? Perhaps if we spent as much time thanking God as we do asking for things, we might receive what we ask for more readily! Petitions, Paul tells the Philippians (4:6), should be presented with thanksgiving. It is so easy to get caught up in our anxieties and needs that we pay scant attention to what God has already done for us, and even less to who God is in himself.

Factions in the Community (1:10–17)

¹⁰I urge you, brothers, in the name of our Lord Jesus Christ, that all of you agree in what you say, and that there be no divisions among you, but that you be united in the same mind and in the same purpose. ¹¹For it has been reported to me about you, my brothers, by Chloe's people, that there are rivalries among you. ¹²I mean that each of you is saying, "I belong to Paul," or "I belong to Apollos," or "I belong to Cephas," or "I belong to Christ." ¹³Is Christ divided? Was Paul crucified for you? Or were you baptized in the name of Paul? ¹⁴I give thanks [to God] that I baptized none of you except Crispus and Gaius, ¹⁵so that no one can say you were baptized in my name. ¹⁶(I baptized the household of Stephanas also; beyond that I do not know whether I baptized anyone else.) ¹⁷For Christ did not send me to baptize but to preach the gospel, and not with the wisdom of human eloquence, so that the cross of Christ might not be emptied of its meaning.

NT: Acts 16:15; 18:24–28; Rom 16:23; 1 Cor 15:17
Catechism: Baptism, sacrament of initiation, 1212; ordinary †ministers, 1256; unity of charity, 814–15
Lectionary: 1:10–13: Votive Mass for the Unity of Christians

From the exalted vision Paul has presented in the address and thanksgiving,   **10**
he now begins to tell his listeners what this means in practice. He will have many
abuses to correct in this letter, but chief among them is that of divisiveness.
He plunges into his subject with a cry of urgency: **I urge you**. The Greek verb
parakaleō here means more than encourage or exhort, but not quite command.
It is almost an adjuration, as the mention of the **name** suggests, yet tempered
with affection and directness by the term **brothers**, which Paul often uses when
he has something painful to relate (1:26; 3:1; 7:29; 10:1; 12:1). The most obvious
symptom of the Corinthians' party spirit is their open wrangling. That **all of you
agree in what you say** is the translation of what is literally "to speak the same
thing," a Classical Greek expression for peace or settling a dispute.[5] The spirit
of concord should be visible and audible in a community bearing the name
of Christ. The divisions are not heresies but factions or cliques that militate
against charity; they could in the long run precipitate defections in graver matters. **United** translates a verb that is elsewhere used for cleansing and mending
fishing nets that have been torn (Matt 4:21; Mark 1:19) or for assembling parts
of a whole, as when persons are brought together and mobilized for a common
task (noun form in Eph 4:12). Paul's concern for the unity of the local church,
like our parishes today, will run throughout his letters (see esp. Phil 2:2).

Paul's concern is based on a recent report from **Chloe's people**. We know   **11**
nothing of Chloe otherwise, but these informants, whom Paul delicately avoids
naming, lest he irritate involved persons even more, belonged to her household
either as members of the family or as slaves, or perhaps as agents of her business
whose duties brought them occasionally to Ephesus.

The divisions are not over doctrine but over personalities. First of all Paul   **12–13**
blasts those who claim him as their hero (**"I belong to Paul"**) in opposition to
others, diplomatically first challenging those most likely to give him ear. Paul's
title to prestige in the Corinthian community lay in his role as founder and
in his labors of nearly two years there. The Roman element of the community
may have especially rallied to Paul's side after the riots of the Jews, the favorable decision of Gallio (Acts 18:12–17), and Paul's choice of the house of Titus
Justus (a Roman name) as headquarters for his preaching (Acts 18:7). When,
after Paul's departure, **Apollos** arrived and began to preach, he must have presented a considerable contrast with his predecessor, especially by the †rhetoric
he had learned in Alexandria (the Oxford of the day). His oratory would have
appealed to the Greek passion for the beautiful and the mystic.

---

5. Aristotle, *Constitution of Athens* 3.3.

The converted Jews would be more inclined to identify with **Cephas** (Peter), for he not only had the prestige of being head of the Twelve but also represented the Palestinian roots of the early Church. If Peter came to Corinth, as Dionysius of Corinth attests[6] (around AD 170), it was certainly after the foundation of the community (3:6, 10; 4:15). That the community knew him would explain the frequent references to Peter in this epistle (3:3–8, 21–23; 4:14–16; 9:4–6; 15:5).

Would not every Christian want to say, **"I belong to Christ"**? This is a puzzle for biblical scholars. In it some see Jews of Palestinian origin who had known Jesus "in the flesh" and who now are appealing to their direct knowledge of Jesus as justification for their party and perhaps for Judaizing practices they wish to promote. Others see it referring to a group of well-intentioned Christians reacting fittingly to the party spirit of the others, though this is unlikely in view of Paul's condemnation of them as well. The best solution appears to be that it is a group who are denying dependence on any human intermediary in favor of their own private relation to Christ.

This party spirit involves an absurdity, and Paul uses ironic rhetorical questions to expose it. **Is Christ divided?** Is Christ cut into pieces, so that each of the four persons would have a part? Or perhaps better, is Christ divided against himself? **Was Paul crucified for you?** Here is one of the earliest written affirmations, though indirect, of the saving power of Christ's death for those who accept it. In Rom 3:22–25, Paul will speak of the shedding of Christ's blood as an atonement for sin, as Matthew will later report Jesus' having said at the Last Supper: "This is [the cup of] my blood of the covenant, which will be on behalf of many for the forgiveness of sins" (Matt 26:28). Paul had surely preached this to the Corinthians, but their championing of different leaders, including Paul, seems to make saviors of those who are only instruments of Christ.

Were you baptized in the name of Paul? further skewers the absurdity. Christians were not baptized in the name of the preacher or the baptizer. The Greek says literally baptized "*unto* the name." Papyrus documents from this period use this expression to mark the transfer of purchased goods from one person to another. Ascribed to the new name, the goods become the property of the new owner. For Paul, that is what baptism does: it signifies that the person is now the property of Jesus Christ. In this case the transfer of ownership is a consecration. In the Old Testament, invoking the divine name on the people means that God has set them apart as his own, thus making them holy (Deut 28:9–10; Isa 63:19; Jer 7:10; 14:9). Thus baptism "into the name" of Jesus (also

---

6. Dionysius of Corinth, *Fragments of a Letter to Rome*, in PG 20:209; ET, http://www.early christianwritings.com/dionysius.html.

Alternate Baptismal Formulas?

The Catholic Church accepts as valid only the Trinitarian formula, as found in Matt 28:19. It is the only place in the New Testament where a baptismal formula is said to be specifically ordered by Jesus. In the Acts of the Apostles, people are said to be baptized "in the name of Jesus" (Acts 2:38; 8:16; 10:48; 19:5), but this does not necessarily mean that such was the formula used. For example, in Acts 19:5 baptism in the name of Jesus is contrasted with the baptism by John the Baptist. This indicates that "baptism in the name of Jesus" was used to distinguish Christian baptism from other types of baptism or ritual baths. Hebrews 6:2 indicates that the initiation of converts included instruction about different kinds of "baptisms" (note the plural). Today some groups do not use the Trinitarian formula for baptism (Unitarian Pentecostals, Mormons, and Jehovah's Witnesses, among others). If at one time the early Church may have baptized "in the name of Jesus," that was not in denial of the Trinity, as is the case in some groups' baptism "in the name of Jesus" today. The quest for inclusive language has led some today to replace the traditional names of the Trinity with "Creator, Redeemer, and Sanctifier," an erroneous move that led the Vatican to declare invalid any baptism so performed, or any other in which the traditional divine names are not used.

used in Acts 8:16; 19:5) is a consecration of the person to God in Jesus Christ. We are not sure whether "baptism in the name of Jesus (Christ)" was the formula actually used in the baptism of converts in the Pauline communities or the communities described in Acts. In Matt 28:19 the disciples are told to baptize "in the name of the Father, and of the Son, and of the holy Spirit." Paul is also clearly Trinitarian (2 Cor 13:13), so if the simple formula "in the name of Jesus" was used, it would clearly imply everything that Jesus revealed about the Father and the Holy Spirit.

Paul left the ministry of baptism to others, having baptized, he says, only **14–16** **Crispus and Gaius**. Acts 18:8 tells us that Crispus was a leader of the synagogue and that he was converted with his entire household. In Rom 16:23 Paul, writing from Corinth, says that Gaius "is host to me and to the whole church." Gaius, therefore, must have been wealthy enough to have a house large enough for the entire community to meet in. Since Paul dictated his letters, we can imagine that after mentioning Crispus and Gaius, he has an "oh, yes" moment, remembering that he **baptized the household of Stephanas also**. Paul singles out Stephanas and his household at the end of the letter as "the firstfruits of Achaia," who have "devoted themselves to the service of the holy ones" (16:15).

What If the Minister Is a Sinner?

In the fourth century a group called the Donatists held that the validity of the sacraments, especially baptism, depended on the holiness of the minister. In this view, if the priest or deacon was in the state of mortal sin, the baptism they performed would be invalid. A serious consequence of this would be that Christians would never know whether they had really received the sacrament. Saint Optatus and later St. Augustine countered the Donatists' position by insisting, as Paul does here, that the minister baptizes only as an instrument of Christ. Although it lasted for a century, Donatism eventually died out.

That means that they were his first converts and that the entire household has been ministering to the fledgling community. Thus they have assumed some kind of leadership role, for Paul urges the church to "be subordinate to such people and to everyone who works and toils with them" (16:16). By the time Paul finishes dictating his letter, he can say that Stephanas has arrived in Ephesus from Corinth, along with Fortunatus and Achaicus (16:17), who may have been bearers of a letter from the community. "Give recognition to such people," he adds (16:18). We can conclude from this that Paul has heard not only from "Chloe's people" (1:11) but also from some of the leaders of the community, and part of the problem he is dealing with seems to be insubordination to the leaders (16:16). Some biblical scholars have proposed that Paul's early communities were so charismatic that they really had little or no authority structure and that the institution of deacons and presbyters came at a later date and then evolved into "early Catholicism,"[7] with its hierarchical structure. This is difficult to sustain in the light of Paul's statement here and also his injunction to the Thessalonians several years earlier: "We ask you, brothers, to respect those who are laboring among you and who are over you in the Lord and who admonish you, and to show esteem for them with special love on account of their work"

7. "Early Catholicism" is a term used by some Protestant scholars to describe a movement they perceive in the early Church, from a charismatic form, in which the imminent end of the world was expected, to a later and more structured institutional form with hierarchical authority, resulting in the quenching of the original inspirational fire. The Epistles to Timothy and Titus, which reflect an ordered community life, are often cited as indications of this tendency. Careful study of the evidence, however, reveals an authority structure in the Christian churches from the beginning, albeit less developed than it appears, for example, in the writings of St. Ignatius of Antioch, from the beginning of the second century. "Early Catholicism" is used by some as a pejorative term to shore up the claim of certain free churches to be closer to the supposedly authority-free original churches.

Writing or Dictating?

Paul did not write his letters. He dictated them. Why? In the ancient world it was common practice for the author of a letter to dictate it to a scribe who was skilled in penmanship and could write rapidly. There is an allusion to this in Ps 45:2: "My tongue is the pen of a nimble scribe," or, literally, "a rapid scribe." Even today in countries like India one can see men sitting in front of a store with a typewriter, ready to listen to the dictation of an illiterate person who wishes to send a letter, for a fee. But even quite literate persons like Paul would prefer dictation, both because it allowed him time to think and also because his own penmanship was not particularly skillful, if we can judge by the note he adds in Gal 6:11: "See with what large letters I am writing to you in my own hand!"

(1 Thess 5:12–13). And in his Letter to the Philippians (1:1) he addresses the "overseers and ministers" (*episkopoi kai diakonoi*).[8]

It appears, then, that as soon as Paul had baptized his early converts, he handed over the baptizing to those he had first baptized, reserving for himself what Christ called him to do—to preach and to found assemblies of "the called," the *ekklēsia*, the church. As the church expanded, there was need for catechists to prepare candidates for baptism, and the rite became more extensive. Paul shows the wisdom of an administrator by delegating responsibilities to others and thus raising up new leaders. As for his preaching, Paul does so **not with the wisdom of human eloquence, so that the cross of Christ might not be emptied of its meaning**. "Emptied of its meaning" is just one word in Greek, *kenōthē*: that the cross of Christ might not be "emptied." The various translations strive to complete the thought, as does the NAB above: "emptied of its power" (NIV, NRSV), "pointless" (NJB). Paul's meaning is that mere rhetoric is hollow, but the cross of Christ is not, nor does its power come from eloquence.

Here Paul announces the theme of the following discourse, where he plays on the difference between the wisdom of mere words, or eloquence ("wisdom of word," *sophia logou*; 1:17) and the message of genuine wisdom ("word of wisdom," *logos sophias*; 12:8). We can see that what is at issue in Corinth is more than simple divisiveness (to which he will return in chap. 3). At a deeper level the penchant of the Greek mind for brilliant discourse (perhaps the Apollos party?) is at issue.

17

---

8. *Episkopoi* will later be used for bishops who have authority over priests, but in the Pauline literature, even in the later letters to Timothy and Titus, the term refers to leaders of the local community, what today would correspond to parish priests. In today's terminology, "episcopal" reflects the Greek *episkopoi*.

Reflection and Application (1:10–17)

Addressed to us, Paul's words challenge our fleshly compulsion to align ourselves with ministers who appeal to us and to make unfavorable comparisons with others. Non-liturgical churches that have only the ministry of the word are more likely to focus their satisfaction or dissatisfaction upon the preacher. Though sacramental churches are not indifferent to preaching, they tend to focus more on the †mystery relived in the liturgy, especially the Eucharist, in which the personality of the priest is less important than the mystery being enacted.

In the Catholic Church, pastors are appointed by the bishop, not elected by the people, and although bishops are certainly aware of how much affirmation the parishioners give their pastor, the ultimate decision as to who is pastor and how long he remains at a given parish is that of the bishop (or the provincial, as the case may be). This policy avoids making the appointment a popularity contest; in its own way it reflects the sacramental nature of the Church, by affirming that leadership in the Church is not primarily a matter of competitive competence but of the grace of God. For centuries the Church had to fight to keep civil authorities and others from interfering with the appointments of bishops, and it still has that problem today in certain countries, such as China and Vietnam.

But more relevant for the mission of the Church everywhere is Paul's condemnation of party spirit. Catholic institutions have not avoided the secular pitfall of internecine rivalries, jealousies, turf fights, backbiting, and other sabotaging of the work of the Lord because of petty personal interests. An institution without any of this is rare indeed; an institution with a lot of it will eventually self-destruct. Many Christians need to learn that maturity means embracing the asceticism of the common good, being willing to sacrifice self-interest for the sake of the body, the Church.

The Gospel, Divine Paradox (1:18–25)

[18]The message of the cross is foolishness to those who are perishing, but to us who are being saved it is the power of God. [19]For it is written:

"I will destroy the wisdom of the wise,
and the learning of the learned I will set aside."

[20]Where is the wise one? Where is the scribe? Where is the debater of this age? Has not God made the wisdom of the world foolish? [21]For since in the wisdom of God the world did not come to know God through wisdom, it was the will of God through the foolishness of the proclamation

to save those who have faith. ²²For Jews demand signs and Greeks look
for wisdom, ²³but we proclaim Christ crucified, a stumbling block to Jews
and foolishness to Gentiles, ²⁴but to those who are called, Jews and Greeks
alike, Christ the power of God and the wisdom of God. ²⁵For the foolishness of God is wiser than human wisdom, and the weakness of God is
stronger than human strength.

OT: Wis 13:1–2
NT: Matt 12:38; Acts 17:19–23; Rom 1:16, 19–20; 2 Cor 12:10
Catechism: Jesus' death on the cross, 619–23
Lectionary: St. Justin Martyr; St. Louis de Montfort; St. Paul of the Cross; St. Peter Chanel; Com-
   mon of Missionaries; Common of Doctors of the Church; Anointing of the Sick; †Mystery of
   the Holy Cross; 1:22–25: Third Sunday of Lent (Year B); 1:23–24: St. Mark

---

What will Paul do with this factious community? He will send them to the   **18**
foot of the cross. He will do this in three ways: first, the message of the cross
itself (1:18–25), then the reception of the message by the Corinthians (1:26–31),
and finally, the cross in Paul's own method of preaching (2:1–5).

Before coming to Corinth, Paul stopped in Athens, where, according to
Luke (Acts 17:22–34), he introduced his message to the Gentiles by appealing
to the best of Greek culture and philosophy, hoping that his listeners would
then be open to what was distinct about his message: that there will be a final
judgment for everyone, and God has given proof of it by raising Jesus from
the dead. Result? Except for a handful of converts, a scoffing rejection of his
message. Luke of course does not give us a full picture of what Paul preached
in Athens (he preached in the Jewish synagogue there too, 17:17). In his speech
to the Gentile intellectuals on the Areopagus, Paul mentions only the resurrection, not the cross. This is Luke's report, not Paul's. Luke wants to stress the
gospel's encounter with the self-sufficient cultured elite, who enjoyed being
entertained by novelties (17:21) and expected Paul's show to be nothing more.
Instead, Paul proclaimed a historical event that demanded conversion. They
were ready neither for the thought of bodily resurrection nor for the cost of
what it meant for their lives.

This lack of success of the "continuity" approach, whether at Athens or elsewhere, must have had an impact on Paul. There is continuity of the gospel with
the best of human reason, yes, and Paul will say that in Rom 1:19. But there is
also discontinuity, a break particularly with reason that has been wounded and
turned in on itself by sin. The gospel collides with that so-called wisdom, and
it is not only the resurrection but also the cross that meets it head-on. Arriving
at Corinth, Paul resolved (2:2) to preach the "scandal" of the cross. Nothing
appears so counter to Greek as well as Jewish thinking than the story of a man

George T. Montague, SM

Fig. 4. The Areopagus. It was here, just prior to his first visit to Corinth, that according to Acts 17:22–34 Paul told the Athenians that their "unknown God" was really Jesus Christ.

condemned as a criminal and subjected to the most painful and shameful death the Romans could devise. But, Paul realized, that's it! As Hamlet said, "The play's the thing wherein I'll catch the †conscience of the King,"[9] so Paul concludes: "It's the paradox that will win souls for the King!" **The message of the cross is foolishness to those who are perishing.** But for those **who are being saved**, it reveals a God of love who thrusts himself into humans' deepest fears, suffering, and death and leads them out of their deepest alienation: sin. That is why **it is the power of God**.

At this point one might ask: is not the resurrection also, even more so, the power of God? Does it not too reveal the love of God? Surely, and Paul would not have avoided mentioning it. But resurrection is a phenomenon that goes beyond our normal human experience. Suffering does not: it is the lot of every human being. That is why we understand the cross better than we understand the resurrection. It is love, sacrificial love to the extreme. And that is quite likely why Paul began his preaching in Corinth with the cross. He will not end there, for neither did God. But that is where God started too. What is at issue here is not so much the objective power of the cross to redeem humankind but especially its *converting* power and hence its importance for preaching.

9. Shakespeare, *Hamlet* 2.2.603–4.

The gospel is power. This will become the central theme of his Letter to the Romans: "The gospel . . . is the power of God for the salvation of everyone who believes: for Jew first, and then Greek" (Rom 1:16). What does that mean? First of all, the gospel is not the kind of †rhetoric that seems to have so enthralled the Corinthians. It is news about an earthshaking event. When we heard and saw the fall of the Twin Towers on September 11, 2001, we did not expect the reporter to entertain us with rhetoric. Give us the facts! The gospel is first of all a witness to the death and resurrection of the Son of God. It is the report of an event that also calls for a decision. It is not mere ideas or †sophistry or philosophy. Second, Paul's preaching of the gospel was accompanied by signs, miracles, and especially healings (Gal 3:1–5). Third and most important, the event of the cross led to changed lives: the power of the cross was not merely the past event of Calvary but also a present event, producing changes in the lives of the Corinthians.

Note that in the present situation both of those who are perishing and those being saved is progressive, suggesting that the end of either path, perdition or salvation, is something not yet attained. Thus one should neither be presumptuous of one's salvation, as if it could never be lost, nor despairing of the salvation of those on the other path, for if they yield to God's grace, their choice can be reversed.

From power Paul moves to wisdom, recalling the words of Isaiah (29:14) in the †Septuagint version: **"I will destroy the wisdom of the wise, and the learning of the learned I will set aside."** In the text of Isaiah, the kingdom of Judah, faced with the menace of Assyria, was turning to Egypt for help. Egypt! The land that had enslaved the Israelites' ancestors, the land from which their ancestors were glad to be free once for all. God promises that he will destroy the misled wisdom of those who supported this plan. Paul applies this text now to the pretenses of a wisdom closed to anything beyond its own horizon, a purely human "wisdom," which God will destroy by the wisdom of the cross.

19

Where is the wise one? is addressed to the Greek. **Where is the scribe?** is addressed to the Jew. **Where is the debater of this age?** "Debater" would typify both, in the pejorative sense of a person constantly discussing and disputing more for the art than for the matter (the Greek for "debater," *syzētētēs*, even sounds like chatter), what Paul elsewhere calls "fleshly wisdom" (2 Cor 1:12).[10] This type of wisdom, **the wisdom of the world**, God has **made . . . foolish**, meaning either

20

---

10. "Fleshly wisdom" is the literal translation of the Greek. Other versions render: "human wisdom" (NAB), "earthly wisdom" (NRSV), "worldly wisdom" (NIV), "human reasoning" (NJB), and "without ulterior motives" (JB).

"addled" or shown to be foolish by his intervention, "like the needle of a compass maddened by the approach of a magnetic force too great."[11] The cross is not human speculation but divine deed. Human wisdom cannot match the deed of God.

21   Up to this point the "wisdom of the world" has been presented in such an unfavorable light that one might think it totally depraved. Yet even prior to God's revealing word in Israel and in the gospel, there was a wisdom offered by God, and it was not totally at odds with human wisdom, for the created universe itself speaks something of the nature of God—enough to make humans' incomprehension and rejection of it a sin and not just a mistake. Thus it was God's plan (his "plan A") that **the world** would **come to know God through** the light of human **wisdom**, as Paul explains in his Letter to the Romans:

> For what can be known about God is evident to them, because God made it evident to them. Ever since the creation of the world, his invisible attributes and eternal power and divinity have been able to be understood and perceived in what he has made. As a result, they have no excuse, for although they knew God they did not accord him glory as God or give him thanks. Instead, they became vain in their reasoning, and their senseless minds were darkened. While claiming to be wise, they became fools. (1:19–22)

Hence, since plan A failed because of sin, it was the will of God through the foolishness of the proclamation to save those who have faith. Saint Thomas Aquinas comments:

> Because of the vanity of man's heart, man went astray from the right path of knowing God. . . . And therefore God led the faithful to a saving knowledge of himself through certain other things that are not found in the patterns of creation. . . . These other things are the facts of faith. God's manner of acting is therefore like that of a teacher who, realizing that his meaning is not being grasped by his hearers, strives to use other words to explain what he has in his heart.[12]

22–23   That other way (plan B) is the way of paradox. The tendency of the **Jews** who opposed the ministry of Jesus and that of Paul (compare Matt 12:38–42; Luke 11:29–32), was to **demand signs**, miracles or spectacular deeds of power, **and Greeks look for wisdom**, something that will captivate but not disturb the cultured mind. Paul here shows his grasp of the psychology of both cultures, which made him an apt instrument for reaching both, but he does so by

11. C. Spicq, "1 Corinthiens" in L. Pirot and A. Clamer, *La Sainte Bible* (Paris: Letouzery et Ané, 1949), 182.
12. Saint Thomas Aquinas, *Commentary on 1 Corinthians* 55.

No Crucified Messiah

In St. Justin's *Dialogue with Trypho*, written in the second century, Trypho says: "Our entire race awaits the Christ, and all the Scripture texts which you have quoted we too recognize as having been said about him. . . . But, as to the question of knowing whether the Christ should be dishonored unto crucifixion, we doubt, for in the law it is said of the crucified that he is accursed [Deut 21:23], and for the present I would not easily believe it. The Scriptures foretell a suffering Christ, evidently; but that this should involve a suffering cursed in the law, we should like to know whether you can demonstrate it."[a]

a. Saint Justin Martyr, *Dialogue with Trypho* 89.1.2.

proclaiming something that goes counter to, because it goes beyond, the natural tastes of each: **Christ crucified**. Jews indeed looked for a Messiah, but the fact that Jesus died on the cross proved that he was not the glorious liberator they desired (see Living Tradition sidebar). For them, the cross was a **stumbling block**, an obstacle to faith.

The Greek understanding of time and history was not †eschatological: it did not have a conception of a goal toward which history was moving. "Time," Aristotle said, "is a kind of circle." Thus a religious founder should be one who more than any other would lead one to contemplate the order and harmony of the universe and lead humanity to a more harmonious subjection to its inevitability. This was at least the view of the Stoics, who were Paul's contemporaries and with whom he argued in Athens (Acts 17:18). In short, such a founder should be a philosopher. A founder who stands the world's values on its head by going to death on a cross—the fate of the criminal dregs of humanity—would indeed have no chance of winning the Greek, even less by claiming that the cross was followed by the resurrection of the body. As for the Jewish critic, the apparent failure of one who claimed to be the Messiah was proof that he was not. That is why it takes a special grace, a divine call, to read in the cross more than stupidity and weakness.

But **to those who are called, Jews and Greeks alike, Christ the power of God and the wisdom of God**. Although Paul condemns rhetoric for rhetoric's sake, here he is a master of rhetoric. Unlike the sophists, who were more concerned with winning a debate by pleasing the audience than with truth in argumentation, the truly great rhetoricians like Cicero, Quintilian, and Seneca

24–25

The Power of the Cross

What was it about the cross that accounted for its power? We do not know how Paul explained his theology of the cross to the Corinthians when he first preached to them, but we can put together elements of his teaching from his letters, realizing that some of what he says later may be more than what he preached in Corinth. Justification comes through the "sacrifice of atonement" of the cross (Rom 3:24–25 NRSV); reconciliation with God and between Jew and Gentile comes through the cross (Eph 2:11–22); the debt of our sins is canceled and "the principalities and the powers" are defeated through the cross (Col 2:9–15). Christ has died, therefore all have died (2 Cor 5:14); the cross is the means by which Jesus cleansed and prepared his bride for himself (Eph 5:25–27); the cross is the means of our dying with Christ in baptism (Rom 6:3–4); it is Christ's death on the cross that we proclaim in the Eucharist (1 Cor 11:26). Beyond these theological implications, Paul must have depicted the horrible suffering and shameful death, which testified to the personal love Jesus had for each one of the Corinthians: He "has loved me and given himself up for me" (Gal 2:20).

the Elder believed that beauty should be in the service of truth. Paul does not hesitate to use it in service of the gospel. **The foolishness of God is wiser than human wisdom, and the weakness of God is stronger than human strength**. Out of concern for inclusive language and proper parallelism, the NAB sacrifices some of the rhetorical impact of verse 25, which reads literally in the Greek, "For the foolishness of God is wiser than men, and the weakness of God is stronger than men."

Reflection and Application (1:18–25)

Truth and beauty. One who is searching for the truth today often has to wade through sound bites and hawking commercials to find it. Politicians spend fortunes to put the right spin on their campaigns, appealing to the emotions sometimes at the expense of the truth. A single image associated with a name can convey a lasting impression, which may ultimately distort reality. But a mature Christian will not be taken in. However, use of the media, modern technology, and the best of rhetoric and art in serving the truth of the gospel is certainly in keeping with effective evangelization. As the Catholic theologian Hans Urs von Balthasar has maintained, entry to the good and the true is through the gate of beauty.

Chrysostom on the Cross

Saint John Chrysostom, himself no slouch at rhetoric, preaching from the vantage point of the fourth century, when the cross had proved its efficacy through two centuries of persecution and the conversion of the empire, could say:

> How greatly did Plato labor, endeavoring to show that the soul is immortal! Yet even as he came he went away, having spoken nothing with certainty, nor convinced any hearer. But the cross achieved persuasiveness by means of unlearned men. Yes, it convinced the whole world—and not about common things but it wrought its conviction speaking about God and the judgment of things to come. And of all men it made philosophers: the very rustics, the utterly unlearned. Behold how "the foolishness of God is wiser than men" and "the weakness stronger"! How stronger? Because it overran the whole world, and took all by force, and while men were endeavoring by tens of thousands to extinguish the name of the Crucified, the contrary came to pass: the name of the Crucified flourished and increased more and more; while the persecutors perished and wasted away. The living at war with the dead were powerless."[a]

a. Saint Chrysostom, *Homilies on 1 Corinthians* 4.3.

Reason and faith. In our world today, after the extreme exaltation of human reason during the Enlightenment, a reaction called "postmodernism" has set in, with many doubting whether truth is objective at all—a fallacy known as relativism. Pope John Paul II confronted this issue in his encyclical *Fides et Ratio* (*Faith and Reason*), and Pope Benedict XVI has written and spoken extensively on the perils of relativism. It is important, therefore, not to interpret Paul as if he is rejecting all philosophy or theology that uses reason, enlightened by faith, to reflect on the meaning of revelation. He is speaking about the self-sufficiency of those who rely on reason alone—and reason distorted by sin and pride—to attain the fullness of truth.

The personal power of the cross. "To us who are being saved [the cross] is the power of God" (1:18). I have seen the power of the cross in many ways in my ministry, especially in its ability to bring the grace of forgiveness. When Rose Mary arrived for the summer program in theology at St. Mary's University, I no longer recognized the bubbly personality I had known in previous summers. Her face was drawn in obvious grief and smiles were forced. After I preached about forgiveness at a retreat she attended, she came to see me.

"I can't do it," she said.

"What can't you do?" I asked.

"Forgive. Six months ago my brother was killed in an automobile accident. He was my closest friend; I loved him dearly. But what makes it worse is that the man who was driving the car claimed—maybe for insurance purposes—that my brother was the driver. I've been filled with grief but also with anger and bitterness toward that man. How can I forgive him for what he has done?"

"Jesus can help us do things we can't do by ourselves. You wouldn't have come to see me if you didn't want to do something about it. I've noticed how drained you are, and now I understand why." After letting her pour out more of her grief, I suggested that she kneel and look at Jesus hanging on the cross. I led her through a meditation on his wounds, not merely his physical wounds but especially the wounds of his heart: put there on the cross by the betrayal of one of his own friends, his disciple of three years; rejected by the leaders of his people, denied by his chief disciple, abandoned by the Twelve, mocked and spit upon.

"And what does Jesus say?" I asked. " 'Father, forgive them. . . .' Now ask Jesus to give you his heart, his forgiving heart. And when you are ready, call that man into this room in your imagination and say to him, 'In the name of Jesus, I forgive you.' " It took a long time, but eventually she was able to do that. And when she stood up, she smiled, a genuine smile, for the first time that summer.

The cross had set her free. The power of the cross had set her free.

I have experienced the power of the cross in similar scenes many times in my ministry. The power of the cross!

A little postscript on Rose Mary. Later that evening I prayed that she would not take back the forgiveness she had given, and I dared to ask the Lord for some kind of confirming sign. Then I went to the kitchen for a glass of milk. It was a large kitchen, and on a distant shelf my eye caught "Rosemary" written on a box. There was smaller print under the name, so I moved closer and read the second line: "Leaves." Then getting a little closer, I could make out the third line. The whole message read: "Rosemary Leaves Whole."

And so it happened. I cut out the words and sent them to her. She has kept them until now, a reminder of the power of the cross.

The Receivers: Divine Paradox (1:26–31)

[26]Consider your own calling, brothers. Not many of you were wise by human standards, not many were powerful, not many were of noble birth. [27]Rather, God chose the foolish of the world to shame the wise, and God chose the weak of the world to shame the strong, [28]and God chose the

**lowly and despised of the world, those who count for nothing, to reduce to
nothing those who are something, [29]so that no human being might boast
before God. [30]It is due to him that you are in Christ Jesus, who became
for us wisdom from God, as well as righteousness, sanctification, and redemption, [31]so that, as it is written, "Whoever boasts, should boast in the
Lord."**

OT: Deut 7:7; Judg 7:2; 1 Sam 16:7
NT: 2 Cor 4:7; Eph 2:9; James 2:5
Catechism: humility in prayer, 2559, 2631; Christ, heart of catechesis, 426
Lectionary: St. Agnes; St. Agatha; Common of Holy Men and Women; St. Vincent de Paul

---

If God has shown a lack of wisdom in determining to save the world by the   **26**
cross, he has shown the same folly in the type of persons he has chosen to receive
the gift. The **calling** that Paul asks them to consider picks up the "called" theme
already introduced in verse 2 and applies it to the concrete circumstances of their
coming to the faith. There were few among them who according to **human standards** were **wise** or **powerful** or **of noble birth**. Though there was a handful of
notables in the community, among whom we know of Erastus, the city treasurer
(Rom 16:23), and Crispus, an official of the synagogue (Acts 18:8; 1 Cor 1:14),
these were the exception in a community made up largely of the lower classes
and slaves. Nevertheless, we should note that the gospel has also appealed to
some in the higher classes in Corinth, lest we be misled by the broad strokes
with which Paul paints the community. The unusual mark of the early Pauline
communities was their embracing all classes—unusual because the intentional
associations of people back then, as now, were usually composed of the same
social class. What accounts for this diversity is that the members of the church
came together not by a simple natural attraction or interest but by a divine call.

Three times Paul says **God chose** (1:27–28), making it clear that it was his gift,   **27–28**
not his prowess or merit, that brought about their new status. God bypassed
the world's wise and powerful in order to select "vessels of clay" (2 Cor 4:7, my
trans.) to show his wisdom and power. The series of the **foolish**, the **weak**, and
the **lowly and despised** climaxes with **those who count for nothing, to reduce
to nothing those who are something**.

For "flesh" (Greek) to **boast before God** is Paul's way of describing humanity's   **29**
self-proclaimed independence from God, priding itself on its talents, wisdom,
and strength as if they were not God's gifts. "What do you possess that you
have not received?" Paul will later ask. "But if you have received it, why are you
boasting as if you did not receive it?" (4:7). God's calling the lowly has turned
human pride on its head.

Boasting in the Lord

LIVING TRADITION

Saint Basil the Great comments:

"The wise man must not boast of his wisdom, nor the strong man of his strength, nor the rich man of his riches." What then is the right kind of boasting? What is the source of man's greatness? Scripture says: "The man who boasts must boast of this, that he knows and understands that I am the Lord." Here is man's greatness, here is man's glory and majesty: to know in truth what is great, to hold fast to it, and to seek glory from the Lord of glory. The Apostle tells us: "The man who boasts must boast of the Lord." He has just said: "Christ was appointed by God to be our wisdom, our righteousness, our sanctification, our redemption, so that, as it is written, a man who boasts must boast of the Lord."

Boasting of God is perfect and complete when we take no pride in our own righteousness but acknowledge that we are utterly lacking in true righteousness and have been made righteous only by faith in Christ. Paul boasts of the fact that he holds his own righteousness in contempt and seeks the righteousness in faith that comes through Christ and is from God. He wants only to know Christ and the power of his resurrection and to have fellowship with his sufferings by taking on the likeness of his death, in the hope that somehow he may arrive at the resurrection of the dead. Here we see all overweening pride laid low. Humanity, there is nothing left for you to boast of, for your boasting and hope lie in putting to death all that is your own and seeking the future life that is in Christ. Since we have its firstfruits we are already in its midst, living entirely in the grace and gift of God.[a]

a. Saint Basil the Great, *Homily 20, On Humility* 3; in PG 31:530–31; trans. Institute for Catholic Educational Leadership, Office of Readings, third Monday of Lent.

30   But there is a boasting "in the Lord" (v. 31), which is quite different, and it is consistent with what has happened in Corinth, where the new Christians now exist **in Christ Jesus**. It is not †rhetoric or championing individual †ministers that counts but a personal relationship with Jesus Christ. He **became for us wisdom from God**. It was a given in the Old Testament that all wisdom is from the Lord (Prov 2:6; Sir 1:1), from whom one should earnestly seek it (2 Chron 1:10–12). Wisdom was even personified as Lady Wisdom, who existed with God before creation (Prov 1:20–23; 8:22–31) and was sent by God to dwell among his people (Sir 24:8–12). The Gospel of John will apply this theme to the preexistent Word, who became flesh and revealed to the human race the God whom no one has seen (John 1:1–18). The bottom line for Paul, too, is that the wisdom from God is the Person of Jesus, who by his example and teaching but, in our present context, most especially by his death on the cross, outshone the most brilliant human wisdom.

Holiness, Consecration, Sanctification

The Bible has an extensive vocabulary connected with the word "holy." The root meaning of "holy" is "set aside," "separate from the ordinary or secular." God is the holy one above all because he is totally other. But things and people can be made holy, the process of which is called sanctification or consecration, the setting aside of a person or object for divine purposes. When one is baptized, one is consecrated, taken from the kingdom of sin and darkness and set aside for the worship and service of God. "Sanctification" refers to the process of making holy, and it can refer either to the initial dedication of the person or object to God or, in the faithful, to our progressive purification and transformation as we grow closer to God in this life.

Jesus is also God's **righteousness**. Sometimes translated "justice," this term will be a major issue in Paul's Letter to the Romans. At one level it means God's saving justice: his faithfulness to his own sworn word, his promise, to save his people. But it also refers to the concrete way he did it by sending his Son to restore humanity's broken relationship with God and thus setting them *right* in his sight. As a Jew and a Pharisee, Paul had sought righteousness through observance of the law, but his dramatic conversion convinced him that righteousness came with accepting in faith the gift of God in Jesus, as shown in the love that led Jesus to his death on the cross (Gal 2:20). "For our sake he made him to be sin who did not know sin, so that we might become the righteousness of God in him" (2 Cor 5:21).

In what way is Jesus our **sanctification**? The Greek word can indicate a process or its result. There is no need to choose between these two meanings here. Jesus has sanctified us, and thus we have become "saints," consecrated people. But sanctification is also ongoing, as 2 Cor 7:1 indicates: "making holiness perfect in the fear of God," and so Paul can pray, "May the God of peace make you holy through and through" (1 Thess 5:23, my trans.). Thus the consecration of baptism, however radical a change it has effected, is not meant to be something static. It calls for a continuing transformation by the Holy Spirit (2 Cor 3:18).

Redemption translates the Greek *apolytrōsis*, originally meaning the buying back of a slave or captive by paying a ransom (*lytron*) to set him free. In the New Testament it refers to Christ's paying the price of his blood to set free those held captive or enslaved by sin (see 1 Cor 6:20). It can also refer to the state of freedom in which the freed find themselves. To the Christians of Paul's day,

Christ the Center

LIVING
TRADITION

For many Christians, religion means "church" with its external practices. But these become chores and routine if one does not have a personal relationship with Jesus Christ. This personal relationship should be the heart of catechesis. After the fourth general synod of Bishops in 1979, Pope John Paul II issued his apostolic exhortation *Catechesi Tradendae* (*Apostolic Exhortation on Catechesis*), which begins (§5) with a reminder that the Person of Christ is the center of all religious instruction: "At the heart of catechesis we find . . . a Person, the person of Jesus of Nazareth, 'the only Son of the Father, . . . full of grace and truth,' who suffered and died for us and who now, after rising, is living with us forever. . . . The definitive aim of catechesis is to put people not only in touch but [also] in communion, in intimacy, with Jesus Christ. Only He can lead us to the love of the Father in the Spirit and make us share in the life of the Trinity."

it was a powerful image of the freedom they now enjoyed as children of God (Gal 4:7) and the challenge to use that freedom in voluntary service through love (5:13).

31   All of these gifts rather than one's own achievements or abilities should be the ground for the Christian's boasting: **Whoever boasts, should boast in the Lord**. This is Paul's abbreviated rendering of the †Septuagint version of Jer 9:22–23: "Thus says the Lord: 'Let not the wise boast of his wisdom, nor the powerful boast of his strength, nor the rich boast of his riches, but let the one who boasts, boast of this: to understand and know that I am the Lord who does judgment and righteousness on the earth.'"

Reflection and Application (1:26–31)

How can we find ourselves in Paul's message to the Corinthians here? It may be helpful to start with Paul's calling them immature, even infants in the faith (3:1). Children grow in self-realization by the affirmation and love of their parents and others and also by their achievements, from beginning to speak to tying their shoes to graduation, and the applause that these achievements bring. In adolescence most teenagers feel a great need for belonging, whether it be to a team, or a youth group, or a gang. Still a bit uncertain of their own identity, they find assurance in an accepting group. At times, however, youth can be so needy of acceptance by their peers that they lose the sense of their individual worth, compromise their values to achieve that acceptance, and engage in put-downs of other persons or groups.

This is a phase that most grow out of, but sometimes adults lapse into adolescence. Such was the case with the Corinthians, and such is the case with some Christians today. Do we make unhealthy comparisons of our parish with other parishes? Of our community with other communities? Of our work with others' work? There is such a thing as a holy rivalry (St. Basil and his close friend St. Gregory of Nazianzus vied to grow in holiness), but there is also an unhealthy better-than-thou attitude, which militates against unity and cooperation. When in a missionary country, where Christians were a tiny and sometimes a suspect minority, I experienced a great fraternal closeness with other religious communities working there, as also with Catholic laypeople and Protestant missionaries, a closeness that I have sometimes missed in other, developed Christian environments.

The Power and the Wisdom

1 Corinthians 2

The first section in this chapter is really a conclusion of the preceding argument. The gospel message was deemed weakness by the humanly "wise" (1:18–25); the receivers were, from a human point of view, the least likely (1:16–31). Now Paul will tell them that even the messenger was beset with weaknesses, but the power of the cross overcame these deficiencies. Then, after this long discourse on the inadequacy of human wisdom, Paul will explain that for those who are mature in their faith, there is a wisdom available from the Holy Spirit.

Weakness and Power in the Herald (2:1–5)

[1]When I came to you, brothers, proclaiming the mystery of God, I did not come with sublimity of words or of wisdom. [2]For I resolved to know nothing while I was with you except Jesus Christ, and him crucified. [3]I came to you in weakness and fear and much trembling, [4]and my message and my proclamation were not with persuasive (words of) wisdom, but with a demonstration of spirit and power, [5]so that your faith might rest not on human wisdom but on the power of God.

NT: 2 Cor 11:6; 12:12; Gal 6:14;1 Thess 1:5
Catechism: Christ, center of catechesis, 426
Lectionary: 2:1–10a: St. Dominic; St. John of the Cross; Common of Doctors of the Church; 2:1–5: Institution of Readers

1   The same divine paradox, shown in the content of the preaching (1:18–25) and in the social position of the hearers (1:26–31), applies equally well to the

preacher from whom they first heard the good news. This good news did not demand but rather forbade pretentious speech and this-worldly **wisdom**, because the gospel has no need of it, any more than a golden statue would need to be decorated with crepe paper. As **the mystery of God** (2:1), it bears its own power.[1] In our language "†mystery" often means something unsolved. In Paul's day the Greek word was often used in referring to the "mystery religions," which kept their rituals secret, and thus it bore the notion of secrecy. For Paul, the gospel is the secret of God's heart, but it is a secret now revealed and proclaimed by the Apostle.

In saying **I resolved**, it appears that Paul made a conscious decision to avoid the "continuity" method of introducing the gospel and went unabashedly for "discontinuity"—an emphasis on how the cross is different from mere human expectations, reasoning, and posturing. Paul has called the cross a stumbling block, or scandal (1:23). That scandal was **Jesus Christ, and him crucified**. While this repeats the content of the message already discussed above, the emphasis here is on Paul's decision **to know nothing** else *among them*. The Corinthians did not need more †rhetorical bells and whistles, and Paul would not entertain them with such. He will later speak about knowing the risen Christ (15:8) and the power of his resurrection (Phil 3:10). But the Risen One is also the Crucified One.

Paul would not appear as a scholar but as the herald of an event. In fact, he appeared with **weakness and fear and much trembling**. He may have had an attack of illness (which he calls "weakness" in Gal 4:13, Greek). But even without that, his situation would have been enough to depress the noblest of souls. Despite remarkable missionary success, he had been forced to leave Philippi, Thessalonica, and Beroea because of persecution (Acts 17:1–15); he had failed to convert the Greeks in Athens (Acts 17:16–34); he had arrived alone in Corinth, without the support of his closest companions; in the depravity of the city and the spirit of the Corinthians, he saw little promise for the call to holiness that he preached; and from his experience of the constant opposition of Jewish leaders, he knew that he should expect little success in the synagogue. But a comforting vision of Christ (Acts 18:9) seems to have been a turning point, teaching Paul that his weakness was the open channel for the movement of the Spirit, the very sacrament of the manifestation of God's power (2 Cor 4:7). In any case, his fear and trembling were surely not due to any uncertainty on his part about

---

1. Although some ancient manuscripts read "testimony" (*martyrion*) in 1 Cor 2:1 instead of "mystery" (*mystērion*), the NAB and most scholars suppose that Paul wrote "mystery" because it prepares for verse 7, which develops the kind of receptivity that the gospel requires.

Beyond Reason

LIVING TRADITION

Saint John Chrysostom remarked on the impossibility of human reason's fully grasping divine revelation because it presents truths like the Trinity or the incarnation, which human beings would never have dreamed of.

> For indeed the excess of folly is in those . . . who consign to reason things that cannot be ascertained except by faith. Think of the smith drawing out the red-hot iron by means of the tongs; if anyone should insist on doing it with his hand, we should vote him guilty of extreme folly.[a]

a. Saint Chrysostom, *Homilies on 1 Corinthians* 5.2.

his gospel; even less was it fear of what the audience might think. Scholars have come up with a great variety of explanations for Paul's "fear and trembling."[2] The best, I believe, is this: Instead of posing with great self-confidence as a powerful speaker was expected to do,[3] Paul was overwhelmed by his own human weakness in the face of the awesome divine message confided to him, like the "fear and trembling" with which he tells us we should work out our salvation (Phil 2:12–13; compare Heb 12:20–21). His reliance not on rhetoric but on the power of the cross, God's own word to the Corinthians, pointed to the message rather than the messenger. Thus he proclaimed what would at first seem to be repugnant to both Jew and Greek: a crucified Messiah.

4–5   The pretense of human wisdom proved to be no match for the **demonstration of spirit and power** that accompanied Paul's preaching. This may refer to the miracles worked by Paul in Corinth (2 Cor 12:12), but most probably it refers to the manifest action of the Holy Spirit in both preacher and hearer, which resulted in the abundant conversions that followed his preaching, and also to the †charisms with which the Spirit filled the community (1 Cor 1:5–7, 12, 14; Eph 1:17, 19; 1 Thess 1:5).

The end or purpose of this proclamation approach is given in verse 5, which climaxes this section and forms an †inclusio with 1:17. There the motive for using this approach was to safeguard the content of the message; here it is to assure authentic faith. Faith, if it is to be divine, cannot rest on human motives alone for its foundation; it is essentially a response to an encounter with the power of God. The experience in Corinth confirmed what Paul knew of

2. David E. Garland, *1 Corinthians*, BECNT (Grand Rapids: Baker Academic, 2003), 85–86, lists and evaluates more than eight.

3. See Quintilian, *Institutio oratoria* 12.5.1–5.

his own gospel. Faith is something that no human appeal can create. His own experience, and that of the Corinthians, has been that it is born in the heart of a paradox reversing the values that blocked both Jew and Greek from embracing the gospel. Though faith may crown the highest achievements of reason, it is totally other than reason. An important lesson: *reason cannot produce faith.* And much less can eloquence do so.

Reflection and Application (2:1–5)

Feeling inadequate for a task we have been given can be a grace, if we admit our fears and trust in God's grace to get us through. A fervent prayer to the Holy Spirit can free us to proceed with trust and boldness. We can take inspiration from Paul's own experience when, after his Athens preaching fell on deaf ears, he arrived in Corinth "in weakness and fear and much trembling" and discovered anew that the gospel, fired by the Holy Spirit, has its own power to move mountains.

The Gospel: Divine Wisdom (2:6–16)

⁶Yet we do speak a wisdom to those who are mature, but not a wisdom of this age, nor of the rulers of this age who are passing away. ⁷Rather, we speak God's wisdom, mysterious, hidden, which God predetermined before the ages for our glory, ⁸and which none of the rulers of this age knew; for if they had known it, they would not have crucified the Lord of glory. ⁹But as it is written:

> "What eye has not seen, and ear has not heard,
>   and what has not entered the human heart,
>   what God has prepared for those who love him,"

¹⁰this God has revealed to us through the Spirit.

For the Spirit scrutinizes everything, even the depths of God. ¹¹Among human beings, who knows what pertains to a person except the spirit of the person that is within? Similarly, no one knows what pertains to God except the Spirit of God. ¹²We have not received the spirit of the world but the Spirit that is from God, so that we may understand the things freely given us by God. ¹³And we speak about them not with words taught by human wisdom, but with words taught by the Spirit, describing spiritual realities in spiritual terms.

¹⁴Now the natural person does not accept what pertains to the Spirit of God, for to him it is foolishness, and he cannot understand it, because it is judged spiritually. ¹⁵The spiritual person, however, can judge everything but is not subject to judgment by anyone.

¹⁶For "who has known the mind of the Lord, so as to counsel him?" But we have the mind of Christ.

OT: Jdt 8:14; Prov 28:5; Wis 9:13; Isa 40:13; 64:3
NT: John 14:26; Rom 11:34; Eph 3:10; Col 1:28; Heb 5:14
Lectionary: 2:10b–16: St. Bede the Venerable; Common of Doctors of the Church

6   If the preceding section roundly skewered the pretensions of human thought and human eloquence to know the divine secret, the present passage balances that principle by another, that the gospel, distasteful in the elementary fact it preaches, becomes in reality the supreme wisdom and has an eloquence all its own. The severity of the cross may be difficult to accept at first, but it bears abundant fruit. Paul here reflects the wisdom teaching of Israel, that rude beginnings bear fruit in joyful harvest:

> For discipline is like her name,
> she is not accessible to many.
>
> Listen, my son, and heed my advice;
>   refuse not my counsel.
> Put your feet into her fetters,
>   and your neck under her yoke.
> Stoop your shoulders and carry her
>   and be not irked at her bonds.
>
> With all your soul draw close to her;
>   with all your strength keep
> her ways. . . .
> Thus will you afterward find rest in her,
>   and she will become your joy. (Sir 6:22–28; see also 4:16–18)

Instead of saying this **wisdom** is proclaimed, the word used for the preaching of the cross in verse 23, Paul here says it is *spoken*, suggesting rather a discussion or conversation. The fact of the cross demands acceptance and commitment—in short, an act of faith in responding to the act of God. Wisdom will never be attained by a discussion whose preestablished horizons are limited to what the human mind alone can see. But once the act of faith is made, it becomes possible to receive and to communicate progressive insights into God's wisdom.

Fig. 5. Corinthian forum.

This can be done, however, only among those who are **mature** in the faith. The Greek word here, sometimes translated as "perfect," appears commonly in the language of Paul's day to describe one who has reached maturity and has acquired the qualities associated with it: strength, virtue, wisdom, understanding, independence—as opposed to the child who remains a minor, dependent on others. This meaning perfectly fits Paul's thought here, that the Corinthians lack the understanding of the mature and show themselves so dependent on one or another preacher (see 1:12) that they are still infants who cannot speak or understand the language of adults.

The mature, then, are not an elite initiated into an esoteric wisdom of which other Christians are deprived—to speak of such would inflame rather than quench the Corinthians' snobbery—but rather those endowed with a deeper understanding of the same truths open to all Christians who have the courage to begin their quest in the humility of the cross. Of this type of wisdom the succeeding chapters of Paul's letter will be a brilliant example. The speaking, according to the NAB, is "to" those who are mature, leaving the possible interpretation that Paul means *his* preaching to the mature. But the Greek says, literally, "We speak *in* the mature." Hence other translations prefer "*among* the mature" (NRSV, NIV), which seems preferable, because Paul is dealing with conversations, prophecies, prayers, and other forms of informal exchange in the community.

Mystery in the Ancient World

In the Jewish tradition of which Paul was heir, the mystery referred to the plan of God or the heavenly council that was revealed to the prophets for the sake of the people (Jer 23:18, 22; Amos 3:7). Hence it was a secret, because it originated in God, but God wanted it to be known, and he made it known through his human spokespersons. The members of the community of Qumran often wrote of the mystery hidden in the writings of the prophets but now revealed in the interpretation given by their founder, the Teacher of Righteousness. Similarly, in Paul, the Christian mystery is God's plan of salvation, the "secret" of his heart, but a secret now revealed in the gospel (Rom 16:25–26; Eph 3:3–9).

This background helps us understand why for Paul the "mystery" is not esoteric or individualistic, as it was in the mystery religions of his day (and in much of the New Age theosophy today). It is open for all, and it is served by public [†]ministers like Paul and his collaborators.

In the Fathers the term "mysteries" is applied to the sacraments, those visible signs of invisible grace that are administered by the priests. This too is more of a development of Jewish thought than of Greek, as we can see in Philo, who says that the prayerful Jew, unlike the initiate into pagan mystery cults, is "initiated into the mysteries of the sanctified life," and that means being immersed in the laws, the prophets, the psalms, "and anything else that fosters and perfects knowledge and piety."[a] The Jewish historian Josephus adds another element when he contrasts the pagan initiation mysteries with the Jewish theocracy, where religion is "the end and aim of the entire community"—not the select few—and "the priests are entrusted with the special charge of it."[b]

a. Philo, *On the Contemplative Life* 25.
b. Josephus, *Against Apion* 2.188–89.

Again Paul insists on the basic and incompatible difference of this wisdom from **a wisdom of this age** and that **of the rulers of this age**. In the light of verse 8, the rulers of this [†]age are those who crucified Jesus, the leaders of both the Jews and the pagans, conceived here as instruments of Satan, the "prince of this world" (John 12:31 NIV). Worldly wisdom, in the light of what God has done, has proved itself bankrupt.

7   This explains the emphatic position of the word "God" in the next verse—**God's wisdom**, not man's, is what **we speak**. And God's wisdom is now no longer to be read merely in the open book of creation; his **mysterious** wisdom has now become accessible. The word "[†]mystery," derived from a word meaning "to close," particularly in the sense of closing the lips, means something

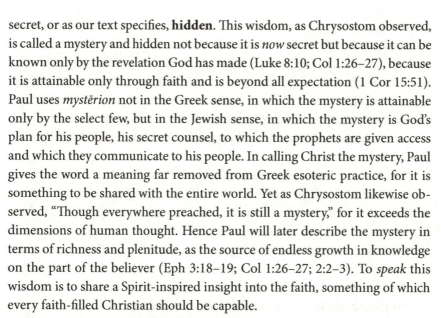

Loved before We Existed

Saint John Chrysostom comments: "And this is what Paul is eager to point out now—that God always loved us even from the beginning and when as yet we were not. For unless he had loved us, he would not have foreordained our riches. Consider not then the enmity that has come between [God and man], for more ancient than that was the friendship."[a]

a. Saint Chrysostom, *Homilies on 1 Corinthians* 7.4.

secret, or as our text specifies, **hidden**. This wisdom, as Chrysostom observed, is called a mystery and hidden not because it is *now* secret but because it can be known only by the revelation God has made (Luke 8:10; Col 1:26–27), because it is attainable only through faith and is beyond all expectation (1 Cor 15:51). Paul uses *mystērion* not in the Greek sense, in which the mystery is attainable only by the select few, but in the Jewish sense, in which the mystery is God's plan for his people, his secret counsel, to which the prophets are given access and which they communicate to his people. In calling Christ the mystery, Paul gives the word a meaning far removed from Greek esoteric practice, for it is something to be shared with the entire world. Yet as Chrysostom likewise observed, "Though everywhere preached, it is still a mystery," for it exceeds the dimensions of human thought. Hence Paul will later describe the mystery in terms of richness and plenitude, as the source of endless growth in knowledge on the part of the believer (Eph 3:18–19; Col 1:26–27; 2:2–3). To *speak* this wisdom is to share a Spirit-inspired insight into the faith, something of which every faith-filled Christian should be capable.

The mystery is God's gift to the human race. There was a time when it was hidden in the heart of God, when humanity passed through the night brought on by sin, but from all eternity God nevertheless planned to dispense this mystery **predetermined before the ages for our glory**.

Verse 8 repeats the thought of verse 6. The **rulers of this age** refers principally to the Jewish leaders and to Pilate but also to the cosmic powers behind them (Eph 1:20–23; 3:10). The human instruments of the death of Jesus were unaware of his true identity. As Jesus himself said of his executioners, "They do not know what they are doing" (Luke 23:34 NRSV); Peter too attributed their tragic deed to ignorance (Acts 3:17). Paul says that if they had known, if they had possessed the secret of divine wisdom, **they would not have crucified the**

8

The Devil Is Tricked

LIVING
TRADITION

The Fathers frequently speak of God's achieving his plan of salvation by tricking the devil. "If Christ had not been put to death, death would not have died. The devil was overcome by his own trophy, for the devil rejoiced when by seducing the first man, he cast him into death. By seducing the first man, he killed him. By killing the last man, he lost the first from his snare."[a]

a. Saint Augustine, *Sermon 263, On the Ascension*, in PL 38:1209–12.

Lord of glory. Paul chooses the most sublime title he can think of to contrast who Jesus really was on the cross with what he looked like—and continues to look like when he is preached as crucified. This title "Lord of glory" or its equivalent, which is used elsewhere in the New Testament only for the Father (Acts 7:2; Eph 1:17), is Paul's way of affirming the divinity of Christ as he hung on the cross. Quite to their surprise, the cosmic powers were defeated and subjected by the very victory they thought they had achieved (1 Cor 15:24–25; Col 2:15).

This mystery, then, was not only hidden from all ages in the heart of God (v. 7). It was also hidden on the cross. And that is why the mere act of Jesus' death on the cross, though it was in fact God's self-revelation to the world, is insufficient to disclose the mystery.

9   What else is needed? Paul builds up to his answer by again affirming, in a more poetic form, how inscrutable the mystery is: **What eye has not seen, and ear has not heard**. Hence it is not comprehended by the senses, nor is the rational mind able to grasp it: **the human heart**, biblically speaking, is the faculty of thinking. The verse is a melding of several Old Testament texts. Moses tells his complaining people: "[T]he Lord has not given you a heart to understand, or eyes to see, or ears to hear until this day" (Deut 29:3). Like the Israelites who were showered by the Lord's favors but still did not understand the implications, so without the Holy Spirit, Christians may not realize the full meaning of the mystery. But the closest text is from Isa 64:3: "No ear has ever heard, no eye ever seen, any God but you working such deeds for those who wait for him." No human being could imagine what God has done for those who love him. Notice that Paul has modified "wait for" in the Isaian text to "**love**." Why the change? The Isaian text speaks of future acts that the people await. But Paul in this text is speaking about the gifts that were hidden in the past but are now present, not requiring

any wait. These he "has revealed" (v. 10) to us. What are they? That God has sent his Son in human flesh; that he died for us; that he rose again and sent the Holy Spirit as the beginning of eternal life, which is the life of the Father, Son, and Holy Spirit—and everything else God has revealed.

To the Christians, identified as those who love God (as in Rom 8:28), God **10** has revealed himself and his gifts **through the Spirit**. Revelation through the historical act of Jesus' dying on the cross and rising from the dead is insufficient without the interior revelation of the Spirit. The external revelation was given to all, even to those who crucified Jesus (Acts 3:13–16). But to perceive the hand of God in the †paschal mystery is the gift of the Holy Spirit, who casts his divine light upon the external event and completes the revelational process.[4] The Holy Spirit opens the gift of Jesus to the believer (1 Cor 12:3; John 14:26; 15:26; 16:13). The Spirit can do this because he fathoms and **scrutinizes everything**. The verb means "to explore, examine, search out" (John 7:52; 1 Pet 1:11). "The one who searches hearts" is God, who knows perfectly the secret of human hearts (Jer 17:10; Rom 8:27). Thus there is nothing hidden in any heart that the Spirit does not know. But more than that, the Holy Spirit casts light upon the darkest areas of the soul, and those who love God (1 Cor 2:9) rejoice to have those areas brought to the light (John 3:21). But it is not only the believer whose heart the Spirit explores.

Here the surprise is that the Spirit reveals **even the depths of God**. The Greek word for "depths" is used in the Old Testament for the depths of the sea or the earth (Ps 69:3; Ezek 26:20). It was easily transferred to mean the obscurity, or better, the transcendent nature of an object's surpassing human power to encompass, and above all in referring to God. "Oh, the depth of the riches and wisdom and knowledge of God! How inscrutable are his judgments and how unsearchable his ways!" (Rom 11:33). The *Titanic* lay unseen on the ocean floor for seventy-five years until searchlights and a television camera, lowered to the depths, revealed it to the explorers and to the world. In like manner the Holy Spirit explores and reveals the depths of God to the believer. One might think also of a person's exploring an unknown cavern for the first time and moving a flashlight over the marvels discovered.

What are these marvels the Spirit reveals? They are found in the paschal mystery to begin with, but then within that, the revelation of Jesus as Lord of glory (1 Cor 2:8; 12:3), God as *Abba*, "Father!" and ourselves as his children (Rom 8:15–16; Gal 4:6). This is not merely an intellectual knowledge; it is also

---

4. Compare Matt 13:13–17, where Jesus presents the same series of negations, eye–see, ear–hear, heart–understand, followed by the conclusion that now, *to you* (believers), perception *has* been granted.

an experiential one, as Gal 4:6 shows by saying that the Christian *cries out* the name *Abba.* If Archimedes could cry out *heurēka!* "I found it!" when he discovered a way of determining the purity of gold, how much more the Christian who experiences the embrace of the divine Father.

Note in passing how the Holy Spirit, who gives knowledge, is associated with love in the heart of Christians (v. 9). There is an implicit link here between love and knowledge, which is explicit in Phil 1:9 and is fully developed in the Letters to the Ephesians and Colossians (Eph 3:17–19; Col 2:2–3).

11–12   Why can the Spirit reveal the depths of God? Because he is God's own Spirit. As an example, Paul points to the human person's spirit by which the person knows **what pertains to** that **person**. So the Spirit of God knows the heart of God because he is the heart of God. And he alone can disclose that heart to us in a way enabling us to **understand the things freely given us by God**. If it were not for the Holy Spirit, the gifts of God would mean nothing more to us than a pot of gold to an elephant. The condition Jesus gave the Samaritan woman, "If you knew the gift of God" (John 4:10), has now been achieved in the Christian. This is no small matter. The Spirit gives us supernatural understanding by which we are drawn into God's own self-understanding in the Trinity. If the universe, with its billions of stars separated by billions of light-years, astounds us, what is to be said of the inner life of its Creator—the interpersonal self-giving love of the Father, Son, and Holy Spirit? The Greek mind was not prepared for this idea. As one poet wrote: "It is not possible for the human mind, sprung from a mortal mother, to fathom the intentions of the gods."[5]

It is this divine Spirit, possessing the divine consciousness, that we have **received**. The Spirit does not replace our natural powers but is received into them as a source of supernatural knowledge, a sharing in the divine light. "The Spirit . . . bears witness with our spirit" (Rom 8:10). That is why the Christian can see in the Crucified One what God himself sees.

13   The gift of the Spirit goes beyond mere knowledge, however. The Spirit enables us to speak in words appropriate to the mystery. It is not that words can ever totally capture the mystery, for that would be to have the infinite mind of God. The gift of tongues is precisely the language that bears witness to the mystery beyond words (1 Cor 14:2). But there are human words that can convey something of the mystery, and Paul will later encourage the use of such words in the gift of prophecy (14:1–5).

We speak about them—the gifts of God—**not with words taught by human wisdom, but with words taught by the Spirit, describing spiritual realities**

---

5. Pindar, *Hymns* 13; see Philo, *On Flight and Finding* 165.

in spiritual terms. The NAB translation understands the Greek to mean using spiritual language to describe spiritual realities, and so do other modern translations: "expressing spiritual truths in spiritual words" (NIV), "we teach spiritual things spiritually" (JB), "fitting spiritual language to spiritual things" (NJB). But it can also mean *interpreting spiritual realities for spiritual persons*: "interpreting spiritual things to those who are spiritual" (NRSV), which would provide a natural lead into the next two verses.[6] A "spiritual person" is equivalent to the "mature" Christian, who is led by the Spirit of God not only in using the charismatic gifts so prized by the Corinthians but also in following the path of virtue and bearing the fruits of the Spirit, with the accompanying ability to crucify his flesh (Gal 5:22–23).

Unfortunately, many a Corinthian Christian is still acting like the **natural**   14
person of his preconversion days. "Natural person" is the NAB's attempt to catch the meaning of the Greek *psychikos anthrōpos*, which means the human person who is moved only by the soul (*psychē*), with its faculties of mind and will, and is closed to the realm of the spirit (*pneuma*). In Paul's thought the human person is made up of body, mind (or soul), and spirit (see Biblical Background). The human spirit is the point of contact with the divine spirit, and when a person opens himself to the Holy Spirit, not only his spirit but also his whole being is renewed, sanctified, and put on the road to continuous spiritual progress (1 Thess 5:23).

However, it is possible for a person to remain in the confines of the purely natural order; to such a one the wisdom of the Spirit will seem **foolishness**, for he or she does not possess the faculty for judging spiritual things. See, for example, the mistaken judgment of Jesus by his fellow Nazarenes (Mark 6:1–6). From this it is clear that in order to understand the Scriptures, for example, one must be in tune with the reality that they are disclosing. If I was born blind, I can have no understanding of color, no matter how well a person with sight might try to explain it to me. Or if deaf, no understanding of the sound of music. Similarly, if I am not attuned to the Spirit's revelation, at least as a seeker, I will not come to understand it.

The spiritual person, however, possesses a faculty by which one can bring   15
a sure judgment not only to the things of the Spirit but also to everything else. In turn he **is not subject to judgment by anyone**. This does not mean that the spiritual person is above criticism or community norms or authority. Paul is

6. Saint Chrysostom understands the expression to be comparing spiritual things of the New Testament with their Old Testament †types or forerunners, such as the resurrection of Christ with the deliverance of Jonah, or Mary's virginal conception of Jesus with Sarah's miraculous conception of a child in her old age, and so on (*Homilies on 1 Corinthians* 7.8).

Body, Soul, Spirit

In 1 Thess 5:23, Paul prays for his readers thus: "May the God of peace make you holy through and through, and may your whole being—spirit, soul, and body—be kept blameless at the coming of our Lord Jesus Christ" (my trans.). Probably drawing on the story of the creation of Adam (Gen 2:7), where God forms the body of man from the earth, then breathes into him the breath of life (spirit), and man becomes a living being (soul), Paul sees the totality of the human person as embracing three dimensions or worlds to which one relates.

The body (*sōma*) is our solidarity with all of material creation—what is solid, lumpy, and collision-prone. It is what enabled St. Francis of Assisi to speak of "brother sun and sister moon." The body especially relates us to other human beings, particularly in the Church, which is the *body* of Christ (1 Cor 12:27). It calls us to think of others, especially the suffering, as belonging to the same body (Heb 13:3). The body is not the same as the "flesh," which, with rare exceptions (1 Cor 6:16; Eph 5:31), Paul uses to mean the tendency of our wounded nature toward sin and selfishness. The body can be the occasion for sin (Rom 6:6), but it is also what will be redeemed (8:23).[a]

The soul (*psychē*) is the natural principle of life, resulting from God's creative act. To it belongs the mind with its ability to reason, to organize, to think. The soul's horizon is what reason can see.

The highest part of the person is the spirit (*pneuma*), which is the person's openness to the transcendent, to mystery, to God. One might compare the human person to a tree. Its roots are sunk in the earth. The trunk organizes the tree's life by channeling it into an identifiable form. Then the limbs and the leaves reach out toward the sky, the sun, and the life-giving rain. In the human person, the body relates us to material creation, the soul organizes our life, and the spirit is our reaching out beyond ourselves. As the limbs and the leaves receive the sun and the rain, so our spirit is an appetite for what is beyond us, and ultimately for God.

The healthy development of the human person happens when all three of these are functioning properly and their activity is integrated. But if one element is neglected or abused, it is difficult for the whole to function. When the body is neglected or abused, the results are evident. When one limits one's life to the body and the rational soul, closing off the spirit, then the person will wither, just as the tree will wither without sun and rain. Now Paul was facing a problem in Corinth with those who felt that their natural wisdom (the wisdom of their *psychē* alone) was adequate to understand and live the mystery of Christ. Not so, Paul says, because without the Holy Spirit's feeding the human spirit, one will never understand the mystery of Christ, and the one who tries to speak about it will talk nonsense. But when the Holy Spirit does feed the human spirit, wonderful things can happen, and one can even speak with words appropriate to the mystery.

a. One of the best books on Paul's theology of the body is still that of J. A. T. Robinson, *The Body: A Study in Pauline Theology* (London: SCM, 1952). On a broader level, see Pope John Paul II's *Man and Woman He Created Them: A Theology of the Body*, trans. Michael M. Waldstein (Boston: Pauline Books & Media, 2006). Saint Thomas Aquinas distinguishes the rational function of the soul from its contemplative function, which in Paul's terms would be the distinction between soul (the rational) and spirit (the contemplative) in *Summa Theologiae* Iae.79.9.

criticizing the Corinthians precisely for lacking submission to authority, which is an essential aspect of spirituality. The spiritual person here, then, is equivalent to the mature Christian, whom the "natural person," lacking the light of the Spirit, cannot judge. Saint Thomas Aquinas uses the analogy of a person asleep not being able to make judgments of a person awake, while the latter can make correct judgments concerning the one asleep.

The concluding verse 16 marks a double advance in thought. **For "who has** **16** **known the mind of the Lord, so as to counsel him?" But we have the mind of Christ**. Paul is quoting a passage in Isaiah (40:13), where the †rhetorical question obviously expects the answer "No one." Paul shifts from "spirit" to **mind** and from the Holy Spirit to **Christ**. "Mind" here stands for the faculty of thought, which involves selecting, comparing, assessing, classifying, and ordering. Since the mind of the Lord involves the formation of concepts and individual judgments, it makes possible an expression of the mystery in human language; God's wisdom is a wisdom, therefore, that is communicable, teachable. Paul in 1 Cor 14:4 will show the superiority of verbal communication to incommunicable experience, and here in 2:16 he evidently wants to show that the Spirit does not depreciate one's intellect and power of speech (14:1–33) but rather engages, directs, and transforms them. The Holy Spirit transforms the mind by causing it to view everything with the mind of Christ: seeing oneself, others, and the whole of creation in the light of the Father's love and desire to have all united with him. This is a goal that is never completely attained in this life, spurring Paul to urge his readers to be constantly "transformed by the renewal of your mind" (Rom 12:2).

Reflection and Application (2:6–16)

Spirit-inspired wisdom is not limited to adults. Children who love the Lord can sometimes astound adults with wisdom that can only come from the Holy Spirit. Audrey, a friend of mine, was holding her three-year-old nephew, Paul, on her knee. She asked, "Paul, did you ever think of giving your life to Jesus?" "How do I do that?" Paul asked. Audrey replied, "Maybe if you ask him, he'll tell you." Little Paul got very serious for a long time, then forming his hands as if he were holding a ball, he tossed the imaginary ball and said, "Catch!"

This passage speaks to us about three important things. First, there is the gift of God's wisdom in the revelation he has given us in Jesus Christ, made effective and personal in us by the Holy Spirit. It is the greatest of treasures, and we should allow the Holy Spirit to be our searchlight as we go deeper with him in prayer and study of the mystery of God. Second, rightly disposed by the Holy Spirit, we can speak and share this wisdom with others. This is not limited to the official teaching by church authorities but is also the heritage and privilege of every believer, as we can see from the charismatic nature of the Corinthian community, where inspirations given by the Holy Spirit were freely shared among those gathered for worship. The Second Vatican Council, in its document on divine revelation, speaks of the "growth in the understanding of the realities and the words that have been handed down. This happens through the contemplation and study made by believers . . . through a penetrating understanding of the spiritual realities they experience" (*Dei Verbum*, §8). Third, this wisdom and its expression sets the Christian apart from the world that is closed and opposed to the light of God's revelation as well as from the worldly wisdom of those who can see no further than human reason.

We live in a world where both faith and reason are imperiled by a subjectivism and relativism that so easily leaks into our way of thinking: "It doesn't matter what you believe" or "One religion is as good as another," or, as I once heard on the radio, "Morality, like beauty, is in the eye of the beholder." It is not uncommon today for individuals to construct their own religion, creating their own "truth," with disregard for the wisdom that humanity has taken millennia to acquire, to say nothing of a divine revelation that might make demands on us—such as the Christian faith, anchored in the self-giving love of the Crucified One. Truth, whether reached through reason or revelation, is an objective reality. It is there whether we like it or not. It is also the only thing that can bring about true community. "Love," Paul will later say, not only bears with those who disagree with us but also "rejoices with the truth" (1 Cor 13:6–7). If we are to be "living the truth in love" (Eph 4:15), it is crucial that we know the truth. In the midst of so much intellectual confusion today, the "mind of Christ" challenges us to constantly "be transformed by the renewal of your mind, that you may discern what is the will of God, what is good and pleasing and perfect" (Rom 12:2).

Our True Boast Is in God, Not Ministers

1 Corinthians 3

Having laid out his magnificent theology of the cross in chapter 1 and his teaching on true, godly wisdom in chapter 2, Paul now tells the Corinthians what these exalted reflections mean for the way they are to live. Rivalries show that they neither understand the cross nor experience the spiritual wisdom that only the spiritually mature enjoy. Since the rivalries are over different †ministers, Paul will now develop a theology of apostolic ministry. On the one hand, he punctures the inflated conception the Corinthians have of the ministry as a popularity contest by insisting that Paul, Apollos, and Peter are only instruments in the hand of God, who gets the credit. On the other hand, he exalts the ministry by stressing its source, which is God, and its end, which is the building of the Church. The Church is not just a social gathering but especially God's field, God's building, God's temple. And all the ministers belong to everyone.

Right View of the Ministry (3:1–9)

[1]Brothers, I could not talk to you as spiritual people, but as fleshly people, as infants in Christ. [2]I fed you milk, not solid food, because you were unable to take it. Indeed, you are still not able, even now, [3]for you are still of the flesh. While there is jealousy and rivalry among you, are you not of the flesh, and behaving in an ordinary human way? [4]Whenever someone says, "I belong to Paul," and another, "I belong to Apollos," are you not merely human?

> ⁵What is Apollos, after all, and what is Paul? Ministers through whom
> you became believers, just as the Lord assigned each one. ⁶I planted,
> Apollos watered, but God caused the growth. ⁷Therefore, neither the one
> who plants nor the one who waters is anything, but only God, who causes
> the growth. ⁸The one who plants and the one who waters are equal, and
> each will receive wages in proportion to his labor. ⁹For we are God's co-
> workers; you are God's field, God's building.

NT: Eph 2:20–22; Heb 5:12–14; James 3:16; 1 Pet 2:2, 5
Catechism: Church as field, building, 755–56
Lectionary: 3:6–10: Mass for after the Harvest

1–2　　Having painted an exalted picture of the wisdom of the mature, Paul now returns to the actual situation of the Corinthians. They are far from that wisdom and spiritual maturity. When Paul came among them, he fed them, like fat-cheeked **infants**, with **milk, not solid food**. The Greek word *sarkinos*, here translated **fleshly** and applied to **infants**, stands in slight contrast with *sarkikos*, translated further on more negatively as "of the flesh" (v. 3). Paul did not expect his converts at first to be capable of more than the rudimentary truths of the faith, any more than an infant would be capable of solid food. Drinking milk, or being nursed, is perfectly appropriate for those who are newly reborn in Christ (1 Thess 2:7; see 1 Pet 2:2). But by now, some three to five years later, they should have become **spiritual people**, that is, mature (see Heb 5:12–13).

3–4　　Instead, they are **of the flesh**, **behaving in an ordinary human way**. The "flesh," for Paul, is the human tendency toward sin and selfishness in resistance to God. To be "of the flesh" is to give way to fleshly drives such as **jealousy and rivalry**, and thus to act in a way that tears down rather than builds up the body of Christ. This is precisely what the Corinthians are doing with their quarreling and disunity. Paul uses "human" here and throughout this section for what is deficient, not in itself but by comparison with what is of God.[1] What is merely human is foolish in contrast with God's wisdom, weak in contrast with God's power.

5　　The Corinthians are bringing their culture's †patron-client pattern of relationships into their community life (see sidebar). Against this, Paul seeks to demote and equalize the "patrons," that is, the †ministers in the church. Thus he turns from the Corinthians' different reactions to the ministers to the ministers themselves. **What** (notice he does not say "Who") **is Apollos, after all, and what is Paul?** They are all simply **ministers**, instruments used by God to

---

1. See 1 Cor 1:25; 2:5, 9, 13–14; 3:3–4, 21.

The Patron-Client System

BIBLICAL BACKGROUND

Greco-Roman society was highly stratified. At the top was the very small governing class, followed by merchants, retainers, and priests, then the artisans, followed by the huge numbers of peasants, and even below them the unclean and degraded, and finally the expendable. Power and privilege ranged from extreme at the top to nothing at the bottom.[a] Social scientists have recently called attention to the patron-client structure of Greco-Roman society. A person would seek security by attaching himself to a patron, whose help, influence, and favors would be repaid by the client's loyalty and service. This arrangement was useful to both. The patron had a company of dependents who could get things done on a lower level, while the client would share in the prestige and influence of his patron. In Corinth the desire for spiritual patronage is possibly what led community members to latch onto Peter, Paul, Apollos, or other important persons who would assure them of their dignity (even without the consent of the supposed patron), but with the attendant effect of promoting their hero as superior to other claimants.

In many underdeveloped countries today, the ancient patron-client system is still common. In Nepal I remember seeing the house of an influential neighbor visited in the early mornings by a line of clients, no doubt seeking favors and promising services.

a. Gerhard Lenski, *Power and Privilege: A Theory of Social Stratification*, 2nd ed. (Chapel Hill: University of North Carolina Press, 1984), 284.

---

bring the Corinthians to the faith. They may not have had equal talent, but that is irrelevant because each one was given his gift by the Lord.

Like laborers in a garden, they came and went, one planting, another watering. But God was always there, giving the growth. And the laborers **are equal**, even though the value of their work may not be, for **each will receive wages in proportion to his labor**. The equality comes not from the differing quality of their work but from their belonging to the Master. Judging the value of their work is God's business. The faithful should focus on the source of all, God, to whom both ministers and faithful belong.

6–8

The ministers are **God's co-workers**. The faithful are **God's field, God's building**. Combining agricultural and architectural images, as later in Col 2:7 and Eph 3:17 ("rooted and built/grounded"), enables Paul to exploit the image of God-given growth on the one hand (the field) and the activity of the co-workers on the other (the building). These images provide a rich source for later development. Here the emphasis falls on the word as "God's," as Chrysostom says (see sidebar).

9

Chrysostom on God's Field, God's Building

If you are God's field, it is right that you should be so called not because of those who cultivate you, but because of God, for the field is not the worker's but the owner's.... Again, the building is not the workman's but the master's. Now if you are a building, you must not be forced asunder. If you are a farm, you must not be divided but be walled in by a single fence, namely, unanimity.[a]

a. Saint Chrysostom, *Homilies on 1 Corinthians* 8.6.

The Work of God (3:10–17)

[10]According to the grace of God given to me, like a wise master builder I laid a foundation, and another is building upon it. But each one must be careful how he builds upon it, [11]for no one can lay a foundation other than the one that is there, namely, Jesus Christ. [12]If anyone builds on this foundation with gold, silver, precious stones, wood, hay, or straw, [13]the work of each will come to light, for the Day will disclose it. It will be revealed with fire, and the fire [itself] will test the quality of each one's work. [14]If the work stands that someone built upon the foundation, that person will receive a wage. [15]But if someone's work is burned up, that one will suffer loss; the person will be saved, but only as through fire. [16]Do you not know that you are the temple of God, and that the Spirit of God dwells in you? [17]If anyone destroys God's temple, God will destroy that person; for the temple of God, which you are, is holy.

OT: Ps 118:22; Isa 28:16
NT: Matt 3:11–12; Acts 4:11–12; 1 Cor 6:19; 2 Cor 6:16; Eph 2:19–22; 1 Pet 1:7; 2:4
Catechism: Church as temple of Holy Spirit, 797; Purgatory, 1030–32
Lectionary: 3:9c–11, 16–17: Dedication of the Lateran Basilica; Anniversary of Dedication of a
    Church; Mass for the Holy Church

10   Dropping the agricultural image, Paul develops the image of the Church as God's building, but from the viewpoint of the builders, meaning the [†]ministers, with Paul himself as the first. Speaking from his own experience, he recalls that it was **according to the grace of God given to me**: thus it was God's choice, not his, that he should be a founder of churches in Gentile territory. He does not hesitate to call himself a **wise master builder**. His task was to lay a **foundation**

The Church as Field and Building

BIBLICAL BACKGROUND

Paul is not unique in his use of the images of field and building. Jesus uses them in his parables: he speaks of his disciples as a field in Matt 13:1–9; and as a vineyard in 21:33–46, where he also presents himself as the cornerstone of the new building, the Church. The agricultural images suggest the wonder of growth given by God, whereas the building image suggests the role of human endeavor in its construction. An important element in both is the emphasis on the movement rather than the finished product. The growth and the building of the Church never stops. Christ empowers the Church to grow and its members to build in such a way that one can never be satisfied that the job is finished (Eph 4:11–16).

on which others could build. That is why Paul did not settle in one place very long. He would invest as much time as necessary to give the new community sufficient stability, appoint local leaders, and move on. This policy shows an enormous trust both in the Holy Spirit and in the fledgling leadership in whose hands he left the community.

11–13 But he warns the Corinthians against any builder who would lay a different foundation than the one Paul has already laid: **Jesus Christ**. This was no small matter in a place like Corinth, where every imaginable cult had its hawkers, and †syncretism—the mixing of elements from various religions—was rife. Others not of apostolic origin could introduce pagan or even Jewish extraneous elements and dilute or transform the gospel into an unrecognizable counterfeit. But even assuming that the minister builds on Paul's foundation, the quality of his work may vary, from **gold** to **straw**. The first three elements Paul mentions are not combustible, the last three are. Paul, then, has been like the master contractor who, after laying the foundation, has let out the rest to subcontractors. If these build well, their work will stand on the day of judgment, biblically associated with fire (Dan 7:9–10; Mal 4:1–2; 2 Pet 3:7).

14–15 If their work is not up to code, it will be burned up. We read frequently of bridges or buildings that collapsed because they were carelessly built or cheaper elements than specified were used. In Paul's image, those who build with "gold, silver," and "precious stones" (v. 12) are probably the ones whose **work stands**. These **will receive a wage**. Paul is more concerned here with the quality of the work than with the virtue of the builders, but for all his theology of grace, he does speak of a reward. The contractor who builds with "wood, hay, or straw" (v. 12) symbolizes the minister whose workmanship is shoddy.

The Fire of Purgatory?

In the text of 3:15 the Church has found a foundation for its doctrine of purgatory, which the Catechism introduces as follows: "All who die in God's grace and friendship, but still imperfectly purified, are indeed assured of their eternal salvation; but after death they undergo purification, so as to achieve the holiness necessary to enter the joy of heaven" (Catechism, 1030). Jesus used undying fire as an image of eternal punishment (Matt 3:12; 18:8; 25:41; Mark 9:43–48; Luke 3:17), but that is not the issue here. Nevertheless, the negligent builder will not escape judgment. Saint Caesarius of Arles (died AD 542) comments: "In that fire it is slight sins which are purged, not serious ones."[a] The person is saved but undergoes a purification in the process. The Church has understood the purification to apply to venial sins and attachments of any sort that need to be burned away. Fire here is understood to be a spiritual fire of purification, the fire of divine love, which the saints often earnestly desired already here on earth so that they might sooner be joined to the beloved.

a. *Sermons* 179.1

Such work will not withstand the final judgment of God; his **work is burned up**, and the person **will suffer loss**. One thinks of a contractor who watches his work go up in flames. But the worker himself **will be saved, but only as through fire**. In the judgment, the careless workman himself will be saved, but only as if running through the burning building and escaping singed. In this case the builder was not destroying the community (as below in 3:17, where the destroyer is destroyed): he was just doing a poor job of building. Paul thus warns all ministers to take their job seriously, for everyone who builds will be responsible for the quality of his work.

16   **Do you not know?** is a stock expression used to introduce a fundamental teaching; here it echoes Paul's frustration with those who do not recognize the exalted nature of the Church. They **are the temple of God**. The Jewish Christians may well have been shocked to hear Paul say this. At the time of the writing of this letter, Herod's magnificent expansion of the Jerusalem temple was nearing completion, the Jewish revolt was eight years away, and the destruction of the temple eleven. Gentile temples were everywhere, housing their gods within, while the people gathered to worship outside. Therefore it must have struck the Corinthians as new to think of *themselves* as the temple of God. But such they are, for **the Spirit of God dwells in** them. Later Paul will use the temple

Fig. 6. The temple of Apollo in Corinth.

metaphor to refer to the individual Christian's body (6:19). But here it refers to the community as such. (Today when we use the word "church" to refer to a building, it is important to remember that originally it referred to the Christian assembly, whether in a building or not.) By applying the meaning of "temple" to the Church, Paul indicates that the Christian assembly is a holy dwelling place where God resides and makes himself accessible to his people, receives their worship and sacrifices, hears their prayers, and speaks through his ministers. "You are . . . members of the household of God, built upon the foundation of the apostles and prophets, with Christ Jesus himself as the capstone. Through him the whole structure is held together and grows into a temple sacred in the Lord; in him you also are being built together into a dwelling place of God in the Spirit" (Eph 2:19–22). "Come to him, a living stone . . . , and, like living stones, let yourselves be built into a spiritual house to be a holy priesthood to offer spiritual sacrifices acceptable to God through Jesus Christ" (1 Pet 2:4–5).

If anyone destroys God's temple, God will destroy that person. The dra- **17** matic Greek sentence structure here is difficult to render in English. Literally, Paul says, "If anyone the temple of God destroys, destroy him God will." Aside from crucifying the Son of God, Paul can think of no more grievous sin than destroying the temple of God. The Corinthians must have been shocked to think that their petty rivalries and turf squabbles could lead to the destruction of the community and God's awesome judgment. But that is what Paul is implying,

God's Temple Is People

The community at Qumran, which judged the temple cult and priesthood in Jerusalem to be apostate, considered itself the new temple in a way that prepared for Paul's teaching here. The Qumranites are "an everlasting plantation, a holy house for Israel, and the foundation of the holy of holies for Aaron, . . . chosen by the will [of God] to atone for the land" (1QS 8.5–6), "a house of perfection and truth for Israel" (8.9). The Qumranites' idea of holiness, however, involved physical and spiritual separation from the world outside, whereas in Paul the Church has a mission to the world.

as if what begins as a tiny crack could bring the collapse of the entire building. The rivalries thus take on the character of sacrilege, because the community is not an ordinary building. It is sacred, it is consecrated: **For the temple of God, which you are, is holy**. The NAB misses the †rhetorical power of the Greek: "For the temple of God is holy, and that temple *you are*."

Reflection and Application (3:10–17)

The Church's foundation. What does it mean that "the Church's one foundation is Jesus Christ her Lord"? Popes John Paul II and Benedict XVI have repeatedly hammered home this point: Jesus Christ is the sole reason for the existence of the Church, and salvation means a personal relationship with him. The applications of this simple truth are many. On the one hand, although the Church sinks its roots in every culture, it forbids syncretism, the mixing of elements of foreign religions or creeds into the purity of its faith. It resists any attempt to teach that other religions are simply equal paths to salvation, as explained in the Vatican document *Dominus Iesus* (*On the Unicity and Salvific Universality of Jesus Christ and the Church*, esp. §§20–23). But even in the ordinary life of a parish, it is easy to get sidetracked into other issues and concerns and lose sight of the central one: promoting one's personal relationship with Jesus Christ. In a parish I know, on Earth Day the homily was totally about ecology, without a single reference to the Scripture readings of the Sunday. The Church is not a club, a philanthropic organization, a social advocacy group, or a business. It is a community called to prepare for the kingdom of God. It does so by inviting all to know the Person of Jesus Christ in the power of the Holy Spirit and thus to be drawn into communion with the Father.

Reverence for God's temple. One morning before the 7:30 morning Mass in St. Mary Magdalen church in San Antonio, a young man smashed three statues, including that of the church's patron saint. A hefty parishioner ran forward and wrestled the youth to the ground, pinning him there until the police arrived. The event shattered the congregation's composure more than it did the statues. Why would anyone do such a thing? Why would one desecrate the holy? Parish congregations might not experience the same shock when petty rivalries make a fissure in the community. But if we take St. Paul seriously, that is what such childish and selfish ways do to the temple that is the community. One would not think of them as sacrileges, . . . but what is Paul saying?

The same reverence for the holy should accompany those who minister to the community. Build with precious stones, not with straw! You are building a temple. There is no place for turf wars or rivalry among the workers. The church is not yours: it is God's.

Everything and Everyone Is Yours (3:18–23)

---

[18]Let no one deceive himself. If anyone among you considers himself wise in this age, let him become a fool so as to become wise. [19]For the wisdom of this world is foolishness in the eyes of God, for it is written:

"He catches the wise in their own ruses,"
[20]and again:

"The Lord knows the thoughts of the wise,
    that they are vain."
[21]So let no one boast about human beings, for everything belongs to you, [22]Paul or Apollos or Cephas, or the world or life or death, or the present or the future: all belong to you, [23]and you to Christ, and Christ to God.

OT: Job 5:13; Ps 94:11; Prov 28:26
NT: Rom 8:10; 1 Cor 1:12; 6:19; 11:3
Catechism: Jesus, Lord of the world, 450

Earlier in the letter Paul introduced the theme of wisdom to counter the **18–20** pretended wisdom of the Corinthians, whose factionalism has shown them to be anything but wise. He countered their estimation of mere human wisdom with the divine "foolishness" of the cross. Now he returns to the wisdom theme, beginning with a line from Job that fits the Corinthians' situation well: God "sets up the lowly on high. . . . **He catches the wise in their own ruses**" (Job 5:11–13). The "lowly" fits with what Paul has said about the lowliness of the cross in 1:18–25 (also Phil 2:6–11), and the low status of most of the community, which contrasts ironically with their self-exaltation (1:26–31). And he adds a line from Ps 94:11, tweaking "the thoughts of *man*" (NIV) to the **thoughts of the wise**. He could also have quoted another line from that psalm, "You fools, when will you be wise?" (Ps 94:8).

21–22   And then, concluding that **no one** should **boast about human beings** (the different †ministers), he suddenly adds his own theological insight: **Everything belongs to you**, he begins, applying this first to the ministers, **Paul or Apollos or Cephas**. The Apostle here reverses the logic of the Corinthians. They had said that *they* belong to one or the other minister, as if that gives them their identity, their importance. Not so, says Paul. The ministers *belong to you*—all of them. The ministers belong to the people, not the people to the ministers. The ministers are servants, not captains of competitive teams. And they are servants of everyone.

That is clear enough. But Paul had said every*thing*, not every*one* belongs to you. And now he goes on to list those things as **the world or life or death, or the present or the future: all belong to you**. What does he mean by this, and what does this have to do with the problem of rivalries? When one feels the need to boost one's ego, one grasps at things that will give one the sense of importance, such as whose coattails do I claim to ride on? But Paul senses that the grasping for identification with one leader over another is symptomatic of a much deeper human compulsion to *possess*, to pad one's security with ownership of things, even of persons like Paul, Apollos, and Peter. Paul wants to convince his people that belonging to Christ has set them free from those compulsions if they will but claim that belonging. This is similar to Jesus' teaching that those who seek first the kingdom of God will attain everything else besides (Matt 6:33).

23   The key to owning everything is, ironically, *being possessed* by Another, a Person: **You . . . belong . . . to Christ, and Christ to God**. It is clear enough that everything belongs to God, for he is the creator of all. And so too all things belong to Christ, whom John identifies as the Word, through whom "all things were made" (John 1:3 NIV), and whom Paul in Col 1:16 identifies as the one "in whom everything in heaven and earth was created" (my trans.; also see 1 Cor 8:6). In addition, Christ possesses all creation by virtue of his redeeming it from its slavery to sin and corruption through his death and resurrection (Matt 28:18; Rom 8:21; Phil 2:11; Col 1:18–20). Thus, belonging to Christ gives the Church, and specifically here the Corinthians, a share is his reigning and

"owning." Later, in Ephesians and Colossians, Paul will call on this linkage in the idea of the overflowing "fullness" of life, grace, and perfection in Christ, as I have shown in my previous books.[2] Like a multitiered fountain that is filled and fills in turn, the †mystery is that all fullness is in God (Eph 3:19), who pours it into Christ, "in whom all fullness dwells" (Col 1:19; 2:9, my trans.), who pours it into the Church and into the cosmos (Eph 1:23). Thus, in reverse, the cosmos receives life from the Church, the Church from Christ, Christ from God. The consequence for the Corinthians is this: You do not have to claim possession of any one minister, because you have them all. In fact, your belonging to Christ means that the entire universe is yours, for you possess it insofar as Christ possesses it, sharing in his creative and redemptive love.

Reflection and Application (3:18–23)

How does one possess everything? The Stoic Seneca said it was by wisdom: "Only the wise man has all things, and has no difficulty retaining them."[3] For Paul as for Jesus, to possess everything means to possess in love. One who loves possesses without controlling. Actually, one who loves another not only does not control that person but even seeks an ever greater spiritual freedom for him or her. Still, it is love that binds the other to us as ours, for we belong to one another, made so by the love of Christ, which we share. As for the ownership of things, I reflect on the ranch of my boyhood. The near eight thousand acres belonged to my father, and because of that I considered the ranch my own, riding or walking wherever I cared and whenever I cared. Similarly, because all creation belongs to our heavenly Father, and our older Brother Jesus is in charge of it, we can consider all of it ours as well. But we possess it as Christ possesses it, in creative and redeeming love. That means we can use it, but we should never lose the contemplative love for creation—animal, vegetable, or mineral. Like St. Francis, the Christian can speak of created things as brother or sister. As a Christian, whatever you love you possess, because you are possessed by the love of Christ. If that is a mystery, so be it.

2. George T. Montague, *Maturing in Christ* (Milwaukee: Bruce, 1964), 221–30; idem, *The Living Thought of Saint Paul* (Beverly Hills, CA: Benziger, 1976), 198–209.

3. Seneca, *De beneficiis* (*On Benefits*) 7.2.

Servants and Stewards

1 Corinthians 4

Paul continues to address the problem of divisions among the Christians in Corinth. They have formed parties around particular leaders. But competition has no place either among the Church's †ministers or among those who champion one over the other. Paul here offers some criteria for genuine ministry and holds his own weather-beaten ministry as an example.

Stewards Judged by the Lord (4:1–5)

---

[1]Thus should one regard us: as servants of Christ and stewards of the mysteries of God. [2]Now it is of course required of stewards that they be found trustworthy. [3]It does not concern me in the least that I be judged by you or any human tribunal; I do not even pass judgment on myself; [4]I am not conscious of anything against me, but I do not thereby stand acquitted; the one who judges me is the Lord. [5]Therefore, do not make any judgment before the appointed time, until the Lord comes, for he will bring to light what is hidden in darkness and will manifest the motives of our hearts, and then everyone will receive praise from God.

NT: Mark 7:1; Luke 12:2–3, 42–44; John 5:44; Rom 2:16; 2 Cor 5:10–11
Catechism: Christ as judge and savior, 678, 680–82
Lectionary: St. Pius V; Common of Pastors

1   Here Paul returns to the subordinate role of ministers. They are servants of Christ and servants of the community in him. But the fact that they serve

the community does not mean they take orders from the community, for they are **stewards**, which means they have authority from the owner to manage the estate for the owner, who in this case is Christ. It is a solemn responsibility, for in their hands are placed the **mysteries of God**. Paul's listeners would be very familiar with the term and the idea of †mystery, because in the Greek society of their day there were all kinds of religions that claimed to offer access to the unknown, not only the mystery religions with their secret rituals—comparable to today's New Age cults—but also fortune-tellers and prophets, just as there are psychics and palm readers today. But for Paul the mysteries he is talking about are those of God, primarily his plan of salvation of the world through Christ. And these mysteries are not hidden and esoteric. They have now been revealed publicly to all.

Paul is here concerned about the varying judgments the Corinthians are   2
making of the ministers. Of course ministers should **be found trustworthy**. But who, in the case of these ministers of Christ, should do the judging? Not the bickering Corinthians.

Not wanting to speak for the other ministers (Peter or Apollos; see 1:12) but   3–4
suggesting they would probably feel the same way, Paul first addresses those who would judge him. Your judgment, he says, **does not concern me in the least**. Paul is not concerned by what people think of him. If he is concerned, as he has been for more than three chapters now, about the way they are comparing ministers, it is for the sake of the unity of the community and not because he sets any value on such judgments. **I do not even pass judgment on myself**. Paul is using judgment in two senses here: as the judgment of his †conscience and as the judgment of the relative value of himself and the other ministers. As far as conscience is concerned, he is **not conscious of anything against** himself. Although his conscience is clear, he does not judge himself **acquitted**, since anyone may have faults that he cannot see (Ps 19:13). He leaves that judgment to the **Lord**. So both for himself and in comparison with others, Paul refuses to judge.

His listeners should follow his example and not pass judgment on the relative   5
value of the ministers. The Lord will do that at **the appointed time**: when **the Lord comes**. "There is nothing concealed that will not be revealed, nor secret that will not be known" (Luke 12:2). Even the greatest works of ministry done without love avail nothing (1 Cor 13:1–3), but that is for the Lord to judge, when **he will bring to light what is hidden in darkness and will manifest the motives of our hearts**. Note that in saying **then everyone will receive praise from God**, Paul does not anticipate condemnation of any of these particular

ministers (Peter, Apollos, or himself), only the relative degree of praise they will receive according to the value of the ministry they have performed, as in 3:10–14.

Reflection and Application (4:1–5)

My brother's family endured a pastor who alienated so many of the parishioners that numbers dwindled and, since there was no other Catholic church in town, some joined local Protestant churches. But my brother and his wife hung in there with others who had the grace to see beyond the acerbic antics of the man, who publicly embarrassed people from the pulpit and told others to get out of his church—until the day he was replaced by a pastor whom everyone loved. Hanging in there was an extraordinary grace. There also is a lesson here for the people of God, who are not always graced with ideal ministers but can hold the faith and the parish together despite them. But the more ordinary situation is the wagging tongue that likes to compare even gifted pastors and gauge cooperation with them accordingly. Paul cautions against pronouncing judgment on Christian leaders: "Who are you to pass judgment on someone else's servant?" (Rom 14:4).

At the same time there is a sense in which each member is a steward: each one has responsibility for the holiness and mission of the church (1 Pet 4:10). In case of serious abuse, one has the responsibility of calling this to the attention of the authority that can do something about it. In a diocese this would normally be the bishop.

Proud Corinthians and Lowly Apostles (4:6–13)

---

[6]I have applied these things to myself and Apollos for your benefit, brothers, so that you may learn from us not to go beyond what is written, so that none of you will be inflated with pride in favor of one person over against another. [7]Who confers distinction upon you? What do you possess that you have not received? But if you have received it, why are you boasting as if you did not receive it? [8]You are already satisfied; you have already grown rich; you have become kings without us! Indeed, I wish that you had become kings, so that we also might become kings with you.

[9]For as I see it, God has exhibited us apostles as the last of all, like people sentenced to death, since we have become a spectacle to the world, to angels and human beings alike. [10]We are fools on Christ's account, but you are wise in Christ; we are weak, but you are strong; you are held in

honor, but we in disrepute. [11]To this very hour we go hungry and thirsty, we are poorly clad and roughly treated, we wander about homeless [12]and we toil, working with our own hands. When ridiculed, we bless; when persecuted, we endure; [13]when slandered, we respond gently. We have become like the world's rubbish, the scum of all, to this very moment.

OT: Ps 116:10
NT: John 3:27; 2 Cor 4:8–12; 6:4–10; 11:23–33; Gal 6:3; 2 Tim 3:10–11
Catechism: suffering, 1506; humility, 525, 2559, 2631, 2706

The problem is not between Paul and Apollos. There is no hint of rivalry **6** between them, nor with Peter. The problem is with the Corinthians. The term **these things** probably refers to most of the argument so far, especially as it has moved toward a conclusion in the preceding verses about the †ministers' not judging one another or even themselves. Paul has **applied** the lesson to himself and Apollos as an example, so that **you may learn from us not to go beyond what is written**. This last expression "beyond what is written" may have been clear to the Corinthians, but it certainly has not been to scholars since then. Perhaps the best suggestion is that it is a popular slogan, because there is no verb: "Not beyond what is written" ("to go" is supplied by the NAB). By quoting this slogan, Paul would be alluding to the practice of an adult's forming letters for his pupils to trace over, admonishing them to stay within the lines. But what is the application of the metaphor? It could refer to this part of the letter that Paul's secretary had just written: the instructions about avoiding divisiveness and the pitting of one minister of the gospel against another. Most scholars, however, believe that "what is written" refers to Scripture. "What is written" is used thirty more times by Paul, always referring to a citation from Scripture. For Paul, Scripture is the Old Testament. But if so, what part of the Old Testament? Since the beginning of the letter, Paul has quoted from it five times, and thus "what is written" would most likely refer to those citations, all of which have to do, in one way or another, with a common theme: God's transcendent wisdom in contrast to human wisdom—which is what the Corinthians are puffed up about. They are **inflated with pride in favor of one person over against another**. However, by the time of the writing of this letter, many of the words of Jesus have no doubt been written down, and they have begun to have the same authority as the Old Testament. Hence there is some support for Chrysostom's interpretation that "what is written" refers to some (by then written) words of Jesus about humility and not judging one another (Matt 7:1–3; 20:26; Mark 10:43).[1]

---

1. Saint Chrysostom, *Homilies on 1 Corinthians* 12.2.

7   This leads Paul to three †rhetorical questions, which have a theological reach far beyond the Corinthians. **What do you possess that you have not received?** In his immediate view, Paul is thinking of the gifts with which the Corinthians have been endowed, the gift of faith first of all, but then also the charismatic gifts he introduced in the initial thanksgiving (1:4–7), and finally the gifts of the series of preachers and teachers they have received. Every one of the latter is a gift, and one is not to be despised in favor of another. In his broader view, however, Paul here reveals his theology of grace, which runs through all his letters and pricks all the puffed-up pride of a humanity forgetting that even its capacity to receive is a gift. But the Corinthians boast as if they **did not receive it**. Richard Hays here quotes a saying that the privileged often "were born on third base and think they hit a triple."[2]

8   With cutting irony Paul says they are **satisfied, . . . rich, . . . and have become kings**. The three traits parallel the three questions of verse 7. They are complacent, like the rich, indolent, and unjust worshipers at the shrine at Bethel, whom Amos condemns (6:1–6). Some scholars think that in addition to pride, the Corinthians, or some of them, have such a realized †eschatology that they think they are already living in the †age of perfection and have no further needs—perhaps, as the sequence suggests, not even any further need for Paul. **You have become kings without us!** Of course their kingship, like their riches and self-satisfaction, is only illusory, for if they truly participated in the kingship of Christ, who got there through the cross, Paul would be reigning with them: **I wish that you had become kings, so that we also might become kings with you**. The play is upon authentic and inauthentic kingship. In baptism they share the royalty of Christ, but their behavior is a travesty of it.

9   It is the path of the cross and humiliation, which is the path of the apostles. To drive the point home, Paul recalls a scene that his listeners had heard of and some may have personally witnessed. When a king returned from battle, the conquered, bedraggled, and chained enemy leaders would often be trailing at the end of his victory parade, displayed for ridicule and sometimes even for execution. If the Corinthians are kings, the apostles are **the last of all, like people sentenced to death, since we have become a spectacle to the world, to angels and human beings alike**. "Sentenced to death" means the apostles follow the way Jesus walked—condemned, sentenced, ridiculed, and crucified. If they wear a crown, it is a crown of thorns like that of the Master. And as Jesus was jeered along the way, so have the apostles been treated. Is Paul going so far as to suggest that the Corinthians are sitting like a king and his court, watching

2. Richard B. Hays, *First Corinthians*, Interpretation (Louisville: John Knox, 1997), 70.

the macabre mortal struggle of gladiators in the arena? Perhaps. Again we have one of Paul's rhetorical triplets: **world, angels, human beings**, suggesting the cosmic nature of what is at issue. The apostolic struggle is a spectacle even to angels, because the combat is not with mere flesh and blood but with the "principalities and powers," with "the evil spirits in the heavens" (Eph 6:12).

Another triplet occurs as Paul reintroduces the theme of the **fools** and the **wise**, the **weak** and the **strong, honor** and **disrepute**. Paul here is in the furrow plowed by Jesus in the Beatitudes, especially in Luke's contrast of the poor and the rich, the hungry and the filled, the praised and the denounced (Luke 6:20–26), the bottom of the seesaw now being ridden by the apostles, the top by the Corinthians. In contrasting fools with wise, Paul associates the apostles with the divine foolishness, in contrast to the Greek †sophists' "wisdom" now rife in the community. The contrast of weak and strong links the ministers to the †mystery of God's weakness, in contrast to human strength (1:18–25). For Paul, this is not a matter of rhetoric but of his personal experience, which he will detail when he speaks about his sufferings in ministry and his "thorn in the flesh" (2 Cor 11:23–33; 12:7–9). This he asked the Lord three times to remove, only to hear the words: "My grace is sufficient for you, for my power is made perfect in weakness." That promise of the Lord leads Paul to conclude: "I will rather boast gladly of my weaknesses, in order that the power of Christ may dwell with me. Therefore, I am content with weaknesses, insults, hardships, persecutions, and constraints, for the sake of Christ, for when I am weak, then I am strong" (12:9–10).

Now follows a series of six characteristic experiences of the apostles and specifically here of Paul. He goes **hungry and thirsty** (2 Cor 11:27; Phil 4:12). He is **poorly clad**, thus being exposed to the elements (2 Cor 11:27). He is **roughly treated**, cuffed about, struck as an insult, as Jesus was (Mark 14:65, the same verb used there). He wanders **about homeless**, as Jesus did during much of his ministry: "The Son of Man has nowhere to rest his head" (Matt 8:20), except on the cross (John 19:30).

His labor is **toil**, heavy and burdensome work with leather or goatskin to make tents, done to support himself and avoid burdening those he would evangelize (1 Thess 2:9). After listing examples of the kinds of hardship the apostles experience, Paul now gives another triplet showing the kind of response he and the authentic apostles give to those hardships. **When ridiculed, we bless; when persecuted, we endure; when slandered, we respond gently.** Paul lives the teaching and example of the Master (Matt 5:44; 1 Pet 2:23) by his own example and teaching. "Bless those who persecute [you], bless and do not curse them"

(Rom 12:14). "Do not repay anyone evil for evil. . . . Do not be conquered by evil but conquer evil with good" (12:17, 21). It was this gentleness that led some of the pagan world to think of the *Christianoi* ("Christians") as *Chrestianoi* ("the kind, loving, merciful"). Gandhi, reflecting the teaching of Jesus, said, "If we lived by the law of an eye for an eye, soon the whole world would be blind."

Finally climaxing the paradox of the apostolic life, Paul says that the mission has made them **the world's rubbish, the scum of all**. Like trash to be thrown in the dumpster or dirt to be wiped from one's feet, the apostles are spurned by the world. All of this is in contrast to the Corinthians, who have the pride of peacocks. **To this very moment** provides an †inclusio echoing "to this very hour" in verse 11, suggesting that in Ephesus, Paul is experiencing the kind of rejection he has just described—perhaps the same situation he describes in 2 Cor 1:8–9: "We despaired even of life. Indeed, we had accepted within ourselves the sentence of death" (see 1 Cor 4:9 above).

This whole section is very similar to 2 Cor 4:7–12, where Paul describes his ministry as a treasure held in "earthen vessels," so "that the surpassing power may be of God and not from us."

The Mixed Emotions of an Anxious Father (4:14–21)

> [14]I am writing you this not to shame you, but to admonish you as my beloved children. [15]Even if you should have countless guides to Christ, yet you do not have many fathers, for I became your father in Christ Jesus through the gospel. [16]Therefore, I urge you, be imitators of me. [17]For this reason I am sending you Timothy, who is my beloved and faithful son in the Lord; he will remind you of my ways in Christ [Jesus], just as I teach them everywhere in every church.
>
> [18]Some have become inflated with pride, as if I were not coming to you. [19]But I will come to you soon, if the Lord is willing, and I shall ascertain not the talk of these inflated people but their power. [20]For the kingdom of God is not a matter of talk but of power. [21]Which do you prefer? Shall I come to you with a rod, or with love and a gentle spirit?

NT: Acts 16:1; 19:22; 2 Cor 10:2; Gal 4:19; 1 Thess 2:11
Catechism: pride, 1866, 2094, 2540

14   Anyone who has had to discipline a child knows the kind of anguish Paul is expressing here. It is as if he feels his words may be misinterpreted as a personal attack. Anyone targeted by what he has said would feel ashamed. But Paul's

aim is correction rather than **shame**, for one can shame others without caring whether they change or not. It is not so with one's children. Calling them his **beloved children** tells of the level of his affection for them and something of his whole emotional state at this point, as he will use the word "beloved" again shortly for Timothy.

There is a claim Paul has on the Corinthians that none of the other †ministers   **15–16**
have: he is the founder of the community, which he considers as a true spiritual begetting. As children should imitate their **father**, so they should imitate Paul precisely in his character of being a crossbearer.

Timothy is precisely the kind of **son** who has been a **faithful** imitator of his   **17**
spiritual father, and in **sending** him to Corinth, Paul hopes that he will **remind** them of his **ways in Christ**, like an elder brother who takes the place of his father in the father's absence. What ways of Paul might Timothy encourage? Certainly strong adherence to the Person of Christ and seeking the common good of the church instead of personal preferences. And as he reminded them in the introductory thanksgiving (1:2), they are part of a much larger reality than their little community in Corinth, for what Paul has taught them is no different from what **I teach them everywhere in every church**.

But after the twinge of paternal compassion, Paul's parental exasperation again   **18–19**
surfaces: he recalls a claim by one of the Corinthian parties that he will not come to see them again. This reference can be understood in two ways. First, in the light of what Paul has just said: if he is father, he has abandoned them! Rather typical of runaway imaginations when there is a delay of an expected arrival, this critique will be shown to be false when Paul arrives. He has sent Timothy to calm their rash judgments and reassure them that he **will come . . . soon**. But, second, in the light of what follows, some may be boasting that they can now run their own show, without having to listen to Paul. Returning again to the themes of pompous talk versus divine power (2:1–4) and human wisdom versus the power of God (2:5), he will show that their **power** is simply inflation, like the witch in *The Wizard of Oz*, who deflates to nothingness when doused with a little water.

The real **power** is the **kingdom of God**. What specifically does Paul mean   **20**
by power here? He has earlier spoken of the cross as the power of God (1:24; 2:5), shown in the conversion of the Corinthians, which was more than words: it was an event. Something happened when Paul preached the word of God. But "power" in the present context has a ring of authority about it, and if necessary Paul will certainly use it.

Finally, returning to the parental image, Paul asks what kind of children they   **21**
want to be, or better, what kind of father they want him to be. A disciplinarian?

89

He evokes the **rod**, the symbol of parental punishment in both the Greek and the Hebrew world ("Whoever spares the rod hates the child, but whoever loves will apply discipline"; Prov 13:24; also see 2 Sam 7:14; Prov 22:15). But this is not Paul's desire, otherwise he would not have spent so much time and effort trying to instruct these recent converts about proper Christian behavior. He would rather come and embrace them, now adequately chastised and corrected by his words, **with love and a gentle spirit.**

Reflection and Application (4:14–21)

Fatherhood in Christ. Even if I had never known my father, I could have learned what fatherhood is from the many mentors, spiritual fathers, I have been blessed with in my life. And I could say as much about my spiritual mothers. As a celibate priest, I have also discovered what a joy and a blessing it is to father others. It is not that I have to be a priest or have to be called "father" to do that, for spiritual fathering or mothering is a role open to everyone. But as I age and continue to teach and form others more perhaps as a grandfather, the awesomeness of this role grows on me. That is why this passage from Paul is dear to me.

My first year of teaching in high school was a disaster. I ended the year exhausted and discouraged. Belonging to a religious teaching order, I knew I would have to be reassigned to another school, where I might try again. But who, I thought, would want to risk taking me on? Yet one of our priests actually went to the provincial and *requested* that I be assigned to his school. On the day before classes opened, he sat me down in his office and said, "George, you have the ability to become a good, an excellent teacher. And there's no reason you can't begin to be that tomorrow." Here was someone who believed in me when I didn't believe in myself. His prophecy was fulfilled, to such an extent that he invited the accrediting inspector that year to visit my class. The inspector returned with high praises, even saying that his experience would be significant in renewing the school's accreditation.

That was fathering. That's what Paul did with Timothy and what he was doing with his beloved Corinthians.

Cleansing the Community

1 Corinthians 5

The length of the section on the disunity in Corinth (1:10–4:21) and the fact that Paul attacks that problem first indicate how seriously he takes it. But other problems in this community must also be addressed, and Paul now turns to them. He begins by targeting the scandalous situation of an incestuous relationship being tolerated in the church. For the first time in Christian literature, we see a case of excommunication: Paul uses his full authority, along with that of the community, to expel the person. As we will note in the commentary, the purpose of this drastic action is not only to preserve the holiness of the community but also to bring the culprit to his senses so that he will be saved. As so often happens in Paul's writings, a moral issue provides him with the opportunity to introduce powerful images that for centuries to come will inspire theological and spiritual development: Christ as the paschal lamb and the Church as fed by "the unleavened bread of sincerity and truth" (1 Cor 5:8).

A Public Case of Incest (5:1–5)

[1]It is widely reported that there is immorality among you, and immorality of a kind not found even among pagans—a man living with his father's wife. [2]And you are inflated with pride. Should you not rather have been sorrowful? The one who did this deed should be expelled from your midst. [3]I, for my part, although absent in body but present in spirit, have already, as if present, pronounced judgment on the one who has committed this deed, [4]in the name of [our] Lord Jesus: when you have gathered

**together and I am with you in spirit with the power of the Lord Jesus, ⁵you
are to deliver this man to Satan for the destruction of his flesh, so that his
spirit may be saved on the day of the Lord.**

OT: Lev 18:8, 29; Deut 13:6; 27:20
NT: Matt 18:20; 1 Tim 1:20
Catechism: incest, 2388–89; excommunication, 1463

1   As far as personal sin is concerned, the case of incest is worse than the factionalism addressed in chapters 1–4, for it calls for excommunication. But if the
community is not united, a strong authoritative intervention by Paul might fail
to win the community's agreement to take the kind of drastic action Paul enjoins.
So the two problems are intertwined. The NAB translation **widely reported**
suggests that Paul has heard of it from several sources, but most translations
render the phrase "actually reported," indicating the shock that Paul experienced
on hearing of the scandal. This seems to fit the sequence better where Paul says
that it is **immorality of a kind not found even among pagans**. The Jews held
the promiscuous culture of the pagan world in abhorrence, but even the pagan
world considered incest with biological or adoptive kin a serious infraction of
the moral order. The Jewish law was clear and carried with it the penalty of
exclusion from God's people. Among the many kinds of incestuous relations
cataloged in Leviticus is the prohibition of intercourse with your **father's wife**
(Lev 18:8), the exact term Paul uses here, meaning stepmother.

2   Paul does not name the individual involved, but what upsets him is the
attitude of the community toward the scandal: **You are inflated with pride**.
Literally "puffed up," they not only tolerate the situation but, it seems, also
consider themselves so spiritually advanced that what one of their members
does in the flesh is of no importance to the others. This split of spirit and body
in the thinking of the Corinthians will surface again in Paul's later critiques. It
is not clear from the text, however, whether they were boasting *because* of the
sin or *in spite of it*. In either case, the community should have taken disciplinary
action. Some scholars have suggested that the incestuous man was a wealthy
patron of the community, which would be loathe to call him to task for this
"private" matter. In any case, the same inflation with pride that Paul targets in
the section above (4:6, 18–19), appears here in the community's heedless failure
to deal with public sexual sin, for which they should **rather have been sorrowful**. Other translations say they should "have mourned" (NRSV) or been "in
mourning" (JB). At issue is not only sorrow for the man's sin but also mourning for the state of the wounded community (often in the Old Testament, as in
the book of Lamentations) that would lead to conversion and action. That is

Paul and the Old Law on Sexual Morality

BIBLICAL BACKGROUND

Incest of the type described here was not the only sexual disorder prohibited by the Mosaic law. There were many others, including homosexual activity (Lev 18:22; 20:13). Inasmuch as Paul seems to abrogate the Mosaic law in Gal 2:15–21; 3:19–25; 4:1–10, 21–31, some authors have maintained that not only the ritual laws but also the moral laws of the Old Testament are no longer binding in the New. This needs a careful response. Paul considered the old law a curse (Gal 3:13), not because it was bad in itself (Rom 7:7), but because it revealed sin in a clearer light than a human's mere wounded †conscience could, and thus became an occasion of greater sin because of God's revealed command (5:13; 7:7–9). In a similar way, a child who knows it is wrong to strike his sister would be additionally guilty of disobedience if his parent told him not to. When Paul declares that the law is replaced with the grace of the Holy Spirit, he sees the law as a hurdle too high to be reached but that can now be leaped over because of the empowering love poured into our hearts through the Holy Spirit (Rom 5:5; Gal 5:18–24). Thus the just demands of the law are not abrogated but fulfilled in us who live by the Spirit (Rom 8:4). Briefly, it is not a question of objective removal of the law but of subjective empowerment that achieves even more than the law required (Gal 5:13).

suggested by the fact that the sorrowing is followed in the Greek by a conjunction of purpose or result: "should have been sorrowful so that . . ." A more literal rendering of the Greek would be: "Your mourning should have been such that you expelled the one who did this thing from your midst." The law in Leviticus was clear—"Whoever does any of these abominations shall be cut off from the people" (Lev 18:29)—and Paul is swift to apply it here. **The one who did this deed should be expelled from your midst**. Even at a distance, Paul exercises his apostolic authority by decreeing the man's excommunication.

But the decree is to be handed down by the community in union with Paul,   3–4
who will be present **in spirit**. The decision has divine authority behind it: **in the name of [our] Lord Jesus** and also **with the power of the Lord Jesus**. This is an apostolic decision with divine sanction. "To deliver this man to Satan" (v. 5) is another way of describing excommunication. Within the church a person enjoys a certain right of sanctuary from Satan because the church is the temple of God, and the Holy Spirit dwells there (3:16). To be excluded is to be deprived of that protection and therefore vulnerable to the attacks of Satan, which God allows for punishment (1 Tim 1:20).

5   This, however, does not mean eternal punishment but the kind of temporal chastisements Satan is skilled at providing (see 2 Cor 12:7 for the "thorn in the flesh," which Paul describes as an "angel of Satan, to beat me"). Such temporal chastisements would, it seems, be more severe outside the community, since the person would be deprived of the sacraments. Thus excommunication is a therapy of privation that hopefully will wake the man up and lead him to repentance and readmission to the community. That is the sense of Paul's goal here: **for the destruction of his flesh, so that his spirit may be saved on the day of the Lord**. A person is openly flouting the moral standards of the Church, which means the law of God, and has thus become a source of scandal, not simply doing something shocking but also setting an example that could easily lead others to follow. In such a case, the community has an obligation to preserve its integrity by calling sin for what it is. Yet when the Church judges that excommunication is called for, it hopes that the exclusion will help the sinner come to their senses before it is too late. "That way he will learn to fear God and to escape the greater punishment that is to come."[1] As in Matt 18:15, the goal is to gain one's brother or sister.

Reflection and Application (5:1–5)

In recent years the Church has suffered because some of its leaders turned a blind eye to the deviant sexual activity of some of its priests and †ministers. And it has had to pay the price, literally, as well as in loss of respect in the public forum, to say nothing of the pain caused to families and many members' loss of trust in bishops who neglected to act. Obviously the Catholic Church is not the only institution that has had this problem, but somehow the world seems to hold the Church to a higher standard—rightly so. The Church must balance pastoral care for the sinner with pastoral care for the community, especially for its more vulnerable members.

Fortunately there are plenty of bishops who watch over their flock with a shepherd's eye. Some years ago in Corpus Christi, Texas, a Catholic woman was operating two abortion clinics. Bishop René Gracida approached her personally, as the Gospel (Matt 18:15) directs, but when she would not change her conduct, the bishop issued a pastoral letter informing his diocese that she had excommunicated herself because of her work in the abortion clinics. (The

---

1. Theodore of Mopsuestia, ACCS 7:46. Severian of Gabala: "This means he should be exposed to the hardship of life"; in *Pauluskommentare aus der griechischen Kirche*, ed. K. Staab, NT Abhundlungen 15 (Münster in Westfalen: Aschendorff, 1933), 243.

excommunication was automatic under canon law, but the bishop formally declared the woman's incurring the penalty.) At least Catholics in his diocese would then know that the Church does not countenance abortion, and the woman was formally notified of the seriousness of her actions.

Clean Out the Corruption for Passover (5:6–13)

⁶**Your boasting is not appropriate. Do you not know that a little yeast leavens all the dough? ⁷Clear out the old yeast, so that you may become a fresh batch of dough, inasmuch as you are unleavened. For our paschal lamb, Christ, has been sacrificed. ⁸Therefore let us celebrate the feast, not with the old yeast, the yeast of malice and wickedness, but with the unleavened bread of sincerity and truth.**

⁹**I wrote you in my letter not to associate with immoral people, ¹⁰not at all referring to the immoral of this world or the greedy and robbers or idolaters; for you would then have to leave the world. ¹¹But I now write to you not to associate with anyone named a brother, if he is immoral, greedy, an idolater, a slanderer, a drunkard, or a robber, not even to eat with such a person. ¹²For why should I be judging outsiders? Is it not your business to judge those within? ¹³God will judge those outside. "Purge the evil person from your midst."**

OT: Deut 13:6
NT: Matt 18:17; John 1:29; Gal 5:9; 17:15; 1 Pet 1:19; Rev 5:5–6
Catechism: Jesus as paschal lamb, 608; paschal mystery, 571–72; feast of Passover, 1164
Lectionary: 5:6b–8: Easter Sunday

Paul now moves into the religious reasons for purifying the community. To **6** say that their **boasting is not appropriate** seems a rather mild rebuke after the strong language of excommunication. But their boasting is probably not about the man's sin; it is their overall arrogant and superior attitude that is willing to condone incest instead of confronting it. **Yeast** makes bread to rise, but it also corrupts. Quite early in Jewish tradition the Feast of Unleavened Bread was joined to that of Passover (Mark 14:1); as Passover approached, Jewish women would scour their kitchen shelves to make sure there was no leaven in the house for Passover (Exod 13:7; Deut 16:4). To eat leavened bread during the weeklong feast of Passover would incur the severest of penalties—being cut off from the people of Israel (Exod 12:15, 19). The only bread permitted during Passover week was and is matzo, the stiff unleavened sheets that recall the haste with which the Israelites escaping from Egypt baked their bread. In the feast

Christ as Passover Fulfilled

When Paul calls Christ the paschal lamb, or Passover lamb, he is
evoking the entire conceptual and emotional world connected
with the Jewish feast of Passover (*pasch*; Hebrew *pesakh*), of which
Christ is the fulfillment. Even today Passover is the most important Jewish feast of the year. It evokes the entire story of Israel's
enslavement in Egypt, the plagues, the night of liberation when
the Israelites slaughtered the Passover lamb, sprinkling its blood
on the doorposts to save their firstborn from being slain, the meal
they ate in haste with unleavened bread, the escape through the
sea to freedom. The New Testament applies these images to various aspects
of what it calls the †paschal mystery: the Passover fulfilled in Christ's death
and resurrection.

the Jews relive their liberation from slavery and the beginning of a new life, a
life of freedom and a new identity as people consecrated to the Lord. **A little
yeast leavens all the dough**. (The saying is repeated in Gal 5:9.) Indeed, it takes
very little compared to the rest of the flour. Paul's point is that one tolerated
scandal can spoil the whole community, both within and as seen by outsiders.

7   The only way to assure that there is no corruption is to become a **fresh
batch of dough**: to start over. But lest they misinterpret that, Paul qualifies
the metaphor by telling the community, **You are unleavened**. The community
does not need to be founded all over again. Their commitment to Christ and
their baptismal consecration have made them a holy people, a people already
set aside for God. They must therefore become what they are. Eliminating
the corrupting influence is the only way to maintain the integrity of their
consecration. The reason they *are* unleavened is that the true **paschal lamb,
Christ, has been sacrificed**. At Passover the lambs were sacrificed, and Paul
here represents the earliest New Testament claim that in his death and resurrection, Christ is the fulfillment of the Jewish Passover. There is a clear causal
connection between their being unleavened and the sacrifice of Jesus, as the
connective **for** indicates. The sacrificing of the lambs in the temple only signaled
the time for the Jews to clean out all leaven from their homes; the slaughtered
lamb did not cleanse the leaven. But the sacrifice of Jesus the Lamb cast out
the leaven and made "a new creation" (2 Cor 5:17), a completely new dough.
That is what the Christian community is. John sees the condemnation and
death of Jesus as happening at the very hour the Passover lambs were being
sacrificed in the temple (John 19:14), and he identifies Jesus on the cross as

fulfilling one of the requirements of the paschal lamb, that none of its bones should be broken (John 19:36).

It is possible that Paul is writing this letter shortly after the Christian feast of **8** Passover, for he speaks later of staying at Ephesus until Pentecost, seven weeks after Passover (1 Cor 16:8). Since Paul mentions Christ as "our paschal lamb," it seems reasonable to conclude that Christians were now celebrating the Jewish Passover as fulfilled in Christ. But the logic of the metaphor calls for something more. Christians' Passover week never ends, and that is why there should never be a corrupting influence in their midst at all. Thus they **celebrate the feast** constantly and should live accordingly, with **sincerity and truth**. This phrase targets the Corinthians' sweeping under the rug the corrupting influence of sin in their midst.

The community should recognize that Paul's teaching here is not new, for **9–10** he had written an earlier letter in which he made it clear: they were **not to associate with immoral people**. One could not, obviously, avoid dealing with them in the marketplace or in the street.

But if any member of the community calls himself a Christian (**anyone** **11** **named a brother**) and is **immoral, greedy, an idolater, a slanderer, a drunk-ard, or a robber**, they should not even eat with such a person. The context, as is clear from the directive to cast out the person in verse 13, indicates that Paul is still thinking in terms of flagrant public sins like the incest condemned above. Thus it indicates one who is living such a lifestyle without remorse, one who needs to convert but has not. "Immoral" here means sexually immoral, probably heading this list because Paul has in mind the incestuous man whose example is eating away at the community like termites. In the ancient world, material goods were limited—unlike our modern industrial society, where if we don't have enough of something, we make more—and thus one's grab-bing more usually meant someone else going with less. Hence the **greedy** are tagged as equally reprehensible. That vice is probably what is leading some of the Corinthians to sue other Christians before pagan courts (6:1–11). Paul will address idolatry in chapters 8–10. With repeated severity the books of Proverbs and Sirach condemn sins of speech, especially slanderous speech, which destroys the reputation of another. The Corinthians may not have gone that far, but surely the dissension Paul targets in the first four chapters involves sins of speech. Paul considers drunkenness as a sin, for it was an abuse of one's body and a blight on any community. It continues to be a moral evil, although today we know that alcoholism is also a disease that can be treated. **Robber** here really covers more than violent grasping of others' goods. It would include "swindler" or "rogue."

The Christian should be careful **not even to eat with such a person**. How does this square with the example of Jesus, who ate with publicans and sinners (Matt 9:10–11; Luke 5:32)? Jesus was reaching out to those not yet converted, not to already-committed disciples who were flaunting their immorality. In biblical times, table fellowship was more than an occasional expression of hospitality. It was a sacred sign of social bonding, the creation of a brotherhood. In the famous shepherd psalm, the phrase "You set a table before me in front of my enemies" (Ps 23:5) means that the host will defend his guest with his own life if necessary. Thus table fellowship was equivalent to community membership. And the vices Paul describes here are ones that exclude a person from the community in the book of Deuteronomy.[2] The fact that the Eucharist accompanied the common meal of the community (1 Cor 11:17–34) gave additional reason for this stricture.

12–13   The Apostle then returns to the community's duty to exercise its judgment and act accordingly for those within the community (Matt 18:17–18). He ends by quoting Deut 13:6: **"Purge the evil person from your midst."**

Reflection and Application (5:6–13)

A little yeast leavens all the dough. I learned this in an unusual way when I was in the Marianist novitiate. Brother Fred, a novice like me, took his turn at cooking. He decided to bake bread, but he was unaware that "a *little* yeast leavens all the dough." He must have mixed the baking powder and the flour in equal amounts. I happened to pass through the kitchen to find Brother Fred frantically trying to control the expanding lumps of dough that were literally taking over the kitchen. Mounds of dough were rising everywhere, claiming every available shelf. We ate pneumatic bread for longer than I can remember.

Confronting sinners. This section is still tightly controlled by the excommunication of the incestuous man, as is clear from 5:13. However, listing as it does several other kinds of public sinners, it raises several questions about what all this means for us today. How do we respond to persons whose immorality is public and therefore scandalous, giving an example that can be an invitation to others to do likewise? How do we deal with a relative living in a sexual relationship outside of marriage? Or with those living in a homosexual relationship? Or with a Catholic who is an abortion provider? Do we say nothing? Do we excuse ourselves on the pretext that we should "not judge"? When Jesus said, "Stop judging" (Matt 7:1; Luke 6:37), it was to those who judged

2. See Deut 17:2–7; 19:15–19; 21:20–21; 22:20–22, 30; 24:7.

others without first judging themselves. He goes on to say, however, that you should "remove the wooden beam from your eye first; then you will see clearly to remove the splinter from your brother's eye" (Matt 7:5), which implies judging, however merciful, and it does not cancel the community's responsibility to judge conduct that is scandalous and injurious to the community (Matt 18:15–18). Whose responsibility is it to confront the person? Obviously parents have this responsibility toward their children. Bishops have it in regard to their priests and laity as well, especially those who are in public office. Pastors are responsible for the uprightness of those who would serve as †ministers, such as lectors, extraordinary ministers of the Eucharist, musicians, and so on. Within one's family one cannot shirk the responsibility of confronting the person, though one needs to pray for prudence that one's approach may have the greatest chance of success. Jesus tells us that we should first approach the person individually, then involve others if necessary (Matt 18:15–17). This is not easy, especially for certain personality types, but it is the loving thing to do, even at the risk of rejection. The Word of God challenges us to live the truth in love (Eph 4:15).

The Court and the Courtesan

1 Corinthians 6

Two other problems are weakening the community. The Corinthians are not only bickering within; they are also taking other community members to court. In addition, they are expressing acceptance of fornication, which is rife in Corinth and considered normal behavior in the culture, but contradicts one's consecration to Christ.

Settle Your Spats at Home (6:1–6)

---

¹How can any one of you with a case against another dare to bring it to the unjust for judgment instead of to the holy ones? ²Do you not know that the holy ones will judge the world? If the world is to be judged by you, are you unqualified for the lowest law courts? ³Do you not know that we will judge angels? Then why not everyday matters? ⁴If, therefore, you have courts for everyday matters, do you seat as judges people of no standing in the church? ⁵I say this to shame you. Can it be that there is not one among you wise enough to be able to settle a case between brothers? ⁶But rather brother goes to court against brother, and that before unbelievers?

OT: Wis 3:8; Dan 7:22, 26–27
NT: Matt 19:28; Rev 20:4

1   The Corinthian Christians' "boasting" (1 Cor 5:6) has shown itself in another way that Paul finds shocking. The word **dare** in the NAB translation is lost in

the middle of the sentence. It occupies the first emphatic position in the Greek: "*Dares* one to . . . ?" The disunity in the church is marked by the fact that some-one has taken another member to secular judges, whom Paul calls **the unjust**. He could have used the word "outsiders," which he had used in 5:12–13, but he chooses the Greek word for "unjust," probably because of the widespread reputation of judges to be corrupt and malleable by bribes. It was taken for granted in the Roman Empire, at least by the masses, that money could win your case. If the one taking his fellow Christian to court was of a higher class or wealthier, it is likely that the judge would rule in his favor, no matter what the evidence. Luke's picture of the persistent widow and the unjust judge was not an unrealistic parable (Luke 18:1–8). The law favored creditors over debtors and landlords over tenants.[1] (See sidebar on the †patron-client relationship.) Thus the poor would have slight chance for justice. James 2:6 reflects this situation: "Are not the rich oppressing you? And do they themselves not haul you off to court?"

Within Greek society were social confraternities that often settled their own disputes internally, and the Jews enjoyed the privilege of judging their members by their own laws. That may be why Luke tells us that Paul could get authoriza-tion from the high priest to fetch the recalcitrant Christian Jews in Damascus and bring them chained to Jerusalem (Acts 9:1–2), and also why Paul himself tells us he suffered thirty-nine lashes five times from the Jews (2 Cor 11:24).[2] The **holy ones**, otherwise translated "saints," means the ones consecrated by the blood of Christ in the sacrament of baptism. See 1:2 above for a discussion of this term.

The holy ones will judge the world, for they will have the privilege of shar- 2–3
ing in Christ's final judgment of the world. Jesus had promised that the Twelve would sit on twelve thrones judging the twelve tribes of Israel (Matt 19:28), and Paul sees all the "saints" doing this, sharing in God's reign, as in Dan 7:22, 27. How do the saints, who were themselves judged worthy to enter the kingdom of heaven, judge others? It is the kind of judgment that victory wins. Chris-tians in glory share the victory of the risen and glorified Jesus, and his victory and theirs is the final judgment upon the good and the wicked. **Do you not know . . . ?** is a †rhetorical question that appears fifteen times in the writings of Paul, six of which are in our chapter; it reminds his readers of something they have forgotten or informs them of something they never learned in the first

1. P. Garnsey, "Legal Privilege in the Roman Empire," in *Studies in Ancient Society*, ed. A. I. Finley (London and Boston: Routledge & Kegan Paul, 1974), 142; quoted in David E. Garland, *1 Corinthians*, BECNT (Grand Rapids: Baker Academic, 2003), 199.
2. Historians question whether the Sanhedrin's authority would have reached as far as Damascus. But local Jewish authorities were free to apply such punishments as Paul said he received.

place. If they are capable of being part of God's supreme court, they ought to be able to judge petty cases among their peers. They have the faith and the light of the Holy Spirit to judge honestly and justly the affairs that would otherwise be taken to **the lowest law courts**. This expression can also be translated "petty cases" (NJB), "trivial cases" (NRSV, NIV), or "trifling cases" (JB)—better in view of the context of verse 3, indicating that the issues in dispute at Corinth are not major, catastrophic kinds, but minor, **everyday matters**.

What does Paul mean by **We will judge angels**? Scholars have offered various interpretations: Christians will share in Christ's rule over everything, even the angels (as in Heb 2:5–9); or the faithful will judge the guardian angels of the nations, implying the judgment of the secular powers of those nations—the very secular powers to whom some of the Corinthians are taking their cases; or at the final judgment Christians will share in Christ's judgment of the devil and his angels in the eternal fire (Matt 25:41; 2 Pet 2:4). Saint John Chrysostom comments, "When the very incorporeal powers shall be found inferior to us who are clothed with flesh, they shall suffer heavier punishment."[3] In any case, Paul is arguing from the greater to the lesser: if you Corinthians are destined to have such an exalted role as judges, how can you be incompetent to judge simple issues ("everyday matters") among yourselves?

4   Two different interpretations of this difficult verse are possible, both depending on the strength given to the Greek word *kathizete*. The normal meaning of the word is "to seat" (as in the NAB), meaning "to appoint" (NRSV, NIV), to place in a position of authority. But are the **courts for everyday matters** actually secular courts, or are they courts within the Christian community? The church would have no authority to **seat as judges** in the secular courts, so "seat as judges" must refer to selecting arbiters or judges within the church. But then what does it mean to select **people of no standing in the church**? The NIV takes the verb as a command: "Appoint as judges even men of little account in the church!"—as do the KJV and some ancient commentators. But why would Paul say that, in light of the next verse, with his recommendation to select someone competent? If the verb is not a command but a statement ("You actually appoint as judges people of no standing in the church"), Paul is scolding them for appointing incompetent Christians for their own courts, which may have led some members of the community to take their cases to secular courts.

These problems, and others, have led other translators to cut the Gordian knot by simply taking the verb "seat, appoint" in an extended sense as "have recourse to," meaning to take their cases to secular courts: "You take your cases

---

3. Saint Chrysostom, *Homilies on 1 Corinthians* 16.5.

to those who have no standing in the church," secular judges. This seems to be the solution adopted by the RSV and NJB.[4]

When the context of a passage points in one direction and a single verb points in another, the interpreter must decide which way to go. Either of the following interpretations makes sense: Taking the verb in the common sense of "appoint": "You have your own courts for deciding everyday matters, but you appoint those in the community who are least competent, thus forcing Christians to take their cases to the secular courts." Or, taking the verb in the sense of "having recourse to": "You are taking your cases to the secular judges, who have no standing in the church."

Either interpretation leads to Paul's rhetorical question: **Can it be that there is not one among you wise enough to be able to settle a case between brothers?** Paul concludes this section by pointing to the real issue: you are all brothers and sisters, and your ability to settle your own issues should be an example to the secular world. But alas, you are taking your spats to the secular world, and that is a scandal. The world cannot say, "See how they love one another!" 5–6

Reflection and Application (6:1–6)

What stands out in this section is how real Paul considers the new family of Christians to be. How much does our being a Christian and our belonging to this family affect our identity? Our identity as citizens of our country is reinforced at every turn: the media, the traffic lights, our taxes on income or sales. If Sunday worship is the only reinforcement we receive for our Christian identity, it is likely to fall far short of what God means it to be. That is why other means—prayer, Scripture reading and study, parish ministry, retreats, faith-sharing groups—are needed to strengthen our Christian identity. If our secular identity is primary, we would probably rather sue than be reconciled within the Christian community, as Paul would expect.

The Demands of a Holy Community (6:7–11)

---

[7]Now indeed [then] it is, in any case, a failure on your part that you have lawsuits against one another. Why not rather put up with injustice?

---

4. For 1 Cor 6:4, RSV has, "If then you have such cases, why do you lay them before those who are least esteemed by the church?" The NJB has, "But when you have matters of this life to be judged, you bring them before those who are of no account in the Church!" Even these translations, though, could mean bringing the cases before those least competent within the community.

Why not rather let yourselves be cheated? [8]Instead, you inflict injustice and cheat, and this to brothers. [9]Do you not know that the unjust will not inherit the kingdom of God? Do not be deceived; neither fornicators nor idolaters nor adulterers nor boy prostitutes nor sodomites [10]nor thieves nor the greedy nor drunkards nor slanderers nor robbers will inherit the kingdom of God. [11]That is what some of you used to be; but now you have had yourselves washed, you were sanctified, you were justified in the name of the Lord Jesus Christ and in the Spirit of our God.

NT: Matt 5:38–42; Rom 12:17–21; Gal 5:21; Titus 3:3–7
Catechism: homosexuality, 2357–59; baptism as washing, 1215; justified by Holy Trinity, 1266

7–8   Having dealt with the scandal of bringing lawsuits before secular courts, Paul now turns to those who would take their brothers or sisters to any kind of tribunal, whether within the community or outside it. The very existence of suits against one another testifies to the immaturity of the community. The Greek word that the NAB translates as **failure** means a loss or a defeat, and it is a triple defeat, for the accused, for the accuser, and for the local church. Nobody really wins, including the community itself. **Why not rather put up with injustice? Why not rather let yourselves be cheated?** This may strike us as caving in before an injustice, as a cowardly surrendering of one's rights. But Paul here is reflecting the teaching of Jesus about turning the other cheek (Matt 5:39), of going the extra mile, or, more relevant here, "If anyone wants to go to law with you over your tunic, hand him your cloak as well" (Matt 5:40). This is also Paul's explicit teaching: "See that no one returns evil for evil; rather, always seek what is good [both] for each other and for all" (1 Thess 5:15). "And for all" shows Paul's concern that the community itself would benefit from this manifestation of wholly benevolent love. In our Corinthian text, however, Paul only recommends this procedure; he does not command it, for the one who seeks redress is not, externally at least, returning evil for evil. He is merely seeking justice. Hence Paul does not say that seeking redress within the community is sinful. He says that the way of love is superior and more helpful for the community. It would raise the issue to another level, as if the one cheated would be saying: "You are my brother, not my enemy, and I love you too much to take you to court." But then in verse 8 Paul slams those community members who do the **injustice** in the first place, made graver because they do **this to brothers**.

9   The mention of "injustice" in the preceding verse provides Paul with a link to the kinds of people who will be excluded from the kingdom, thus laying down principles valid for all times, including our own. He begins with the **unjust**. **Do not be deceived** suggests that some of the Corinthians are indeed being

deceived—about wisdom, power, incest, and now about other vices that Paul will mention. **Fornicators** (*pornoi* in the Greek, from which comes our word "pornography") refers here to various types of sexual sins other than adultery, which is mentioned separately. Sirach 23:16–22 lists three kinds of sins of the flesh: solitary sins (perhaps alluding to masturbation), fornication, and adultery. If **unjust** refers back to the cheaters just discussed, **fornicators** looks forward to 1 Cor 6:12–20. In mentioning **idolaters** Paul may have in mind those members of the community he will address in chapters 8–10 who are courting idolatry by their syncretistic lifestyle. **Adulterers** are those who violate their own or another's marital relationship by intercourse. **Boy prostitutes** (Greek *malakoi*) refers to those who offer themselves to be penetrated by males.

The next term, *arsenokoitai*, translated here as **sodomites**, has in recent years been the subject of much discussion in the light of our culture's heightened awareness of homosexuality. Attempts to say that the word does not refer to homosexual acts have fallen short, however.[5] The term is unknown before Paul, who has apparently compounded two terms found in the †Septuagint: "You shall not lie [*koitēn*] with a male [*arsenos*] as with a woman; such a thing is an abomination" (Lev 18:22; see also 20:13). The ancient world was not as aware, as we are today, of the distinction between homosexual attraction and homosexual acts. Clearly our text refers to homosexual conduct. Neither were the ancients aware of any kind of therapy for those with same-sex attractions who might want to change their orientation, as indeed some have in our time.[6]

The rest of the list merely echoes that in 5:11: **nor thieves nor the greedy nor drunkards nor slanderers nor robbers**. But the conclusion is categorical: none of these **will inherit the kingdom of God**, meaning salvation, eternal life. God alone is judge of individuals, whose †consciences may be warped either by their own bad choices or by circumstances not of their own choosing. But Paul's warning is drastic: the consequences of these sins are eternal.

That is what some of you used to be. The Church is the table fellowship of redeemed sinners, who praise the mercy of God. That mercy is not a cheap

10

11

5. See Raymond E. Brown, *Introduction to the New Testament* (New York: Doubleday, 1997), 528–40; Garland, *1 Corinthians*, 212–15. Earlier editions of the NAB (as in 1986) used the term "practicing homosexuals," which was accurate and clearer for most people than "sodomites."

6. There are those who are insulted by the suggestion that healing might be pursued, since they claim that their homosexual orientation is determined genetically. But despite years of research, no gene has been discovered that predetermines same-sex attraction, though certain other factors such as a genetic predisposition to shyness might easily be manipulated by a homosexual encounter or environment. Other factors have been cited: parental influences, childhood sexual abuse or trauma, peer labeling, early experimentation, repeated behavior, and others. See Benedict Ashley and Kevin O'Rourke, *Health Care Ethics*, 4th ed. (Washington, DC: Georgetown University Press, 1997), 390–91; and John F. Harvey and Gerald V. Bradley, *Same-Sex Attraction: A Parents' Guide* (South Bend, IN: St. Augustine's Press, 2003).

gift. It cost the death of the Son of God. It is more than a sentiment. Here Paul proclaims his frequent theme, that God has transferred sinners from one kind of existence to another (see Col 1:13). The change has been radical, and it happened through their conversion to Christ, sealed by baptism. **Washed** refers to the baptismal rite and the interior cleansing by the Holy Spirit that baptism signifies and achieves. **Sanctified** means consecrated, for they are the temple of God (1 Cor 3:17). **Justified** means set in a right relation with God and with one's fellows. Justification by faith in Jesus Christ will become a major theme of Paul's Letter to the Romans. The triple "washed, sanctified, justified" is matched by a triple reference to God the Father, Jesus, and the Holy Spirit: **in the name of the Lord Jesus Christ and in the Spirit of our God**. This is one of the several references that laid the basis for the later development of the doctrine of the Trinity. What began with Paul's shock at the Corinthians' behavior ends by recalling that they have been placed in the heart of the Holy Trinity. Christian morality derives from that center.

Reflection and Application (6:7–11)

God's intention for sexuality. The gospel upholds the dignity of every human being, created in the image and likeness of God himself (Gen 1:26). It further proclaims that every person is called to share intimately in the life of the Holy Trinity as a child of God the Father, a brother or sister of Jesus Christ, and a temple indwelt by the Holy Spirit, God's own Trinitarian love. God's glory is man fully alive, as St. Irenaeus put it.[7] And consequently the Church teaches that society must promote the full development of human persons and preserve the institutions that make for their integral development. Primary among these is marriage, the union of one man and one woman, which is made sacred in the Church through the sacrament uniting the two in a permanent union open to the transmission of life. In that context the person reaches fulfillment in the total gift of self to the other. The Church remains faithful both to revelation and reason in condemning whatever would demean the divine intention for sexuality.

The Body Is for the Lord (6:12–20)

---

[12]"Everything is lawful for me," but not everything is beneficial. "Everything is lawful for me," but I will not let myself be dominated by anything.

---

7. *Against Heresies* 4.20.7.

¹³"Food for the stomach and the stomach for food," but God will do away with both the one and the other. The body, however, is not for immorality, but for the Lord, and the Lord is for the body; ¹⁴God raised the Lord and will also raise us by his power.

¹⁵Do you not know that your bodies are members of Christ? Shall I then take Christ's members and make them the members of a prostitute? Of course not! ¹⁶[Or] do you not know that anyone who joins himself to a prostitute becomes one body with her? For "the two," it says, "will become one flesh." ¹⁷But whoever is joined to the Lord becomes one spirit with him. ¹⁸Avoid immorality. Every other sin a person commits is outside the body, but the immoral person sins against his own body. ¹⁹Do you not know that your body is a temple of the holy Spirit within you, whom you have from God, and that you are not your own? ²⁰For you have been purchased at a price. Therefore, glorify God in your body.

Fig. 7. Votive relief dedication to Asklepios.

Public domain / Wikimedia Commons

NT: Rom 6:12–19; 8:9–10; 1 Cor 10:23, 31; 15:12–13; Col 2:22; 1 Thess 4:8
Catechism: goodness of every creature, 339; fornication, 1852, 2353
Lectionary: rite of marriage; 6:13c–15a, 17–20: St. Maria Goretti

The previous section has laid the groundwork for this more detailed treatment of sexual immorality (*porneia*). As the previous section ended with the Trinity, so will this one. If there is an *ought* in the Christian life, it is only because there is first an *is*, a new existence in the Trinitarian life of God. In this, Paul is breaking new ground for Jew as well as Gentile. For the Jew, whose adherence to the law already restricted sexual activity to marriage, it was the Trinitarian foundation of sexual ethics that was new. For the Gentile, it was new moral ground as well: the pagan world had no censure for extramarital intercourse but even a positive rationale for it. "Mistresses we keep for pleasure, concubines for the sake of daily intercourse, wives to bear us legitimate children and to be our faithful housekeepers."[8] Though this attitude was certainly not universal in Paul's day, and Caesar Augustus had initiated legislation to improve family life, nevertheless the prevailing attitude toward sex was casual, and prostitution thrived. When Paul first introduces the topic here, he uses *porneia* in its broadest sense for all forms of unlawful sex, properly translated in 1 Cor 6:13 not as "fornication" (NRSV), but as "immorality" (NAB) or "sexual immorality" (NJB, NIV). By this he means any use of sex outside of marriage. Only later does he apply the principle to union with a prostitute, the temptation to which the Corinthian men would be most vulnerable. It would not be immediately obvious to converts that Christian initiation meant a sudden abstinence, since the contemporary mystery religions made no such demand on their initiates. In this section Paul shows first that sexual immorality is not an indifferent matter (6:12–14) and then that it is an outrage to Christ (6:15–17) and to the Holy Spirit (6:18–20), already named in verse 11.

12   In saying **"Everything is lawful for me,"** Paul is repeating a principle of Christian liberty he especially cherished (7:35; 10:23), one that he had no doubt given in regard to foods, as indicated in what follows (see also 8:8; 10:23). Some in the community seem to have taken it as applying to sexual activity as well. Without withdrawing the principle, Paul hastens to clarify it. The use of the principle should not lead to the absurdity of enslaving oneself under the pretense of becoming free. Our new existence in Christ makes all things belong to the Christian (3:22); all things are "within my power," that is, I have the power and the freedom to make moral decisions, but for that very reason I should not allow myself to "fall under the power" of anyone or anything. Thus runs a play on words in the Greek that escapes the NAB's translation: **I will not let myself be dominated by anything**. The Cynic-Stoic ideal of "things for me, not me for things"—this is what Paul skillfully turns on these †sophists, who were taking specious advantage of Paul's principle. One might equate their reasoning with those today who consider sex as nothing more than recreation.

13–14   But the equation is impossible, says Paul. The matter of sexual satisfaction is subject to another principle. It involves the whole body and thus the whole person. The body is not for sexual satisfaction in the way that the stomach is for food. Reason tells us that sexual activity is designed for union with a person, not, like eating, for the consumption of an object. And the whole **body**, which is somehow involved in sexual activity, has an even nobler end, a divine end: it is **for the Lord**. It is destined ultimately to be united and conformed to the

8. Pseudo-Demosthenes, *Against Neaera* 122; trans. A. Murray, *Private Orations III*, Loeb Classical Library (Cambridge, MA: Harvard University Press, 1939), 445–46.

glorious body of Christ, now living in heaven (Phil 3:21). **And the Lord is for the body**. That is, in his glorified state his purpose now is to be the principle of resurrection for the Christian's body: **God raised the Lord and will also raise us by his power**.[9] There is a †rhetorically powerful contrast here:

Food is for the stomach, and the stomach is for food,

but

the body is for the Lord, and the Lord is for the body.

Elsewhere Paul shows that the risen life that Christ gives is not merely a future one but is already begun now and is meant to grow through the Holy Spirit's being constantly poured out (see 2 Cor 3:18; 1 Thess 4:8). Thus as one regularly nourishes one's body with food, so Christ nourishes his body, the Church (Eph 5:29, which probably alludes to the Eucharist). It is significant that Paul does not here use Christian marriage to argue against sexual immorality—he would take for granted that one should exercise sexuality only within the sacred bonds of matrimony—but rather he appeals to the consecrated character of the individual's body and its transcendent destiny. Thus his injunction applies to all, married and single.

And that is what he develops as he asks, **Do you not know that your bodies are members of Christ?** Here we are thrown into the highly realistic way Paul understands the Christian's union with Christ. It is not a spirit-to-spirit union only. It is also a body-to-body union. Even in its present earthly condition, the Christian's body is united to the risen body of Christ. This flies in the face of the Platonic notion of the body as a cage from which the soul is freed at death,[10] a view that could lead to dismissing anything done in the body as irrelevant to one's eternal destiny. Some scholars think that some members of the Corinthian community used this Platonic soul-body dichotomy to justify bodily actions such as fornication. Thus they would see it reasonable and justifiable to give one's body to a prostitute and one's spirit to Christ. Paul demands, **Shall I then take Christ's members and make them the members of a prostitute?** That what belongs to Christ so intimately would be snatched away through an act of violence is unthinkable. The Greek verb here translated "Shall I take?" is not the ordinary word for "take" but is used more often for taking by force or injustice (Luke 6:29–30; 11:22; John 19:15). But that is precisely what the Christian does

15

---

9. The "his" could refer to God or to the Lord, or it could be inclusive of both, just as the two are governed by a single pronoun and verb in 1 Thess 3:11.

10. Plato, *Phaedo* 80–85; *Phaedrus* 250c.

who unites himself with a prostitute. Stealing from Christ, he makes himself a member of the prostitute, her property. And for one who has been freed by Christ through belonging to him, this is an enslavement, a "falling under the power of," the type of thing that Paul excluded in verse 12. Union with a prostitute is not the only type of fornication, but Paul uses it here as the most typical and that which the city of Aphrodite presented as the most common temptation to the male converts to the new faith.

16   The fornicator **becomes one body with her**, for **"the two," it says, "will become one flesh"** (Gen 2:24). Sexual union, whether within marriage or not, involves the whole person of each partner. It leaves an imprint on the soul as well, because of the partners' psychosomatic nature. The libertines cannot say that in giving the body what it lusts for, the soul remains free and unengaged. Today this still is no small matter, given the currency of casual sex in our society. Sex is not a merely biological activity: it is a communion of persons.

17   **But whoever is joined to the Lord becomes one spirit with him**. Here the words "is joined" are the same words used for union with the prostitute, indicating the stark realism with which Paul considers the Christian's union with the Lord. Thus "becoming one spirit" with Christ does not deny the bodily union just expressed (our "bodies are members of Christ"; v. 15). Rather, the effect of bodily union with Christ is the opposite of bodily union with the prostitute. It has a spiritualizing effect. The Holy Spirit, who inhabits the body of the risen Christ, is passed on to the body of the Christian, much in the way electricity runs to the lamp once the lamp is plugged into the socket. Though union with the prostitute makes a person more "flesh," bodily union with Christ effects a transforming union with the Holy Spirit. In Paul's thought, the opposite of "spirit" is not the physical body but "flesh." Never does Paul consider "spiritual flesh" possible; a "spiritual body" is not only possible, but it is also the destiny of Christians (1 Cor 15:44). The reason is that, already now, their bodies are united to the body of Christ, which in its risen state is "life-giving spirit" (1 Cor 15:45), and thus in their very bodies Christians become "one spirit with him."

18   The only possible conclusion is to *flee fornication*. The NAB translation, **Avoid immorality**, though admissible, loses the strength that Paul intends here: shun, escape from, flee. *Porneia* may be translated "immorality," but the context suggests more specifically sexual immorality or fornication. Following Saint Thomas Aquinas, spiritual writers have advised that while other vices call for a tactic of resistance, fornication calls for the tactic of flight, lest passion be enkindled by toying with the occasion.

The next sentence is difficult to interpret: **Every other sin a person commits is outside the body, but the immoral person sins against his own body**. Would not overeating, drunkenness, and drugs also be sins against one's own body? Paul is obviously saying that there is something unique about sexual sin. Perhaps an example might help: A husband who drinks to excess is harming his relation with his wife, but one who commits adultery directly attacks their relationship, their being "one body"—a point made by Bishop Oecumenius at the end of the tenth century.[11] When you are one body with Christ, sexual immorality is adultery, a violation of the one-body union with Christ.

As in the previous passage, Paul concludes by placing the whole issue in the **19** context of the Trinity. Being one spirit with Christ means that the Christian shares in Christ's own character as a temple of the Holy Spirit. The very **body** of each Christian then becomes a **temple of the holy Spirit**. Paul does not say that the soul is the temple. Philo, an Alexandrian Jew who was a contemporary of Paul, spoke of the intelligence as being a temple, but he never applied the image to the body. But in the Christian view, it is the body itself that enjoys union with the divine persons. In relation to Christ, the believer's body is a member (v. 15); in relation to the Holy Spirit, the body is a temple. The emphasis is on the *Holy* Spirit, which makes sexual immorality a sacrilege. The Spirit is **from God**, but he is also truly possessed by the Christian (**you have** the Holy Spirit from God).

Christians may not dispose of their body as something of their own. Each **20** believer has **been purchased**. The whole theology of redemption is contained here. There was an ancient practice of freeing a slave by a rite in the temple of the gods. He was declared "servant of Apollo" and thus entered the state of freedom from slavery to his human masters. Much was made of the price paid on this occasion, and the term used for slave was *sōma*, "body." When we realize that the majority of the population of Corinth were slaves, and that many in the Christian community were either slaves or freed slaves, we can understand how meaningful would be the allusion to the liberating ransom of redemption by Christ (1:30; Gal 4:5; 5:1). When Paul adds **at a price**, he is intentionally using understatement. Let the listener and the reader fill in: by the blood of the Son of God (Eph 1:7; 1 Pet 1:19)! If the body of the Christian is a temple, it is the place where God is worshiped and glorified (Ps 29:9). **Therefore, glorify God in your body**. The very physical life of the Christian is a liturgy (Rom 12:1), and chastity envelops each one, body and soul, with a brilliance that reflects the glory of God (2 Cor 3:18; Phil 1:20; 3:21).

11. See ACCS 7:59.

You Belong to Another

LIVING
TRADITION

Chrysostom offers this analogy: "Supposing you had a daughter and in extreme madness had let her out to a pimp for hire and made her live a prostitute's life, and that a king's son were to pass by and free her from that slavery and join her in marriage to himself; after that you would have no power to bring her into the brothel. For you gave her up once for all and sold her. Such as this is our case also. We let out our own flesh for hire unto the devil, that grievous pimp: Christ saw and set it free, and withdrew it from that evil tyranny; it is not then ours any more but his who delivered it. If you are willing to use it as a King's bride, there is none to hinder you; but if you take it where it was before, you will suffer just what they ought to suffer who are guilty of such outrages. Therefore you should adorn rather than disgrace it."[a]

a. Saint Chrysostom, *Homilies on 1 Corinthians* 18.3. Pope John Paul II's "theology of the body" has had a powerful impact on the Christian understanding of the body and sexuality. The full text of his presentations is available in *Man and Woman He Created Them* and in a shorter, popular rendition by Mary Healy, *Men and Women Are from Eden* (Cincinnati: Servant Books, 2005).

Reflection and Application (6:12–20)

A member in the Italian parliament of a party that represents Christian values was caught in a Rome hotel room in the summer of 2007 with two prostitutes and a large amount of cocaine. When asked by the authorities how this fits with his Christian values, he responded, "Of course, I recognize Christian values. But what has that got to do with going with a prostitute? It is a personal matter."[12] The man would have felt at home in Corinth. In our times we have witnessed sexual failings of public officials and, lamentably, even of some of the clergy. Perhaps they did not bother to look for philosophical justification of this split between private and public morality, but the fact that they kept their failings hidden as long as they could shows that some kind of practical split was at work in their conscience. Jesus' teaching about purity of heart (Matt 5:8, 27–30) calls for an integration of body, soul, and spirit on the part of all of us. Paul teaches the same truth as the Master by awakening his people to the exalted state of their consecration as members of Christ and temples of the Holy Spirit. If we are to follow Paul's example, we need to go beyond medical and psychological reasons for chastity and focus on the holiness of our state as Christians, which derives from our intimate relation with the Father, the Son, and the Holy Spirit.

12. *New York Sun*, quoted by the *San Antonio Express-News*, August 12, 2007, H-1; original in the Italian newspaper *La Stampa*.

Marriage and Virginity

1 Corinthians 7

After spending a third of the letter addressing abuses in the community, Paul now turns to questions the Corinthians have sent to him or areas of concern that have been reported to him. The questions are quite honest ones, questions of conscience, some of which seem to be prompted by those more ascetically inclined who want to do the most perfect thing and are perhaps an irritant to those less so inclined. If the previous chapters exposed a number of Christians still unconverted in the areas of rivalry and sexuality, these chapters show that there were also those with the zeal of converts who might go to excess. In any case, there is considerable confusion in the community over marriage and virginity (7:1–40), meat offered to idols (8:1–11:1), proper attire for women in church (11:2–16), behavior at the Eucharist (11:17–34), the exercise of spiritual gifts (12:1–14:40), and most important, the resurrection (15:1–58).

Paul's treatment on the states of life in chapter 7 is carefully crafted: The ideal of chastity (7:1); the married, unmarried, and formerly married (7:2–16); fidelity to one's vocation (7:17–24); the not yet married (7:25–38); summary (7:39–40).

To the Married and the Unmarried (7:1–11)

---

¹Now in regard to the matters about which you wrote: "It is a good thing for a man not to touch a woman," ²but because of cases of immorality every man should have his own wife, and every woman her own husband. ³The husband should fulfill his duty toward his wife, and likewise

the wife toward her husband. [4]A wife does not have authority over her own body, but rather her husband, and similarly a husband does not have authority over his own body, but rather his wife. [5]Do not deprive each other, except perhaps by mutual consent for a time, to be free for prayer, but then return to one another, so that Satan may not tempt you through your lack of self-control. [6]This I say by way of concession, however, not as a command. [7]Indeed, I wish everyone to be as I am, but each has a particular gift from God, one of one kind and one of another.

[8]Now to the unmarried and to widows, I say: it is a good thing for them to remain as they are, as I do, [9]but if they cannot exercise self-control they should marry, for it is better to marry than to be on fire. [10]To the married, however, I give this instruction (not I, but the Lord): a wife should not separate from her husband[11]—and if she does separate she must either remain single or become reconciled to her husband—and a husband should not divorce his wife.

NT: Matt 5:32; 19:9, 12; 1 Tim 5:11–14

Catechism: conjugal love, 1643; periodic continence, 2370; indissolubility, 1644–48; conjugal fidelity, 2364–65; divorce, 2382–86

1   If we had at hand the letter the Corinthians sent to Paul, the task of interpreting his responses would be much easier. As it is, like listening to only one side of a telephone conversation, we have to reconstruct the questions from the answers, and that has to be done with care. In any case, from the start it is important to observe that Paul is not giving his whole thought on any of these questions. He does not, for example, here put marriage in the kind of Trinitarian context he did in dealing with the litigious and sexual problems above (6:1–20). We can assume, though, that he would consider that theological context as continuing also here, and we have in Eph 5:21–33 a quite profound theology of the marriage union.

The NAB follows most contemporary scholars by considering the statement **"It is a good thing for a man not to touch a woman"** as part of the Corinthians' letter and thus fittingly put in quotation marks. "Touch" in this context means to have sexual relations; in view of the fact that Paul disposed of sex outside of marriage in the previous section, the question must have to do with complete abstinence within marriage, probably posed by the overly but mistakenly zealous. Does the new Christian life require or recommend abstinence from sex for everybody?

2   Paul will uphold voluntary celibacy a few verses later, so he does not say that the statement is utterly false, **but**, he says, considering the currency of **immorality** (*porneia*) in the surrounding culture, which he has discussed above, the Christian who is married should find sexual fulfillment with one's own spouse. He is *not* saying that one should marry to avoid fornication. This is an interpretation that a number of scholars have embraced, judging Paul's theology of marriage to be very negative and one-sided. But for the Apostle, marriage is a †charism, a gift of God (7:7), as much as celibacy is. The one who marries does well (7:38). As the context indicates, Paul is telling married couples that they should not abstain from relations lest they be tempted to seek satisfaction outside of their marriage. Origen sees this caution not merely for one's personal benefit but especially as a loving service to the *other*, lest the other be tempted to adultery.[1]

3–4   Paul buttresses this by saying that **the husband should fulfill his duty toward his wife, and likewise the wife toward her husband**. Paul indicates there is no warrant for one spouse's deciding unilaterally to abstain from normal marital relations for spiritual reasons. The spouse's body belongs to the other, who therefore in the matter of intercourse has **authority** to expect consent from the marriage partner. It is mutual authority, however, which means that the authority is not absolute and should be exercised with thoughtfulness and love. Gordon Fee comments: "Paul's emphasis, it must be noted, is not on 'You owe me,' but on 'I owe you.'"[2]

There is a clear mutuality here that will run through this entire chapter. The husband is not lord of the wife, as was often assumed in the culture, but her equal in mutual belonging. Paul, following Jesus, is establishing a new, countercultural, and revolutionary equality between husband and wife. This is an important principle to remember when later Paul speaks about the husband being head of the wife (11:3).

5   **Do not deprive each other** means that one should not refuse the other, nor should they both abstain for extended periods of time, lest their **lack of self-control** tempt them to seek satisfaction elsewhere. He does, however, allow for abstinence **by mutual consent for a time, to be free for prayer**. It is significant that Paul expects prayer to accompany periods of mutually agreed abstinence. In fact, it is the only purpose of abstinence that he envisions. Great pastoral wisdom is this, because prayer can sublimate the sexual drive and bring about a deeper spiritual union.

6   At certain times in the Old Testament, sexual abstinence was required when approaching the holy (Exod 19:15) or for a holy mission (1 Sam 21:4–6; 2 Sam

---

1. Origen, *Homilies on 1 Corinthians*, in *JTS* 9 (1908): 500–503; quoted in Judith L. Kovacs, trans. and ed., *1 Corinthians: Interpreted by Early Christian Commentators*, The Church's Bible (Grand Rapids: Eerdmans, 2005), 108–9.

2. Gordon D. Fee, *The First Epistle to the Corinthians*, New International Commentary on the New Testament (Grand Rapids: Eerdmans, 1987), 280.

11:11–13). This suggests that abstinence is best directed toward a time of worship. But Paul wants his people to know that his allowing periodic abstinence is not a command: it is indeed a **concession**. In this section the whole question is whether abstinence is "good" (7:1). Some Corinthians think so. But Paul says it is not good for the married, *except by way of concession* for a time to devote themselves to prayer. A commitment to celibacy is good only for those who have the gift (Matt 19:12), as the next sentence makes clear.

7   **Indeed,** Paul says, still in the line of concession, **I wish everyone to be as I am,** that is, celibate. However, **each has a particular gift from God, one of one kind and one of another.** The word "gift" here is *charisma*, "charism," the same word that Paul uses elsewhere for the spiritual gifts such as tongues, prophecy, healing, and the rest.[3] Charisms are gifts given to individuals for the building up of the body, the Church. In the context, then, and as an introduction to what follows, marriage is a charism, and so is celibacy. Some argue that since marriage is a natural state and celibacy is a special gift of God, marriage should not be considered a charism. But why then would Paul say that each one has a particular gift from God, clearly comparing marriage and celibacy as particular gifts? Paul surely is thinking of marriage in the Lord, which brings grace also to the children and even to an unbelieving spouse (7:14).

8   Clearly marking off verse 8 from the preceding question of abstinence within marriage, Paul now addresses those who are not married, either because they are not so yet or because the spouse has died. In saying that it is a **good thing** for **the unmarried** and **widows . . . to remain as they are,** Paul is further responding to the question of the Corinthians about what is "good" about abstinence (7:1). In saying that celibacy is a good thing, Paul is not saying it is the *only* good thing. He will indicate under what conditions celibacy might be embraced.

9   "Not good" summarizes his response to lengthy or permanent abstinence within marriage. But yes, it is good for the unmarried to remain celibate, provided they can **exercise self-control**, if they are capable of being chaste in the celibate state. Interpreters are divided on exactly what Paul means by saying **it is better to marry than to be on fire**. Does this mean the eternal fire of hell? Or does it mean that a person's passions might be so strong that they are difficult to contain, and therefore one's attempts to observe celibacy would leave the person burning with desire? In favor of the former, which was held in earlier times by many commentators and is still held today by some, is the fact that no mention is made of what one burns *with*. However, it is now recognized

3. See Rom 12:6; 1 Cor 1:7; 12:4, 9, 28, 30–31.

Quenching the Sexual Fire

As for the rest of the New Testament, for Paul the only legitimate intercourse is within marriage. Not so in the Greco-Roman world. The Stoic philosopher Epictetus writes: "And indeed when a man out of passionate love is under the compulsion to do something contrary to his right sense, . . . he is in the grip of something violent, and, in a manner of speaking, divine."[a] And Achilles Tatius: "However angry you make me, I still burn with love for you. . . . Make a truce with me at least for now; pity me. . . . A single consummation will be enough. It is a small remedy I ask for so great an illness. Quench a little of my fire."[b] This view of sex as a compulsion that must be fulfilled, so frequent in our day, is a far cry from the sacredness with which Paul views the gift of sexuality and the respect and sensitivity that *agapē*, divine love, brings to it.

a. Epictetus, *Discourses* 4.1.14.
b. Tatius, *Leucippe and Cliotophon* 5.26.2; quoted in David E. Garland, *1 Corinthians*, BECNT (Grand Rapids: Baker Academic, 2003), 274.

that "burning" was a common figure in Greek literature for sexual desire, and it appears also in Sir 9:8 (see also Prov 6:27–29):

> Avert your eyes from a shapely woman;
> > do not gaze upon the beauty that is not yours—
> Through woman's beauty many have been ruined,
> > for love of it burns like fire.

For Paul, as for all the biblical authors, the proper outlet for sexual passion is within marriage, not outside it. That was not at all obvious in the surrounding culture. One could satisfy the strong sexual urge simply by having sex wherever one could get it (see sidebar). For Paul, the only proper sexual expression is in marriage, which involves the total gift of oneself to the other.

Next Paul turns to the married. He recalls the command of Jesus forbidding divorce. Ordinarily in this chapter, Paul begins with the duties of the men and then those of the women. But here he puts the woman first. Perhaps it was because the question posed by the Corinthians came from a particular case in the community in which a woman was contemplating divorce. If Paul had been writing for a Jewish community, the issue would not have been raised, since among the Jews only the man could initiate divorce. But most of the Corinthian Christians were Gentiles, and in Corinth, as in Rome, women had the legal right to initiate a divorce. But for Christian couples the word of the

10–11

Fig. 8. Ancient Roman marriage.

Lord is authoritative: Neither husband nor wife may initiate divorce, for divorce itself is forbidden (Matt 5:31–32). (The word **separate** is equivalent to **divorce**: see Mark 10:9.)

When we look back over this opening section of chapter 7, we notice that it is all about duties and not about rights. If the obligation of the one spouse assumes a right over the other, this is not Paul's emphasis. He has said that each spouse belongs fully to the other, in service of his argument that neither spouse has the right to unilaterally decide that the couple will not have sexual relations. By declaring that the spouses do belong to each other, he establishes an approach to marriage in which each spouse should be entirely devoted to the good of the other. This mutuality is detailed in the reciprocal duties of both husband and wife. Paul's teaching here is revolutionary. It will be given an even

Mutuality of Husband and Wife

LIVING TRADITION

The Church Fathers universally follow Paul in the matter of mutual rights of husband and wife. In the Roman world, wives were expected to keep marital chastity, but the same was not expected of husbands. So Theodoret of Cyr writes: "Human laws demand that women be chaste, and if they are not they are punished for it, but they do not demand the same from men. Since it was men who made the laws, they did not make themselves equal with woman but allowed themselves extra indulgence. The holy apostle, however, inspired by divine grace, was the first one who made the law of chastity apply to men as well."[a]

On the issue of abstinence within marriage, Chrysostom writes: "Unless there is mutual consent, abstinence in this case is really a form of theft."[b] Augustine says that the partner who wishes to practice abstinence but yields to the other's request for intercourse gains before God the merit of abstinence anyway.[c] We can presume that Augustine understood the intention of abstinence here to be for a good purpose, such as prayer.

a. Theodoret of Cyr, *Commentary on 1 Corinthians* 201; in PG 82:271.
b. Saint Chrysostom, *Homilies on 1 Corinthians* 19.3.
c. Saint Augustine, *Letter 262, To Eudicia*; quoted in ACCS 7:61, where "continence" is used instead of "abstinence."

deeper theological dimension in Eph 5:21–33, where marriage is regarded as an icon of Christ and the Church.

Reflection and Application (7:1–11)

Because of the complexity of issues surrounding marriage, the Church has an extensive section on it in the Code of Canon Law. The Church does not recognize as valid a marriage of a Catholic before a civil court. The marriage of a Catholic to a non-Catholic requires a special dispensation. The Church does not recognize the dissolution of a valid marriage by civil divorce. However, the Church does recognize that there are sometimes sufficient reasons for separation (violent abuse, for example), either temporary or permanent.[4] The Church does allow for the annulment of a marriage that lacks a necessary component for validity, as determined by the appropriate Church authority.

4. United States Conference of Catholic Bishops, *Marriage: Love and Life in the Divine Plan* (Washington, DC: USCCB, 2009), 1.3.

While rejecting contraception as contrary to God's plan for marriage, the Church does accept natural family planning, which is abstinence in periods of fertility as a means of appropriately spacing procreation. This suggests that there might be reasons other than prayer for periodic abstinence. Serious reasons of health would be an obvious one.

For a concise summary of the Church's teaching on marriage and the laws applicable to it within the Church, see the Catechism, 1601–66.

Paul's Judgment for Particular Situations (7:12–16)

¹²**To the rest I say (not the Lord): if any brother has a wife who is an unbeliever, and she is willing to go on living with him, he should not divorce her; ¹³and if any woman has a husband who is an unbeliever, and he is willing to go on living with her, she should not divorce her husband. ¹⁴For the unbelieving husband is made holy through his wife, and the unbelieving wife is made holy through the brother. Otherwise your children would be unclean, whereas in fact they are holy.**

¹⁵**If the unbeliever separates, however, let him separate. The brother or sister is not bound in such cases; God has called you to peace. ¹⁶For how do you know, wife, whether you will save your husband; or how do you know, husband, whether you will save your wife?**

NT: 1 Pet 3:1

Catechism: marriage and divorce: unbeliever made holy by spouse, 1637; disparity of cult, 1633–35, 1637; annulment, 1628–29

12–14   **To the rest**, as we will see from the context, refers to those who converted to Christianity while married to an unbeliever, whether Jew or Gentile. Paul is not referring to an unmarried believer who wishes to marry an unbeliever, since a marriage entered into by a Christian should be "in the Lord" (7:39). Judging from the culture of the day and from the passages in Acts that speak of a whole household converting when the head of the household becomes Christian (Acts 16:15, 31–34), we can guess that many married couples converted together. But our present passage indicates that this was not always the case. Now Paul launches out on his own apostolic authority, making clear that this is what **I say (not the Lord)**. Because Jesus' teaching did not address this circumstance, Paul is free to use his authority to resolve the issue. If one spouse converts and the other does not, what is the newly baptized Christian spouse

Christians Should Marry "in the Lord"

BIBLICAL BACKGROUND

Paul's insistence that Christians should marry "in the Lord" so that the couple practice the same religion finds an echo in Hellenistic culture. The involvement of women in secret religious rites not open to men, such as in some of the mystery religions, is denounced by Plutarch in his "Advice to Bride and Groom": "A wife ought not to make friends of her own, but to enjoy her husband's friends in common with him. The gods are the first and most important friends. Wherefore it is becoming for a wife to worship and to know only the gods that her husband believes in, and to shut the front door tight upon all strange rituals and outlandish superstitions. For with no god do stealthy and secret rites performed by a woman find any favor."[a]

a. Plutarch, *Moralia* 140D.

to do? Is the new consecrated state of the baptized such that the marital union with the unbeliever should be dissolved?

Paul's response is that if the other does not convert, that is no grounds for divorce, as long as the **unbeliever . . . is willing to go on living with** the Christian. From what follows we can assume that "to go on living" means to live peaceably (7:15). Instead of the Christian's being defiled by the unbeliever (a concern that may have been voiced by some of the Corinthians, particularly in light of the Jewish fear of contamination with idolaters, which Paul himself warns against; 5:9–13), the opposite is true. The unbelieving partner **is made holy through** the Christian spouse. Exactly how this happens Paul does not say. Perhaps some of the holiness, the new and beautiful lifestyle of the Christian partner, would rub off on the other. However, a better clue is given by the perfect tense of the Greek, which does not appear in the NAB translation: "The unbelieving husband *has been* made holy through his wife, and the unbelieving wife *has been* made holy through the believing husband." However ongoing the process of sanctification might be, the text speaks of a sanctification that has already happened, and that must refer to some kind of extension of the baptismal holiness of the believer to the unbeliever. Certainly Paul does not mean to imply the unbeliever has no need to convert. Unlike the defiling union with the prostitute (6:12–20), the union of spouses is something instituted by God (Gen 2:24). In this case that bond, far from causing defilement to the believer, becomes a conduit in the other direction for the radiation of the Christian's holiness to the unbeliever. The effect on the unbeliever is not of the same order as faith and baptism, but because of the natural marriage bond and physical union of husband and wife, something of the holiness of the body of Christ touches the unbeliever. Perhaps Paul is thinking of a passage like Exod 29:37, where the altar, once consecrated, makes holy whatever touches it.

The holiness of the believer conveys a certain holiness on the **children** as well. This is a mysterious saying of Paul. How does it happen? Paul does not say that they can become holy through the example or training of the Christian parent. He says they **are holy**. It must be on the basis of the same principle as for the couple. Not only is the Christian not defiled by either spouse or children, but because of being a member of the body of Christ, the Christian becomes a conduit of blessing for the children. Nothing is said here about the baptism of these children, whether already born or yet unborn, nor the issue of whether the consent of the partner is needed to have them raised as Christians. These are questions that subsequent tradition will deal with.

15   **If the unbeliever separates**, the believer has no choice but to accept the separation. Roman law did not permit contesting a divorce. But the believer is now free to remarry, for **the brother or sister is not bound in such cases**. One is set free from any obligation to remain faithful to the marriage if the other departs. Of itself, that says nothing about a Christian's initiating divorce. Much depends on how the next sentence is translated. **God has called you to peace** appears to indicate that the Christian vocation ("called") brings with it a right to peace in the practice of one's faith, so that, combined with 7:12–13, it would justify initiating divorce if the unbeliever harasses the believer over the faith or makes the believer's life intolerable. Saint Justin Martyr records the case of a Christian wife who remained married to an abusive unbeliever in the hopes of converting him, but eventually she divorced him.[5] In this case, "if the unbeliever *departs*" means something broader than initiating divorce. It could apply to making the marriage intolerable for the believer. Support for this position can be found in the word "bound" ("the believer is not bound"). It is not the usual word for something legally binding, but a word indicating the bondage of slavery.

On the other hand, the clause can be translated, "*But* God has called us *in* peace," which would revert to the idea expressed in 7:12–13, that if you were in marital peace when you were called, then do not try to get out of it now that you are a Christian. Paul is concerned that some of his faithful might too readily seek divorce because of marital difficulties or just because they are now Christian, so he encourages them to hang in there in the hopes of saving the marriage. Whichever translation is taken, it carries over its influence into the next verse.

5. Saint Justin, *Second Apology* 2.

The Pauline Privilege

LIVING
TRADITION

This text is the foundation for what in the Catholic Church is called the Pauline Privilege, which is described in Canon 1143 as follows:

> 1. A marriage entered by two non-baptized persons is dissolved by means of the Pauline privilege in favor of the faith of a party who has received baptism by the very fact that a new marriage is contracted by the party who has been baptized, provided the non-baptized party departs.
> 2. The non-baptized party is considered to have departed if he or she does not wish to cohabit with the baptized party or does not wish to cohabit in peace without insult to the Creator unless, after receiving baptism, the baptized party gave the other party a just cause for departure.

The phrase "without insult to the Creator" refers to conditions that make fulfillment of the obligations of the Christian life difficult or impossible for the baptized party.[a]

a. The explanation is found in the commentary on Canon 1143 in *The Code of Canon Law: A Text and Commentary*, commissioned by the Canon Law Society of America (Mahwah, NJ: Paulist Press, 1985), 814–15.

How do you know, wife, whether you will save your husband; or how do you know, husband, whether you will save your wife? If the preceding sentence urges staying in the marriage, then the question is to be taken in a positive sense: "If you stay in the marriage, you have a chance to save your husband or wife." If the preceding sentence approves separation, then this sentence is understood negatively: "Chances are slim that you will save your spouse." Here is another case where we wish Paul would have been clearer. Perhaps the Corinthians knew well what he meant. The Church has taken the text to justify the Pauline Privilege, which allows the dissolution of a marriage under certain conditions (see sidebar), with freedom to remarry. However, even if the Christian spouse is free to remarry, that believer may choose to remain in the marriage with the hope of converting the unbeliever, as did the woman for a while in the case that St. Justin reports (above).

16

Stay Put (7:17–24)

¹⁷**Only, everyone should live as the Lord has assigned, just as God called each one. I give this order in all the churches.** ¹⁸**Was someone called**

after he had been circumcised? He should not try to undo his circumcision. Was an uncircumcised person called? He should not be circumcised. ¹⁹Circumcision means nothing, and uncircumcision means nothing; what matters is keeping God's commandments. ²⁰Everyone should remain in the state in which he was called.

²¹Were you a slave when you were called? Do not be concerned but, even if you can gain your freedom, make the most of it. ²²For the slave called in the Lord is a freed person in the Lord, just as the free person who has been called is a slave of Christ. ²³You have been purchased at a price. Do not become slaves to human beings. ²⁴Brothers, everyone should continue before God in the state in which he was called.

OT: 1 Macc 1:15
NT: Rom 2:25–29; 6:18–22; Gal 5:6; 6:15
Catechism: slavery forbidden, 2414

17   At first sight this section seems to be a digression from Paul's discussion of marriage and celibacy. Such digressions would not be surprising in a letter that is being dictated and perhaps interrupted by some external circumstance. But in fact this section provides a theological reason for what Paul has been discussing. Just becoming a Christian does not demand or entitle a change of status. God's call transcends all categories. The heart of this section is God's call, referred to eight times in these eight verses. It is our common call to the faith that creates our identity both as individual Christians and as the body of Christ. This call relativizes all distinctions of race, gender, ethnicity, and social standing (Gal 3:28). **Everyone should live** the Christian life in whatever state a person was when called, the state that God's providence **has assigned**. The discussion of marriage and celibacy falls under this broader rule, which is an **order** Paul gives **in all the churches**. Though it is a matter of discipline rather than doctrine, it is not a suggestion but a rule grounded in Paul's apostolic authority. Becoming a Christian is not a title or an invitation to move to a different social level. Paul is trying to keep the call to the faith from being obscured by a compulsion to see it as a call to a different state of life. All are equalized by the common call.

18   Those who were Jews when called should not try to rewrite their history and **undo** their **circumcision**. (Concealing their circumcision was practiced by the Jews who cooperated in the propagation of Greek culture under Antiochus IV; 1 Macc 1:15.) Those who were Gentiles (**uncircumcised**) when **called** should not try to become a more original Christian, as the Jewish Christians could claim to be, by being **circumcised**. Paul faced the latter problem with the Galatians

Jewish Attachment to Circumcision

**BIBLICAL
BACKGROUND**

Saint Justin expresses well the attachment of the Jews to circumcision. In his *Dialogue with Trypho*, chapter 10, he quotes Trypho: "Have you not read that that soul shall be cut off from his people who shall not have been circumcised on the eighth day? And this has been ordained for strangers and for slaves equally. But you, despising this covenant rashly, reject the consequent duties and attempt to persuade yourselves that you know God, when, however, you perform none of those things which they do who fear God." Justin responds by quoting the Scripture's foretelling of a new covenant and recalling Paul's doctrine that Abraham received God's call and responded in faith without circumcision.

who were being persuaded by Judaizers to submit to circumcision. His reaction was swift and uncompromising (Gal 5:2–6).

For Paul the Jew to say that **circumcision means nothing** is really astound-   19–20
ing, for it was a sign of the covenant that God made with Abraham, which the Jews considered eternal, and it was one of the commands to be observed in every generation (Gen 17:9–14; see sidebar). It superseded even the command-ment not to work on the Sabbath, so that a child could be circumcised on the Sabbath if it was the eighth day from birth (John 7:22). Since Jews considered it the essential sign separating them from other people and committing them to the Mosaic law, the question arose as to whether Christians would take it as their boundary-setting initiation too. The consequences of doing so Paul found intolerable: it would compromise the uniqueness of the new thing begun in Jesus Christ. Baptism, furthermore, unlike circumcision, was available to women and men alike. Circumcision would impose an unnecessary burden on Gentiles that would diminish the attraction of the gospel. Paul saw all this with a clarity that the Jewish Christians in Jerusalem did not, but he was able to convince the leaders in Jerusalem that his view was from the Holy Spirit (Acts 15).

What matters is keeping God's commandments. Why does Paul say this instead of saying that what matters is belief in Jesus Christ? Circumcision was a sign of the Jew's covenant commitment to the Lord, which meant keeping the commandments, and it was a countersign if one did not keep the command-ments. Paul is concerned to emphasize that Christians too are committed to holiness. In the moral climate of Corinth, Paul wants to insist on the high moral ground required of those who believe in Jesus Christ, no matter whether one is circumcised or not. Thus when Paul states in verse 17, "Everyone should live as the Lord has assigned," he means more than just staying put in the state in which one was called. He means to *live the gospel*, which includes the commandments of God, to its fullest in whatever state. Just being circumcised or uncircumcised is not going to assure one of salvation. In the moral climate of the Corinthian community, Paul wants to insist on the holiness required of those who believe in Jesus Christ. This little section closes with an †inclusio of verse 20 with verse 17: **Everyone should remain in the state in which he was called**. This is a broad statement, to which Paul will soon give some qualifications regarding marriage and celibacy (7:25–35). What he says here seems to be largely shaped to prepare for what he is now going to say about slaves.

21   The same principle applies to slaves. **Do not be concerned** means that the slave should not consider that slavery makes him a second- or third-class citizen, since everyone is both slave and free in Christ (v. 22). **But, even if you can gain your freedom, make the most of it**. What does "make the most of it" mean? Does this mean that slaves should stay slaves even if they can become free? Or does it mean that if they have an opportunity for freedom, they should take it? The NAB translation is probably intentionally ambiguous because the meaning is not perfectly clear. The NJB chooses the sense to remain as a slave: "Even if you have a chance of freedom, you should prefer to make full use of your condition as a slave." The NRSV translates: "Even if you can gain your freedom, make use of your present condition now more than ever." But the Greek here can also mean "if indeed," so that the idea would be, "But if indeed you can gain your freedom. . . ." And so the NIV translates: "If you can gain your freedom, do so."

Greater clarity is offered by the fact that in the frequent Greco-Roman practice of setting the slave free, the choice was not in the power of the slave, only the master. Hence the best interpretation seems to be this: if you gain your freedom, use that state, just as you used the state of slavery, as an opportunity to live and bear witness to your Christian faith. Again, Paul is saying that one's social state contributes nothing to salvation, nor does it compromise salvation. What matters is to make the most of the grace God gives, whatever one's state in life.

22–24   **The slave . . . is a freed person in the Lord**, and **the free person . . . is a slave of Christ**. This is because both are **called in the Lord**. And that call is rooted in the fact that they both have been **purchased at a price**, a term for the purchase of slaves. To understand Paul's thought here we need to put off our twenty-first-century glasses and put on those of the first-century Greco-Roman world. Slavery evokes to us today the images of Africans hauled like animals in the hold of a slave ship, then sold in the market (see sidebar). Unfortunately, slavery still occurs today in some countries. Being a slave in the ancient world was hardly a desirable situation. Slaves were not legally permitted to marry, and Quintilian says that children should not be beaten, for beating is "fit for slaves."[6] This type of servitude was the lot of a huge number of the population—estimates for Corinth are that one-third to two-thirds of the population were slaves. Still, slavery did not always mean an abject state of life. Some slaves were better educated than their masters, and sometimes selling oneself into slavery brought a betterment of status, especially if the master was a person of high social rank.

There was a distinction between a freeborn person and a freed person, a distinction important for our text, which speaks of both. A freedman or freedwoman still retained a relation with the former master or mistress, who now was the free person's patron (see sidebar on †patron-client relationship), with reciprocal obligations. The freed person owed the patron respect, a certain amount of service, gifts, and other duties. The patron in turn assured the freed person of sponsorship, protection, and welfare. Perhaps because of this enduring relationship, Paul prefers the term "freed person" to "freeborn" when applying the analogy to the Christian slave, for he is not like an untethered balloon. He moves to a higher state but remains in a relationship with Christ, who has set him free but remains his patron. By the same token, the person born free, having no human master, becomes a slave of Christ, a lower state than the freed person. Paul uses here the †rhetoric of the seesaw, in the same spirit of Jesus' saying, "Whoever exalts himself will be humbled, and whoever humbles himself will be exalted" (Matt 23:12). Paul is using every tool he can find to convince his readers of the surpassing reality of their new state, which makes preoccupation with their worldly state inconsequential. **Do not become slaves to human beings**, then, can have a double meaning. On the one hand, it can mean "Do not sell yourself into slavery," whether as an act of heroism (for example, to pay off someone's debt) or to pursue some benefit (for example, for financial gain). On the other hand, another meaning is probably better: if they evaluate themselves according to human status markers, they become slaves to worldly values, but now they are free in Christ.

Everyone should continue before God in the state in which he was called. This is an inclusio with verse 17, a general principle that Paul has applied analogously to the different states.

---

6. Quintilian, *Institutio oratoria* 1.3.13–14.

The Lot of Slaves

How did one come to be a slave? Capture in war often peopled the victor's land with many slaves. When the Greek-speaking king of Syria, Antiochus III, lost a war with the Roman Empire in 188 BC, slaves were brought to the capital of the empire as prisoners, among them many Jews. Vespasian took six thousand prisoners in the Jewish War (in AD 67) and sent them as slaves to Nero for work in digging a canal across the Corinthian isthmus. Other persons became slaves simply by being kidnapped and sold. Still others fell into unpayable debt and sold themselves into slavery, usually according to a contract for a certain number of years. Some did this simply because their lives of poverty were so miserable that they preferred to belong to someone's household, even as a slave. Children who were abandoned and exposed by their parents, if found alive, were sometimes adopted as slaves. At times parents sold their children, especially their daughters, into slavery. Finally, some were born into slavery, children of parents who were slaves. Slavery was so important a factor in the society and economy of the first-century Mediterranean world that scholars estimate that one-third of the populace of the major cities were slaves. In short, slavery was largely an economic arrangement.[a]

The slave was the master's property (a "body"), and the owner was free to do with him or her what he wished with impunity. Sexual abuse, even death, was within the unchallenged power of the master. Obviously the manner of treating slaves differed greatly from owner to owner. When the head of a household became Christian, the whole household frequently followed suit, including the slaves,[b] but there were cases where the slave was Christian and his owner was not. First Timothy 6:2 supposes both possibilities. If some masters were known for cruelty, slaves were also known for lying, so much so that laws required their testimony in court to be (supposedly) verified by torture.

a. See Muhammad Dandamayev and S. Scott Bartchy, "Slavery," *ABD* 6:58–73.
b. Acts 16:15, 31–34; 18:8; 1 Cor 1:16; 16:15.

The Case of Virgins (7:25–35)

[25]Now in regard to virgins, I have no commandment from the Lord, but I give my opinion as one who by the Lord's mercy is trustworthy. [26]So this is what I think best because of the present distress: that it is a good thing for a person to remain as he is. [27]Are you bound to a wife? Do not seek a separation. Are you free of a wife? Then do not look for a wife. [28]If you marry, however, you do not sin, nor does an unmarried woman sin if she marries;

Slavery Forbidden

On the matter of slavery, the Catechism of the Catholic Church is clear and categorical: "The seventh commandment forbids acts or enterprises that for any reason—selfish or ideological, commercial, or totalitarian—lead to the *enslavement of human beings*, to their being bought, sold and exchanged like merchandise, in disregard for their personal dignity. It is a sin against the dignity of persons and their fundamental rights to reduce them by violence to their productive value or to a source of profit. Saint Paul directed a Christian master to treat his Christian slave 'no longer as a slave but more than a slave, as a beloved brother, . . . both in the flesh and in the Lord' (Philem 16)" (#2414).

but such people will experience affliction in their earthly life, and I would like to spare you that.

²⁹I tell you, brothers, the time is running out. From now on, let those having wives act as not having them, ³⁰those weeping as not weeping, those rejoicing as not rejoicing, those buying as not owning, ³¹those using the world as not using it fully. For the world in its present form is passing away.

³²I should like you to be free of anxieties. An unmarried man is anxious about the things of the Lord, how he may please the Lord. ³³But a married man is anxious about the things of the world, how he may please his wife, ³⁴and he is divided. An unmarried woman or a virgin is anxious about the things of the Lord, so that she may be holy in both body and spirit. A married woman, on the other hand, is anxious about the things of the world, how she may please her husband. ³⁵I am telling you this for your own benefit, not to impose a restraint upon you, but for the sake of propriety and adherence to the Lord without distraction.

NT: Matt 19:12; Luke 10:40; Rom 13:11; Heb 13:14; 1 John 2:16–17
Catechism: consecration of virgins, 922–24; consecrated life, 914–33
Lectionary: St. Mary Magdalene de Pazzi; Common of Virgins; Ritual Mass for the Consecration of Virgins and Religious Profession; Votive Mass for the Holy Church; 7:29–31: Mass for the Beginning of the Civil Year

---

If everyone is to remain in the state in which they were called (7:17, 24), **25** what of one's unmarried daughters? Must they never marry? And what about unmarried men? The word **virgins** here must apply to men as well as women, since verse 27 addresses men. The state of male virginity was unheard of in pagan antiquity. The closest the word came was its use in the neuter for things not yet used, as today we say "a virgin forest." But in the book of Revelation (14:4) it is used of both men and women, as here. On this issue Paul says he has **no commandment from the Lord**. Paul shows no awareness of Jesus' recommendation of celibacy for those who are called and willing (Matt 19:11–12), but he arrives at the same teaching. Jesus certainly did not command celibacy, and neither does Paul. Note Paul's awareness of the distinction between his words and those of the Master—a principle often overlooked by the biblical scholars who say that the early Church created most of the sayings of Jesus found in the Gospels. Even so, his words do have apostolic weight, though in this case it is his **opinion**. Lest the word "opinion" be taken too lightly, he reminds the Corinthians that he was called **by the Lord's mercy**, and that call has made him **trustworthy**. And in a gentle understatement in 7:40, he will say, "and I think I too have the Spirit of God." Jesus left to his apostles the application of his teaching to many specific circumstances, but they would do so with his authority.

26 **I think best** means obviously that this is not a command, but it is an excellent and beautiful thing (the rich word *kalos*, which Paul uses twice here, conveys both goodness and beauty) for one to remain as he or she is. Thus the apostle repeats the general principle he has explained at length earlier in the chapter. In this section he gives several reasons for his recommendation, the first of which is **the present distress**. What does he mean by that? Two interpretations are possible: (1) the difficulties to which any life in this world is subject, especially marriage—an interpretation that enjoyed the favor of the ancient commentators—or (2) the crisis of the final times preceding the †parousia. On the first interpretation, the expression would be equivalent to the "affliction in their earthly life" of verse 28. On the second, it would be equivalent or parallel to the time that "is running out" in verse 29. Both interpretations are possible, but the second seems preferable in that Paul uses the term *anankē*, "distress," here not for his personal afflictions (as in 2 Cor 6:4; 12:10; 1 Thess 3:7) but for the distress in which the Church finds herself in the final times (Luke 21:23), which are already unfolding in the life of the Church ("the present distress"). The Greek word suggests compulsion or compression. Time itself has been compressed by the resurrection of Jesus on one end and his second coming on the other, and that gives the present life an urgency of which unbelievers are unaware. In that context the life of virginity becomes particularly desirable because the meaning of time has been changed now that the Lord is on its horizon.

27 In verse 27 Paul speaks of men, since in that culture it was the man who took the initiative in pursuing marriage. The one **bound to a wife** should **not**

seek a separation. Unfortunately, this translation makes the text a mere repetition of the command of 7:10–11: don't divorce. But the Greek word translated "separation" (*lysis*) is different from the words Paul used above for divorce; it means the loosing of a bond or a commitment. Hence, other scholars have suggested that Paul has in mind a betrothal, a promise to marry. And since the Greek word translated "wife" (*gynē*) can also mean "woman," the sense would be, "Are you already committed to a woman? Do not seek to be released from your commitment."

Are you free of a wife? Then do not look for a wife is a repetition of his preference stated in the preceding verse (26). This verse should not be isolated from the context of verses 7 and 9, which take for granted that not all are called to celibacy.

Marriage is a †charism, and Paul will extol its profound meaning in Eph 5:21–33, but those who marry will **experience affliction in their earthly life** (literally, "will have tribulation of the flesh"). These are not the tribulations of the final times but the anxieties, cares, difficulties, and sufferings that are inseparable from the married state. They can be avoided without spiritual detriment. And for this reason Paul says that for his part, **I** (the emphatic "I," *egō* in the Greek) **would like to spare you that**.

28

But now Paul raises their thoughts beyond daily trials to a much broader horizon. **The time is running out**. Literally, "the time has been shortened." The NAB uses a contemporary expression that means there is not much time left. But the Greek suggests that time itself has suffered a dramatic reduction by some external force. This we know from elsewhere is the event of the resurrection of Jesus and the second coming, which it entails (Acts 17:31; 1 Thess 1:10). Paul in no way specifies the exact duration of remaining time. But for Christian faith these two great events have contracted time, like an accordion or a fluted curtain closed to its shortest, because we see both ends of time at once—and thus its ultimate meaning—in a way that the nonbelieving world does not.

29–30

This means that the Christian enjoys a unique freedom in relation to the things of this world. In saying **Let those having wives act as not having them** he certainly does not mean they should live celibately (7:5), nor that those **weeping** should not weep nor those **rejoicing** should not rejoice, nor that those **buying** should not possess. But none of these things has lasting value; the danger is that one may become absorbed or engrossed in them at the expense of what is meant to last: one's state as a Christian. This principle of interior liberty applies to all. Hold everything you have with a relaxed grasp!

31   The succession of paradoxes climaxes with the play on words between "using" (*chrōmenoi*) and "using up" (*katachrōmenoi*; NAB: **using it fully**), that is, making use of the things of the world but not pouncing upon them like a greedy child devouring the proffered sweets and grasping for more. Christians hold their goods with a light grasp, not because they pursue a Stoic ideal of emotional detachment, but because they wait for their returning Lord. The text does not discourage human initiative (Paul had corrected the Thessalonians on this point: 1 Thess 4:11–12; 2 Thess 3:6–12) and, of course, the kingdom of God demands the best of one's efforts (1 Cor 3:10–15). But **the world in its present form is passing away**. The word translated "present form" here is *schēma*, which frequently means what appears in contrast to what is real. A writing attributed to Plato uses it for pretense in contrast to truth or virtue;[7] Plutarch uses it in a phrase meaning "under the *show* of."[8] Euripides uses it of the theater: "The world is a scene which is quickly going to change."[9] The viewer of a play knows that nothing is more changeable than the scene on the stage. To make such a temporary episode the object of a total commitment is to live in a dream world. Euripides' meaning is probably closer to Paul's sense here. It is not that what you daily experience in the world is unreal (*maya*, "illusion," as in Hinduism). It simply is passing, temporary. The psalmist already said so: "Teach us to count our days aright, that we may gain wisdom of heart" (Ps 90:12). But the Christian accepts this truth with joy, knowing that the resurrection and parousia of Christ brings eternal life.

32   It is this universal law of Christian liberty that inspires Paul's praise of virginity: **I should like you to be free of anxieties. An unmarried man** (this could refer to widowers as well as to those never married) is concerned **about the things of the Lord, how he may please the Lord**. This means that he would be freer to pray and to serve the church and his neighbor. Obviously Paul means that such a man is free to be occupied with the interests of the Lord, not that every unmarried person will automatically be so occupied.

33–34   **But a married man is** necessarily concerned about such temporal matters as the support of his family and **how he may please his wife**. Then Paul applies the same principle to an **unmarried woman or a virgin**, on the one hand, and the **married woman** on the other. In both cases Paul acknowledges that seeking to please one's spouse and concern about temporal matters goes with the territory of married life. He recognizes that the individual who embraces celibacy

---

7. Plato, *Epinomis* 989C.
8. Plutarch, *Dion* 16.
9. Cited by Spicq, "1 Corinthiens," 221.

A Sign of the Kingdom to Come

LIVING TRADITION

In his Apostolic Letter *Vita Consecrata* (*The Consecrated Life*), §26, Pope John Paul II points to the "†eschatological nature of the consecrated life":

> "Where your treasure is, there will your heart be also" (Matt 6:21). The unique treasure of the Kingdom gives rise to desire, anticipation, commitment, and witness. In the early Church, the expectation of the Lord's coming was lived in a particularly intense way. With the passing of the centuries, the Church has not ceased to foster this attitude of hope: she has continued to invite the faithful to look to the salvation which is waiting to be revealed, "for the form of this world is passing away" (1 Cor 7:31; cf. 1 Pet 1:3–6).
>
> It is in this perspective that we can understand more clearly the *role* of consecrated life as an *eschatological sign*. In fact it has constantly been taught that the consecrated life is a foreshadowing of the future Kingdom. The Second Vatican Council proposes this teaching anew when it states that consecration better "foretells the resurrected state and the glory of the heavenly Kingdom" (*Lumen Gentium*, §42). It does this above all by means of the *vow of virginity*, which tradition has always understood as *an anticipation of the world to come*, already at work for the total transformation of man.

does so as a way to "please the Lord" (v. 32) and to avoid having his attention be divided. Thus remaining single has no superior value in itself; its advantage resides in the undivided life it makes possible, but that must be deliberately embraced. Above all it must not be clung to out of selfish motives. The thought prepares Augustine's statement: "What we praise in virgins is not the fact of being virgins but of being consecrated to God by a religious celibacy."[10]

Augustine also makes clear that when Paul says virginity enables the person to be **holy in both body and spirit**, he is not saying that married couples cannot be holy. These words, Augustine says, "do not mean that the chaste wife is not holy in body. Paul asks each of the faithful, 'Do you not know that your body is a temple of the holy Spirit within you, whom you have from God?' (1 Cor 6:19). Holy, therefore, are the bodies also of married people who are faithful to each other and to the Lord."[11] And the saint adds: "I do not hesitate to prefer the humble wife to the proud virgin,"[12] which means that, although the state of consecrated celibacy can foster holiness and closeness to the Lord, in the end

---

10. Saint Augustine, *Holy Virginity* 11; in PL 6:401.
11. Saint Augustine, *On the Good of Marriage* 13.
12. Saint Augustine, *On the Good of Marriage* 8; quoted in Kovacs, *1 Corinthians*, 130.

it is virtue that makes saints. "The end which makes virginity a virtue is the liberty to occupy oneself with divine things."[13] While Paul does not mention a vow of any kind, he does imply a conscious embracing of the state of celibacy, either temporary or permanent, out of a religious motivation.

35   These recommendations Paul has made **not to impose a restraint upon you**—literally, "to throw a noose about you." Even in the matter of vocations, there is freedom. He simply wants to present what is *ideal*. The root meaning of the word translated here as **for the sake of propriety** means what is beautiful in appearance, and in the moral sense, what is honorable, noble, hence ideal. Specifically celibacy is beautiful as an expression of readiness for the coming of the Lord and the future life, where "they neither marry nor are given in marriage" (Mark 12:25). The Christian life may be lived in any state, and great sanctity may be attained there, but no *state* comes closer to the ideal form than that of virginity. It was the state that Jesus himself chose, as well as that of his mother and, as tradition has it, that of the beloved disciple. A second advantage is that it promotes intimacy with the Lord. The Greek word translated **adherence** means what is "well placed," "well situated," like the beloved disciple who was next to the Lord at the Last Supper. It can also mean readiness to serve. And, along with that, a third advantage is that one is less prone to **distraction**. Intimacy with the Lord without distraction would also mean greater availability for the service of the Lord, his people, and his kingdom, as the Christian experience of millennia has shown.

Reflection and Application (7:25–35)

This passage, along with Jesus' commendation of celibacy (Matt 19:12), forms the Magna Carta of the consecrated life. It is primarily a declaration of independence and freedom. The great good of charity, the love of God, which alone outlasts the changing scenery of this world, is worth committing oneself to in celibate consecration as a state of life. If Paul coincides with Plato in saying that the figure of this world is passing away, he does not make the philosophical principle of the changeableness of temporal things the main motive for his praise of virginity. Rather, we are living in a segment of time marked at either end by the Christ event. In the resurrection, which is behind us, the glorious consummation of salvation is forecast and guaranteed. Thus we are living in a new kind of time, because its goal as well as its beginning has been revealed. So radically has the meaning of time been changed that

13. Saint Thomas Aquinas, *Summa theologiae* IIa.IIae.152.5.

unnecessary involvement in essentially transitory states can be a curtailment of freedom. Virginity, then, is the visible symbol of Christ's lordship over time. In the consecrated virgin the Church proclaims that time is no longer secular but sacred. It is no longer a circle but an arrow. It is bathed already in the glory of the resurrection and the dawn of the parousia. The virgin is the witness to this divine fact, much like the snowcapped peak that catches the first light of the sunrise and heralds the day to a sleeping world. Thus the virgin serves even the state of marriage by being a continual reminder of the end of all Christian life. Celibacy for the kingdom demonstrates that marriage is not a biological or emotional necessity but is a vocation given by God and freely chosen. My theology professor said it in a striking way: "Celibacy safeguards the freedom of marriage." Celibacy reveals that God's love can fully satisfy the human heart; people do not need sex, or even the intimacy of marriage, to be happy. It is a reminder that marriage is only a sign of the heavenly wedding and the infinitely greater communion of persons that we will enjoy with the Trinity and all the saints forever. It is a symbol of the life to which *everyone* is called for eternity.

But note that Paul's preference of celibacy has to do with the *state* of celibacy. He says nothing about the actual holiness of individuals who live in that state. The state *facilitates* holiness and intimacy with the Lord, and that is why as a state it is preferable. But it does not mean that everyone in that state is holier than the married. Like marriage, intentional celibacy is a gift, a charism (7:7), and therefore a matter of God's prior call. And if the call was a grace, so is perseverance in the call. As a religious, I am humbled and powerfully challenged by the extraordinary holiness of many married couples I have known. Paul would disapprove of a competitive comparison between the states. On the contrary, because we are one body, the body of Christ, everything in the Church belongs to everyone ("all things are yours"; 3:22–23 NIV). My celibacy is a gift to the married, and the married are a gift to me, and together we reflect the glory of God. Our gifts are complementary and necessary for each other. Like the positive and negative poles of a generating dynamo, when we dance together the Holy Spirit produces energy for the city of God.

A Particular Case (7:36–38)

36If anyone thinks he is behaving improperly toward his virgin, and if a critical moment has come and so it has to be, let him do as he wishes. He is committing no sin; let them get married. 37The one who stands firm in

his resolve, however, who is not under compulsion but has power over his own will, and has made up his mind to keep his virgin, will be doing well. [38]So then, the one who marries his virgin does well; the one who does not marry her will do better.

OT: Sir 7:24–25

36–38   This passage is what the exegetes call a *crux interpretum*, a cross (annoyance) for interpreters, because practically every phrase is open to different interpretations. There are basically three possible overall meanings, each of which is championed by some scholars: (1) It refers to the father of a virgin daughter who has come of age or is advancing in age, and in a culture where the father has ultimate authority (*patria potestas*), he is free to give her in marriage or not. (2) It refers to a "spiritual marriage," where the two have vowed or promised to live together as brother and sister, hence celibacy within a marriagelike arrangement. If the man finds he cannot control his sexual drive, they may assume a regular marriage relationship. (3) It refers to engaged couples who are attracted to celibacy and are asking themselves whether they should go ahead with the marriage or not.

In favor of the first view is the fact that in verse 38 the Greek verb *gamizō* ordinarily means to give (a woman) in marriage, not to marry (*gameō*). Thus the Jerusalem Bible translates, "The man who sees that his daughter is married has done a good thing." The two verbs are distinguished in the saying of Jesus that in heaven people do not marry or give in marriage (Matt 22:30 and parallels). However, the distinction was breaking down in the popular Greek of Paul's day, so that the NAB is justified in translating verse 38, **The one who marries his virgin does well** (so also NIV; the NJB and the NRSV even translate: "he who marries his fiancée"). A further problem with this interpretation is that, at the end of verse 36, where we would expect Paul to advise the father, "Let him give her in marriage," we find instead, **Let them get married**, thus bringing in a third party. And the expression "his virgin" is unaccompanied by "daughter," where we might normally expect it (Acts 21:9).

Thus other scholars have maintained that the phrase envisages the practice of a spiritual marriage in which, for mutual support, a couple decides to live together without intercourse. But this practice is nowhere attested in any first-century document. Although the practice existed later, probably initially with good intentions, it was condemned by St. John Chrysostom, St. Jerome, and church councils because of abuses. It would be surprising for Paul to approve of such a situation, given the danger he signaled about extended abstinence for married couples (7:5). Moreover, the "husband" in this supposed situation has the sole right to decide whether to consummate the marriage, which also conflicts with the idea of mutual consent in 7:5.

In the third solution, it is a question of engaged couples who think, in view of the "present distress" (7:26), that they should refrain from marrying. It is true that Paul deals with the question from the viewpoint of the fiancé, but **Let them get married** seems to assume that it would apply to the woman as well. It is likely that Paul approaches it from the man's viewpoint because the sexual urge in males is usually the stronger. **Behaving improperly toward his virgin** would then mean that he is having difficulty controlling his sexual drive. Despite Paul's preference for celibacy, he makes it clear that there is no sin in getting married. But should the person not experience the imperiousness of the sexual drive and have the gift of self-control, he **will be doing well** to remain celibate. But what then does it mean that the celibate **has made up his mind to keep his virgin**? That would seem a strange way to say he has decided not to marry her. But it can mean that he has decided to keep her inviolate or to "keep her virginity" and not touch her sexually.[14]

Absolute certainty in interpreting this text has evaded the scholars. But the third seems to be the most probable. In any case, it is clear that Paul does not approve of sexual relations outside of marriage, and he returns at the end to state his preference for the state of celibacy because of the freedom it gives a person to be at the disposition of the Lord and his service: **one who does not marry her will do better.**

Fidelity and Widowhood (7:39–40)

39A wife is bound to her husband as long as he lives. But if her husband dies, she is free to be married to whomever she wishes, provided that it be in the Lord. 40She is more blessed, though, in my opinion, if she remains as she is, and I think that I too have the Spirit of God.

NT: Rom 7:2; Eph 3:4
Catechism: indissolubility of marriage, 1644–45

Though separated from the above by our division, this short section is not an afterthought. It continues Paul's practice of alternating advice or directives to men and to women, which, in a patriarchal †age, is remarkable for the equality

39

---

14. See the references in Garland, *1 Corinthians*, 342.

it gives women.[15] As the preceding section approached the question from the man's standpoint, now Paul turns to the case of a married woman. She **is bound to her husband as long as he lives**. The same principle would apply to men who must remain with their wives as long as they live (7:11). But upon the death of the spouse, one is free to remarry, **provided that it be in the Lord**, that is, in the Church. It is not clear whether Paul intends the directive to marry a Christian as a command or as a strong preference. Surely many of the Christians in Corinth were married to non-Christians when they converted, so that mixed marriages were common in the early days of the nascent church. But what if the non-Christian dies? Paul certainly expects the Christian who then wishes to marry to do so "in the Lord." This would obviously apply to the Christian whose Christian spouse dies. Although Paul does not consider an alternative, it is still not clear whether Paul would admit any exception to the rule, or whether "in the Lord" would also cover the marriage of a Christian to a non-Christian being blessed by the Church, as is done today.

As Paul already indicates in his reciting of various cases, marriage involves many variables, certainly more than the Apostle envisages here. That is why the Church is needed to judge how the apostolic tradition on marriage applies in various situations.

40   But, speaking of the woman, **she is more blessed, . . . in my opinion, if she remains as she is**, not remarrying. The reasons would be the same as those given above for celibacy. Although Paul has just said that it is his opinion, he gently and modestly qualifies that by saying, **I think that I too have the Spirit of God**, which suggests that his opinion can hold ground against any other person claiming to know what the Spirit is saying to the churches.

First Timothy 5:14 will bring an adjustment of Paul's opinion about widows remaining celibate. Pastoral experience has apparently shown that it is better for young widows to remarry, both for their own support (versus support by the church) and to give them a focused commitment.

Reflection and Application (7:1–40)

This chapter is remarkable from many points of view. First, it is the down-to-earth application to the states of life of the new thing that has happened in the resurrection of Jesus. How do Christians live out this ⁺mystery in their daily lives? Since the resurrection means that Jesus is Lord of history and that he is coming soon, should married couples so live in the future glory that they

---

15. See the whole of 1 Cor 7:1–16.

abandon normal relations in the present? Should all become celibate? Should single persons forget about marrying? Paul wants the Corinthians to keep their feet on the ground and does not let them pursue a false asceticism that is unrealistic in their state of life. In so doing, Paul creates a beautiful, and, in the culture, a novel understanding of marriage. It is a reciprocal relationship. In the midst of a patriarchal society, he does not favor the man over the woman. "Be subordinate to one another out of reverence for Christ" (Eph 5:21).

Second, celibacy takes on a new meaning. It is not an ideal of self-mastery, as the Cynics and Stoics would have it. Nor is it a forlorn and pitiable state. It is a witness to the new meaning of time because of the resurrection and the imminent †parousia, and it is possible for those who have the †charism, the call. It frees them to be more available to the Lord, to contemplate him, and to serve him and his kingdom.

Idols: Freedom and Conscience

1 Corinthians 8

In the next three chapters Paul will deal with the question of eating meat offered to idols. This might seem to be of little interest to the twenty-first-century reader. Although the topic may be antiquated, the underlying gospel message is one the contemporary world and above all Christians need to hear. The question is clear: Do we live for ourselves or for others? Is the Christian community like a billiard table, where we bounce off one another—or is it like a cluster of grapes clinging together and to the vine?

Missionaries know what a struggle it is to wean recent converts from their former habits or lifestyles, which might involve superstition or idolatry. Converts would like to be Christians, but the old ways still have their attractions. In a somewhat different form today, our culture is offering a dazzling array of alternatives to the Christian faith, options to which poorly instructed faithful are vulnerable, often because some of those alternatives are a hybrid with some Christian elements. In Corinth some converts have even found a theological rationale for participating in the sacrificial banquets of pagans. Others, perhaps the Jewish converts, are shocked that Christians would even accept an invitation to a nonbeliever's meal at home, since the meat served may have been offered to an idol. Paul himself may have been accused of eating such meals. How will Paul deal with this situation?

Since Paul was raised in strict monotheism, he would normally strike out vociferously, condemning those Corinthians who, under the pretext that idols are nothing, are continuing their involvement in idolatrous rites. Instead, he waits three chapters till he says outright "avoid idolatry" (10:14). Why this delay? Because there is something more urgent than avoiding idolatry: it is love. And love means thinking of others. Paul will spend chapters 8 and 9 on that issue, first showing the scandal that the bull-in-the-china-shop behavior can cause other members of the community, and then citing his own example of sacrifice for the sake of the common good.

Knowing Is Not Enough (8:1–6)

¹Now in regard to meat sacrificed to idols: we realize that "all of us have knowledge"; knowledge inflates with pride, but love builds up. ²If anyone supposes he knows something, he does not yet know as he ought to know. ³But if one loves God, one is known by him.

⁴So about the eating of meat sacrificed to idols: we know that "there is no idol in the world," and that "there is no God but one." ⁵Indeed, even though there are so-called gods in heaven and on earth (there are, to be sure, many "gods" and many "lords"), ⁶yet for us there is

> **one God, the Father,**
> > **from whom all things are and for whom we exist,**
> **and one Lord, Jesus Christ,**
> > **through whom all things are and through whom we exist.**

OT: Exod 20:2–3; Deut 6:4
NT: John 1:3; Rom 11:36; 14:1–23; 15:2; Gal 4:8; Col 1:16–17
Catechism: only one God, 212–27; idolatry, 212–14; Jesus as Lord, 446–51

Todd Bolen / BiblePlaces.com

Fig. 9. Meat market in Corinth.

1   Like all Greek cities of Paul's day, Corinth was awash with temples, altars, and idols. The Acrocorinth mountain, dominating the city from a height of some 1,800 feet, housed the ancient temple of Aphrodite, the Greek goddess of love (the Roman Venus). Animal sacrifices were part of the regular fare of Gentile life. The Jews who lived there abhorred the idolatrous practices of their compatriots, so for those Jews who became Christians, participation in anything idolatrous was out of the question. Probably, too, as Jews they would have had only the minimal social contacts necessary with the Gentile citizenry (see Acts 10:28). For the Gentile converts, it was a different story. Many of them had belonged to guilds, ancient trade associations that had their patron gods or goddesses, with festivals in their honor. They had participated in offering the pagan sacrifices, eaten meat that had been sacrificed, and done this often either in a temple or in the homes of friends or fellow guild members. Sometimes the meat they bought in the market had been previously sacrificed in a pagan temple. Now suddenly they had come to know the one God and Jesus as his Son and only Lord. What now of their social contacts? If a pagan friend invites them to the temple (see illustration) to participate in a sacrifice and to eat meat that was offered there, how should they respond? If a friend invites them to their home for a meal, should they accept, or should they decline because the meat may have been offered to an idol? It was a case of †conscience, and the Corinthians were divided on how to respond to it. Some in the community claimed that "**all of us have knowledge**," meaning that they are enlightened about the fact that "there is no idol in the world" and that "there is no God but one" (1 Cor 8:4). Hence, they reasoned, what difference does it make if they eat **meat sacrificed to idols**? There is no reality in or behind the idol. Yet others in the community, fresh from their conversion, were convinced they were contaminating themselves with sin if they had any brush with idols, even if quite indirect. Probably these were strongly influenced by the Jewish Christians, whose traditions were strict in the matter.

      What interests Paul is not so much the pastoral solution he will offer as the attitude of those who cavalierly flaunt their knowledge that the idols are nothing, holding that there is no divine reality or power in the idols. These know-it-alls are possibly even deriding those members of the community who have a lingering sensitivity to the reality of the idols or are convinced that they must avoid any social contact with idol worshipers. Thus he addresses himself to those who claim they have knowledge. The translation **knowledge inflates with pride, but love builds up** falls short of the †rhetorical impact of the Greek: "Knowledge puffs up, but love builds up." The Greek for "inflates" is *physioi*, which takes an inflating sound to pronounce. It is not that knowledge is evil.[1] Paul praises the Corinthians for their knowledge (1:5) and the Romans for theirs (Rom 15:14). "The expression of knowledge" is a gift of the Holy Spirit (1 Cor 12:8); and Paul prays that his readers may grow in knowledge (Eph 1:17; Col 1:9–10), especially through love (Phil 1:9). But knowledge without love reduces one to nothing (1 Cor 13:2). It is like a balloon that bobs in the wind but is useless for building anything. Love, the divine *agapē*, on the other hand, builds community. Love is sensitive to the needs of others, applauds their gifts, seeks to connect with them, and fosters solidarity.

The more the truly wise person knows, the more he realizes how little   2–3 he knows. After saying, **But if one loves God**, we would expect Paul to say something like, "one knows him" or "one knows all that needs to be known." Instead, we read that if one loves God, **one is known by him**. This sudden reversal casts the whole discussion in a new light. What is important is that God knows us; if we know him, it is because he first knew us. God's knowledge of us, biblically speaking, is equivalent to his loving choice of us. This counts both for the individual ("Before I formed you in the womb I knew you, before you were born I dedicated you"; Jer 1:5) and the people ("You alone have I known, among all the families of the earth"; Amos 3:2). Obviously God knows everything, but the knowledge Paul is talking about here is the knowledge of loving intimacy bound by covenant. It is not that we have decided to love God, and then he took notice of us. If we love God, this is a sign that God has loved us first. More important than any earthly knowledge is being known by God. And the text suggests that only love gives us the right knowledge of God, of self, of others, and of the world, because only love adequately reflects God's knowledge, which is inseparable from his love. Heaven will be the consummation of this knowledge and this love: "At present I know partially; then I shall know fully, as I am fully known" (13:12).

So what relevance does this have for the question of eating meat offered to   4 idols? Quoting what was probably part of their first instruction in the faith, a maxim that the Corinthians may have repeated to justify their sharing in idol feasts, Paul says, **We know that "there is no idol in the world," and that "there is no God but one."**

---

1. Some scholars have thought that the problem at Corinth was with early gnostics, who were promoting a kind of individualized knowledge that would supposedly elevate them above their peers. But in this section Paul does not say that the knowledge these Corinthians claim is false. Like Paul, they "know" that an idol is nothing (8:4). Yet the behavioral consequences that they justify by this knowledge are hurting the community.

5   He then expands on each of these parts, first by discussing idols. Paul grants
that **there are so-called gods in heaven and on earth (there are, to be sure,
many "gods" and many "lords")**. The ancient Greek geographer Pausanius lists
the following gods and goddesses worshiped at Corinth: Chronos, Poseidon,
the Sun, the Calm, the Sea, Aphrodite, Artemis, Isis, Dionysus, a tree, Fortune,
Apollo, Hermes, Zeus, Asclepius, Bunaea, and others.[2]

6   Although Paul and the Corinthians "know" that these deities do not exist
and that therefore their idols are nothing, still, the deities do have an existence
in the minds of their worshipers, and their worship can become instruments
of demons who seek to destroy faith in the one true God (10:20). The context
makes clear that the words **for us** in no way imply an equality between the
beliefs of the pagans and the faith of Christians, as if Paul were saying, "They
have their gods, but we have ours." Quite the contrary, the idols of the pagans
are false and are even the instruments of Satan. Paul quotes what is probably
an early creedal formula that may have been part of the baptismal instruction
given to the Corinthians. There is **one God**. This was already the Jewish faith
(Deut 6:4; Isa 45:5), and in the later Old Testament books God is called "Father," the formal title *Ab* (Hebrew),[3] which Jesus changes to the intimate *Abba*
(Aramaic; Mark 14:36). Here it is God's role as creator that is highlighted, in
view of the Corinthians' former and present involvement with the culture of
idols. Not only is the one God and Father the one **from whom all things are,**
but he is also the one **for whom we exist**. Implicit, therefore, is that we do not
exist to worship anyone or anything else. By his previous reference to "many
lords," Paul has prepared for the contrast with the **one Lord, Jesus Christ**. The
statement that Christ is the one **through whom all things are and through
whom we exist** is the earliest written affirmation of Christ's preexistence and
his role in creation—a role that later councils will theologically define. Indeed,
Paul may be quoting an earlier creedal formula.

What This Means for Community (8:7–13)

> [7]But not all have this knowledge. There are some who have been so
> used to idolatry up until now that, when they eat meat sacrificed to idols,
> their conscience, which is weak, is defiled.
>   [8]Now food will not bring us closer to God. We are no worse off if we do
> not eat, nor are we better off if we do. [9]But make sure that this liberty of

2. Pausanius, *Description of Greece* 1–5.
3. Pss 68:6; 89:27; 103:13; Isa 63:16; 64:8; Jer 3:4, 19; 31:9; Mal 1:6; 2:10.

yours in no way becomes a stumbling block to the weak. [10]If someone sees
you, with your knowledge, reclining at table in the temple of an idol, may
not his conscience too, weak as it is, be "built up" to eat the meat sacrificed to idols? [11]Thus through your knowledge, the weak person is brought
to destruction, the brother for whom Christ died. [12]When you sin in this
way against your brothers and wound their consciences, weak as they are,
you are sinning against Christ. [13]Therefore, if food causes my brother to
sin, I will never eat meat again, so that I may not cause my brother to sin.

OT: 2 Macc 4:7–22
NT: Matt 10:40–42; Rom 6:15–19; 14:13, 17, 20–21; Heb 13:9; Rev 2:18
Catechism: †conscience, 1776–94

Paul has aligned himself with the "knowledge" of those who know that idols **7**
do not really exist and that God is one (1 Cor 8:4). **But not all have this knowledge.** If "this knowledge" refers to that dogmatic fact, it would be surprising
that there would be a group uninstructed in this basic Christian catechesis.
The knowledge seems then to refer to the implications of that knowledge and
the kinds of practice that could or should flow from it. Does the fact that idols
do not exist authorize considering the meat offered to them as just ordinary
meat, the pagan ritual having no effect whatever, and therefore it is legitimate
to eat such meat? Or is there a real detriment to the Christian faith to eat such
meat? If unbelievers eating the meat believe they are communing with a god,
should the Christian abstain? Paul continues to address the "knowers" here,
and interestingly enough, he does not try to correct or complete the instruction of the other group he will soon call "the weak" (v. 9). Instead, he comes to
their defense. They are the ones who, fresh from idol worship themselves, do
not fully grasp that idols are nonentities and have no effect on meat sacrificed
to them. These Christians' conversion was not complete. So it has happened
in the later history of the Church. Fresh converts at the Franciscan missions
in the southern United States would at times run off to celebrate the feasts of
their tribal gods. I knew a Catholic in Nepal who went to pray at the temple of
Saraswathi on the goddess's feast day. The examples limp, because the issue here
is meat offered to an idol, yet the parallel stands because the danger of one's
acting in that situation is that the convert is taking a step backward, giving the
god some credit, and thus possibly falling back into idolatry. That is what Paul
means when he says that **their conscience, which is weak, is defiled.** Paul uses
the word †conscience (*syneidēsis*) twenty times, including eight times in 1 Cor 8
and 10. It means the faculty by which one judges whether an action is right or
wrong. These are fresh converts who are not out of the woods of idolatry yet.

For them to revert in the slightest would weaken their conscience even further and could lead to their embracing idolatry again.

8–9   So what consequence should this have for those who "know"? Paul first of all grants that food of itself is indifferent: it **will not bring us closer to God**, whether we eat or abstain. But the symbolic context of eating is not indifferent. If it provides **a stumbling block to the weak**, the consequences are deadly serious. The image of the stumbling block is frequent in the Bible. It may cause a complete fall, or it may simply trip up the person on the journey. Sometimes translated "scandal," it does not mean "something shocking" but rather that which causes another to sin. In the book of Exodus the Israelites are warned not to make a covenant with the gods of Canaan, "lest they become a snare among you" (Exod 34:12; also 23:33). "Snare" is the Greek word *proskomma*, "stumbling block," the same word Paul uses here.

10   What exactly Paul means by "the weak" (v. 9) is explained in verse 10. It is these fresh converts who still have in their consciousness some sense that the idols are real. If they see **you, with your knowledge** " 'that there is no idol in the world' and that 'there is no God but one' " (8:4), **reclining at table in the temple of an idol**, they might be encouraged to eat the idol offerings in violation of their understanding of their Christian commitment. It is clear that here Paul is speaking about participation in a pagan religious practice, not about visiting in homes and eating meals that have no explicit religious symbolism—a situation he will discuss later (10:25–28).[4] Paul uses the words **"built up"** ironically

---

4. The temples in Corinth sometimes provided dining facilities. According to Jerome Murphy-O'Connor, although such facilities would be used for sacrificial meals, they could also be rented out to groups that would not use them for such purposes; see his work *St. Paul's Corinth: Texts and Archaeology*, 3rd ed. (Collegeville, MN: Liturgical Press, 2002), 189–90. Paul obviously is referring to participation in

here as the opposite of the true building up that comes from love (8:1). Does Paul envisage one or several of his "enlightened" disciples actually dining with impunity in one of a temple's banquet halls and thus participating in idol worship? He will categorically condemn such activity in 10:20–22, where he says that to do so would be to share fellowship with demons. But here he chooses to address himself first to the responsibility each Christian has for the building up of each other, to awaken the Corinthians out of their individualism and pride, to think of their new identity as a corporate identity in Christ.

But we may ask: Is not eating idol meat in a temple a sin in itself and not just because it might cause "the weak" to sin? Why doesn't Paul begin with that and then deal with the consequential issue of scandal later? The clue is in the mention of love at the very beginning of the discussion (8:1, 3), developed at length and lyrically in chapter 13. Love means sacrifice, however distressful. For converts to break their usual social ties would have been extremely painful. It would ostracize them from their fellow citizens and make life exceedingly difficult for them. Hence Paul eases into the discussion by (1) appealing first to their concern for their fellow Christians, members of the body of Christ, who have a prior claim to their social bonding now (chap. 8); (2) appealing to Paul's own example of giving up his rights for the sake of the gospel (chap. 9); and (3) finally addressing the sin of idolatry directly by appealing to the sacrificial meal that is proper to Christians, the Eucharist (chap. 10).[5] Here, then, it is the misuse of this "liberty of yours" (8:9) that is at issue. Actually the word the NAB translates "liberty" is *exousia*, meaning "authority," with the nuance of "right" (as in 9:4–6), which suggests that they are acting with complete disregard for the effect their action might have on others.

Their **knowledge** thus becomes a source of **destruction** for the one who   11–13
is not merely **the weak person** but also **the brother for whom Christ died**. This text powerfully marks the fact that Christ did not die for humanity in the abstract but for each individual person, for you and for me. Paul could think of no more powerful motivation than Christ's gift of himself upon the cross (recalling the cross as an antidote to the divisions in 1:18–25), so that to **wound** the **consciences** of one's **brothers** amounts to despising what Christ has done for them and thus **sinning against Christ**. Christ's passion and death is also the supreme model of concern for others, the kind of solidarity with "the

---

directly sacrificial meals, which would be idolatrous, but he may have also intended to exclude the taking of nonsacrificial meals in a pagan temple because of the possible confusion such an action might create.

5. Saint John Chrysostom already noted Paul's tactics here: "He began from the lesser topics and so made his way to the sum of all evils: since thus that last point also became more easily admitted, their mind having been smoothed down by the things said before" (*Homilies on 1 Corinthians* 24.6).

Chrysostom: The Four Charges

LIVING TRADITION

Saint John Chrysostom points to the charges Paul here lays upon the "strong" who lead the "weak" into sin: "The charges are four, and they are extremely heavy: that it was a brother, that he was weak, and one whom Christ treasured so highly as to die for him, and that after all this, for a morsel of meat he was destroyed."[a]

a. Saint John Chrysostom, *Homilies on 1 Corinthians* 20.10.

weak" that Paul hopes the "knowers" will embrace. The new community of the church is infinitely more precious than the fellowship of the pagans, their guilds, and their banquets, because it has been formed at an infinite price. For that reason, Paul says that **if food causes my brother to sin, I will never eat meat again**. Introducing his own commitment in this matter prepares for the lengthy exposition on his own example, which now follows.

Reflection and Application (8:7–13)

In the Christian community it is not sufficient to be right: one must also be loving. In our culture today we hear a lot about rights and less about duties. Parents know that, while they have a right to discuss certain sexual matters, to do so in front of their children at an age at which they are not prepared could well prove harmful. But even more so, if one engages in pornography and leaves magazines lying around for others to see, that is not only a sin in itself but a sin of scandal as well. Jesus said that those who cause others to sin should have a millstone attached to their neck and be thrown into the sea (Matt 18:6). Using the excuse "Everybody is doing it" indicates that the person has submitted to scandal, has been led into sin.

Paul's Personal Example

1 Corinthians 9

Example speaks louder than words. Jesus lived the message he preached and told his disciples to do the same. He called some people "hypocrites" if they did not live the lifestyle they preached. Following Jesus means walking in his footsteps. Paul here appeals to his own example of delicate concern for others, even when it means forgoing his own rights.

Paul's Rights as an Apostle (9:1–12a)

¹Am I not free? Am I not an apostle? Have I not seen Jesus our Lord? Are you not my work in the Lord? ²Although I may not be an apostle for others, certainly I am for you, for you are the seal of my apostleship in the Lord.

³My defense against those who would pass judgment on me is this. ⁴Do we not have the right to eat and drink? ⁵Do we not have the right to take along a Christian wife, as do the rest of the apostles, and the brothers of the Lord, and Cephas? ⁶Or is it only myself and Barnabas who do not have the right not to work? ⁷Who ever serves as a soldier at his own expense? Who plants a vineyard without eating its produce? Or who shepherds a flock without using some of the milk from the flock? ⁸Am I saying this on human authority, or does not the law also speak of these things? ⁹It is written in the law of Moses, "You shall not muzzle an ox while it is treading out the grain." Is God concerned about oxen, ¹⁰or is he not really speaking for our sake? It was written for our sake, because the plowman should

plow in hope, and the thresher in hope of receiving a share. [11]If we have sown spiritual seed for you, is it a great thing that we reap a material harvest from you? [12a]If others share this rightful claim on you, do not we still more?

OT: Deut 25:4
NT: Luke 8:2–3; 12:6, 24; Acts 9:17–19; 18:3; Rom 15:27
Catechism: support of church and clergy, 2043

If Paul spent the previous chapter reproving the "knowers" for giving bad examples to their "weaker" brothers and sisters, he now offers his own example as an alternative. There are two plausible reasons why Paul chooses to motivate the Corinthians by his personal example rather than by appealing to his authority. First, he is sensitive, particularly in regard to his Gentile converts, to the delicate social situation in which they find themselves: friendships, relations within extended families, guild memberships, and even the hopes of bringing others to Christ without creating obstacles. Second, the issue is not what is right or wrong in itself but rather the situation in which what might be permissible in itself is not the right thing to do because it would be misinterpreted and acted upon by other Christians against their †conscience. Hence Paul at this point prefers to motivate by means other than laying down the law. He believes his own example is a chief means to achieve this. But there is a risk in doing so. Would the Corinthians think of him as a boaster? Plutarch, who lived in the same century as Paul, wrote an essay on how to praise oneself in a way acceptable to the audience. Three of the conditions he lists are met by Paul in this chapter: (1) he is defending himself against charges (9:3); (2) he is doing so under compulsion (9:16–18); and (3) he shows that it is for the good of others that he is admonishing them (9:24–27). Though Plutarch lived a generation after Paul, this comparison does show that the Apostle knew and used the proper †rhetorical tools of the day.[1]

1–2   The opening sentence of this chapter makes sense in light of the last verse of the preceding one: "If food causes my brother to sin, I will never eat meat again, so that I may not cause my brother to sin" (8:13). If eating meat is a natural right, being an apostle surely entitles Paul to other rights, authorized as he was by Christ himself: **Am I not free? Am I not an apostle? Have I not seen Jesus our Lord?** Though he had not been with Jesus during the public ministry, his vision and commission by the risen Lord (14:8–11) fully accredited him as equal with the Twelve. In their midst he has worked all the signs of an apostle (2 Cor

---

1. David E. Garland, *1 Corinthians*, BECNT (Grand Rapids: Baker Academic, 2003), 406.

12:12). By God's grace he is founder of the community: **Are you not my work in the Lord?** Earlier he had said that the community was "God's field, God's building" (1 Cor 3:9), "God's temple" (3:16–17). Thus he does not say "You are my work" but "You are my work in the Lord." The fields of apostolic labor were laid out by the Lord, and though Paul was not given the fields of others to plant and cultivate, Corinth was given to him. Much like the founders of religious orders but more so, he has a prior title to exercise his authority over his foundation. The very existence of the flourishing community attests to Paul's authentic mission from Christ. All these reasons give him a number of rights, not least of which is to be supported by the community, as he will soon affirm. They are the **seal of** his **apostleship in the Lord**. Just as a seal testifies to the authenticity of a document, so also the community itself confirms the divine origin of Paul's preaching by embodying the word in a new and holy way of life.

Suddenly in verse 3 we find Paul in a courtroom setting, answering accusers: **my defense against those who would pass judgment on me**. The translation "pass judgment" is perhaps a bit strong for the Greek here, which ordinarily means "to examine, to interrogate," as a lawyer or judge might do *before* passing judgment. Since Paul has given us no evidence of opponents among his faithful, we can assume that the "examiners" or "interrogators" are hypothetical and serve as a rhetorical device to introduce his claim to the several rights he will now detail.

The first is that he has the **right to eat and drink**, probably meaning the right to eat and drink at the expense of the church he serves, but it could also mean to eat food that had been offered to idols. (Later he will specify under what conditions Christians might do so.) The second is the right **to take along a Christian wife**, literally, a "sister woman" or "sister wife." In the apostolic writings the word "sister," like "brother," refers to a Christian. Although several of the Fathers of the Church thought Paul was referring to a woman attendant, like the women who attended to the needs of Jesus and his disciples in Luke 8:1–3, this would make the word *gynē* ("woman, wife") redundant, and hence the NAB translation "wife," with the consensus of modern scholars, is correct. It is not clear whether **the rest of the apostles** refers only to those who have "seen the Lord" (9:1) or whether it extends to a broader group such as Barnabas (Acts 14:14) or Andronicus and Junia (Rom 16:7), who are called apostles, probably in the original meaning of "ones sent." For the present purpose it does not matter, for Paul has forgone that right, remaining celibate (7:8). The †**brothers of the Lord** are mentioned several times in the New Testament (Mark 3:31–35; 6:3; John 2:12; 7:3, 5, 10; Acts 1:14), and James is one specifically named (Gal 1:19).

3–5

Celibacy and Ministry

We know that Peter was married because Matthew, Mark, and Luke report the story of Jesus' healing Peter's mother-in-law (Matt 8:14; Mark 1:30; Luke 4:38). Since it was a normal expectation that every Jew should marry, and since the first disciples were adults, we can assume that most of the apostles were married and that their wives, as Paul intimates, accompanied them on their missions. Luke mentions a number of women who accompanied Jesus during his public ministry, and some of them may have been wives of the male disciples (8:1–3). Still, it is the same Luke who has the addition of "wife" among the persons one might leave for the sake of the kingdom of God (18:29). But this might refer to those who choose not to marry.

Clerical celibacy is not therefore a requirement of apostolic origin, though Jesus and Paul were celibate. However, quite early there were those who embraced celibacy as a means of belonging more totally to the Lord and his service, a recommendation of both Paul (1 Cor 7:25–35) and Jesus, according to Matt 19:12. In some of the Eastern Catholic and Orthodox churches, a man can marry before ordination to the priesthood but not afterward. Permanent celibacy is generally required of bishops. This tradition, it seems, rests on the symbolism of the bishop being married to the Church. In both the East and the West, celibacy was voluntarily embraced by monks and women religious. It became a requirement of diocesan priests in the Western Catholic Church only in the twelfth century. Aside from the freedom it gives to be more available to the people, celibacy of priests is a witness to the transcendent goal of the Christian life, the heavenly glorified state (†age), where there will be neither marriage nor giving in marriage (Matt 22:30; Mark 12:25) and where all will be the bride of the Lamb (Rev 21:2, 9–10). That indeed is the witness of all who profess celibacy for the sake of the kingdom.

(See sidebar.) **Cephas** (*Kēphas*) is the Aramaic name "Rock" for Peter, who was seemingly known to the Corinthian community (1:12).

6   The second right, to which Paul devotes a lengthier discussion, is the right to be supported by the faithful among whom and for whom he works. The Corinthians had seen Paul work to support himself during his ministry among them. Some may have thought this strange, since pagan priests were supported by the offerings of their people. However, if he had accepted money for his services, they may have thought that he was "selling" the gospel or the Holy Spirit (see Peter's response to Simon Magus, who wanted to buy the Holy Spirit; Acts 8:18–24). Though he and **Barnabas** had the right to receive support, they gave it up for the sake of a clearly unselfish witness to the gospel.

Brothers of the Lord

Although the early Reformers Luther, Calvin, and Zwingli held that Mary was "ever Virgin," Protestants since then have generally thought that the "brothers and sisters" of Jesus were his full blood brothers and sisters and hence were other children of Mary. The Catholic Church, invoking Mary as "ever Virgin" from early centuries, has maintained that Jesus was her only child. In the early second century there was already a tradition that the brothers of Jesus were sons of the widowed Joseph by a previous marriage. The New Testament never says that these "brothers and sisters" are children of Mary. Furthermore, in Mark 15:40 and Matt 27:56 one of the women at the cross is another "Mary, the mother of James and of Joses/Joseph," but these are listed as brothers of Jesus in Matt 13:55 and Mark 6:3. Hence they are sons of a *different* Mary, though they are called Jesus' brothers. This strongly suggests that, since the writers of these expressions were Jews, they followed the general Near Eastern custom of referring to any close relatives as "brothers" or "sisters," as we can see from Gen 13:8; 14:16, where Lot is called the brother of Abraham, although he was actually Abraham's nephew. Similarly, the Hebrew term for "brother" is used in Gen 29:15 to mean simply "relative." Today in India and Africa this tradition is still followed, as I know from personal experience. On one occasion, one of my novices in Nepal introduced a visitor as his "brother," but after some conversation with the visitor, I discovered he was a third or fourth cousin.

Paul now buttresses his right to compensation with two arguments, the first from common sense, the second from Scripture. For the first he uses three examples: the **soldier**, the planter, and the shepherd. The sense is clear: all three have a right to be recompensed for their labor. Similarly, those who "fight" for Christ, who plant the gospel (as Paul did in Corinth; 3:6), or who shepherd God's people—these have a right to the fruit of their labor. For the second argument, Paul goes beyond **human authority** and appeals to **the law of Moses**. The quotation is from Deut 25:4. Like a true rabbi, since there is no Old Testament text explicitly covering the question, he uses a *qal wahomer* (from the lesser to the greater) argument: If God says that the **ox** that treads out the **grain** should not be muzzled, that is, should be allowed to eat of the grain it is treading, how much more should one who works in the field of the Lord be entitled to share in its resources. Indeed, when Paul asks, **Is God concerned about oxen?** he doesn't mean God doesn't care about them at all, but rather how much more is he concerned that the human laborer receive his wage. Thus

7–12a

Barnabas

According to Acts, Barnabas, a Levite from Cyprus, was an out-standing member of the early Church in Jerusalem, where the apostles changed his name from Joseph to Barnabas, meaning "son of encouragement." That seems to be linked to the fact that he had sold a piece of his property and given the money to the apostles to be distributed to those in need (Acts 4:35–37). After Paul's conversion the disciples in Jerusalem were afraid to meet the former persecutor, but Barnabas reached out to him and gave him a favorable introduction (9:27).

When the Jerusalem church heard that the church in Antioch was making converts of the Gentiles, they sent Barnabas to investigate. He encouraged the church there and then went and fetched Saul from his hometown, Tarsus, and together they spent a whole year teaching in the church of Antioch (Acts 11:20–26). When famine struck, Paul and Barnabas carried a collection to the Jerusalem community (11:27–30). Later the two of them were sent by the church in Antioch on their first missionary journey to Cyprus and Asia Minor (13:2–3), which was crowned with successful founding of communities there. After their return to Antioch, some people from Judea arrived, insisting that all Gentile converts must be circumcised, meaning that all converts must also become Jews if they wished to be saved. Paul and Barnabas went to Jerusalem and there argued strongly against requiring circumcision of the Gentiles, taking the Gentile convert Titus along with them (Gal 2:3). Their arguments, strengthened by the very presence of the uncircumcised Titus, won the day.

Back in Antioch the two planned to revisit the churches they had founded in Asia Minor, but a "sharp disagreement" arose when Barnabas wanted to take his cousin John Mark (Col 4:10) along again, and Paul would not hear of it because the younger missionary had abandoned them on their first trip. It is possible there was more to it than that, since Barnabas had sided with Peter about eating separately with Jews when he came to Antioch (Gal 2:13). But the reference here in 1 Cor 9:6 seems to indicate that there was a reconciliation, since Barnabas holds to the same practice as Paul in the matter of supporting himself in his ministry.

the text is **speaking for our sake**. As the **plowman** and **the thresher** work in hope of receiving a share of the produce, so **we** who **have sown spiritual seed for you, is it a great thing that we reap a material harvest from you?** As the one who first sowed the faith in Corinth, Paul has a right to receive material support from them, more so than the **others** who **share this rightful claim** on them. Here Paul is probably referring to other laborers in Corinth who have accepted support, and rightfully so. Apollos may have been one such person, since he preached there (1:12; 3:5).

The Gospel Is Free (9:12b–18)

> [12b]Yet we have not used this right. On the contrary, we endure everything so as not to place an obstacle to the gospel of Christ. [13]Do you not know that those who perform the temple services eat [what] belongs to the temple, and those who minister at the altar share in the sacrificial offerings? [14]In the same way, the Lord ordered that those who preach the gospel should live by the gospel.
>
> [15]I have not used any of these rights, however, nor do I write this that it be done so in my case. I would rather die. Certainly no one is going to nullify my boast. [16]If I preach the gospel, this is no reason for me to boast, for an obligation has been imposed on me, and woe to me if I do not preach it! [17]If I do so willingly, I have a recompense, but if unwillingly, then I have been entrusted with a stewardship. [18]What then is my recompense? That, when I preach, I offer the gospel free of charge so as not to make full use of my right in the gospel.

NT: Matt 10:10; Acts 9:15–16; 22:14–15; 26:16–18; 1 Cor 4:12; 2 Cor 11:7–9
Catechism: support of church, clergy, 2043
Lectionary: 9:16–19, 22–23: St. Francis Xavier; Common of Pastors; Admission to Candidacy for Diaconate and Priesthood

Yet we have not used this right. Paul now comes to the point of his argument. **12b** The strong and lengthy case he has made for his rights now makes his renunciation of them more telling. Why has he not used this right? He did not want to do anything that would **place an obstacle to the gospel of Christ.** "Place an obstacle" (NAB, NRSV), "obstruct" (JB, NJB), is a milder word than "scandal," used by Paul in reference to the idol offerings, but it is Paul's parallel to it. Even though what he might have done would in itself be legitimate, he would not do it if it would occasion some to turn away from the gospel. Paul is willing to sacrifice anything that could rightly be sacrificed to gain persons for Christ.

In the next verse (13) we have a sign that this letter is being dictated. For **13** Paul suddenly switches back to the idea of his rights and finds two more reasons for having them: (1) In the Jewish temple as in pagan temples, those who serve there are given a share of the temple offerings and the sacrificed meat. Paul is likely thinking of the legislation of the Pentateuch. **Those who perform the temple services** probably refers to the Levites (Num 18:21–32; Deut 18:6–8), and **those who minister at the altar** to the priests (Num 18:8–32; Deut 18:1–8). These allusions take on even more significance when we note that in Romans, Paul uses the example of temple service and priestly sacrifice as an image of his own ministry: "the grace given me by God to be a †minister of Christ Jesus to the Gentiles in performing the priestly service of the gospel of God, so that the offering up of the Gentiles may be acceptable" (Rom 15:15–16).

14   (2) Finally, the climactic and definitive argument: **The Lord ordered that those who preach the gospel should live by the gospel**. Was this a word of Jesus that has come down to us through Paul rather than in the Gospels? Perhaps. In any case it is a summary of Jesus' teaching in Matt 10:1–15; Mark 6:7–11; Luke 9:1–15; 10:1–12. The proclaimers of the good news should take nothing with them and depend on the hospitality of the hearers for food and lodging. Since none of the Gospels was written at the time Paul was dictating this letter, he must have known at least the gist of these sayings from pre-Gospel oral or written tradition. Although Paul uses the word "ordered," he interprets it not as requiring him to demand support but rather as giving him the right to it, a right that he could, for the benefit of the gospel, forgo. We notice how Paul has skillfully built up his argumentation: from common sense (the soldier, the planter, the shepherd) to the Old Testament (the ox, the temple ministers) and finally to Jesus.

15–16   Repeating **I have not used any of these rights**, he wants to make it clear that if he has spent so much time proving his right to support, it was not to evoke sympathy and not so that they would begin to support him now. **I would rather die**. Here the Greek reveals not only Paul's emotion but also a break characteristic of dictation. Literally: "For it is better for me to die than—" and instead of finishing the sentence he concludes, **no one is going to nullify my boast**. Boasting in the Greek world was at times approved, at other times condemned. In the †Septuagint, which was Paul's Bible, boasting is often used for glorying in God's gift. "He is your boast, and he is your God, who has wrought in the midst of you these great and glorious things, which your eyes have seen" (Deut 10:21).[2] "All who love your name will boast in you" (Ps 5:12). "You are the boast of their strength" (Ps 88 [89]:18). "Let him who boasts boast in this—in understanding and knowing that I am the Lord who exercises mercy and judgment and righteousness upon the earth" (Jer 9:23), which Paul quotes in 1 Cor

---

2. This and the following translations are directly from the Septuagint, not from the NAB. Since the NAB generally does not follow the Greek Septuagint but rather the Hebrew text, the reader should not expect translations directly from the Septuagint to be equivalent to the NAB. Also, since there are differences in numbering in some of the Psalms, the corresponding number in the NAB is given in brackets after the Septuagint number.

1:29, 31. Paul's boast, his pride, is in the gospel that he serves, not as a job for which he will be paid but as a divine commission that he must fulfill. He is under a compulsion, for the gospel is an overwhelming power that drives him on, as if he is galloping full speed as he is bearing the banner of Christ, and it is the banner, not the rider, that is the boast. There are, of course, pathological compulsions, but there are other compulsions, the drives of mission, such as the kind we have seen in Gandhi or Martin Luther King Jr. or Mother Teresa of Calcutta. Long before them, Paul had that drive: "The love of Christ impels us" (2 Cor 5:14). Paul cannot think of not preaching the gospel: **Woe to me if I do not preach it!** This is truly a prophetic experience, like that of Jeremiah, who said that the word of God was like a fire inside him that he could not contain (20:8–9). But Paul, instead of complaining as Jeremiah did, says his call from God to proclaim the gospel is his boast, however costly it may be.

To preach the gospel was not Paul's idea or initiative. This seems to be the best understanding of **If I do so willingly**, that is, by my own choice. Then it would be like a service for which I should demand and receive a **recompense** from those to whom I preach. A well-known speaker addressing a convention should receive a stipend for his talk. But in this, Paul is a slave of Christ, and Christ's call meant that he was **entrusted with a stewardship** that he must manage for his master. He will not be paid by those whom he serves in the name of the Master; his **recompense** will come from the Master himself. And what is that recompense? Paul could have said, as in 2 Tim 4:8, that it is "the crown of righteousness" that awaits him "on that day." But instead, he says his recompense is precisely to preach the gospel free of charge. The reward for preaching the gospel is the very preaching of it—free of charge. Giving up his rights was not a burden to him if it promoted the gospel.

17–18

Reflection and Application (9:12b–18)

Our family had a retriever named Jeb, a maroon-spotted dog that loved nothing more than fetching whatever one would toss. Whenever I would visit my family on the ranch, Jeb would come running to meet me, knowing that I would give him another chance to show his skill. I would take a stick or rock, throw it, and Jeb would take off like a jet at full speed, sometimes catching the stick or rock as it bounced. Then he would proudly return it and drop it at my feet. Did he want a pat on the head in appreciation for what he did? Or a bone to chew on or a morsel of meat? Not at all. He wanted me to throw it again. And if perchance I was distracted in conversation with a family member, he would eventually paw at my foot until I would reach down and toss the object again. His reward for fetching it? Fetching it again. He would do this over and over, not until he got tired but until I did. I think of Jeb when I think of Paul's preaching the gospel. He looks for no further reward than preaching it again—free of charge.

Reaching Out to Others (9:19–23)

> ¹⁹Although I am free in regard to all, I have made myself a slave to all so as to win over as many as possible. ²⁰To the Jews I became like a Jew to win over Jews; to those under the law I became like one under the law—though I myself am not under the law—to win over those under the law. ²¹To those outside the law I became like one outside the law—though I am not outside God's law but within the law of Christ—to win over those outside the law. ²²To the weak I became weak, to win over the weak. I have become all things to all, to save at least some. ²³All this I do for the sake of the gospel, so that I too may have a share in it.

NT: Matt 20:26; Rom 15:1; 1 Cor 10:32–33; 2 Cor 11:29
Catechism: inculturation 854, 1204
Lectionary: 9:16–19, 22–23: St. Francis Xavier; Common of Pastors; Admission to Candidacy for Diaconate and Priesthood

Having discussed the privileges he has renounced, Paul now returns to the theme of freedom announced in 9:1: "Am I not free?" He did not develop the theme of freedom there; instead, we now realize that it was just the first side of an arch that, completed with this section, would encase the whole discourse on Paul's self-renunciation. This is technically called an †inclusio. This side of the arch reveals what he was up to all along: the overall image is of freedom freely surrendered for the sake of love. The free apostle makes himself a slave. It is precisely what Paul says in Gal 5:13: "For you were called for freedom, brothers. But do not use this freedom as an opportunity for the flesh; rather, serve one another through love." The verb translated "serve" (*douleuō*) in Gal 5:13 is the same verb translated "made myself a slave" here in 9:19, so it can be translated "make yourselves slaves of one another through love." True love, the love of *agapē*, is sacrificial. The coin of the kingdom is love. One side is delight in the beloved, the other sacrifice for the beloved; the more one uses the coin, the more it becomes transparent as delight and sacrifice blend into one. Jesus went to his death out of love.

19–20   Notice how often Paul uses the word "all" in this section. He is **free in regard to all**, that is, he is not indentured to anyone, but he has freely chosen to become

a slave to all so as to win over as many as possible. He could have said "to win over all," and that certainly is his desire. But he is a realist and knows from his own experience that not everyone will accept the gospel. Is Paul abandoning his own self-identity or sacrificing a principle by making himself a slave to everyone? No, this is the same Paul who elsewhere says, "Am I now currying favor with human beings or God? Or am I seeking to please people? If I were still trying to please people, I would not be a slave of Christ" (Gal 1:10). The context is obviously different, for in Galatians he is fighting for the right of Gentile Christians to avoid circumcision, whereas here it is a question of letting go of his personal rights in order to reach more people with the gospel. **To the Jews I became like a Jew to win over Jews; to those under the law I became like one under the law—though I myself am not under the law—to win over those under the law**. Obviously Paul was already a Jew, so here he must mean that when he was with Jews, he ate as they ate and probably even washed his hands as Jews did. He did not flaunt his freedom from these things, nor did he condemn the Jews for continuing their customs, even circumcision, as long as it was clear that none of these things counted for salvation but were only a testament to their heritage, and as long as they did not impose these matters on the Gentile converts. It is faith in Christ that saves Jew and Gentile (Gal 2:16). What Paul *did* say was that Jews and Gentiles are now meant to form one community and now should eat together—the point of his dispute with Peter in Gal 2:11–14. After Jesus and Peter, the wall between Jew and Gentile was first broken down in Paul himself. It was probably the most painful problem he had to deal with in trying to win over the Jews.

To those outside the law, the Gentiles, **I became like one outside the law**.   21
When he was with Gentiles, Paul followed Gentile customs, especially in matters of food. As he writes to the Romans: "The kingdom of God is not a matter of food and drink, but of righteousness, peace, and joy in the holy Spirit" (Rom 14:17). Lest the Corinthians misinterpret what he means by "outside the law," Paul hastens to add that he is **not outside God's law but within the law of Christ**. It is clear here, then, that Paul is not tossing out the Ten Commandments. On the contrary, the law of Christ is even more demanding. But at the same time it is easier because it is the law of love, and that love is God's love "poured out into our hearts through the holy Spirit that has been given to us" (Rom 5:5). We cannot measure up to the holiness that God expects of us by our own efforts to observe his law. Nor does he expect us to. The Holy Spirit enables us to go even beyond the limits of the law, because what is impossible to the human person is possible with the grace of God.

22–23   Why does Paul now bring in **the weak**? Actually, he seems to slip this in precisely because it is the Corinthians' problem. They have probably followed him in agreement up to this point, but now he touches on the neuralgic issue: the weak are those who could be led into sin by the swashbuckling, bull-in-the-china-shop activity of those who "know" that an idol is nothing and therefore claim and exercise the right to eat idol-offered meat, disregarding the effect it might have on their brothers and sisters in the community. Paul holds up his conduct as an example here. He will abstain any time his eating might lead others into sin. Then he concludes this rhythmic, poetic section with an inclusio, echoing the same thought with which the paragraph began: **I have become all things to all, to save at least some**. But then verse 23 adds another thought. Not only is his preaching of the **gospel** something that offers salvation to others; but Paul himself knows that he also will **have a share in** its fruit himself as he shares it with others. This not only picks up the inexorable mandate laid upon him (9:16) but also adds that it is by sharing the gospel that one enjoys its fruits. When given away, material gifts no longer belong to the giver; when shared, spiritual gifts grow in the one sharing.

Reflection and Application (9:19–23)

There is a physical and spiritual law that what we don't use we lose. A muscle that is never used withers. A conviction never shared will grow weaker in the one who holds it. This is also true of one's Christian faith. That is why you will find the strongest faith in those who give themselves to some kind of ministry, even if it is an active sharing of their faith with their families, their friends, and co-workers. The waters of the Jordan River feed two seas, the smaller Sea of Galilee and the much larger Dead Sea. Fish live in abundance in the Sea of Galilee; nothing lives in the Dead Sea. The difference? The Sea of Galilee passes on the water it receives; the Dead Sea just receives without giving.[3] A parable of life. A parable for gospel living.

Athletes Can't Be Cocky (9:24–27)

---

[24]Do you not know that the runners in the stadium all run in the race, but only one wins the prize? Run so as to win. [25]Every athlete exercises

---

3. Due to more recent damming at Deganya and along watercourses in Jordan, today very little water flows into the Jordan south of Chinnereth (the Sea of Galilee). Along that stretch the Jordan is no longer fresh water but largely waste water, and little of it. During part of the year virtually nothing flows from the Jordan into the Dead Sea. The Dead Sea level is falling by about one meter a year.

discipline in every way. They do it to win a perishable crown, but we an
imperishable one. ²⁶Thus I do not run aimlessly; I do not fight as if I were
shadowboxing. ²⁷No, I drive my body and train it, for fear that, after having preached to others, I myself should be disqualified.

OT: Wis 5:16
NT: Gal 5:7; Phil 3:14; 2 Tim 4:7–8; 1 Pet 5:4; Rev 2:10; 3:11

Paul now introduces another facet of his ministry that he hopes will inspire
the Corinthians to take the high road of sacrifice for the sake of others. The
Apostle is not complacent. Using the metaphors of the footrace and the boxing
match, where complacency means defeat, Paul prepares for the next chapter,
where he will show the same lesson from Israel's desert experience.

24   Corinth was the venue for the popular Isthmian games every two years.
They were modeled on the Olympics and drew many of the same contestants.
Footraces and boxing were a regular part of the fare. Hence the two metaphors
would be especially meaningful to Paul's community, as Paul applies them to
the Christian life. It is a race, as Paul loves to insist elsewhere (Gal 5:7; Phil
2:16; 2 Tim 4:7) and a boxing match. It is not against our fellow Christians that
we compete but simply against the flesh that would invite us to saunter down
the track, if on the track at all, assuming that everyone will automatically be
crowned. Some of the Corinthians have fallen into this complacency—not uncommon even among Christians today—that assumes victory will be granted
to anyone who enters the race by being baptized in the Church, no matter how
they live thereafter. No, says Paul, you must run so as to receive the prize. In
Phil 3:13–14 Paul writes: "Forgetting what lies behind but straining forward
to what lies ahead, I continue my pursuit toward the goal, the prize of God's
upward calling, in Christ Jesus." In Delphi, Greece, there are the well-preserved
remains of the footrace stadium (see photo) where the finish line is clearly
etched in stone, and at an elevation in the stands one can still see the bench for
the dignitaries who bestowed the crown. This coming forward and "upward" to
receive the victor's crown is what Paul has in mind by Christ's "upward calling."
But it belongs only to the one who runs **so as to win**.

25   Effort in the race will not suffice if there has not been intense discipline be-
forehand: **Every athlete exercises discipline in every way**. Epictetus, the late
first-century Stoic philosopher, writes to a would-be athlete:

You have to submit to discipline, follow a strict diet, give up sweets, train under
obedience, at a fixed hour, in heat or cold; you must not drink cold water, nor
wine just whenever you feel like it; you must submit to your trainer precisely as

George T. Montague, SM

Fig. 10. Paul loved the image of the race (9:24; Phil 3:12–16; 2 Tim 3:7–8). In the footrace stadium at Delphi, one can see, midway in the stands, the seat for the officials from whom the winners would receive the "perishable crown" (1 Cor 9:25).

you would to a physician. Then when it is time for the contest, you have to "dig in" next to your opponent. You will sometimes dislocate your wrist, sprain your ankle, swallow quantities of sand, take a scourging [the penalty for a foul]; yes, and then sometimes get defeated along with all that. After considering all this, go into the games, if you still wish to.[4]

If these are the kinds of things Paul's readers would think of as they listen to his words about the discipline of athletes, they would probably have recognized an allusion to abstinence from the idol offerings (8:10–13). While victors in the Olympic games won a crown of laurel, in the Isthmian games they were given a diadem of celery, often already beginning to wither. Perhaps the perishability of the crown was to contrast with the joy of victory itself. Seneca, the philosopher and statesman contemporary of Paul, contrasts the fame that athletes win after enduring the agonies of their profession with that of the Stoics whose reward is "not a garland or palm or a trumpeter who calls for silence at the proclamation of our names, but rather virtue, steadfastness of soul, and a peace that is won for all time."[5] For Christians, the reward is even more than human virtue. It is **imperishable** because it is the crown of eternal life. "From

4. Epictetus, *Discourses* 3.15.2–5.
5. Seneca, *Moral Epistles* 7.16.

now on the crown of righteousness awaits me, which the Lord, the just judge, will award to me on that day, and not only to me, but to all who have longed for his appearance" (2 Tim 4:8). "Hold fast to what you have, so that no one may take your crown" (Rev 3:11).

Applying the metaphor to himself, Paul says, **I do not run aimlessly**. Then he introduces his second example. He is not only a racer but also a boxer. However brutal professional boxing may seem to us today, it cannot compare with the brutality of the ancient sport. In Roman times boxers fought with leather bands around their fists and sometimes wore metal-filled leather hand coverings called *caesti*, which resulted in bloody duels to death. Facial disfigurement was not the least of the effects, as we know from the grotesque representations of ancient boxers. Paul is not just going through the motions; he is not pretending, he is not flailing the air, **as if I were shadowboxing**. He is "giving himself a black eye," the literal meaning of **I drive my body**. And **train it** is literally, "I make it my slave." Though this text has inspired asceticism of various kinds in the history of the Church, it refers here to the sacrifices Paul is willing to make for others, in this case forgoing his rights for their sake. For if he did not exert his full energy in what is in reality a combat against his own flesh, he fears not just losing the match but actually being thrown out of the ring. Thus, having **preached to others**, he entertains a wholesome distrust of self **for fear that . . . I myself should be disqualified**. "Disqualified" is the translation of most versions, thus continuing the image of the boxing match. But the Greek word also means being proved false, being shown to be counterfeit, a fake. This latter sense goes well with the image of shadowboxing. Looking exteriorly as if one is fighting is not enough. A real victory supposes a real battle. So too, Paul does not count on his call as an apostle nor on his preaching to assure his salvation. He must live out his call to the very end. Just as it was insufficient to get on the track or enter the ring in order to win, it is insufficient to pretend to be a Christian (shadowboxing) and live as if not. And in that state to presume salvation is presumptuous indeed—as Paul will demonstrate next from the example of his ancestors in the desert.

Reflection and Application (9:24–27)

Paul practiced self-discipline, especially the discipline of seeking the common good in preference to his own advantage, in order to avoid hypocrisy and remain faithful to Christ. Not a bad attitude to have, especially if one has a widespread reputation. How often we find public figures shamed by their public and private scandals, and this is particularly shocking when such persons are clergy or †ministers. The great temptation facing many is to be more concerned about looking good than being good. One can be led to think that being popular with others is all one needs to be secure—or, in theological terms, to be saved. The Corinthian Christians are tempted, on the one hand, not to lose face with their pagan friends by refusing to participate in pagan banquets, and on the other hand, to run over the tender †consciences of their weaker brothers and sisters in the community. Are our temptations today much different? On the one hand, are we inclined too easily to blend in with the secular culture in which we live? And on the other, do we insist on our rights even when the common good would invite us to refrain from asserting them? It isn't sufficient to be right: we must also be loving. Although Paul is slowly and gently building up to his black-and-white condemnation of idol worship, he wants to make it clear, from his own example, that the Christian life involves the cross, a cross that is not ascetical mountaineering but self-sacrifice for the common good of the Church.

"For fear that, after having preached to others, I myself should be disqualified." These words of Paul are a sober alert to us against presumption. If Paul, who had seen the risen Christ and had been sent by him to evangelize the nations, worked out his own salvation "with fear and trembling" (Phil 2:12), what of us? Today the belief that everybody will be saved is little short of universal. It is easy for us to lose a sense of the transcendence of God, his otherness, and blissfully ignore the words of Jesus about entering "through the narrow gate; for the gate is wide and the road broad that leads to destruction, and those who enter through it are many" (Matt 7:13). Our contemporary world has created what I would call the religion of the self, in which "I" create reality according to my tastes, including the reality of what will be my ultimate destiny. Jesus says that road leads to destruction. The Church calls it the sin of presumption. Some Protestants teach the doctrine "once saved always saved," which is another kind of presumption.

Having cited his own example, Paul in the next section will warn his faithful by using examples from the history of God's people.

Warnings and the Eucharist

1 Corinthians 10

In chapter 8 Paul has urged those with knowledge about idols to think of the common good and give greater value to love. In chapter 9 he reinforced this exhortation by showing how he himself sacrifices his rights for the good of others. Now he will bring out the big guns: Scripture, God's Word, as the ultimate argument. He will go to the central act of God in the history of Israel, the exodus, and show that the Corinthians are on the brink of falling into the same sin of presumption as their spiritual ancestors, who, after being delivered from slavery and fed miraculously in the desert, perished without reaching the promised land because they indulged in idolatry. The Corinthians are facing the same kind of challenge now: to cling to the one sacrifice of Christ celebrated in the Eucharist, which is incompatible with even feigning idolatry.

Learning from the Exodus (10:1–13)

¹I do not want you to be unaware, brothers, that our ancestors were all under the cloud and all passed through the sea, ²and all of them were baptized into Moses in the cloud and in the sea. ³All ate the same spiritual food, ⁴and all drank the same spiritual drink, for they drank from a spiritual rock that followed them, and the rock was the Christ. ⁵Yet God was not pleased with most of them, for they were struck down in the desert.

⁶These things happened as examples for us, so that we might not desire evil things, as they did. ⁷And do not become idolaters, as some of them did, as it is written, "The people sat down to eat and drink, and rose up to revel."

[8]Let us not indulge in immorality as some of them did, and twenty-three thousand fell within a single day. [9]Let us not test Christ as some of them did, and suffered death by serpents. [10]Do not grumble as some of them did, and suffered death by the destroyer. [11]These things happened to them as an example, and they have been written down as a warning to us, upon whom the end of the ages has come. [12]Therefore, whoever thinks he is standing secure should take care not to fall. [13]No trial has come to you but what is human. God is faithful and will not let you be tried beyond your strength; but with the trial he will also provide a way out, so that you may be able to bear it.

OT: Exod 13:21; 14:22; 16:4–35; 17:5–6; Num 11:4, 34; 14:16; 20:7–11; 21:5–6; 25:1–9
NT: Matt 6:13; 26:41; Acts 5:9–10; Heb 4:2–3
Catechism: Baptism, 1213–84; the Eucharist, 1322–419; with grace, virtues forge character, 1810
Lectionary: 10:1–6, 10–12: Third Sunday of Lent (Year C)

After trying to motivate the Corinthians to seek the common good, first by showing them how scandal violates love (8:1–13) and then by his own example of sacrificial love (9:1–26), Paul continues to build his arguments toward the climax by appealing to the witness of Scripture, where the Israelites' complacency in the matter of idolatry had devastating effects. Working with a typological interpretation of the exodus account (see sidebar), he sees fulfilled in Christ, and therefore in the Christian community, some of the major experiences of "our ancestors" in the desert. In saying "our ancestors," Paul considers the Gentile Christians indistinguishable from the Jewish ones: all have the same ancestors, for the Church is the Israel of God (Gal 6:16) and Abraham "is the father of all of us" (Rom 4:16). An ancient Jewish tradition held that the convert to Judaism should say, "Our God and the God of *their* fathers,"[1] thus maintaining the distinction even after conversion, but not so with Paul: all are one in the new Israel.

Paul reads the exodus story and the Christ event like a double exposure. In so doing he immensely enriches both. God already had in mind the liberating effects of baptism when he delivered the Israelites through the Red Sea. With Moses he already had Jesus in mind as leader of the new exodus. With the manna he was preparing for the Eucharist. In the rock from which the water flowed in the desert, he was thinking of Jesus, from whom the waters of life would flow, the Holy Spirit. The typology can be outlined thus:

Now let us look at each of these elements in turn. The **cloud** is a classic symbol in the Old Testament for the presence of God. A cloud led the people by day and concealed them at night as they made their way to the Red Sea

---

1. *Mishnah Bikkurim* 1:4. The Mishnah is a collection of Jewish sayings compiled around AD 200.

†Type: The Exodus Ancestors	Antitype: The Church
The cloud	The Holy Spirit
The sea	Baptism
Baptized into Moses	Baptized into Christ
Spiritual food: manna	Spiritual food: the Eucharist
Spiritual drink: water	Spiritual drink: the Eucharist or the Holy Spirit
Rock: source of water	Rock: Christ, source of the Holy Spirit
Rock followed them in space	Rock: Christ present with the Church, followed the ancestors in time

(Exod 13:21–22; 14:19–20; Ps 105:39). The Lord came down in a cloud over Mount Sinai at the time of sealing the covenant with his people (Exod 19:16; 24:15, 18). When Moses built the tabernacle, the cloud came down and overshadowed it, and "the glory of the LORD filled the Dwelling" (Exod 40:34–35). Paul sees the cloud of the exodus as a prefigurement of the Holy Spirit, whom Christians receive when they are baptized. And as the Israelites crossed the sea to freedom, Christians have escaped the tyranny of sin and death through the waters of baptism.

The expression **baptized into Moses** would make no sense apart from its parallel "baptized into Christ." Paul sees the New Testament fulfillment already present in the Old Testament type: it was only in being united to Moses that the people escaped Egypt, just as it is only in being united to Jesus that one is saved (1 Cor 12:13). As the manna was **spiritual food** in the sense that it was not the product of human hands but a sheer gift from heaven, so the Eucharist is spiritual food, and not only because it is a heavenly gift but also, being the body of Christ, it is the source of the Holy Spirit (1 Cor 6:17; 12:13; 15:45). This typology has furnished the Church with a rich source for theology of the sacraments.

The **spiritual drink** of which the Israelites partook was the water that flowed from the rock when struck by Moses (Exod 17:1–7; Num 20:2–13). It was spiritual in the sense that it was miraculously provided by God. The fulfillment is in the Holy Spirit, as Paul makes explicit in 12:13: "We were all given to drink of one Spirit." In this Paul reflects the same theme found in the Gospel of John: "Whoever drinks the water I shall give will never thirst; the water I shall give will become in him a spring of water welling up to eternal life" (4:14). " 'Let anyone who thirsts come to me and drink. Whoever believes in me, as scripture says: "Rivers of living water will flow from within him." ' He said this in reference to the Spirit that those who came to believe in him were to receive" (7:37–39). And most graphically, when the soldier pierced Jesus' side after his death on

2–3

4

the cross, "blood and water flowed out" (19:34). John's linking of blood to water may symbolize the Eucharist along with baptism and the Holy Spirit. So it is also possible that the spiritual drink of which Paul speaks may at least hint at the eucharistic blood of Christ. As Chrysostom comments, "The same Person brought them through the sea and you through baptism; and before them set the manna, but before you his body and blood."[2]

There is a rabbinic tradition that helps explain Paul's curious expression, **They drank from a spiritual rock that followed them**. The rabbis wondered how the Israelites were able to have water during the forty years of their journey. They concluded that the rock struck by Moses became a kind of movable well, "like a rock traveling with them,"[3] "and wherever they journeyed it rolled along."[4] Assuming that Paul knew this tradition, he plays on the idea of "following." The rock indeed *followed* them, not in space but in time—that is, it came later chronologically—**and the rock was the Christ.** The Fathers of the Church understood that the type really contained the antitype, that is, Christ was actually present in the rock, and that presence was revealed in the New Testament.

5–7   The point of all this reflection is that the ancestors had received great gifts, indeed supernatural gifts. **Yet God was not pleased with most of them, for they were struck down in the desert.** Some of them perished by being swallowed into the earth (Num 16:30–33) or by fire (16:35), some of those who engaged in worship of the golden calf were slaughtered (Exod 32:25–28), and the rest of that generation died in the desert, unable to enter the promised land (Num 14:20–24; Deut 1:34–35). But the primary point that Paul wishes to make here is that the know-it-all Corinthians who participate in idolatrous meals are sinning like their ancestors and are consequently inviting the same catastrophic results. And all the more so because the gifts that Christians enjoy infinitely surpass the gifts of their ancestors. Baptism, the Eucharist, and the Holy Spirit will not save them unless they live in a way that corresponds to the holiness of these gifts. Hence they should read the danger sign staring at them from the pages of Scripture before it is too late. For **these things happened as examples for us, so that we might not desire evil things, as they did.** The Greek word for "examples" is *typoi*, literally, "types." Typology—understanding Old Testament

---

2. Saint Chrysostom, *Homilies on 1 Corinthians* 23.3.

3. *Tosefta Sukkah* 3.11–12; quoted in David E. Garland, *1 Corinthians*, BECNT (Grand Rapids: Baker Academic, 2003), 470.

4. *Numbers Rabbah* 1.5 on Num 21:17; quoted in Garland, *1 Corinthians*, 270. The written form of this tradition is post-Christian, but it relays an earlier tradition.

events or persons as prefigurements of New Testament realities—includes not only heralds of salvation but also warnings of judgment (see sidebar).

Paul proceeds to highlight five examples: desiring evil things, idolatry, immorality, testing Christ, and grumbling. The golden calf incident (Exod 32:1–6) alluded to here—**"The people sat down to eat and drink, and rose up to revel"**—parallels the situation in Corinth, which also involved a sacrificial banquet. Paul does not mention the slaughter of those who participated (Exod 32:28), focusing rather on the similarity with the pagan sacrificial meals in Corinth.

The indulging **in immorality** refers to the fornication of Israelite men with   8
Moabite women, who then induced them to participate in the "sacrifices of their god, and the people ate of the sacrifices and worshiped their god" (Num 25:2). The †Septuagint, which was Paul's Bible, has an even closer parallel to Paul's situation: "They invited [the Israelites] to the sacrifices of their *idols*; and the people ate of their sacrifices and worshiped their *idols.*" God's anger flared and **twenty-three thousand** died.[5]

Paul next recalls Num 21:4–9, where the people "complained against God   9–10
and Moses" about the "wretched food" and lack of water in the desert, in response to which God sent fiery serpents among them "so that many of them died." We would have expected Paul to say that they tested *God*, but just as he spoke of the rock being Christ, here he says the target of their complaint was **Christ**, thus tightening the identification of Old and New Testaments. Note here how Christ takes the place of God. Although Numbers does not call the complaining "testing" (Greek *peirazō*), their action is characterized as testing in the LXX version of Ps 77 [78]:18: "They tested [*peirazō*] God in their hearts by demanding the food they craved." Instead of commanding them at this point, the Apostle chooses the exhortatory verb form "Let us not," thus including himself and again seeking to win them over by persuasion. But in verse 10 he returns to the command form in telling them, **Do not grumble as some of them did**. The best way to understand this verse is by seeing it as an expansion of verse 9. There Paul has called the people's sin as a way to "test Christ," but now he says the "test" was specifically complaining or grumbling (Num 21:4–9). Who or what was the **destroyer**? That was the biblical description of the one who destroyed the firstborn of the Egyptians (Exod 12:23), whom Paul sees as now executing a death sentence via the serpents upon the faithless of the Lord's own people.

5. Both the Hebrew and the LXX mention twenty-four thousand; perhaps Paul had a memory lapse, or he may have had a different manuscript copy. This minor discrepancy does not alter the lesson he is teaching.

Typology

BIBLICAL BACKGROUND

Typology is the understanding of how persons, things, and events in salvation history prefigure God's future purposes, especially the culmination of his plan in Jesus Christ. In light of the gospel, the persons, things, and events of the Old Testament are recognized as "types" that point forward in a veiled way to Christ and his †paschal mystery. The Catechism notes that "the Church, as early as apostolic times, and then constantly in her Tradition, has illuminated the unity of the divine plan in the two Testaments through typology, which discerns in God's works of the Old Covenant prefigurations of what he accomplished in the fullness of time in the person of his incarnate Son" (128).

Typological interpretation is present even in the Old Testament. The Jews' return from exile in Babylon is understood as a new exodus (Isa 41:17–20; 43:16–17); the Messiah will be a new David (9:7); God will make a new covenant (Jer 31:31). The prophets continually present God's past saving deeds as the pattern for his future acts.

In the New Testament, Jesus reveals himself as the transcendent fulfillment of all Scripture and all salvation history (Mark 14:49; Luke 24:25–27; John 5:46). He is the new Moses (Mark 9:2; John 1:17) and the new David (Mark 11:10). He is lifted up like the bronze serpent in the wilderness (John 3:14); his body is the temple (2:21); he is the ladder of Jacob's dream (1:51), the Passover lamb (1 Cor 5:7; †paschal meal), and the Suffering Servant of the Lord (Matt 20:28). The crossing of the Red Sea prefigures salvation by baptism (1 Pet 3:21); the manna in the desert foreshadows the Eucharist, the true bread from heaven (John 6:32). In the words of the medieval theologian Hugh of St. Victor, "All Sacred Scripture is but one book, and this one book is Christ, because all divine Scripture speaks of Christ, and all divine Scripture is fulfilled in Christ" (Catechism, 134).

11   It is possible that among the Corinthians were those who complained that Paul's condemnation of their participation in idol worship was too severe. But Paul hopes that these stories will serve as an **example** and a **warning**, all the more convincing since Christians live in the †age of fulfillment, where the realities foreshadowed have come to pass. If our ancestors offended Christ in shadow, how much more the offense for us in broad daylight! That is the sense of describing **us** as the ones **upon whom the end of the ages has come**. The "end of the ages" here does not mean the end of time or the second coming of Christ. It refers to the age opened up by the resurrection of Jesus, so that we are living in the final times.

12   A false sense of security can be fatal. This applies to all but especially to those who are overconfident in their "knowledge" that allows them to partake in what they now consider to be meaningless ritual—pagan sacrificial meals—for the sake of conviviality. To **fall** means to die (10:8; Num 14:3), and that means to lose one's eternal salvation. But actually Paul will also mean physical death for those who are abusing the Eucharist (11:30).

At first sight the sudden reference to trials may seem out of place. However, if   **13** we consider the social consequences of rejecting idolatry, the verse is a beautiful conclusion. The Corinthians are thinking of their friends, relatives, and business associates, especially of their patrons in the †patron-client culture, who are going to be shocked by this sudden retreat from what had been their custom until now. To decline invitations, and to do so habitually, would not only invite alienation but perhaps even persecution. Thus Paul wishes to reassure them that it is possible to stand firm on their Christian confession in the face of these potential consequences. So far they have not suffered more than other human beings have suffered: **No trial has come to you but what is human**. And even if matters should get worse, **God is faithful and will not let you be tried beyond your strength**, for his faithfulness will engender their faithfulness. It is significant that Paul does not promise that they will escape the trial (or be raptured out!); but **with the trial**, God **will also provide a way out**, and paradoxically the way out is simply to **be able to bear it**.

Reflection and Application (10:1–13)

This last verse indicates that the way God answers our prayers is not always the way we expect. We may ask to be released from a heavy cross, and often enough the Lord removes it from us. But often too his answer is instead to give us the strength to endure the suffering and even to offer it as a sacrifice for others, saying with St. Paul, "I rejoice in my sufferings for your sake, and in my flesh I am filling up what is lacking in the afflictions of Christ on behalf of his body, which is the church" (Col 1:24). The word "tried" can also be translated as "tempted." God does not allow us to be tempted beyond our strength. Thus when tempted, we should look for the way out that his providence is supplying. If we do succumb, then the way out is through repentance and confession.

The Table of the Lord (10:14–22)

---

¹⁴**Therefore, my beloved, avoid idolatry.** ¹⁵**I am speaking as to sensible people; judge for yourselves what I am saying.** ¹⁶**The cup of blessing that we bless, is it not a participation in the blood of Christ? The bread that we break, is it not a participation in the body of Christ?** ¹⁷**Because the loaf of**

bread is one, we, though many, are one body, for we all partake of the one loaf.

¹⁸Look at Israel according to the flesh; are not those who eat the sacrifices participants in the altar? ¹⁹So what am I saying? That meat sacrificed to idols is anything? Or that an idol is anything? ²⁰No, I mean that what they sacrifice, [they sacrifice] to demons, not to God, and I do not want you to become participants with demons. ²¹You cannot drink the cup of the Lord and also the cup of demons. You cannot partake of the table of the Lord and of the table of demons. ²²Or are we provoking the Lord to jealous anger? Are we stronger than he?

OT: Lev 3:1–17; Deut 4:24; 32:17; Ps 106:37

NT: Matt 26:26–27; 1 Cor 11:23–26; 12:12

Catechism: real presence in the Eucharist, 1088, 1377–81; the Eucharist makes the Church one body, 1396

Lectionary: Mass for Blessing of Chalice and Paten; 10:16–21: Mass for Dedication of an Altar; 10:16–17: The Body and Blood of Christ; Mass for Institution of Acolytes; Mass for Viaticum; Mass of the Most Holy Eucharist

14–15   Paul's approach to the topic of participation in Corinth's sacrifices and sacrificial meals has been centripetal. He has moved from what is less important but might be more acceptable to the Corinthians (8:1–13), to his own example (9:1–27), and then to the Old Testament warnings (10:1–13). But here now he has arrived at the center of his argument: the Eucharist. **Therefore** indicates he is concluding his previous arguments and is ready to make his concluding demand. He wants them first to know the strong affection he has for them (**my beloved**), which inspires his tough love: **Avoid idolatry**—literally, "Flee from idol worship." The addition of *from* (Greek *apo*) makes the expression still more emphatic than the "Flee fornication" of 6:18 (KJV). It is no longer merely a question of prudence and charity (8:10). Sharing in such a sacrificial meal is sacrilege. Paul does not want their compliance to be an act of blind obedience, however. He wants them to **judge for yourselves what I am saying**. Paul realizes that demanding obedience without a rationale is no more effective than a parent who never explains the reason for a command. That reason Paul will give as the climactic and fully sufficient reason for avoiding idolatry. Christians should avoid the pagan sacrificial banquets because they have a sacrificial banquet of their own!

16   **The cup of blessing** may be interpreted as meaning the cup that obtains and imparts all blessings. The direct reference, however, is to the third ceremonial cup of the †paschal meal, poured after eating the paschal lamb, over which the father of the family would pronounce a thanksgiving before drinking, saying,

Chrysostom on the Cup

LIVING TRADITION

In Jewish thought, which carries over into the Eucharist, "blessing" means a praise of God for some specific gift received. Noting that "blessing" means "thanksgiving," Chrysostom writes: "Recounting over the cup the unspeakable mercies of God and all that we have been made partakers of, so draw near to him, and communicate, giving him thanks that he has delivered from error the whole race of mankind; that being afar off he brought them near; that when they had no hope and were without God in the world, he made them his own brothers and fellow heirs. For these and all such things, giving thanks, thus we approach." These words sound much like the prefaces of our Roman Rite eucharistic prayers (esp. Eucharistic Prayer IV); indeed, they are found in one form or another in the Byzantine liturgies of St. John Chrysostom and St. Basil and in those of other Eastern rites.

Then, paraphrasing Paul, Chrysostom continues: "What is in the cup is that which flowed from His side, and of that we partake. But he called it a cup of blessing, because holding it in our hands, we so exalt him in our hymn, wondering, astonished at his unspeakable gift, blessing him, among other things, for the pouring out of this same drink . . . to us all. Therefore, if you desire blood, he says, redden not the altar of idols with the slaughter of brute beasts, but My altar with My blood."[a]

a. Saint Chrysostom, *Homilies on 1 Corinthians* 24.3.

"Blessed art thou, Lord our God, king of the universe, who dost create the fruit of the vine." But by saying, "the cup of blessing **that we bless**," Paul is contrasting it with both the Passover cup and whatever drinking was done in the pagan meals. It doubtless refers to the eucharistic cup, the "cup of the Lord" of verse 21. The †*Didache*, a late first-century Christian document, gives examples of such prayer accompanying the Communion (chaps. 9 and 10). The verb Paul uses here (*eulogeō*) is also used in 1 Sam 9:13 LXX for the priestly action of consecrating a victim in the name of the people. It points to the sacrificial nature of the blessing, hence the Eucharist as sacrifice. The cup is mentioned before the bread either because Paul wishes to draw the Christian contrast with the pagan sacrifices that began with a libation or, more probably, because he wishes to develop further his thoughts on the bread. The *Didache* gives a prayer of thanksgiving over the chalice first.

The union effected by the blood and the body of Christ is a **participation**. This Greek term *koinōnia* has a richness difficult to express in a single word. The

NAB, RSV, and NIV translate it as "participation." Others translate it "sharing" (NJB, NRSV) or "communion" (JB). In documents contemporary with Paul, *koinōnia* is a favorite expression for the marital relationship as being the most intimate between human beings.[6] Depending on the structure of the Greek, it can mean union with a person, as Paul has already in this letter spoken of a *koinōnia* with the Son of God (1:9), or a common sharing in something, such as in the faith (Philem 6), in sufferings (Phil 3:10), or in a work of service (2 Cor 8:4). Both senses converge in the *koinōnia* of the Holy Spirit (2 Cor 13:13). The term can also stand for the community created by the sharing. All of these senses can be seen in Paul's use of the word here. The *koinōnia* of the Eucharist is (1) a common sharing or participation in the body and blood of Christ; (2) an intimate union with the person of Christ; (3) a "community" brought about by the Eucharist, as will be specified in verse 17. Is the Eucharist a simple meal, or is it also a sacrificial meal? The separate consecration of cup and bread, one signifying the blood and the other the body, certainly points to sacrifice, since the separation of the animal's blood from its body was essential to sacrifice. In addition, the comparison of the Eucharist with the pagan sacrifices suggests that Paul is saying, "We have our own sacrifice." This will become clearer in what follows.

17   **Because the loaf of bread is one, we, though many, are one body, for we all partake of the one loaf.** How is this to be understood? The Greek word translated "bread" can also mean "loaf." The NAB translates it first as "loaf of bread" and then switches to "loaf," perhaps to bring out the symbolism of the local community's sharing in a single loaf. Certainly the early Christian community found in Christ's gesture of distributing a single loaf, now liturgically repeated (Luke 24:35; Acts 2:42, 46; 20:7, 11), a symbol of its own new oneness. But Paul surely also means a unity that goes beyond the local community. "We, though many" includes all Christians who share in the Eucharist. How are we to understand the unity of the Church made by the one bread? Is it only symbolic? For Paul, the reality of the unity is as real as the body of Christ, for that is what the Eucharist is. "Because the loaf of bread is one, we . . . *are* one body." The Eucharist effects what it signifies. We have already seen how realistically Paul envisions Christians' union with the risen Christ. We are his members, so truly that union with a prostitute is equivalent to adulterous infidelity to Christ (6:13–17). Our union with him is effected by baptism, for we are "baptized into one body," the body of the risen Lord (12:13); what baptism does in a constitutive way, the Eucharist does in a progressive way. We become what we

6. Josephus, *Jewish Antiquities* 1.304; *3 Macc* 4:6; see Isocrates, *Oration 3, Nicoles* 40.

One Eucharist, One Body

The †*Didache* sees in the very constitution of the bread a symbol of the unity of the Church: "As this broken bread, once scattered upon the mountains, was gathered to make one whole, may your Church be thus gathered from the extremities of the earth into your kingdom" (9:4). Chrysostom adds: "As the bread consisting of many grains becomes one, so that the grains nowhere appear; they exist indeed, but their difference is not seen by reason of their conjunction; so we are conjoined with each other and with Christ."[a]

Augustine comments:

> "The body of Christ," you are told, and you answer, "Amen." Be members then of the body of Christ that your amen may be true. Why is this †mystery accomplished with bread? We shall say nothing of our own about it, rather let us hear the Apostle, who speaking of this sacrament says: "We being many are one body, one bread." Understand and rejoice. Unity, devotion, charity! One bread: and what is this one bread? One body made up of many. Consider that the bread is not made of one grain alone, but of many. During the time of exorcism, you were, so to say, in the mill. At baptism you were wetted with water. Then the Holy Spirit came into you like the fire which bakes the dough. Be then what you see and receive what you are. Now for the chalice, my brethren, remember how wine is made. Many grapes hang on the bunch, but the liquid which runs out of them mingles together in unity. So has the Lord willed that we should belong to him, and he has consecrated on his altar the mystery of our peace and our unity.[b]

a. Saint Chrysostom, *Homilies on 1 Corinthians* 10.17.
b. Saint Augustine, *Sermon 234*; in PL 38:1116.

consume, the body of Christ. We become, in the words of St. John Damascene, *concorporeal*, one body, with Christ.[7]

The Apostle now strengthens his point with proof from the Jews' under- **18–20** standing of sacrifice, which Paul as a Jew had subscribed to and which was still practiced in the temple when he wrote this letter. The **Israel according to the flesh** is pre-Christian Israel, fulfilled in the "Israel of God" (Gal 6:16), the Christian Church. It was a commonplace in Jewish theology that to eat the meat of a sacrificed animal was to partake in the sacrifice itself (**the altar**).[8] And since the altar was a figure and symbol for the Lord himself (Deut 12:11–12; 18:1–4; Heb 13:10), eating the sacrificial meal was a union with the Lord. This does not mean, Paul hastens to say, that he considers the idols

7. John Damascene, *De fide orthodoxa* (*Exposition of the Orthodox Faith*) 4.13; in PG 94:1153.
8. Philo, *Special Laws* 1.221.

Fig. 11. Pagan altar.

of Corinth to be anything real or the pagan sacrificial meals as having any inherent efficacy. Quite the contrary: **What they sacrifice, [they sacrifice] to demons**. Paul is quoting Deuteronomy: "They sacrificed to demons, to 'no-gods'" (Deut 32:17; see also Ps 96:5; Bar 4:7). However well intentioned the Gentile converts may have been, and their compatriots may still be, Paul says that the Christian, having come to know the true God, sees the idols for what they are. To return to them, even if you are "enlightened" as to their nonexistence, would be to make yourselves **participants with demons**. *The point is the significance of the act.* The idols may be nothing, and the Christian participants may know that they are nothing, but to engage in an act that expresses belief in them is not only scandalous but also opens people up to the darkness whose prince is Satan.

21   The incompatibility of pagan sacrificial meals with the supper of the Lord is absolute: whence the contrast between the **cup of the Lord** and **the cup of demons**, and between **the table of the Lord** and **the table of demons**. Here "table" has replaced "altar" of verse 18, but this in no way diminishes the sacrificial nature of the meal, for "table" is a frequent equivalent of "altar" in the Old Testament (Isa 65:11; Ezek 41:22; 44:16; Mal 1:7–12).[9]

9. The Council of Trent had good reason for declaring that in this text Paul is comparing altars; Session 22, *De sacrificio Missae.*

The Real Presence

The Catechism (1377–81) repeats what has been the constant faith of the Catholic Church in the real presence of Christ in the Eucharist: "The Eucharistic presence of Christ begins at the moment of the consecration and endures as long as the Eucharistic species subsist. Christ is present whole and entire in each of the species and whole and entire in each of their parts. . . . In the liturgy of the Mass we express our faith in the real presence of Christ under the species of bread and wine by, among other ways, genuflecting or bowing deeply as a sign of adoration of the Lord. . . . Saint Cyril says: 'Do not doubt whether this is true, but rather receive the words of the Savior in faith, for since he is the truth, he cannot lie.'"[a]

a. Cyril of Alexandria, *In Luc.* 22.19; in PG 72.912.

Finally, **are we provoking the Lord to jealous anger?** God's anger is not　**22** just that of a lawmaker's wrath at disobedience. It also comes from his jealousy! How could God, being perfectly happy, be aroused to jealousy? The Old Testament already makes this bold claim (Deut 6:14–15; 32:21; Josh 24:19–20; Ps 78:58–64) because he has bound himself to his people by a marriage covenant, in which infidelity is adultery (Hos 1:2–2:25).[10] Paul is saying that to participate in the pagan sacrifices is to invite the holy jealousy of a lover who loves us infinitely. It is to pretend to be "stronger than" Christ. Human weakness is no match for the power of God (Job 9:32; 37:23; Isa 10:15), and Paul applies this sober †rhetorical question to himself as well as to others by using "we" instead of "you": **Are we stronger than he?** "It is a fearful thing to fall into the hands of the living God" (Heb 10:31).

This text shows the nature of the Eucharist as "communion" in the triple sense described above. But it also shows that the Eucharist is a sacrificial meal. This becomes apparent from (1) the double mention of body and blood in the sacrificial context; (2) the contrast between the Lord's cup and table on the one hand, and the cup and table of demons on the other; and particularly (3) the point of the whole contrast, which is not the sacrificial nature of the pagan meals versus the nonsacrificial nature of the Eucharist, but rather the *union*

10. See also Isa 54:5–10; 62:4–5; Jer 2:2; 6:1–10, 20; Ezek 16:8, 28. As John Paul II put it, "Breaking the covenant signifies not only an infraction of the 'covenant' connected with the authority of the Supreme Legislator, but [also] unfaithfulness and betrayal: a blow that directly pierces his heart as Father, Bridegroom and Lord"; see John Paul II, *Man and Woman He Created Them: A Theology of the Body*, trans. Michael M. Waldstein (Boston: Pauline Books & Media, 2006), 536.

| **BIBLICAL** |
| **BACKGROUND** |

Drinking the Sacrificial Blood

South of Kathmandu, Nepal, there is a Hindu temple called *Dakshin Kali*, or Kali of the South, where I witnessed animal sacrifices that were offered every Tuesday and Saturday. The men would queue up, some with a goat, some with a chicken if they were poorer. When they reached the head of the line, they would present the animal to the priest, who would slit its throat and squirt the blood on the stone idol. Then the one who brought the offering would take the goat or the chicken, clean it, cook it, and picniclike, share it with family and friends. Once I also saw a woman drinking the fresh blood of the sacrificed goat. (My one thought is that there must have been a lot of flies around the Corinthian temples, as there were at this Hindu shrine.) This was the kind of sacrifice or communion to which Paul refers in Corinth; he forbids the faithful to attend because they have the infinitely superior unbloody memorial of the blood shed for them on Calvary.

---

that is effected: on the one hand with Christ, or on the other with demons. Paul forbids Christians to partake in the pagan sacrifices because we have our own.

Reflection and Application (10:14–22)

To us today all this talk about idolatry may seem antiquated and boring. But that may be because we have been so numbed by the relativism of our †age that we do not realize how crucial this teaching of Paul is. Of course the idols are nothing. That is not the point. The point is this: To believe one thing and do another—for whatever reason, like being social—is to erode even what belief you may have started with. Today it can take the form of the disastrous postmodern idea that words and gestures are not related to anything real—including words and gestures about God. They are just creations of the human mind, and no one creation has more value than another, since it is all wordplay, or in the case of ritual, simply ceremony. This frees one from the need to make a decision about any truth claim. One can make up one's own religion or value system because truth is what I want it to be, not what is *there* whether I like it or not. The price of that "freedom" is surely the ultimate severing of human community, which presupposes a common agreement about self-transcending truth. It is here that the martyrs are witnesses in the radical sense of the word. They give their lives because of a reality worth dying for. Their faith is not just words: their religious acts are not just rituals.

The Eucharist as Sacrifice

LIVING TRADITION

"The sacrificial character of the Eucharist is manifested in the very words of institution: 'This is my body which is given for you' and 'This cup which is poured out for you is the New Covenant in my blood' (Luke 22:19–20), . . . the very blood which he 'poured out for the forgiveness of sins' (Matt 26:28)" (Catechism, 1365). The Mass is not a new sacrifice every time it is celebrated. "The Eucharist is thus a sacrifice because it *re-presents* (makes present) the sacrifice of the cross, because it is its *memorial* and because it *applies* its fruit" (Catechism, 1366).

But Paul has an even more sinister warning: involvement in idolatrous practices, even if just for fun, can open a person to the demonic. Pastoral experience has shown that even seemingly innocent playing with Ouija boards, tarot cards, palm reading, fortune-telling, and similar windows to the occult can lead to spiritual bondage.

Freedom to Seek the Good of Others (10:23–11:1)

²³"Everything is lawful," but not everything is beneficial. "Everything is lawful," but not everything builds up. ²⁴No one should seek his own advantage, but that of his neighbor. ²⁵Eat anything sold in the market, without raising questions on grounds of conscience, ²⁶for "the earth and its fullness are the Lord's." ²⁷If an unbeliever invites you and you want to go, eat whatever is placed before you, without raising questions on grounds of conscience. ²⁸But if someone says to you, "This was offered in sacrifice," do not eat it on account of the one who called attention to it and on account of conscience; ²⁹I mean not your own conscience, but the other's. For why should my freedom be determined by someone else's conscience? ³⁰If I partake thankfully, why am I reviled for that over which I give thanks?

³¹So whether you eat or drink, or whatever you do, do everything for the glory of God. ³²Avoid giving offense, whether to Jews or Greeks or the church of God, ³³just as I try to please everyone in every way, not seeking my own benefit but that of the many, that they may be saved. ¹¹:¹Be imitators of me, as I am of Christ.

OT: Ps 24:1; Sir 37:28
NT: Rom 14:19; 15:2; 6:12; Phil 2:4; Col 3:17; 1 Tim 4:4

Catechism: †conscience, 1776–94
Lectionary: 10:31–11:1: St. Ignatius of Loyola

23–24   Up to this point Paul has zeroed in on participating in the pagan sacrificial banquets, which he denounces as idolatry. But what is one to do in purchasing meat in the market? Must one inquire whether it was offered to an idol? And if one is invited to a friend's dinner in their home, should one decline in case the food served there had been offered to an idol? Here Paul shows the insight of a moral theologian, making distinctions that will help the faithful navigate between the Scylla of idolatry and the Charybdis of isolation and social rejection. He repeats the slogan of 6:12, **"Everything is lawful,"** calling his listeners to think outside the box of legalism or license and outside the box of self-interest. But whereas in chapter 8 it was the other, unenlightened members of the community that they should be aware of, here it is the relation with outsiders that is Paul's concern—and no doubt the primary concern of his listeners, for they are wondering how to live out their covenant commitment to Christ as well as their desire to evangelize their friends in the midst of idols and idol offerings everywhere.

25–27   Two scenarios present themselves. First, if you are shopping for meat **in the market**, there is no need to ask if it has first been offered to an idol. All meat belongs to God, who owns everything on earth. The meat is not contaminated by being offered to an idol—unless someone drags it back into that context by pointing out that it has been offered to an idol (see vv. 28–29 below). The same holds **if an unbeliever invites you and you want to go**, presumably to his home for a meal and not to a sacrificial meal (since Paul has already excluded that; 10:21), **eat whatever is placed before you, without raising questions on grounds of conscience**. Paul is aware of the reality of the Greco-Roman world, highly structured according to †patron-client relationships that were necessary for service and protection; he knows that it would be impossible to isolate oneself from all contacts with nonbelievers, or for the Christian community to become a ghetto. Furthermore, wholesome relations with nonbelievers could provide a bridge for introducing them to the Christian faith. One does not have to initiate an investigation into the history of the food when there is no public insistence on it.

28–29a   **But if someone says to you, "This was offered in sacrifice"**: Paul does not identify who the informer might be—the host, an unbeliever guest, or another Christian guest—and it really does not matter. This situation changes the significance of the eating: **do not eat it on account of the one who called attention to it and on account of conscience; I mean not your own conscience, but the**

other's. Who is this "other"? It could be another Christian guest or a servant with a "weak . . . conscience" (8:7) who perhaps has whispered to his fellow Christian that it is idol meat and who would be scandalized by the other's partaking of such food. That would mean that although I know that the idol meat is nothing, I don't want to scandalize my Christian brother or sister by eating it. Alternatively, if the nature of the meat is publicly known, and the Christian knowingly partakes of the idol-offered food, in addition to scandalizing fellow Christians, this endorsement would confirm, or at least not challenge, the nonbeliever in his idolatrous convictions.

The second half of verse 29 looks like a bomb blowing up all that went before, for at first sight it seems that Paul is adopting the objection of those who know that an idol is nothing, and therefore he could eat without caring what others think. Thus exegetes scramble to find a way to explain it within the context of all that has gone before. The best solution is to see it as connected with verse 27, with the intervening verses 28–29a being a parenthetical qualification. At this point it would be helpful to read the verses in the following order: 27, 29b–30 ("For why . . . ?"), 28–29a. Hence Paul would be saying that his and any Christian's right to eat without asking questions should not be constrained by the conscience of the weaker ones who would forbid eating *any* meat in the unbeliever's house. The unknown food is blessed or cleansed, if need be, of its original cultic purpose by the Christian's prayer of thanksgiving. It seems that some scrupulous members of the Corinthian community have criticized Paul precisely on this point: **Why am I reviled for that over which I give thanks?** *29b–30*

This interpretation—a defense of eating without questioning meat of unknown history—leads best into what follows, which shows Paul's desire to minimize offense to non-Christians. Christians who live **for the glory of God** should **avoid giving offense**: they should do what is possible within the limits of the faith so as not to offend those they hope to evangelize. **To Jews**, by avoiding idolatry; to **Greeks**, by being open to their dinner invitations while abstaining from food identified as an idol offering; to **the church of God**, by not scandalizing "the weak" but also by not shutting out social contacts and friendships that present opportunities for evangelization. This is Paul's personal program, to **try to please everyone in every way** ("all things to all"; 9:22), **not seeking my own benefit but that of the many, that they may be saved.** The Apostle does not want to sacrifice his great hope of winning others to the gospel by excessive scrupulosity. Drawing all to the gospel was the program of Jesus, which Paul is following, and which he urges the Corinthians to follow as well: **Be imitators of me, as I am of Christ.** *10:31–11:1*

181

Reflection and Application (10:23–11:1)

The entire unit of chapters 8 through 10 is a masterpiece of moral and pastoral insight and persuasion. On the one hand, Paul is dealing with headstrong people who think their knowledge about the nonexistence of idols gives them a right to share in pagan sacrificial meals. On the other hand, he is dealing with the scrupulous who think that eating in a nonbeliever's house is fraught with the likelihood of idolatry. The headstrong need to be persuaded that they are engaging in idolatry, and the scrupulous need to be persuaded that they can maintain their Christian integrity and build bridges with nonbelievers by accepting invitations to nonbelievers' meals in their homes. Realizing that the headstrong are more difficult to persuade, Paul begins by appealing to their love for their Christian brothers and sisters, that is, the good of the community over personal advantage (chap. 8). This is not Paul's primary reason for avoiding idolatry; it is what he judges his readers would be most inclined to accept as a starter. They now belong to a new community, which has a prior claim on their commitments. He then appeals to his own example of self-sacrifice (chap. 9). And finally in chapter 10 he categorically tells them to flee from idolatry because of the Christian sacrificial meal, the Eucharist, which allows no †syncretism. *The whole issue has to do with the body of Christ.* I came to this realization as I puzzled over why Paul did not simply tell the headstrong at the beginning that what they were doing was idolatry, and therefore a serious sin in itself, but appealed instead to the concern they should have for their weaker brothers and sisters in the Lord, "for whom Christ died" (8:11). Paul appeals not to the first commandment but to their identity in the body of Christ. He begins the section with the ecclesial body of Christ and climaxes with the eucharistic body of Christ. Their Christian experience in the body of Christ, ecclesial and eucharistic, overrides their old habits of sociability among their pagan compatriots.

But then he corrects those whose scruples would prevent them from reaching out to unbelievers. He finds a way between the extremes to provide a common ground for the Church to stand on, living in truth and charity both for those within and those without.

We may not find ourselves in exactly the same circumstances today as the Corinthians did, but we are often faced with perplexing decisions: Should I attend the wedding of a Catholic relative getting married outside the Church? Under what conditions might I attend a non-Catholic service? Should I accept an invitation to travel that would make it impossible to attend Sunday Mass? In these and many other decisions of daily life, we need the Holy Spirit's gifts of wisdom and discernment, as well as the apostolic authority of the Church, like the directives Paul gives here.

Problems in the Community at Worship

1 Corinthians 11

At this point Paul turns to three issues regarding the church's liturgical assemblies: the proper attire for women, behavior at the Lord's Supper (chap. 11), and the use of the spiritual gifts, or †charisms (chaps. 12–14). As fresh converts, the Corinthians have a lot to learn. In the process of Paul's dealing with them, we too can learn much.

In chapter 11 Paul treats two liturgical problems. The first has to do with proper attire for women and men when gathered for worship. Although cultural norms have changed, the underlying principle of respect for the sacredness of the liturgy has not. The second problem concerns proper behavior at the Eucharist. The Corinthians regularly celebrated a love feast, or potluck supper, along with the Eucharist, where serious disorder was dishonoring the Lord's Supper and the holy nature of the assembly. Paul will recall Jesus' institution of the Eucharist and warn the Corinthians of the peril of receiving the body of the Lord unworthily.

Women's Headdress (11:2–16)

---

²I praise you because you remember me in everything and hold fast to the traditions, just as I handed them on to you.

³But I want you to know that Christ is the head of every man, and a husband the head of his wife, and God the head of Christ. ⁴Any man who prays or prophesies with his head covered brings shame upon his head.

⁵But any woman who prays or prophesies with her head unveiled brings shame upon her head, for it is one and the same thing as if she had had her head shaved. ⁶For if a woman does not have her head veiled, she may as well have her hair cut off. But if it is shameful for a woman to have her hair cut off or her head shaved, then she should wear a veil.

⁷A man, on the other hand, should not cover his head, because he is the image and glory of God, but woman is the glory of man. ⁸For man did not come from woman, but woman from man; ⁹nor was man created for woman, but woman for man; ¹⁰for this reason a woman should have a sign of authority on her head, because of the angels. ¹¹Woman is not independent of man or man of woman in the Lord. ¹²For just as woman came from man, so man is born of woman; but all things are from God.

¹³Judge for yourselves: is it proper for a woman to pray to God with her head unveiled? ¹⁴Does not nature itself teach you that if a man wears his hair long it is a disgrace to him, ¹⁵whereas if a woman has long hair it is her glory, because long hair has been given [her] for a covering? ¹⁶But if anyone is inclined to be argumentative, we do not have such a custom, nor do the churches of God.

OT: Gen 1:26–27; 2:21–23
NT: 1 Cor 4:17; 7:17; 14:33; Eph 5:23; 1 Tim 2:12–13
Catechism: proper attire for the liturgy, 1387

2   This passage has spawned an immense amount of literature in recent years, particularly because of the question it raises about Paul's view of the respective roles of men and women. Even to summarize the different positions would take more space than this commentary allows. For that reason, we will simply try to explain the text without exaggerating its value for one position or the other. The text is a unit, indeed an †inclusio, with beginning and end matching, verse 2 referring to the traditions of the churches and verse 16 to their universal customs. To begin with, Paul praises the Corinthians because they **hold fast to the traditions, just as I handed them on to you**. Not everything in the community needs correction, for Paul thanked God for the gifts bestowed on them in 1:4–7. "Traditions" can refer to the basic teachings he has passed on to them, or specific practices, like the Eucharist—probably both. He expects unity in doctrine and practice among the churches he has founded.

But now in response either to one of the questions about which they wrote to him (7:1) or about which Chloe's people told him (1:11), Paul wants to clarify the proper attire of men and women when at worship. It is possible that some of the women in the community had taken their new liberty in Christ as authorizing them to break with the social customs of the day, which expected women in public to wear veils over their hair.[1] Otherwise they could seem to be giving the same availability as prostitutes. The veil symbolized the married woman's belonging to her husband, the unmarried daughter's belonging to her father. Since the first churches met in homes and not in public venues, some women may have thought they (or at least the women hosts, who had some authority in the home) were permitted to be unveiled. In the Roman world of the first century, there was a movement of "new women," who were testing the limits of the culture by going unveiled. Although this was generally not well regarded, Paul's own teaching that after baptism "into Christ, . . . there is not male and female; for you are all one in Christ Jesus" (Gal 3:28) may have been taken as theological support by the Christian women who wanted to tout their freedom in Christ.

In response, Paul first argues from his understanding of "head": **Christ is the** **head of every man, and a husband the head of his wife, and God the head of** **Christ**. This whole complex passage (vv. 3–16) has evoked so many differing interpretations that our commentary will try to illustrate the complexity and then simply choose the interpretation we think best. The complexity begins as follows: (1) The Greek word *anēr* can mean either man (the male) or husband, and *gynē* can mean either woman or wife. In this first line the NAB takes the two words to mean husband and wife, though they could mean man and woman, which is the way the NAB translates the terms in verses 4–15. (2) The word *kephalē* can mean (a) "head" (either physical head or metaphorical head, like the head of a business); or (b) "source," as we might speak of the source or headwaters of a river (though this is a less frequent use of the term). "Head" would suggest authority or prominence (being first); "source" would suggest origin. Paul is thinking of origin in verse 8, where he recalls the formation of the woman from the man in Gen 2:21–23. But then he seems to reverse this order when he says, "Just as woman came from man, so man is born of woman" (v. 12). So we are on a better track in taking *kephalē* as "head."

But then what does the statement mean? I agree with the NAB and the commentators who understand Paul as referring to marriage and the need to preserve proper order in the assembly. In the Greco-Roman culture of the day, as mentioned above, for a woman to appear in public unveiled was to manifest the same availability as a prostitute. Another clue in the text is the word "glory," used for both the glory of God and the glory of man. Biblically speaking, when applied to God, "glory" is the outward manifestation of his magnificence, holiness, and beauty. The wife is the husband's glory, she is *his* beauty rather than

3

---

1. Paul is speaking about veiling of the head, not the face, as some Muslim women do today.

that of another, and as God will not give his glory to another (Isa 42:8), so the husband has a unique claim upon the "glory" of his wife, reflected particularly in her hair. Similarly, the Church is the glory of Christ; as the preceding section on idolatry has shown, Christ will not allow his glory, the Church, to be given to another. Thus Paul finds a scriptural rationale for the prevailing custom of women being veiled in public, and here specifically for their veiling in the assembly.

4–5   This gives the reason why **any man who prays or prophesies with his head covered brings shame upon his head**. Most scholars agree that the head that is shamed is the metaphorical head, Christ, just as any woman who prays or prophesies with her head unveiled brings shame upon her head, that is, her husband.[2] In the light of what we have said about "glory," we can see how this would fit the woman, whose "head" is her husband. As in the Old Testament, the woman is her husband's "nakedness," that is, she should be exposed only to him (Lev 18:8);[3] so also here in the culture of the day, public exposure of a woman's hair was equivalent to suggesting her availability to anyone, as a prostitute might be.

6   Thus the shame is equivalent to having her own **head** (in the physical sense now) **shaved**, which means the rejection of her own glory. To expose her hair, which belongs to her husband, is to lose the very glory she has. The sacredness of the marital bond is at issue here, and it is reinforced by the sacredness of the liturgy. The veil, then, symbolizes that the woman is one flesh with her husband. Perhaps it is not too much to say that it is the tent of intimacy in which both of them live.

7   But how is the **man** the **glory of God** by having his head uncovered? We are in the system of liturgical symbols that reflect the marital relationship depicted in Gen 2:7–25. The first man, Adam, is a †type of Christ, who is the image, the icon, of God (2 Cor 4:4). Since here the husband fulfills the liturgical role of Christ (as Paul says here in v. 3), Paul sees it as fitting to say that the husband is the image of God and the woman his "glory," as is suggested by Adam's lyrical rejoicing in Eve (Gen 2:23).

8–9   The origin of Eve from Adam sets the pattern for the relation of husband and wife: **For man did not come from woman, but woman from man; nor**

---

2. One might ask whether Paul means that his prescriptions apply only to the moment of praying or prophesying or to the entire time of the worship service. Given the culture of the day, it is most likely that he is thinking of the entire service, mentioning the activity of praying or prophesying because the attention of the congregation would be drawn to the person so doing.

3. In Lev 18:8, the NAB translates "uncover the nakedness" as "have intercourse," the NIV as "have sexual relations," but the RSV and NRSV maintain the literalness of the Hebrew.

was man created for woman, but woman for man. In the Genesis account Adam was created from the clay of the ground and Eve from Adam's side, which means that God created Eve through the material instrumentality of Adam. The purpose of the account was not to teach the superiority of man to woman (Adam, after all, was from dirt, and Eve from Adam's side), but to show woman's superiority to the animals, her equality in dignity to man, their complementarity, and their attraction to each other. But Paul also knows that after the creation of the first couple, man now is born of woman, as he says in verse 12, and he qualifies what he says about "woman for man" in verse 11 by teaching their interdependence.

What does it mean that **a woman should have a sign of authority on her** 10 **head, because of the angels**? This is an obscure and notoriously difficult passage to interpret, and scholars have proposed dozens of explanations, which space does not allow us to detail. We should first note that the text says, literally in the Greek: "A woman should have *exousia* on her head." The RSV translates this as "veil," on the assumption that it is a mistranslation of an Aramaic word for veil. But most translations, like the NAB, have "authority," which is the clear meaning of *exousia*. Some take this as meaning *submission* to the authority of her husband. However, nowhere in Greek does the word have that passive meaning. It always means authority to do something. In the context it could mean authorization to pray and prophesy. In our interpretation this would mean that the veil protects the marital priority, without which she would be out of order to pray or prophesy. Unveiled, she would attract men's attention to herself rather than to the word of the Lord that she is speaking; consequently, unveiled, she has no authority to pray or prophesy. Veiled, she respects the conventional order, which indicates her belonging to her husband, and this gives her authority to use her word gifts in ministry. This seems to be confirmed by the equally obscure mention of the "angels." The best explanation appears to be that the angels were understood to be present during the worship of the community (as was the case with the Qumran community: "the angels of holiness are [with] their [congregation]")[4] and would be offended by disorder. Since prophecy was considered to be an inspired revelation, it was an earthly manifestation of an angelic function. Since the earthly liturgy is a participation in the heavenly liturgy, where all is harmony and order (see the book of Revelation throughout), the angels would be offended by disorder in the earthly liturgy.

But lest this be understood as a one-way street, giving the man, or husband, 11–12 complete autonomy, Paul hastens to add that **in the Lord**, that is, in the Christian

---

4. See 1QSa (*Rule of the Congregation*) 2.8–9; see also 1QM (*War Scroll*) 7.5–6.

BIBLICAL
BACKGROUND

Men's Effeminate Dress

A comment by the Greek philosopher Epictetus reflects what Paul's contemporary world thought about the "natural order of things." Confronting a young man with hair styled like a woman's, Epictetus tells him to live "rationally. And what is rationally? In accordance with nature and perfectly. . . . Adorn as a man, not a woman."[a]

a. Epictetus, *Discourses* 3.1.25–27; see also Philo, *Special Laws* 3.7.37–38.

economy of things, **woman is not independent of man or man of woman**. Instead of insisting that they are free of each other by reason of their newfound faith (see Gal 3:28), he speaks of their connectedness. They are brought into a new realm of interdependence by their union in the Lord. This caveat indicates that Paul is aware of the tension between the traditional restraint on women's behavior and the new equality of all in Christ, and thus he wishes to balance the previous comment about the husband's headship with the positive one of the new creation in Christ. Paul seems to feel a bit of discomfort with the tension, which reappears in his treating of marriage in Ephesians, where he speaks of the woman's submission to her husband (5:22), but puts this under the umbrella of mutual submission (5:21). In the Adam and Eve story, though woman came from man, it is obvious in the present order of creation that **man is born of woman**, and that is the way it has been since the birth of Eve's first child. This caveat indicates that Paul is aware that the man's being "head" in the sense of origin can deteriorate into domination, which was not God's plan but results from the fall (Gen 3:16). Neither man nor woman must forget that they are not the ultimate source: **All things are from God**.

13–14   Paul trusts that his listeners will be sufficiently swayed by his scriptural arguments that they can **judge for** themselves. But in case they cannot, he appeals to the cultural norms of the day. **Nature** here does not mean the physical law of hair growth. It means rather what the society of Paul's day—and we might add, the culture of most people in the world—considered to be the natural order of things.

15   The woman's **long hair** is **her glory** (see v. 7), but it is also her **covering**, since a woman with no hair would find baldness to be a source of shame (see v. 5).

16   Finally, as if all the above arguments might fall on deaf ears, Paul finally comes down on the side of the **custom** of his other churches (**we**) and the **churches**

of God, that is, the early communities in Judea (1 Thess 2:14). Just as in the matter of idol offerings Paul appealed to the Corinthians' sense of solidarity with other members of the community, so here he concludes by calling them to solidarity with the other Christian communities, an early indication that the local church is not autonomous but is part of a much larger community called Church, which has its own universal norms.

Easily overlooked in this passage is the importance of the very fact that women publicly prayed and prophesied in the Pauline communities. The exercise of prophecy was itself one of the ways the Christian community distinguished itself from the synagogue, where there was praying, reading, and teaching but not prophecy, which most Jews of the time held was no longer given in the present †age but would belong to the age to come.[5] With the resurrection of Jesus and the gift of the Holy Spirit, Christians believed the age to come had already begun and the prophecy of Joel had been fulfilled, that "your sons and daughters, . . . your male and female servants" would prophesy (Joel 3:1–2). This gave women a new role not allowed in the synagogue, where public discourse was reserved to men. All that is taken for granted here, where the focus is the proper attire in doing it. But Paul's instruction is very clear. Liturgical action never justifies bypassing the marital relationship, which is a symbol of Christ's relationship with his bride, the Church.

Reflection and Application (11:2–16)

It is obvious that cultural norms have changed considerably since Paul called for women to be veiled at the liturgy. Though some women may still choose to wear veils at Mass (as is sometimes done by Hispanic women as part of their culture), and some women religious wear them as part of their habit, no one today would think that the absence of a veil means sexual availability, as it did in Paul's day.[6] This raises the important distinction between doctrine and discipline. The dogmatic and moral teaching of the Church does not change, but the discipline of the Church has changed with different times and social circumstances. Fasting during Lent used to be required on all the Lenten weekdays,

---

5. *Tosefta Pesahim* 2.15; *Jerusalem Talmud Shevi'it* 90.1, 1.4; *Leviticus Rabbah* 21.8. This evidence is later than the first century but may reflect earlier tradition.

6. One of my young women students, of Hispanic background, was touched by this passage in Paul and wrote: "Women who wear veils can use them to show the Lord, in a special way, that His glory is greater than theirs. They cover their hair, often a source of beauty and pride for women (their glory, 1 Cor 11:15), before the Source of All Beauty." This particular student did not wear a veil at Mass, probably because of the reverse of the Corinth culture: to do so would have unduly attracted attention to herself!

but the requirement now applies only on Ash Wednesday and Good Friday. The injunctions regarding kosher meat in Acts 15:20 were formulated to facilitate the unity of Jew and Gentile in the early Church, but those circumstances no longer hold, and it is not even certain that they were universally applied in Paul's day. The Council of Florence in 1442 explicitly declared that the injunctions on kosher meat were no longer binding. In a similar way, the Church today has regarded Paul's discipline about the veiling of women to be precisely that: a disciplinary measure that was needed in view of the cultural norms of the time. Paul himself says as much when he ends by saying, "We do not have such a custom" (11:16).

So is there nothing to be gained from this passage for today? It invites reflection on the deeper principle of proper dress and behavior when the Christian community gathers for worship. The meaning of certain gestures differs from culture to culture. North Americans would consider someone deliberately coming to Sunday Mass barefoot to be disrespectful of the sacredness of the event. But in Nepal wearing shoes at the liturgy was considered to be a sign of either ignorance of the culture or disrespect. Though cultures differ, the principle of propriety at worship is the same. Men and women both need to attend to this. "Is That a Naked Woman in That Pew?" ran the headline in the Archdiocesan Catholic Newspaper of San Antonio. The editor, Martha Brinkman, had asked herself that question at a recent Mass when she saw a woman in a pew ahead of her. All that Martha could see was a bare back and bare legs, the rest being blocked by the pew. Although a homeless man should never feel unwanted because of his poor attire, and a late-morning Mass in some places like my hometown is offered to hunters welcomed from their early morning hunt, common sense and respect should rule in normal situations.

Abuse of the Eucharist (11:17–22)

> [17]In giving this instruction, I do not praise the fact that your meetings are doing more harm than good. [18]First of all, I hear that when you meet as a church there are divisions among you, and to a degree I believe it; [19]there have to be factions among you in order that [also] those who are approved among you may become known. [20]When you meet in one place, then, it is not to eat the Lord's supper, [21]for in eating, each one goes ahead with his own supper, and one goes hungry while another gets drunk. [22]Do you not have houses in which you can eat and drink? Or do you show contempt for the church of God and make those who have nothing feel

**ashamed? What can I say to you? Shall I praise you? In this matter I do
not praise you.**

OT: Deut 13:3
NT: 1 Cor 1:10; James 2:6; 2 Pet 2:1; 1 John 2:19
Catechism: right dispositions for communion, 1355

Although at the beginning of this chapter, Paul praised the Corinthians for   **17**
holding fast to the traditions he had given them (11:2), there are some areas
of conduct that call for censure. **This instruction** evidently refers not to the
preceding but to what follows. The divisions over personalities cited by those
of Chloe's household are now overshadowed by the divisions in the very celebration of the sacrament of unity. The Corinthians seem to have no concept
of the real nature of this meal.

When they **meet as a church**, as the *ekklēsia*, the assembly of the called,   **18–19**
there are divisions among you. This is what **I hear,** Paul says, **and to a
degree I believe it.** He mitigates his judgment, as if the real situation could
not be as bad as reported. When he says, **There have to be factions among
you**, what kind of necessity is he talking about? Certainly factions are not
the direct will of God; otherwise Paul would not have so vigorously scolded
the Corinthians for their divisions in chapters 1–3. It seems rather that he
means a certain inevitability of the kind Jesus described in his parables about
the sower (Mark 4:1–20 and parallels), where not everyone responds well to
the word, and the parable of weeds among the wheat (Matt 13:24–30). He
knows that God can bring good out of evil (Rom 8:28), including **that [also]
those who are approved among you may become known** and vindicated.
One of the effects of scandals in the Church is to make the good and faithful
members surface more clearly. This assumes that there is condemnation and,
where possible, repairing of the scandal, at least by the Church authorities,
as Paul did here.

The early Christians met in homes, like that of Gaius (Rom 16:23), **to eat**   **20**
the Lord's supper. From the context it is evident that part of the celebration
was a meal (held either before, during, or after the Eucharist: †paschal meal),
later called an †*agapē* meal, or "love feast." It was a kind of potluck supper that
was meant to symbolize and effect a solidarity in the community joined at a
common table and in so doing to care for the poor in the community. But the
opposite was taking place: the meal had the appearance not of a banquet but of
a series of picnicking circles or individual dinner groups as in today's restau-
rants or cafeterias, separated, however, not by convenience but by class. This
practice, whereby individuals would bring their own food to eat at a common

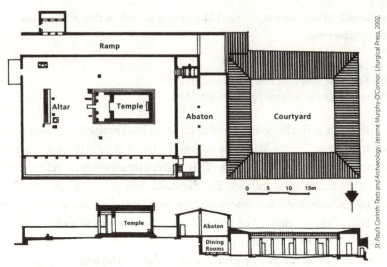

Fig. 12. Layout of the Asclepion Temple in Corinth. Note the dining rooms.

meal, was well known in the Greek world. But that is exactly what Paul finds unconscionable in the eucharistic assembly.

21   **Each one goes ahead with his own supper** can mean either that the first arrivals consumed the available food without waiting for the others to arrive, or that each had brought their own food, and those with more did not share with those with less or nothing. In any case, there is a shocking disparity between those who gorged themselves unto drunkenness and the poor, who were left to go **hungry**. This could not be called the Lord's Supper, the Eucharist.

22   If you are going to eat your own supper, do it in your private homes, Paul says. Their present practice fails on two counts: First, **you show contempt for the church of God**. "For," as Chrysostom comments, "it was made a church [*ekklēsia*, "assembly"], not that we who come together might be divided, but that they who are divided might be joined; and this the act of assembling shows."[7] And this is not just any assembly; the church is a temple sacred to the Lord (3:16–17). Second, you **make those who have nothing feel ashamed**. It is astounding that a community so divided could stay together at all. Jerome Murphy-O'Connor suggests that only the home of a wealthy person would be large enough to accommodate the growing community. In such a home the host may have reserved the *triclinium*, the dining room, for his wealthier guests, who had the leisure to arrive early and where they could "recline" (8:10), while leaving the larger *atrium* as second-class accommodations for the poor, laborers arriving from their work who would have to sit (see 14:30). He also cites

7. Saint Chrysostom, *Homilies on 1 Corinthians* 27.4.

several texts showing that in the Greco-Roman world the social class to which one belonged often determined the quality of food one might receive at the same meal.[8] It is likely that because of abuses such as these, the Eucharist was eventually separated from the *agapē* meal, though in today's parishes food is often served after Mass, and a festive dinner may follow the Eucharist in more solemn celebrations.

Reflection and Application (11:17–22)

The celebration of the Eucharist is a communion with the body of Christ, not only in the host and the cup, but also in his members gathered at the particular assembly. Thus we do not approach the table of the Lord without first exchanging the greeting of peace. A Benedictine monastery has a stained-glass window of two monks embracing each other, with the inscription in Latin, "Do not give false peace." It may be easy to give peace to the person next to us, but the kiss of peace means reconciliation, or at least a willingness and a desire to be reconciled with everyone before we approach the altar. "Therefore, if you bring your gift to the altar, and there recall that your brother has anything against you, leave your gift there at the altar, go first and be reconciled with your brother, and then come and offer your gift" (Matt 5:23–24).

This sign of peace means not only that we surrender our resentments and forgive but also that we reach out to those on the fringes of the assembly—the poor, the shabby, the smelly, the lonely. In a big parish it may not be easy to spot such persons unless we are close to them. Do we follow our natural tendency to avoid them, to associate only with our kind? If we come to the Eucharist only to be fed, that is what we will do. But if we come also to feed, we will reach out to those who are hungry for love—and this may be done after the Eucharist.

The Tradition of the Eucharist (11:23–26)

[23]For I received from the Lord what I also handed on to you, that the Lord Jesus, on the night he was handed over, took bread, [24]and, after he had given thanks, broke it and said, "This is my body that is for you. Do this in remembrance of me." [25]In the same way also the cup, after supper, saying, "This cup is the new covenant in my blood. Do this, as often as you

8. Jerome Murphy-O'Connor, *St. Paul's Corinth* (Wilmington, DE: Michael Glazier, 2002), 159–61.

Tradition and Traditions

Tradition and traditions is a common theme running through Paul's Letters and frequent in this Letter to the Corinthians. He is concerned to ensure that the traditions received and held in other Christian assemblies be followed in Corinth too (11:2, 16; 14:36). The term "traditions" is a common one in ancient rabbinic usage (see Gal 1:14). In Paul's writings it stresses that the content of the teaching or practice is not the whim of his personal fancy (1 Cor 11:2)—even though the Apostle himself could legislate with full authority when the need arose—but a sacred deposit (1 Tim 6:20) received from the Lord (1 Cor 11:23) or the first apostles (1 Cor 15:3), to which Paul himself felt bound (Gal 2:2). Such traditions were received and transmitted in their integrity, and—surprisingly, for Paul is the apostle of liberty—they had the force of law. These "traditions" were universal Christian customs (1 Cor 11:2–3; 14:34) or liturgical rites, such as the Eucharist (1 Cor 11:23–25), or dogmatic or moral teachings (Rom 6:17; 1 Cor 7:10, 12, 25; 9:14; 15:3–4; 2 Thess 3:6).

---

drink it, in remembrance of me." ²⁶For as often as you eat this bread and drink the cup, you proclaim the death of the Lord until he comes.

OT: Exod 12:14; 24:8; Deut 16:3; Jer 31:31–34

NT: Matt 26:26–29; Mark 14:22–25; Luke 22:14–20; Heb 8:6–13

Catechism: the institution narrative, 1353; pledge of glory to come, 1402–5

Lectionary: Holy Thursday; The Body and Blood of Christ; Mass for Institution of Acolytes; Mass for Viaticum; Mass for Blessing of Chalice and Paten; Mass for Priests; Mass of the Most Holy Eucharist

23   The **for** introducing this section ties the institution of the Eucharist (†paschal meal) tightly to the preceding. The disorders that Paul has lamented in the community are all the more grave because the Eucharist, memorial of Christ's death, is something the Lord himself has established. It was not a creation of Paul or of the Palestinian Christians. **I received from the Lord** at first sight seems to say that Paul received it in a personal revelation from the risen Jesus. Three considerations, however, make this highly improbable: (1) The Greek verbs for "I received" and **I also handed on** are the normal terms used for the process of receiving and handing on a tradition in a human way; they correspond exactly to the rabbinical terms *qibbel* and *masar* for this process. When Paul wishes to speak of revelation, he uses nouns like "revelation" or "†mystery" (1 Cor 15:51) or the verb "appear" (Rom 16:26; 1 Cor 4:5). (2) One might ask when this revelation could have taken place. Three days after his conversion,

Chrysostom on Jesus' Betrayal

For even if one be a very stone, yet when he considers that night, how he was with his disciples, "very sorrowful," how he was betrayed, how he was bound, how he was led away, how he was judged, how he suffered all the rest; one becomes softer than wax and is withdrawn from earth and all the pomp of this world. Therefore Paul leads us to recall all those things, . . . putting us to shame and saying, Your Master gave even his own self for you; and you do not even share a little food with your brother.[a]

a. Saint Chrysostom, *Homilies on 1 Corinthians* 27.5.

according to Acts, Paul was in full contact with the community at Damascus; he was instructed and even began preaching the new faith in the synagogue. It is hardly conceivable that he would not have been instructed about the breaking of the bread. (3) The Greek preposition *apo* ("from") in "from the Lord" does not necessarily imply direct communication, as would the preposition *para*, which Paul omits, contrary to his custom with the verb *paralambanō* ("receive") used here. The sense then is "I received as a tradition going back to the Lord himself."

What follows is the first historical witness to the institution of the Eucharist, predating the Gospel of Mark by at least five to ten years. But Paul already affirms that it is well-anchored tradition even in the details, the first of which is that it was instituted on the night on which Jesus **was handed over**, which should alert the Corinthians to the gravity of the occasion they are commemorating. See Chrysostom's comment in the sidebar. The translation "handed over" instead of "betrayed" has the advantage of ambiguity about it, since Jesus was "handed over" not only by Judas (Mark 14:10, 42, 44) but also by the chief priests (to Pilate; Mark 15:1), and by Pilate (to crucifixion; Mark 15:15). It can also refer to God's handing over Jesus for the salvation of the world (Rom 8:32).

24–25

Paul's version of the words of institution are more than Mark's and Matthew's, which lack **that is for you**, and less than Luke's (in 22:19), which has "given for you." **This cup is the new covenant in my blood** echoes "This is the blood of the covenant" in Exod 24:8. The parallelism with the sacrifice's sealing the old covenant demands taking "that is for you" as an affirmation of the sacrificial nature of this body, which brings salvation. The separate consecration of the bread and the wine signifies the separation of the blood from the body of Christ in death (though in reality the whole Christ is present under both species: bread and wine). The death of Christ is treated as a

sacrifice in the Synoptics (Matt 20:28; Mark 10:45) and repeatedly in St. Paul.[9]
Here, then, the body of Christ is identified with the body immolated on the
cross (so likewise John 6:51).

The words **Do this . . . in remembrance of me** do not appear in Mark
or Matthew and only once in Luke (22:19), whereas Paul has them twice
(vv. 24–25). The oral tradition fluctuated slightly, but not the basic narrative
of the event. With the Corinthians, Paul wants to insist that the continuation
of Jesus' sacrificial meal was intended by the Lord, just as the Passover of the
Jews was celebrated regularly to recall the great saving events (Exod 12; 13:9).
Paul seems to have written this letter around the time of the Jewish Passover,
in the spring of AD 57 (see 1 Cor 5:7). The book of Deuteronomy speaks of
the Passover meal as an important remembrance: "that you may remember
as long as you live the day you left the land of Egypt" (Deut 16:3, 6; see also
Exod 12:14, 17; 13:3). The Jews thought very realistically of their memorial as
a representation of the mystery of their deliverance from Egypt. As Deut 16:6
says to the later generations, the exodus was "the very time you left Egypt."
The Jewish Passover in remembrance of the day *you* came forth from Egypt
(see Deut 16:1–3) has now become the Christian Passover **in remembrance
of me**, the Lord Jesus Christ. The same idea of representation of the mystery
carries over into the celebration of the Eucharist, and the Church sees in the
invocation of the Holy Spirit upon the bread and wine (called the *epiklēsis*) the
divine power enabling the elements to be transformed into the body and blood
of Christ, thus making really present the mystery of the Christian exodus, the
death and resurrection of Christ.[10]

Jesus' words over the cup evoke two important passages from the Old Testament. As Jesus spoke of the **blood** of the **covenant**, the disciples would remember the blood by which the covenant of the Lord with his people was sealed
(Exod 24:5–8):

> Then, having sent young men of the Israelites to offer burnt offerings to the LORD,
> Moses took half of the blood and put it in large bowls; the other half he splashed
> on the altar. Taking the book of the covenant, he read it aloud to the people, who
> answered, "All that the LORD has said, we will hear and do." Then he took the

9. Rom 3:24–25; 5:6–8; 8:32; 14:15; 1 Cor 1:13; 15:3; Gal 2:20; 3:13; Eph 5:25; 1 Thess 5:10;
Titus 2:14.
10. Saint John Damascene comments: "You ask how the bread becomes the Body of Christ, and the
wine . . . the Blood of Christ. I shall tell you: the Holy Spirit comes upon them and accomplishes what
surpasses every word and thought. . . . Let it be enough for you to understand that it is by the Holy
Spirit, just as it was of the Holy Virgin and by the Holy Spirit that the Lord, through and in himself,
took flesh" (*De fide orthodoxa* 4.13; in PG 94:1145A; quoted in the Catechism, 1106).

blood and splashed it on the people, saying, "This is the blood of the covenant which the LORD has made with you according to all these words."

The covenant was sealed by the blood of animals. But Jesus spoke of the shedding of his own blood, and it would seal a **new** covenant. "New covenant" is a phrase found in only one place in the Old Testament, Jer 31:31–33:

> See, days are coming—oracle of the LORD—when I will make a new covenant with the house of Israel and the house of Judah. It will not be like the covenant I made with their ancestors the day I took them by the hand to lead them out of the land of Egypt. They broke my covenant though I was their master—oracle of the LORD. But this is the covenant I will make with the house of Israel after those days—oracle of the LORD. I will place my law within them, and write it upon their hearts; I will be their God, and they shall be my people.

Jeremiah does not say how that New Covenant would be ratified, but Jesus does. Like the Old Covenant, the new one will be sealed with blood, his blood. And it will not be sprinkled on the people but given to them to drink, as his body will be given to them to eat. He will be a sacrificial meal, which the New Covenant people will consume.

The Greek word for "covenant" is *diathēkē*, which has the added meaning of "testament," and in this sense the New Covenant has, by the death of the Testator, taken on an unbreakable character (Gal 3:15–16; Heb 9:16). Hence it is impossible to change the nature of the Lord's Supper or caricature it as the Corinthians are doing. Paul certainly hopes his recalling of the institution of the Eucharist will awaken in the community the sense of solidarity with others, especially with the poor, to which this sacrificial meal calls them.

The Eucharist is not merely the presence of the body and blood of the Lord; **26** it is also the solemn representation of his death. Elsewhere in the New Testament, the verb **proclaim** means to make a solemn and public proclamation of some new order of things now in effect.[11] It is by both word and action that the Eucharist proclaims **the death of the Lord until he comes**. In this short phrase, sung or recited in the Roman Catholic Mass immediately after the consecration, Paul sums up three great mysteries: the death of Christ, which is past; the presence of the risen Christ ("Lord" here refers to the risen Lord, as in Rom 10:9); and the future coming of Christ. According to Joachim Jeremias, the early Jewish Christians, carrying over a Jewish belief and hope that the Messiah would come at Passover, continued to celebrate the feast with the

11. See 1 Cor 9:14; also Acts 3:24; 4:2; 13:5; 15:36; 16:21.

hope that Jesus the Messiah would return as they celebrated it. They would read and pray into the night, and then, if Jesus had not shown up by 3:00 a.m., they would celebrate the Eucharist.[12] The meaning of this is profound: the Eucharist is the best thing the Church can do until Jesus returns. While waiting to see him face-to-face, the Church celebrates his real but hidden presence in the sacrament.

Consequences and Remedies (11:27–34)

[27]Therefore whoever eats the bread or drinks the cup of the Lord unworthily will have to answer for the body and blood of the Lord. [28]A person should examine himself, and so eat the bread and drink the cup.

[29]For anyone who eats and drinks without discerning the body, eats and drinks judgment on himself. [30]That is why many among you are ill and infirm, and a considerable number are dying. [31]If we discerned ourselves, we would not be under judgment; [32]but since we are judged by [the] Lord, we are being disciplined so that we may not be condemned along with the world.

[33]Therefore, my brothers, when you come together to eat, wait for one another. [34]If anyone is hungry, he should eat at home, so that your meetings may not result in judgment. The other matters I shall set in order when I come.

OT: Prov 3:11–12
NT: Acts 5:9; Heb 6:6; 12:5–13; 1 Pet 4:17; Rev 3:19
Catechism: unworthy communion, 1385, 1457

27 The consequences of abuse of the eucharistic meal are dire. **Whoever eats the bread or drinks the cup of the Lord unworthily will have to answer for the body and blood of the Lord.** "Unworthily" could mean any state of serious unrepented or unconfessed sin, but here it refers to the disorder and selfishness shown in the context of the Eucharist itself, a sacrilegious disrespect for the sacrament, sinning against "the body and blood of the Lord." The NAB translates the Greek word *enochos* as "answer for" ("answerable for" NRSV, NJB), the NIV the milder "guilty of sinning against." The former is more exact, because the idea of divine judgment is clearer. Sacrilege invites divine judgment, as Paul indicates is already happening in the community (11:29–30). The body is also the body of Christ that is the Church, and thus to receive the sacrament in the

12. Joachim Jeremias, *The Eucharistic Words of Jesus* (Philadelphia: Fortress, 1966), 123.

LIVING TRADITION

Chrysostom on "Unworthily"

Saint John Chrysostom uses this text to exhort his faithful to works of mercy. Speaking of the unworthiness of the one who chronically disregards the needs of the poor yet comes to receive communion, he says: "How can it be other than unworthily when it is he who neglects the hungry? Who besides overlooking him puts him to shame? For if failing to give to the poor casts one out of the kingdom, . . . consider how great the evil will prove, to have done so many sacrileges? . . . You have partaken of such a Table, and when you should be kinder than any and like the angels, you have become more cruel than any. You have tasted the blood of the Lord, and not even at that moment do you acknowledge your brother. Of what forgiveness then are you worthy? For even if before this you had not known him, you should have come to know him from the Table; for he has been deemed worthy to partake of it—and you do not even judge him worthy of your food!"[a]

a. Saint Chrysostom, *Homilies on 1 Corinthians* 27.6.

state of disharmony with the community, as some are doing, is sacrilegious (see Reflection and Application below).

Some commentators go further in specifying what the guilt is. To be "guilty of the blood" of someone is a biblical expression for being responsible for another's death (Gen 4:10; Deut 21:7; Matt 27:24–25). David Garland comments:

> The Lord's Supper proclaims the Lord's death. Those whose behavior at the Lord's Supper does not conform to what that death entails effectively shift sides. They leave the Lord's side and align themselves with the rulers of this present †age who crucified the Lord (1 Cor 2:8; cf. Heb 6:5). This explains how they make themselves so vulnerable to God's judgment.[13]

In this view the text provides the basis for saying that sins are the cause of the death of Christ, even if the sins have been committed after the historical time of his death. This is more explicit in Heb 6:4–6, which discusses the apostasy of those who have "once . . . tasted the heavenly gift": "they are recrucifying the Son of God for themselves and holding him up to contempt."

A person should examine himself to see if he is in the state of sin, particu-   28
larly whether there is a block to charity in his heart. Implicit here is, of course, that repentance comes as a result of the examination.

13. David E. Garland, *1 Corinthians*, BECNT (Grand Rapids: Baker Academic, 2003), 550.

29   **For anyone who eats and drinks without discerning the body, eats and
drinks judgment on himself**. Again "body" here has the twofold sense of
the eucharistic body, which is the body of the risen Lord Jesus present in the
sacrament, and also the body of the church, the community gathered for the
Lord's Supper, for it too is the body of Christ (12:27). The two are inseparable:
"Because the loaf of bread is one, we, though many, are one body, for we all
partake of the one loaf" (10:17). To "discern" is literally to "judge through,"
to perceive and assess the true nature of the body in both senses. One who
receives unworthily brings judgment on himself. Chrysostom comments: "Not
discerning the body, that is, not searching, not bearing in mind, as he ought,
the greatness of the things set before him, not estimating the weight of the
gift. For if you should come to know accurately who it is who lies before you
and who he is who gives himself, and to whom, you would need no other argument, but this is enough for you to use all vigilance, otherwise you would
be altogether lost."[14]

30   "Judgment" does not exclude the final judgment, but the focus here is on
the judgment being felt in the community here and now. **That is why many
among you are ill and infirm, and a considerable number are dying**. The
bread of life and the cup of salvation have become the bread of death and the
potion of destruction. Paul, who earlier recalled the deaths of the Israelite
idolaters who ate the manna in the desert (10:3–10), does not hesitate to at-
tribute the illnesses and deaths in the community to unworthy reception of
the Eucharist! Chrysostom anticipates an objection here that there may be
people who are sinning but are not receiving these punishments. " 'How is
it that they do not suffer punishment?' you ask. Because there [in hell] they
shall suffer a severer one. But we, if we would [discern the body], neither
here nor there need suffer it."[15] On the positive side, in the history of the
Church's saints and mystics, there are those who have sustained themselves
on the Eucharist alone.

31   **If we discerned ourselves, we would not be under judgment**. Or: "If we
judged ourselves, we would not be judged" (NRSV). The second part of the
sentence is a Jewish way of saying, "God would not judge us." Repentance and
reform in this present life can erase God's judgment both in this life and in the
next. But when we experience the evil fruits of our sin—as the Corinthians are
in illness and death—this is not God's vindictive judgment but actually an act
of his mercy, urging us to repentance and conversion.

14. Saint Chrysostom, *Homilies on 1 Corinthians* 28.2.
15. Saint Chrysostom, *Homilies on 1 Corinthians* 28.2.

The Eucharist and Health

LIVING TRADITION

The Catechism (1509) comments: "'Heal the sick!' (Matt 10:8). The Church has received this charge from the Lord and strives to carry it out by taking care of the sick as well as by accompanying them with her prayer of intercession. She believes in the life-giving presence of Christ, the physician of souls and bodies. This presence is particularly active through the sacraments, and in an altogether special way through the Eucharist, the bread that gives eternal life and that St. Paul suggests is connected with bodily health (cf. John 6:54, 58; 1 Cor 11:30)."

But since we are judged by [the] Lord, we are being disciplined so that   **32** **we may not be condemned along with the world**. God's judgment upon us when we are in sin is his discipline, as one would discipline one's child out of love (Heb 12:5–11). When our evil choices bear rotten fruit, this is God's way of signaling us that something is wrong. It is like the hunger the prodigal son began to feel when he ran out of money and food; he began to come to his senses (Luke 15:17).

Wordplay appears in the Greek of this whole section, which cannot be rendered in English. The words "discerning," "judgment," "discerned," "judged," "condemned"—all are related to the root verb *krinō*, "judge," which makes a strong †rhetorical effect.

Providing an †inclusio with verse 17 and thus tying the whole section of   **33** verses 17–34 together, Paul concludes: **Therefore, my brothers, when you come together to eat, wait for one another**. In the light of what has gone before, more is clearly at issue than mere "waiting." Even if they should wait to consume their own food, this would still not be the Lord's Supper (v. 20). At a dinner the Greek word behind "wait for" means "welcome, show hospitality to one another."[16] The idea is that all food should be shared. If one who arrives early cannot delay his gratification, "he should eat at home" (v. 34).

Otherwise **your meetings may ... result in judgment**, in the sense men-   **34** tioned above in verses 29–32. We do not know, and probably the Corinthians did not either, what Paul meant by **the other matters** he said he would **set in order** when he came. Perhaps they referred to the Eucharist, perhaps to matters they had asked about, perhaps to matters Paul would only learn about upon his arrival.

---

16. See references in Garland, *1 Corinthians*, 554.

Reflection and Application (11:27–34)

In the Byzantine tradition, before distributing Communion the priest holds up the elements and says: "Holy things for holy people." The Roman Catholic liturgy calls for the exchange of the kiss of peace before receiving the Eucharist. It is a sign of reconciliation and welcome to the ecclesial body of Christ before receiving his sacramental body. This goes back at least to the time of St. Justin in the mid-second century: "Having ended the prayers, we greet one another with a kiss" (*First Apology* 65). If fraternal peace is a condition for receiving the Eucharist, however, approaching the table with unrepented sin adds sin to sin. And sin has its consequences. It may not be physical illness or death, as Paul says is the case with the Corinthians, but the Eucharist cannot be the life-giving bread that Jesus meant it to be; instead, it deals spiritual death. But that need not be the case. Repentance, confession of sin, the will to reconcile and to embrace the needy—these are the threads of the red carpet that we roll out to welcome the eucharistic Lord. Though it is wrong to receive Communion without confession and absolution of serious sins, Communion does have the effect of cleansing from venial sin. Indeed, in the Byzantine liturgy, Communion is given with the words, "The servant of God, [*name*], partakes of the precious, most holy, and most pure body and blood of our Lord, God, and Savior Jesus Christ for the remission of sins and for life everlasting."

One might wonder whether Paul's judgment on the physical and even fatal effects of the Corinthians' unworthy Communions would apply to our Christian lives today. Although we cannot generalize with certainty from this one case, there certainly is a warning here to make sure we are rid of serious sin before receiving the Eucharist. The sin that Paul discusses here was the breakdown in love among the Corinthians, their disregard for the poorer members among them, and their unwillingness to share at a meal that was meant to be a love feast. The moment of the greeting of peace is an appropriate time to examine ourselves to see if there is any unforgiveness in our heart, anyone excluded from our love, any buried resentment that we have not dealt with. If we are aware of any serious unrepented sin, we should not approach the altar until we have repented and confessed. If we do receive unworthily, then we should not be surprised if we fall victim to maladies such as Paul describes.

Many Gifts, One Body

1 Corinthians 12

At the beginning of this letter, Paul gave thanks for how richly the Corinthians have been endowed with spiritual gifts, especially "with all discourse and all knowledge" (1:5), adding that in fact they do not lack "any spiritual gift" (1:6). As the letter progressed, though, it was evident that they lack much in maturity and even in awareness of their new identity as Christians. The Corinthians' divisiveness and insensitivity to the common good of the community is compromising their effective use of the gifts. Hence Paul now returns to the spiritual gifts—"the spirituals" (*pneumatika*), as he calls them here—first to clarify the source and purpose of these charismatic gifts in chapter 12 and then in chapter 14 to give practical directions on how to use them. In the center of this section Paul places his classic Magna Carta on love (chap. 13).

For a long time, understanding and interest in these gifts waned in the Church; but in recent years, particularly since Vatican Council II, the emergence and flourishing of the charismatic renewal and other renewal movements and a revitalization of the mission of the laity have led to a great resurgence of interest in this treasure of the Church's heritage. Paul insists that every Christian is endowed with one or more of these gifts of the Holy Spirit for the building up of the Church, and he urges the Corinthians to seek the gifts and exercise them, but in a way that is orderly and effective.

The Spirit and Jesus (12:1–3)

¹Now in regard to spiritual gifts, brothers, I do not want you to be unaware. ²You know how, when you were pagans, you were constantly

attracted and led away to mute idols. ³Therefore, I tell you that nobody speaking by the spirit of God says, "Jesus be accursed." And no one can say, "Jesus is Lord," except by the holy Spirit.

OT: Num 11:25–29; 1 Sam 10:5–6; Pss 115:4–5; 135:15–17; Joel 3:1–2; Mic 3:8
NT: Luke 1:67; Acts 2:17–18; 19:6; Rom 10:9; Rev 19:10
Catechism: discerning revelations, 67; discerning †charisms, 801

1   Paul is obviously beginning a new topic here, probably referring to a question the Corinthians wrote to him about. The word translated in the NAB as **spiritual gifts** (*pneumatikōn*) can also mean "spiritual persons," and some scholars have translated it that way, holding that Paul is referring to those he mentioned earlier in the letter who can judge spiritually (2:15), unlike the immature who cannot (3:1). However, the context of the entirety chapter 12 favors the translation of the majority of scholars as "spiritual gifts" (JB, NAB, NIV) or "gifts of the Spirit" (NJB). Further, in 14:1 the Greek form is not personal but neuter plural, clearly referring to the gifts, so that *pneumatika* ("spirituals") is virtually identical with *charismata* ("charisms") in 12:4. The term *pneumatika* emphasizes the source of the gifts in the Holy Spirit; *charismata* focuses more on the gifts themselves.

2   Paul's Gentile converts are fresh from their pagan worship of idols, to which they were **constantly attracted and led away**. This is the NAB's handling of a difficult redundancy in the Greek: literally, "You were [repeatedly] led, led away." The latter verb suggests more than attraction. It is sometimes used for prisoners being dragged away to execution. The Greek oracles—priestesses of ancient Greece through whom a deity was believed to speak, like the prophets of Baal in 1 Kings 18:26–29—often worked themselves into a frenzy, where their loss of rational control was taken as evidence that they were possessed by a god or a daimon. This "supernatural" behavior was a magnet to the common people's appetite for the marvelous. But it was really being out of control, and Paul calls it capitulating to an evil, enslaving force, from which they have now been set free. The idols, of course, could not speak—they were **mute**, a point of mockery for the psalmists and prophets: "They have mouths but do not speak" (Pss 115:5; 135:15–18; see Isa 46:6–7). Elijah taunts the prophets who call upon Baal for a whole day, with no answer forthcoming (1 Kings 18:26–29). Paul implies a contrast of these deaf-and-dumb gods with the God who hears and speaks, the God of the Word.

3   To today's reader, it may seem strange that Paul would have to tell the Corinthians something so elementary as that the **spirit of God** would never inspire one to say, **"Jesus be accursed."** First, we should observe that there is no "be"

in the Greek here, just as there is no connecting "is" in "Jesus is Lord." Some authors suggest that the parallel with *Kyrios Iēsous* (literally, "Jesus Lord," would mean that the translation of *Anathema Iēsous* should be "Jesus is cursed" or "Jesus is a curse" (supplying the indicative verb). That would be a milder form than "Jesus be accursed" (supplying the optative), since it could mean that the speaker is stating that the Old Testament curse had fallen on Jesus (Deut 21:23; see Gal 3:13). However, both these expressions are acclamations, not just statements, and Paul says that the *anathema* could never come from the Holy Spirit. So we judge the better translation is as the NAB gives it, the invoking of a curse. Is this something that might be blurted out by a Christian in a paranormal or ecstatic state? The **therefore** at the beginning of verse 3 connects that verse with the preceding one about being under the influence of idols (an influence that Paul says is demonic; 10:20–22). But Paul later says that "the spirits of prophets are under the prophets' control" (14:32), and nowhere else in these chapters does he deal with ecstatic manifestations. Some scholars have suggested that an early, undeveloped form of gnosticism has invaded the community, leading some members to overvalue the spiritual to the degradation of the human Jesus, who was limited by the flesh; now, possessing the Spirit, they would no longer need Jesus; in fact, they could curse him. But gnosticism did not flourish until the second century, and the texts invoked to support this position are much later than Paul.

Well, then, was there any place where Jesus was cursed? In his second-century *Dialogue with Trypho*, Justin tells us that a main obstacle for the Jews' coming to faith in Jesus was the fact that Scripture itself said, "Anyone who is hanged is a curse of God" (Deut 21:23).[1] Paul quotes this text in Gal 3:13 to illustrate that Christ became a curse for us, and here in 1 Corinthians, Paul portrays Jesus crucified as a scandal to the Jews (1:23). For them, "crucified Messiah" was an oxymoron, self-contradictory. This Scripture passage would also give them warrant to curse both Jesus and Christians, as Justin reports sometimes occurred.[2] *Anathema*, the word used for curse here, is a typically Jewish word. Some scholars therefore make the case that verse 2 refers to pagans, verse 3a to Jews, and verse 3b to Christians.[3]

Another view is that Paul is imagining a hypothetical case, the worst possible scenario, cursing Jesus (which any Jew or Gentile might do), as a

---

1. Saint Justin Martyr, *Dialogue with Trypho* 89.1–2.
2. Saint Justin Martyr, *Dialogue with Trypho* 16.4; 47.4; 96.2; 127.2.
3. Charles H. Talbert, *Reading Corinthians: A Literary and Theological Commentary on 1 and 2 Corinthians* (New York: Crossroad, 1987), 81–82; David E. Garland, *1 Corinthians*, BECNT (Grand Rapids: Baker Academic, 2003), 571.

foil for the confession of faith that the Holy Spirit makes: "Jesus is Lord." The "therefore" introducing verse 3 would indicate that any denigrating statement about Jesus, no matter who said it, would be the kind of thing said under the impulse of idol worship, which Paul has already said was the work of demons (10:20).

As with a number of Paul's texts, we simply do not have enough information concerning the context of his discussion with his readers to make an unqualified decision. The most plausible solution would seem to be this: As pagans, the Corinthians were led off like unwitting prisoners to dumb idols. But the movement of the Holy Spirit is quite different: it is liberating. The Spirit's movement can be discerned thus: Negatively, any condemnation or denigration of Jesus does not come from the Spirit of God. And positively, any sincere confession that **Jesus is Lord** comes from the **holy Spirit**.[4] "Witness to Jesus is the spirit of prophecy" (Rev 19:10). In preparing to discuss the charisms, Paul sets a foundation for all movements of the Spirit: it is the basic Christian confession of Jesus as Lord. Thus there are no grounds for elitism or for competition, as Paul will explain in what follows. Whatever gifts one might have, they all find their source in what is common to all, as Paul will make clear in the following (12:4–13): one Spirit, one Lord, one God, one body, one baptism. He will do the same in Eph 4:4–16, where he prefaces a discussion of the charisms by recalling that there is "one body and one Spirit, . . . one hope of your call; one Lord, one faith, one baptism; one God and Father of all."

The Gifts (12:4–11)

---

[4]There are different kinds of spiritual gifts but the same Spirit; [5]there are different forms of service but the same Lord; [6]there are different workings but the same God who produces all of them in everyone. [7]To each individual the manifestation of the Spirit is given for some benefit. [8]To one is given through the Spirit the expression of wisdom; to another the expression of knowledge according to the same Spirit; [9]to another faith by the same Spirit; to another gifts of healing by the one Spirit; [10]to another mighty deeds; to another prophecy; to another discernment of spirits; to

---

4. Could a false prophet proclaim "Jesus is Lord" while giving a false prophecy? Certainly the mere use of Jesus' name does not guarantee the divine origin of his prophecy. Paul is not referring to the mere repetition of words but to a sincere confession of Jesus as Lord. "Not everyone who says to me, 'Lord, Lord,' will enter the kingdom of heaven. . . . Many will say to me on that day, 'Lord, Lord, did we not prophesy in your name?' . . . Then I will declare to them solemnly, 'I never knew you. Depart from me, you evildoers'" (Matt 7:21–23).

another varieties of tongues; to another interpretation of tongues. ¹¹But one and the same Spirit produces all of these, distributing them individually to each person as he wishes.

OT: Num 11:29; Isa 11:1–5; 32:15–17; 44:3; 61:1–4; Joel 3:1–3
NT: Mark 16:17–18; Rom 12:4–8; Eph 4:7–16; 1 Pet 4:10
Catechism: communion of †charisms, 951
Lectionary: 12:3b–7, 12–13: Pentecost Mass during the Day; Mass for the Holy Church; Mass for †Ministers of the Church; Mass for the Laity; 12:4–11: Mass for Admission to Candidacy: Diaconate and Priesthood; 12:4–13: Mass for Confirmation

Here Paul describes these "spirituals" (*pneumatika*; 12:1) by three other terms: **4–6** they are "charisms" (*charismata*, translated here as **spiritual gifts**), different **forms of service**, and different **workings**. A fourth term is used in verse 7, "manifestation of the Spirit." Each depicts a different aspect of one and the same phenomenon. On the one hand, they are gifts, not something one produces by one's own efforts, and hence we should be careful not to equate them with acquired skills, although the gift could bring a new and Spirit-filled anointing to such abilities. A musical ability could, for example, become a gift of the Spirit to the degree that it is placed lovingly at the service of the community, so that it is no longer entertainment but a ministry that truly builds up the body and is recognized as such (see 14:26).

That the gifts are **different forms of service** indicates that they are not given primarily for the benefit of the individual, though if a gift is a work of the Spirit, there would normally be a good effect in the one exercising the gift, as Paul will later say about praying in tongues (14:4). Nor are they given to establish a spiritual ranking or elitism. Rather, they are given for the good of the community and should be governed by that purpose. **Different workings** refers to activities that take place in the community and that are inspired by God.

In all of these terms, the emphasis is on variety, extending the understanding of gifts to include whatever ministries build up the community, yet with all having a common source. From a theological point of view, most significant is the fact that Paul parallels the **Spirit**, the **Lord**, and **God** (the Father), giving a clear Trinitarian dimension to the gifts. Though he may not have had the intention of teaching the equality of the three Persons here, the fact that he attributes to them equal functions points in that direction. It does not mean that charisms are given only by the Spirit, gifts of service only by the Lord Jesus, and workings only by the Father. Paul simply attributes to one or the other divine Person the aspect that he thinks is most appropriate to each. Gifts are attributed to the Holy Spirit because they are *spiritual* gifts. Forms of service suggest the Lord Jesus, both as the one for whom the service is performed even as it ministers to

LIVING
TRADITION

Vatican II on Charisms

It is not only through the sacraments and Church ministries that the same Holy Spirit sanctifies and leads the People of God and enriches it with virtues. Allotting His gifts "to everyone according as he will" (1 Cor 12:11), He distributes special graces among the faithful of every rank. By these gifts He makes them fit and ready to undertake the various tasks or offices advantageous for the renewal and upbuilding of the Church, according to the words of the Apostle: "The manifestation of the Spirit is given to everyone, for profit" (1 Cor 12:7). These charismatic gifts, whether they be the most outstanding or the more simple and widely diffused, are to be received with thanksgiving and consolation, for they are exceedingly suitable and useful for the needs of the Church. (*Lumen Gentium*, §12)

the community, and also because Jesus, though Lord, became servant for our sakes (Mark 10:45), giving us an example to follow (John 13:14–15). Finally, "workings," or activities—a rather comprehensive summary—are attributed to the Father, the first cause of all.

7   **Manifestation of the Spirit** means that the gifts are visible, outward evidences of the work of the Spirit. They are not merely interior graces of prayer. We might think of a crystal-ball chandelier that sparkles as it turns. This kind of manifestation would tell the unbeliever visiting the church that God is truly in their midst (14:24–25). **Is given**, repeated in verse 8, indicates that the manifestation cannot be attributed to a natural talent, nor does it indicate that the receiver is a holier person who merited the gift. This is quite important because many Christians believe that the charisms are only for canonizable saints. No, they depend on God's choice and generosity (v. 11). **For some benefit** ("the common good," NIV, NRSV; "the general good," NJB; "for a good purpose," JB) again means that the purpose of every gift is to build up the church in faith, hope, and love and to empower its outreach.

8   Now follows a list, not intended to be exhaustive, of the gifts most commonly in evidence in the early communities and in Corinth in particular. Wisdom is the first of the gifts with which the messianic king was to be anointed (Isa 11:2). Inasmuch as the gifts listed by Isaiah were for holy governance, we can assume that here in Paul **the expression of wisdom** ("the utterance of wisdom," NRSV; literally, "the word of wisdom") would be a gift of giving practical counsel, of the kind recorded in the books of Proverbs and Sirach but now purified and completed by the light of the Holy Spirit. It might not seem wise from a

purely human point of view to advise forgiving one's enemies, but that is what the supernatural gift of wisdom and the advice of wisdom would inspire. Like knowledge and the other gifts, its charismatic nature is revealed only when it is exercised, when the counsel is given. Jesus promises to give the disciples wisdom in speaking when they are dragged before governors and magistrates (Luke 21:15): "The holy Spirit will teach you at that moment what you should say" (12:12).

"Knowledge," often teamed with wisdom (Rom 11:33; Col 2:3), is also listed among the gifts of the Messiah in Isa 11:2. Here **the expression of knowledge** could mean either an understanding of the mysteries of God (1 Cor 13:2), an insight into some aspect of the faith (for which Paul more often uses a related Greek word, *epignōsis*),[5] or knowledge of a fact otherwise hidden, such as Jesus' revealing to the Samaritan woman her past relationships (John 4:18). It enables one to instruct others (Rom 15:14), and thus it involves speaking (1 Cor 14:6). Paul finds the Corinthians richly endowed with this gift (1 Cor 1:5; 2 Cor 8:7). He repeats again and again that these gifts come **through the Spirit** (as in v. 8) or "by the same Spirit" (as in v. 9), thus tying each gift to the source that all Christians have in common. Paul's repeated insistence on the one and the same Spirit, which runs through the next verses, suggests that some of the Corinthians perhaps thought of their inspirations as coming from various unconnected spirits, angels perhaps.

Here **faith** cannot refer to the faith that saves, which is necessary for all, but rather to an extraordinary movement of expectant faith, the faith that moves mountains (Mark 11:23). Jesus was speaking hyperbolically, but the lives of the saints testify to moments of this kind of faith and their extraordinary results.[6]

Gifts of healing, a sign of God's kingdom in the ministry of Jesus, continued in the early Church. Though all the baptized are empowered to pray for healing in the name of Jesus, some members appear especially endowed with these gifts, so that healing becomes a ministry for them. As in the life of Jesus (Matt 4:23–25), the ministry of healing became an important tool for evangelization in the early Church (Acts 3:1–26; 9:32–43), based as it was on the mission he gave his disciples (Mark 16:18; Luke 9:2). It responds to a most basic human need on the physical level but also draws persons into the deeper level of spiritual and emotional healing as they discover the Lord as the source of forgiveness and peace.

9

---

5. As in Eph 1:17; 4:13; Phil 1:9; Col 1:9, 10; 2:2; 3:10.

6. For an outstanding illustration of the power of faith and prayer in the most impossible circumstances, see the story of Immaculée Ilibagiza, survivor of the Rwandan genocide, in her books *Left to Tell* (New York: Hay House, 2006) and *Led by Faith* (New York: Hay House, 2008).

10   **Mighty deeds**, which most scholars interpret as miracles, might be the kind
of on-the-spot manifestation of the Spirit's power that Paul exercised in casting a temporary blindness on the magician Elymas, which brought about the
conversion of the proconsul Sergius Paulus (Acts 13:8–12), or Peter's raising
of Tabitha from the dead (9:36–42). Padre Pio's bilocation, confirmed by witnesses, would probably fit here, as would the miraculous multiplication of food
that has occurred in the lives of several saints and even in our own time in the
feeding of the poor on the garbage dump in Juárez, Mexico, as I know from the
personal testimony of several eyewitnesses.

Many today think of **prophecy** as foretelling a future event. Although
there are examples of such forecasting both in Jesus' prediction about the fall
of the temple (Mark 13:2) and in Agabus's telling of a coming famine (Acts
11:28) and Paul's imprisonment (21:10–11), the term in the New Testament
has the broader meaning of speech inspired by the Holy Spirit. This activity
of the Holy Spirit was new and unsettling to those among the Jewish scribes
who by New Testament times considered prophecy to be a thing of the past,
now safely and sufficiently enshrined in the Scriptures. In Paul's communities
such spontaneous inspirations of the Spirit were expected, and Paul told his
earliest readers that they should not quench the Spirit or despise prophesying,
but test everything (1 Thess 5:19–21). For more details see the commentary
below on 14:1.

Discernment of spirits is the gift for the testing that the Apostle told the
Thessalonians they should do with every manifestation of the Spirit. The use of
"spirits" here indicates that not every movement one might think to be inspired
by the Holy Spirit, even in the context of worship, is necessarily so. Certainly
if someone should say "Jesus is cursed," the entire community could readily
identify that as demonic. But there are other situations that are not clear-cut—
the history of the Church and our own daily experience are full of them—and
these call for discernment. Is this thought from God, or is it merely of my own
invention, or is it a mixture of both, or is it from an evil spirit? Paul seems to
be saying that certain persons in the community are gifted with a spiritual insight that will enable the community to gain clarity in the matter. The story of
Jesus' temptation in the desert shows that Satan can even quote Scripture for
his purpose (Matt 4:1–11). Paul will say that Satan can disguise himself as an
angel of light (2 Cor 11:14). "Our struggle is not with flesh and blood but with
the principalities, with the powers, . . . with the evil spirits" (Eph 6:12). That is
why the community and the individual cannot depend on their natural powers
to discern but need the light of the Holy Spirit.

Varieties of tongues come second to last, perhaps because Paul wants to temper the Corinthians' overestimation of their importance. Because Paul treats them at length in chapter 14, here I will simply describe the gift of tongues as preconceptual prayer or speech, delaying the demonstration until that chapter, as also with the **interpretation of tongues**.

But one and the same Spirit produces all of these, distributing them individually to each person as he wishes. This verse provides an †inclusio with 12:4–6, which insists on the single source of all the gifts. It also makes clear that who gets what gift and when he or she gets it is God's business ("as he wishes"), not that of the Corinthians. The spirit of competition already noticed at the beginning of the letter has shown up in the free-flowing worship of the community. And that leads to the next section.

11

Reflection and Application (12:4–11)

The spiritual gifts, or charisms, are first of all a manifestation of the life of the Trinity. That means that their source and goal is the interpersonal life of Father, Son, and Holy Spirit. Natural gifts, like music or public speaking, are not a revelation of God's innermost life in the same way that these gifts are. These spiritual gifts, which may build on nature but essentially go beyond it, are aimed at bringing persons into intimate communion with the Holy Trinity. That is why they are not to be despised but to be sought after (12:31; 14:1). They are part of the divine endowment of the Church.

The charism of faith. In the midst of a terrible drought in northern India in the 1980s, the little village of Sokho and its neighboring village were suffering from hunger. One Sunday the Scripture text was about the Lord's providing quail in the desert for the hungering Israelites. After celebrating Mass in Sokho, Father Dan got on his motorcycle with his catechist and sped to the neighboring village, where at the prayer of the faithful, a man got up, walked up to the altar, threw off his outer garment, and prayed aloud, "Lord, you gave your people food in the desert. We are your people too, and we are starving. Our children are starving! Do for us what you did then. I believe you will." As Father Dan and his catechist were returning to Sokho, lightning and thunder struck from a menacing storm cloud overhead. "What is God saying?" Father Dan asked the catechist. (In that culture, as in biblical times, people think of thunder as the voice of God.) Back came the answer: "He is saying, 'Where do you want it to rain?'" Father Dan shouted, "Right where we're starving!" but by this time he had lost his catechist, who was running toward the jungle, where people were shouting with glee because hail had knocked down a flight of Siberian geese, providing abundant food as well as rain for the villages. Father Dan attributed this extraordinary response of the Lord to the extraordinary faith of the simple villager who believed that God would act.

What One Body Means (12:12–26)

[12]As a body is one though it has many parts, and all the parts of the body, though many, are one body, so also Christ. [13]For in one Spirit we were all baptized into one body, whether Jews or Greeks, slaves or free persons, and we were all given to drink of one Spirit.

[14]Now the body is not a single part, but many. [15]If a foot should say, "Because I am not a hand I do not belong to the body," it does not for this reason belong any less to the body. [16]Or if an ear should say, "Because I am not an eye I do not belong to the body," it does not for this reason belong any less to the body. [17]If the whole body were an eye, where would the hearing be? If the whole body were hearing, where would the sense of smell be? [18]But as it is, God placed the parts, each one of them, in the body as he intended. [19]If they were all one part, where would the body be? [20]But as it is, there are many parts, yet one body. [21]The eye cannot say to the hand, "I do not need you," nor again the head to the feet, "I do not need you." [22]Indeed, the parts of the body that seem to be weaker are all the more necessary, [23]and those parts of the body that we consider less honorable we surround with greater honor, and our less presentable parts are treated with greater propriety, [24]whereas our more presentable parts do not need this. But God has so constructed the body as to give greater honor to a part that is without it, [25]so that there may be no division in the body, but that the parts may have the same concern for one another. [26]If [one] part suffers, all the parts suffer with it; if one part is honored, all the parts share its joy.

OT: Num 20:8–11
NT: John 7:37–39; 10:1–15; 15:1–6; Rom 12:15; 1 Cor 3:16; 10:2–4; Gal 3:28
Catechism: union in the body of Christ, 789–91
Lectionary: Anointing of the Sick; Christian Initiation apart from the Easter Vigil; Mass for Infant Baptism

12   In this section, it is not a matter of some kind of metaphoric "unity in diversity" that could be applied to any group. It is a matter *of the kind of unity and diversity that exists in the body of Christ*. It is not a question of how the many can be one but how the One, Christ, can be many. This emerges from Paul's shorthand at the end of this verse. After saying, **As a body is one though it has many parts, and all the parts of the body, though many, are one body**, he could have said "so also the body of Christ," meaning the Church. Instead, he says **so also Christ**, indicating that God's plan since the resurrection of Jesus is that he be many: the whole Christ, including his members. Here we strike a vein deeply rooted in Paul's conversion experience, when the risen Lord asked him, "Saul, Saul, why are you persecuting me?" (Acts 9:4). The unity of the Church with Jesus is so intimate that whatever Saul did to the least of Jesus' brothers, he did to Jesus (Matt 25:40). This is indeed a †mystery: as we saw in 6:12–20, Paul thinks of the union of Christians with Christ in realistic and, as it were, physical terms.

This becomes evident again here when he says that **in one Spirit we were all**   13
baptized into one body. In our way of thinking today, we would understand this as becoming members of a group, a collectivity like the student body of a school. But in Paul's mind, if we become one, it is because each of us is joined sacramentally and bodily to the risen body of Christ. This is clear from the following: (1) Paul's realistic contrast between union with Christ and union with a prostitute in 6:12–20; (2) the parallelism of "body" here with "Spirit" at the end of the verse (13). If the Spirit is the Holy Spirit, then "body" would normally stand for the individual body of Christ, for it, not the Church, is the source of the Spirit. (3) The participation in the eucharistic body effects the unity of the Church (10:17). That unity far transcends a tribal or ethnic or class unity. Traditional walls have collapsed as all became one, **whether Jews or Greeks, slaves or free persons**. Through the new experience, these groups found themselves to be brothers and sisters around the eucharistic table. The person of Jesus had now created a new and universal—catholic—community. As in 6:12–20, the result of this baptismal union with the body of Christ is that **we were all given to drink of one Spirit**. Paul returns to the image of the water flowing from the rock in the desert, which he used in 10:4 to illustrate Christ's gift of the Spirit: "All drank the same spiritual drink, for they drank from a spiritual rock that followed them, and the rock was the Christ." This allusion to Christ as the rock further confirms the physical sacramental union with the risen Christ that makes the many into the one Christ.

It is this sacred unity that now enables Paul to extend the image of the **body**   14–20
and draw conclusions about the relation of its diverse members to one another. It appears that the tendency to form cliques, condemned by Paul at the beginning of the letter (1:12–13), shows up here in a different form. As Garland puts it: "The segmentation of the Corinthian congregation into cliques . . .

Baptism and the Charisms

Paul introduces his long discussion of the †charisms by underlining their source in our baptismal union with the body of Christ and the Holy Spirit given through that union. The Fathers of the Church understood that charismatic grace comes with baptism, and it simply needs to be activated by prayer and cooperation with the gift. Thus at the end of the second century, Tertullian addresses the catechumens at the baptismal font: "Therefore, you blessed ones, for whom the grace of God is waiting, when you come up from the most sacred bath of the new birth, when you spread out your hands for the first time in your mother's house [the church] with your brethren, ask your Father, ask your Lord [Jesus] for the special gift of his inheritance, the distributed charisms, which form an additional, underlying feature [of baptism]. Ask, he says, and you shall receive. In fact, you have sought, and you have found; you have knocked, and it has been opened to you."[a]

And around AD 364 St. Hilary of Poitiers, an adult convert and doctor of the Church, writes: "We who have been reborn through the sacrament of baptism experience intense joy when we feel within us the first stirrings of the Holy Spirit. We begin to have insight into the mysteries of faith, we are able to prophesy and to speak with wisdom. We become steadfast in hope and receive the gifts of healing. Demons are made subject to our authority. These gifts enter us like a gentle rain, and once having done so, little by little they bring forth fruit in abundance."[b]

Practically speaking, this means that the charisms are the rightful inheritance of everyone who is baptized. However, as Tertullian suggests, they are to be sought (as Paul himself said: "Strive eagerly for the spiritual gifts"; 1 Cor 14:1) and activated. A homely example: when you receive a new credit card, you must activate it before you can use it. So with the spiritual gifts: learn about them, ask for them, activate them, use them.

a. Tertullian, *Baptism* 20; quoted in Kilian McDonnell and George T. Montague, *Christian Initiation and Baptism in the Holy Spirit: Evidence from the First Eight Centuries*, 2nd rev. ed. (Collegeville, MN: Liturgical Press, 1994), 108.

b. Hilary of Poitiers, *On Psalm 64:15*; as translated in McDonnell and Montague, *Christian Initiation and Baptism in the Holy Spirit*, 184, 186.

spurs individuals to treat their differing spiritual experiences as a pretext for reinstating class divisions—now employing spiritual classifications—so as to elevate themselves over others."[7]

Paul's analogy first addresses those who think that because their gift is less sensational, they do not belong to the body. **If a foot should say, "Because I**

7. Garland, *1 Corinthians*, 592, 745–46.

Irenaeus and Cyril on the Charisms

About AD 180 St. Irenaeus, bishop of Lyons, wrote, "Those who are truly [Jesus'] disciples, receiving grace from him, perform [miracles] in his name for the well-being of others, according to the gift which each one has received from him. For some truly drive out devils, so that those who have thus been cleansed from evil spirits frequently believe [in Christ] and join themselves to the Church. Others have foreknowledge of things to come: they see visions and utter prophecies. Others still heal the sick by laying their hands upon them, and they are made whole. Yes, moreover, the dead even have been raised up, and remained among us for many years. And what more shall I say? It is not possible to name the number of the gifts which the Church [scattered] throughout the whole world has received from God, in the name of Jesus Christ who was crucified under Pontius Pilate, and which she exerts day by day for the benefit of the Gentiles, not practicing deception on anyone, nor receiving any reward from them on account of such miracles. For as she has received freely from God, freely also she †ministers."[a]

Saint Cyril of Jerusalem urged the catechumens preparing for baptism: "Let each one prepare oneself to receive the heavenly gift of prophecy. God grant that you may be worthy of the †charism of prophecy."[b] In the last instruction before baptism, he exhorts them: "My final words, beloved ones, in this instruction are words of exhortation, urging all of you to prepare your souls for the reception of the heavenly charisms" (18.32).

a. *Against Heresies* 2.32.4.
b. *Catechetical Lectures* 17.19, 37.

---

am not a hand I do not belong to the body," it does not for this reason belong any less to the body**. This is obviously an encouragement to the weaker members of the community, who are needed just as much as the apparently stronger ones are. Verse 18 elevates the disposition of this diversity by affirming that it is God who has so arranged the body: **God placed the parts, each one of them, in the body as he intended**. As God willed the human body to have many interdependent parts, so it is with the Church. There is no unimportant member. Against our culture's deification of independence, Paul stresses *inter*dependence. God's plan for unity is not uniformity but harmony—the interaction of many different members with very diverse gifts, learning to use their gifts to upbuild and support one another.

Paul now turns to those who think their gift is so important that they can do   21–24
without the others, or at least without some of the other gifts that they consider

inferior. Quite the contrary, **the parts of the body that seem to be weaker are all the more necessary**. Some scholars have taken the apparently weaker but all the more necessary member to mean the genitalia. Artemidorus in his book *The Interpretation of Dreams* (second century) speaks of the "necessary member" as the male organ.[8] We actually honor those organs by covering them, out of respect, as we honor the Eucharist by a tabernacle or a veil. **Those parts of the body that we consider less honorable we surround with greater honor**. The members that are sometimes considered "less honorable" are in reality the most important for the continuation of the human race—they are "all the more necessary" (12:22). Thus we honor them by covering them, since they are ordered to give life in the intimacy of marriage. The NAB catches this nuance quite well by translating **our less presentable parts are treated with greater propriety**. But we can also think of other members of the body that we honor by adornment: for example, rings that ennoble ear lobes, or in several cultures nose rings, or . . . painted fingernails and toenails.

25–26   Paul suddenly shifts his thought here to show not only that the different parts are necessary and complementary **but** also **that the parts may have the same concern for one another**. The quality of life in the body of Christ can be judged by how much care the stronger members have for the weaker. A secular model of a corporation may be marked by individuals climbing over others to get to the top; yet in the family of the Church, what counts is not competition but compassion for one another; in fact, the most important person is the most needy—the poor, the sick, the handicapped, the elderly, the lonely—the ones to whom Jesus was sent to bring the good news (Luke 4:18–19). Just as in the human body, when one member **suffers**, the rest of the members of the body **suffer with it**, so it should be in the body of Christ. And by the same token, the honor of one brings **joy** to all. This last line is a direct challenge to the competitiveness of those Corinthians who boast of their gifts (or their favorite preachers; 1:11–13) to exalt themselves over others.

Reflection and Application (12:12–26)

Why does Paul say that members who are weaker—the more needy—are actually the more necessary? The best answer can be given by a family who has a severely handicapped daughter named Cecilia. When their other daughter, a very talented and beautiful young woman, wrote her college application essay

8. Artemidorus, *Oneirocritica* (*The Interpretation of Dreams*) 1.45, 79, 80; Garland, *1 Corinthians*, 595.

on the person who had taught her the most, she wrote about Cecilia, who taught her about love, about our worth not being in what we can do, about not focusing on our needs but on the needs of others. Is it the needy who need us—or we who need the needy?

Gifts in the Body of Christ (12:27–31)

²⁷**Now you are Christ's body, and individually parts of it.** ²⁸**Some people God has designated in the church to be, first, apostles; second, prophets; third, teachers; then, mighty deeds; then, gifts of healing, assistance, administration, and varieties of tongues.** ²⁹**Are all apostles? Are all prophets? Are all teachers? Do all work mighty deeds?** ³⁰**Do all have gifts of healing? Do all speak in tongues? Do all interpret?** ³¹**Strive eagerly for the greatest spiritual gifts.**

But I shall show you a still more excellent way.

OT: Num 11:16–29
NT: Luke 6:13; Rom 12:15
Catechism: diversity of gifts, 791; †charism of healing, 1508

Finally Paul arrives at the application for which he has set up the metaphor   **27–28** of the body. The members of the community are members of the body of Christ. What Paul was talking about in the previous section was the attitude of those who judged their personal value by the kind of gifts they had. In this section it becomes evident that he was not saying there is no hierarchy of gifts. For that is exactly what he says here, and in verse 31 he urges the Corinthians to strive for the greatest gifts. The diversity of gifts, and even the order of them, is God's determination, and that too is a gift. Paul will now explain how God has designated the different persons to have such gifts.

Apostles, meaning "those who are sent," refers primarily to the twelve men chosen and appointed by Christ to continue his work, either during his lifetime (Matt 11:2–4; Luke 6:13–16) or after his resurrection (Matt 28:16–19; Acts 1:2, 26).

Although the term is used loosely of Barnabas (Acts 14:14) and of the couple Andronicus and Junia, who are "prominent among the apostles" (Rom 16:7), indicating that others could be "sent," one of the requirements of the apostles was that they had seen the risen Jesus and were sent by him. That is why Paul can consider himself an apostle: he saw Jesus and was sent by him (Acts 22:14–15; 1 Cor 9:1). **Prophets** were speakers especially inspired by the Holy Spirit who had a recognized ministry. Apparently they were not officially commissioned or ordained, but their gift of prophetic utterance was sufficiently recognized that it became an office, or formal position, in the church. Thus they would be different from members of the community who only rarely or occasionally exercised the gift of prophecy. God designated some by a more habitual gift of inspired speech, and this was recognized by the community.[9] **Teachers** were those who instructed others in the faith. They too had a recognized office, all the more important as the number of converts grew. God worked, therefore, both through the gift and its recognition and authorization by the community. The fact that Paul speaks of prophets rather than prophecy, and of teachers rather than teaching, and lists them as second and third indicates that these were now roles or ministries and not passing inspirations or gifts. Although the rest are not numbered, the use of **then . . . then** does indicate an order, but they do not appear to be stable offices, for the nouns are not personal but refer to gifts.[10]

Mighty deeds ("miraculous powers," NJB) and **gifts of healing** were described above, in 12:9–10. New here are **assistance** and **administration**. The former refers to gifts of service, especially service to the poor or needy in the community. (One thinks of the St. Vincent de Paul Society or other works of service in a parish.) The latter comes from a root meaning the rudder of a ship, and it is used for piloting (a meaningful metaphor for a seafaring community like Corinth). It probably refers to those who have a gift for guidance, visioning, and setting a direction for the community, and today what we might call organizational skills. It is likely that these gifts build on natural skills but also manifest the Spirit's power by the grace and joy with which they are fulfilled and the degree to which they build up the community. Last come **varieties of tongues**, which the Corinthians would not have put last, and yet, as we will see in chapter 14, it is not a gift to be despised.

29–30   All these †rhetorical questions expect the answer no. Not everyone is called or gifted for every role in the community. Hence Paul reinforces what he has earlier said about the variety of gifts. One should not be envious of the gifts of others but rejoice in the diversity in the body of Christ.

---

9. Already the Old Testament recognized the need for norms for distinguishing true from false prophets (Deut 13:2–4; 18:21–22), and this carried over into the New Testament, where prophecy has to be tested (1 Thess 5:20–21) according to the norm of faith in Jesus Christ (1 Cor 12:1–3), and the existence of false prophecy is recognized (Matt 24:11–12). The †*Didache* 11.3–12 lists several signs of a false prophet.

10. The NIV of 1 Cor 12:28 expands the gifts into †ministers, e.g., "workers of miracles, also those having gifts of healing," and so forth, but this is taking liberties (perhaps legitimate) with the Greek text.

Saint Clement to Later Corinthians

Some forty years after Paul wrote this letter, the church in Rome sent a long letter to the Christians in Corinth, who still showed some of the same problems Paul had faced, but this time rebelling against their leaders. Tradition has attributed this letter to Clement, the third bishop of Rome. He uses the same image of the body: "Let us take our body as an example. The head without the feet is nothing; likewise, the feet without the head are nothing. Even the smallest parts of our body are necessary and useful for the whole body, yet all the members work together and unite in mutual subjection, that the whole body may be saved. So in our case let the whole body be saved in Christ Jesus, and let each man be subject to his neighbor, to the degree determined by his spiritual gift (*charisma*)."[a] Although Clement exhorts them to obey superiors, he also urges submission to each other's gifts.

a. See *1 Clement* 37–38.

Suddenly it seems as though Paul's thought skips a beat. Having ranked the spiritual gifts, he says, **Strive eagerly for the greatest spiritual gifts**.[11] He could hardly mean that they should strive to be apostles, for that depends on Christ's appointment. But he has listed the ministry of prophet immediately after apostle (12:28), and in 14:1 he urges them to seek the gift of prophecy. It appears, then, that Paul is urging those who overly prize the gift of tongues to seek also those gifts that are more useful for the community. But what does striving mean if the charisms are gifts? Surely it would mean praying for the gift and the docility to receive it. And it would mean exercising the gift, stirring it up, since charismatic grace is given, in seed at least, with the Holy Spirit already in baptism (compare 2 Tim 1:6–7).[12]

And while he is thinking of higher things, Paul's mind immediately goes to **a still more excellent way**. This provides the bridge to the next chapter, on love. Nevertheless, he does not describe love as a charismatic gift but as a *way*. It is the high road that all must travel, and if you really want to excel, excel first in love.

11. The words in 1 Cor 12:31 could be read as an indicative, "You strive eagerly for the spiritual gifts," but the parallel with 14:1 rules this out. Instead of the superlative form "greatest," other translations stick more closely to the comparative form of the Greek *meizona*: "the greater gifts" (NIV, NRSV), "the higher gifts" (JB, NJB).

12. The relation of the grace of the charisms to baptism is developed by McDonnell and Montague in *Christian Initiation and Baptism in the Holy Spirit*; and idem in a short pastoral document, *Fanning the Flame* (Collegeville, MN: Liturgical Press, 1991).

In the Greek the expression is not comparative, as if Paul were saying that love is better than the charisms. He uses the superlative. He does not describe love as a charismatic gift but as a *way* beyond comparison: it is the best of all. Not everyone has every spiritual gift, but everyone is called to live in love. All the gifts are to be exercised in love. The charisms are the slaves, love is the master.

Reflection and Application (12:27–31)

Was Paul's exhortation to strive eagerly for the spiritual gifts, stated in verse 31 and repeated in 14:1, for the Corinthians only or for Christians of all times? The Church unfortunately has gone through periods where the gifts Paul speaks of here fell into disuse, at least by the majority of Christians, and that is still the case today with many Christians. I must confess that when I wrote my first textbook on Paul, subtitled *An Intensive Study of Key Texts*, I skipped chapters 12 to 14 of 1 Corinthians (even, would you believe it, chapter 13!) because I thought the gifts as described by Paul would be irrelevant to today's audience, whether college students or Bible study groups. But there is so much evidence of the importance of the spontaneous movement of the Holy Spirit in the New Testament (Rom 12:3–8; Eph 4:7–16; 1 Pet 4:10; the Acts of the Apostles throughout), reinforced by the Second Vatican Council (*Lumen Gentium*, §12; *Apostolicam Actuositatem* [*Decree on the Apostolate of the Laity*], §3), that this vital element cannot be ignored. Since the council, many renewal movements have flourished in the Church, the charismatic movement being the one most obviously finding its inspiration in the scriptural witness to the spiritual gifts. Paul was not suggesting that the gifts are for the few. What he says to the Corinthians is addressed to Christians of all times: *strive eagerly for the spiritual gifts!*

Love, the Heart of the Gifts

1 Corinthians 13

Perhaps the most popular part of the New Testament, this chapter evokes wedding bells, the bridal march, and confetti. But it appears here as the jeweled centerpiece of Paul's discourse on the †charisms. Some interpreters think that chapter 13 was inserted later either by Paul or a disciple. If chapter 13 is momentarily deleted, there is a smooth transition from 12:30 to 14:1. However, the chapter perfectly fits Paul's concern that the charisms should build up, and they do so only if inspired by love (8:1). Far from being a digression, this chapter provides the foundational principle that must order all the exercise of gifts in the body of Christ. It is love that gives charisms their value. Furthermore, it is typical of New Testament †rhetorical style to arrange a presentation to highlight the centerpiece, which certainly happens with chapters 12 and 14 serving like companion jewels for the central diamond: love.

There are several words for love in Greek. *Eros* means romantic or sexual love.[1] *Philia* means the love of friendship. *Philadelphia* is brotherly/sisterly love. *Storgē* is parental love. The word Paul uses for love here is none of these: it is *agapē*. In the New Testament this means a wholly benevolent, disinterested love. If the other kinds can be tainted with selfishness, this kind is loving just for the sake of loving, not seeking any reward or return of the love except in the measure it benefits the other. In the New Testament it is used primarily for God's love for us, which, shown in Jesus' self-gift on the cross, is "poured into our hearts through the Holy Spirit which has been given to us" (Rom 5:5 RSV).

---

1. For an excellent treatment of the difference and the unity of *eros* and *agapē*, see Pope Benedict XVI, *Deus Caritas Est* (*God Is Love*), §§1–8.

This love, God's own perfect love, arouses love for God in return (Rom 8:28; 1 Cor 2:9). This could be called the vertical dimension of *agapē*, descending from the Father and ascending back to him from those who love him in return. This Trinitarian trait of Christian *agapē* sets it apart from even the highest form of love understood in the Greco-Roman world.

Agapē is inseparably love for everyone, for one cannot share in God's love if one does not love all that God loves—even one's enemies (Matt 5:43–48)! It is this horizontal dimension of love that is Paul's concern in this chapter. It falls neatly into three parts: (1) Love is essential (13:1–3). (2) Love births all virtues (13:4–7). (3) Love lasts forever (13:8–13).

Love Is Essential (13:1–3)

---

¹If I speak in human and angelic tongues but do not have love, I am a resounding gong or a clashing cymbal. ²And if I have the gift of prophecy and comprehend all mysteries and all knowledge; if I have all faith so as to move mountains but do not have love, I am nothing. ³If I give away everything I own, and if I hand my body over so that I may boast but do not have love, I gain nothing.

OT: Lev 19:18; Tob 4:13
NT: Matt 5:43–48; 22:39–40; John 15:12; 1 Cor 8:1–3; 16:14; Phil 2:1–2
Catechism: love needed to practice justice, 1889; love is essential, 1826
Lectionary: 12:31–13:8a: Mass for Conferring Sacrament of Marriage; 12:31–13:13: St. Joseph Calasanz; Common of Holy Men and Women; Reception of Baptized Christians into Full Communion; Mass for the Promotion of Charity

1 Some authors suppose that Paul's "I" here stands for a hypothetical person. But he has already used his own example as a means of persuading the Corinthians (1 Cor 9). He turns to it here again, associating himself with their experiences, all of which he has already had: he speaks in tongues more than any of them (14:18), he certainly knows the †mystery of Christ, he has proclaimed the word prophetically and worked accompanying miracles (2 Cor 12:12), and he beats his body and brings it to subjection (1 Cor 9:27). Thus instead of speaking of their use of the gifts without love, Paul imagines himself doing so with gifts to the extreme, thus hoping to get a sympathetic hearing. Although he has put **tongues** last in his earlier lists (12:10, 30), here he puts them first, possibly because the Corinthians are prizing them as the highest, thus giving those who use them a claim to superior spirituality. By **human and angelic tongues** Paul is probably using hyperbole, intentional exaggeration, and the order of the Greek words even suggests that "if I speak with all the languages known to humanity, and even all the languages used by angels." Angels praise God (Pss 103:20; 148:2), and a Jewish tradition held that they had their own languages.[2] But angels were also bearers of heavenly messages. Thus the Corinthians might think that it is angelic language they are speaking when speaking in tongues, either to praise God or to convey a heavenly message. Interpretation, then (see 14:5), would be a rendering of the angelic prayer or message in understandable human language. In any case, the point is how useless such tongues would be without love. In our Western culture a **resounding gong or a clashing cymbal** suggests jarring noise, at least when it is not a discreet accompaniment to an orchestra. Plato and many following him used such musical instruments as figures for an empty †sophist.[3] However, in the Middle East of Paul's day, including the Jewish temple, as even in a number of cultures today, such instruments were also used in religious celebrations. In 14:9 he says that speaking in tongues without interpretation is meaningless. Here he says that it is meaningless without love. Gong and cymbal, then, stand for meaningless sound. He intends to belittle not the gift of tongues but its use without **love.**

Prophecy Paul regards as the gift most to be desired (14:1), and it too is　　**2** meant to foster love in the community and in the one who exercises it. But the speaker might use it in a harshly condemning way or for the speaker's own glory. It is not clear whether the power to **comprehend all mysteries** is a further specification of the gift of prophecy or whether it goes with the following: **all knowledge.** The latter seems more likely, in which case the charismatic gift of **knowledge** is insight into the revealed mysteries of God, a special insight granted by the Holy Spirit. What the speaker needs to know is that the God who gives light into the mysteries is also the God who gives love in the heart. Knowledge without love inflates (8:1). Thus, as Paul insists, one's knowledge must be used with love.

In hypothesizing **all faith so as to move mountains**, Paul shows that he is aware of the saying of Jesus recorded in Matt 17:20 and Mark 11:23, that faith is capable of moving mountains. By adding "all" the Apostle imagines having the strongest faith conceivable. Paul is not referring to the faith that saves but to a charismatic faith enabling miracles. If I have all these gifts—tongues, prophecy, knowledge, and mountain-moving faith—**but do not have love, I am nothing.** Not useless, but *nothing.* Whatever effect my exercise of the gifts might have on others (probably very little, though sometimes God can use quite

2. *Testament of Job* 48–50.
3. Plato, *Protagoras* 329A.

imperfect instruments), without love I diminish my own being. I am like the Wicked Witch of the West, annihilated by a dash of water.

3   It is hard to imagine how one might **give away everything** one owns and not have love. Paul is not thinking only of great acts of philanthropy but also of giving up all that one has, reducing oneself to poverty to help others. Some might have the charismatic gift of distributing goods to the poor, but if this is done for vainglory or to show one's superiority to others—hence without love—it is useless in the sight of God. **If I hand my body over that I may boast** appears in other translations as "surrender my body to the flames" (NIV), "deliver my body to be burned" (RSV), "give up my body to be burned" (NJB). This is one of those texts where the difference of a single Greek letter changes the meaning. *Kauchēsōmai* means "that I may boast"; *kauthēsōmai*, "that I may be burned."[4] The better Greek manuscripts read "boast," but others read "burned." The problem is not only a possible scribal change, inadvertent or intentional, but also the fact that both meanings make good sense. "That I may be burned" would evoke the story of the three young men in Dan 3:15–23 who offered themselves to the fiery furnace rather than worship the false god ("they gave their bodies to be burned"; 3:28 LXX), a situation repeated in the martyrdom of many Christians, especially under Nero, who made torches out of the Christians to illumine his gardens. (The Roman catacombs frequently depict the three men in the fiery furnace as an image of the Church's suffering and being preserved amid persecution and martyrdom.) As Ceslas Spicq comments, Paul "contrasts the totality of the gift with the nothingness of the result."[5]

However, the better manuscripts have the other reading, "that I may boast," the one chosen by the NAB. In either case, the idea is that Paul envisages the most heroic self-gift done for a motive other than love. T. S. Eliot, in his imaginative interpretation of the temptations of St. Thomas Becket in *Murder in the Cathedral*, presents the final tempter as offering Thomas the crown of martyrdom so that he may enjoy a human glory, a triumph of his own pride. To which Thomas answers, "The last temptation is the greatest treason: to do the right deed for the wrong reason." A true martyr goes to his death because there is no other way to be faithful to God, not because it will be the ultimate triumph of his human pride. The ego can feed on anything—even martyrdom. Only love makes it real.

4. It takes two letters in English to render each of the Greek letters transcribed by the English *ch* (for χ) and *th* (for θ).
5. Ceslas Spicq, *Agape in the New Testament* (St. Louis: Herder, 1965), 2:149.

Reflection and Application (13:1–3)

Though Paul would not be thinking of the later Christian martyrs as he wrote 1 Cor 13, there were plenty of stories around about pagan self-immolation by fire, the latest of which would have been the suicide by fire in Athens of a Hindu, Zarmanochegas, around AD 20, when Paul was a youth.[6] The Corinthians would have remembered the legend about the capture of the city by Dorian invaders when Hellotis and one of her young sisters threw themselves into the flames of the burning temple of Athena—commemorated by the *Hellotia*, a funereal feast.[7] In our own time, during the Vietnam War a Buddhist monk doused himself with gasoline and set himself on fire to protest the war. Suicide bombers became common in the Middle East in the late twentieth and early twenty-first centuries, and hijackers killed almost three thousand people by crashing two planes into the Twin Towers in New York in 2001. Though many of the bombers may have thought of themselves as martyrs, the carnage they wreaked was a travesty of love.

Love Births All Virtues (13:4–7)

> [4]**Love is patient, love is kind. It is not jealous, [love] is not pompous, it is not inflated, [5]it is not rude, it does not seek its own interests, it is not quick-tempered, it does not brood over injury, [6]it does not rejoice over wrongdoing but rejoices with the truth. [7]It bears all things, believes all things, hopes all things, endures all things.**

OT: Exod 34:6; Num 14:18
NT: Gal 5:22; Titus 3:4
Catechism: love of enemies, 1825

This section begins with two positive traits of love, next lists eight faults that it is not, then returns with five positive traits. Love here is personified, and commentators point out that these are traits of Jesus. To take on these traits is to become more like him. In the Greek, Paul expresses each trait as a verb (e.g., "love patients"), which is impossible to render in English. The effect of the verb in Greek is to show that love is active. "Unlike other loves, which can remain hidden in the heart, it is essential to charity to manifest itself, to demonstrate itself, to provide proofs, to put itself on display, so much so that

4

6. Strabo, *Geography* 15.1.73.
7. Spicq, *Agape in the New Testament*, 2:148.

in the NT it would almost always be necessary to translate *agapē* as 'dem-onstration of love.' "[8]

Love is patient. In our modern language "patience" covers a wide range of experiences, all the way from waiting in line at the checkout counter to refraining from honking the horn in a traffic jam. The biblical term goes beyond response to these types of annoyances. It means to be patient in suffering (Rom 12:12; Col 1:11). In addition to being slow to anger, it also includes the disposition not to return injury for injury (1 Thess 5:14–16) but to suffer injustice with goodwill (1 Cor 6:7). It was the kind of patience that Jesus showed in his passion. It does not mean merely hiding an inner anger under a pleasant exterior: it extends to the heart. Love is never bitter. It does not desire to get even.

Love is kind. In our modern usage, the word "kindness" has become worn so thin that it often suggests mere external courtesy. Paul is so concerned to describe the uniqueness of love in this trait that he uses a word not found else-where in the Bible and before Paul's time only in the *Psalms of Solomon* (not part of the Bible). It suggests warm and benevolent welcome, magnanimity, hospitality and generosity with time and service, an eagerness to make one's brother and sister in the Lord experience their preciousness. In the Greek the two traits just mentioned are arranged in a poetic †chiasm difficult to capture in English but highlighting the word "love" at both beginning and end: "Love is patient, kind is love."

Love **is not jealous**. Jealousy or envy was the root of the Corinthians' cliques and their competitiveness in using the charismatic gifts. The jealous person says, "I wish I had what he or she has." The envious person becomes sad because of others' gifts. But what mother is envious of her children's gifts, even when they outshine her? Because she loves them, she considers their gifts her own. So with *agapē*. Love makes us one with the beloved, and the beloved's gifts become ours. But jealousy and envy isolate (see Reflection and Application below).

Love **is not pompous**. "Pompous" translates another word not found else-where in the Bible or even in profane Greek. Other translations: "Love is not boastful" (JB, NJB); "it does not boast" (NIV). The Greek word means to be a braggart or a windbag. Jesus was humble of heart (Matt 11:29) and said that only the humble would be exalted (18:4; 23:12), as Mary proclaimed in her Magnificat (Luke 1:46–55). Love is the opposite of posturing like a peacock, as some of the know-it-alls in Corinth were doing (1 Cor 8:1). He who boasts must boast only in the Lord and what the Lord has done (1:31). For "what do

8. Ceslas Spicq, *Theological Lexicon of the New Testament*, trans. and ed. James D. Ernest (Peabody, MA: Hendrickson, 1994), 1:12.

you possess that you have not received?" (4:7). When we know we are loved by God (Rom 8:39; Gal 2:20), that is our treasure, and we need resort to no other means to assure us of our importance.

It is not inflated ("conceited," JB, NJB; "proud," NIV; "arrogant," NRSV). The Greek *physioutai* even has a hissing sound like the air being pumped into a tire or balloon. The image suggests a false or exaggerated sense of self-importance, very different from the effect of the breath of the Holy Spirit. The Corinthians have competed in spiritual gifts, comparing themselves with others and claiming a superiority that is illusory. Those moved by love, however, gladly associate themselves with the lowly, the neglected, the wallflowers, like water that always seeks the lowest level first and rises only as the lower part is filled.

It is not rude. Love is never the bull in the china shop. As much as possible it avoids giving offense (10:32; 2 Cor 6:3). It is tactful and considerate in fraternal relations. It is never indecent or obscene or disrespectful. It avoids whatever might be shameful, such as suing other members of the community before pagan courts (6:1–11), the scandal of incest (5:1–5), or excessive drinking during the Eucharist (11:21–22).

It does not seek its own interests ("is not self-seeking," NIV; "never . . . selfish," JB; "never seeks its own advantage," NJB; "does not insist on its own way," NRSV). The different translations catch the varying nuances of this word, which must be understood in the context of Paul's admonishing the Corinthians about their disregard of other members in the community. It could hardly mean that one must never assert the interests of one's own well-being, health, survival, and other such matters that would come from authentic love of self as God's creation and God's child. It is rather the conceited selfishness that is the opposite of divine love, which seeks not its own advantage but the good of others without return. This self-sacrificing love is the kind of ideal kingdom living that Jesus proposed. "Whoever wishes to come after me must deny himself, take up his cross, and follow me. For whoever wishes to save his life will lose it, and whoever loses his life for my sake and that of the gospel will save it" (Mark 8:34–35). One should let go of one's possessions, even rights, when love and discipleship prompt that (Matt 5:38–42; Luke 14:33), even lending without expecting return (Luke 6:35). It is the kind of divesting of self that made the first community to be of one heart and one soul (Acts 4:32), a contrast to the Corinthians, whom Paul advises: "No one should seek his own advantage, but that of his neighbor" (1 Cor 10:24). It is the kind of relinquishing of rights that Paul exemplified in not expecting payment for his preaching of the gospel (9:3–27). And so would he urge the knowing Corinthians to do

5

in regard to their brothers' weak †consciences (8:1–13). He even says they should be disposed to let themselves be cheated instead of battling a brother in a secular court (6:7). In short, since Jesus did not please himself (Rom 15:3), love forbids his disciples to do so.

Love **is not quick-tempered** ("does not take offence," JB, NJB; "is not easily angered," NIV; "is not irritable," NRSV). There is, of course, a just anger at evil, which Jesus himself showed (Mark 3:5). But there are also those who are touchy, who fly off the handle at the slightest provocation, who take a personal offense as a warrant for war. Charity, the gift of God's love, knows how to turn wounds into intercessory prayer and forgiveness.

Love **does not brood over injury** ("does not . . . store up grievances," NJB; "keeps no record of wrongs," NIV; "is not . . . resentful," JB, NRSV). The Greek verb *logizomai*, a favorite of Paul's, has a repertoire of meanings. It means to calculate, to add up, estimate, ponder, let one's mind dwell on, take notice of. Akin to the preceding verb, here it could mean that it does not take account of evil done to oneself; love is so strong that wrongs received roll like water off a duck's back and thus are not even remembered. It can mean that one does not weigh the evil done to oneself, with a tendency to put one's thumb on the scale. It can also mean that one does not ponder the evil one notices in the neighbor and certainly does not gossip about it. Since Paul did not specify any more specific nuance, there is no need to exclude any of those senses. But the most probable one is that caught by the NAB, the NJB, and the NIV. Love does not keep a record of wrongs. This suggests compiling a list of offenses, locking them up in the safety-deposit box of one's memory, and bearing an ongoing resentment or bitterness against the offender. Love will have none of that. Like Jesus, love forgives and desires nothing more than to embrace the offender (see Reflection and Application below).

6 　　　Love **does not rejoice over wrongdoing but rejoices with the truth**. Here Paul's treatment of divine love crosses the divide from the negative to the positive traits. If love pays little or no attention to harm done to oneself, it is highly sensitive to harm done to others and to any form of injustice. Jesus said, "Blessed are they who mourn" (Matt 5:4), and that would include those who mourn and pray for those who do evil. Even if the harm is done to oneself and others see it as meriting punishment, one is saddened by it. "Do not rejoice when your enemies fall, and when they stumble, do not let your heart exult" (Prov 24:17). Not given to vengeance, the one who loves always wishes a blessing. "Bless those who persecute [you], bless them and do not curse them" (Rom 12:14). On the other hand, when confronted by what is true, the one who loves applauds

Giving Love, Rejoicing with the Truth

Pope Benedict XVI writes: "In God and with God I love even the person whom I do not like or even know. . . . This [help] I can offer them not only through the organizations intended for such purposes, accepting it perhaps as a political necessity. Seeing with the eyes of Christ, I can give to others much more than their outward necessities; I can give them the look of love which they crave."[a]

With regard to 1 Cor 13:6, the Pope comments: "All people feel the interior impulse to love authentically: love and truth never abandon them completely, because these are the vocation planted by God in the heart and mind of every human person. The search for love and truth is purified and liberated by Jesus Christ from the impoverishment that our humanity brings to it, and he reveals to us in all its fullness the initiative of love and the plan for true life that God has prepared for us. In Christ, *charity in truth* becomes the Face of his Person, a vocation for us to love our brothers and sisters in the truth of his plan. Indeed, he himself is the Truth (cf. John 14:6)."[b]

a. *Deus Caritas Est*, §18.
b. Ibid.

and congratulates. "Truth," here contrasted with wrongdoing, means truthful conduct, morally upright behavior, beautiful and exemplary deeds. No matter who does them, there is no envy or jealousy (v. 4) because love unites one with all the good in the beloved. Because human persons live in society, to rejoice in the truth means to support all social initiatives that respect the dignity of the human person and the common good.

Love **bears all things, believes all things, hopes all things, endures all**   7
things. The Greek word for "bears" can mean "endures," but this is basically the same as the fourth verb in this verse. Thus the other sense of the verb seems more likely—"to cover, pass over, keep confidential"—which is rendered by the NIV as "always protects," by the JB as "is always ready to excuse," by the NJB as "is always ready to make allowances," or, as Adolf von Harnack long ago offered, love throws a cloak of silence over what is displeasing in another person. Love resists passing on negative comments about another. Since the entire context here has to do with relations with others rather than with God, "believing" and "hoping" must fit the same pattern. "All things" is †rhetorically hyperbolic: an intentional exaggeration permitted in a poetic hymn such as this is. "Belief" here has the sense of trust. Although not naively credulous, one who loves is inclined to believe the best about others, to trust their motives and actions. But

as Spicq points out, even if the evil in another is evident and undeniable, *agapē* still does not despair of the future: it hopes all things. It trusts the basic goodness and potential of the person; it counts on the final triumph of the good. Thus Jesus saw in the woman caught in adultery the promise of a beautiful future, in a way that her accusers did not.

Reflection and Application (13:4–7)

Love is not jealous. I saw love's exclusion of jealousy in a way that embarrassed my rash suspicion once when I was teaching at the Franciscan University of Steubenville. Allison, one of the students, had just produced a commercial recording of her original music, and she had scheduled a performance in the bookstore to celebrate its release. Since there were a lot of other good musicians on campus, I wondered whether any of them would show up. I'm ashamed to say that I really thought they would be jealous that Allison had made it in a way they had not. I went to hear Allison, partly out of pity because I thought few of her peers would be there. Instead, I could hardly get into the bookstore. The performance was wonderful, and the applause was loud and long. It said, "Allison is ours!" This is the kind of attitude that Paul is trying to instill in the Corinthians. When we love, there is no room for jealousy because others' gifts become ours.

Love does not brood over injury. After I had preached on the parable of the unforgiving debtor in Matt 18:21–35, a woman shared with me her struggle with forgiveness. When her husband returned from the Vietnam War, he was emotionally crippled and frequently resorted to fits of anger. On one occasion he even hit her on the head, making a bobby pin shoot a sharp pain in her skull. Although he never hit her again, she took out the pin and, to remind her of what he did to her, she placed it in a wall crack near the refrigerator, where she could see it every day—for twenty-seven years! "But tonight," she said, "when I go home, I'm going to throw that bobby pin away and forgive him. I want to set him free. I want to set myself free."

Love hopes all things. If I am interviewing a candidate for a job, one of the questions I would ask myself is, Can I trust this person? To answer that question, I would look for the history of his or her previous performance in consultation with previous employers and any other source of helpful information, the purpose being to minimize the risk of employing the person. But that is hardly trust; it is more like logic, and any employer will be prudent to do so (Sir 6:6–17). Real trust means a willingness to risk with the other without evidence or even with evidence to the contrary. Would I risk hiring an ex-convict, giving him the chance of a better future? It would mean believing and hoping in that person's future.

Love Lasts Forever (13:8–13)

[8]Love never fails. If there are prophecies, they will be brought to nothing; if tongues, they will cease; if knowledge, it will be brought to nothing. [9]For we know partially and we prophesy partially, [10]but when the perfect comes, the partial will pass away. [11]When I was a child, I used to talk as a child, think as a child, reason as a child; when I became a man, I put aside childish things. [12]At present we see indistinctly, as in a mirror, but then face to face. At present I know partially; then I shall know fully, as I am fully known. [13]So faith, hope, love remain, these three; but the greatest of these is love.

OT: Gen 32:31; Num 12:8; Deut 34:10
NT: Rom 8:35–39; 1 Thess 1:3; 5:8; Heb 10:22–24
Catechism: the theological virtues, 1813–29

Love never fails is sometimes translated, "Love never ends" (NRSV), "does not come to an end" (JB). Both meanings can be retained. Love never ends: unlike the †charisms, which will pass away, love will last forever, into eternity. There is no essential difference between *agapē* in this life and in the life to come; here it is in the obscurity of faith, there in the brilliance of vision, but it is the same love. Love never fails. In this life as well, love never stumbles or falls. The literal meaning of the Greek word *piptō* is to fall or collapse, and in the moral sense to fail, as when one sins (Prov 24:16). Love perseveres to the end. As Jesus approached the Last Supper, John writes: "He loved his own in the world and he loved them to the end" (John 13:1). Where there is *agapē*, there is fidelity unto death. Romantic love, *eros*, can be fickle;[9] and friendship, *philia*, can break down. But if you love someone with *agapē*, you will never cease to love them, no matter what they do. That is why the Church seals a couple's love with Christ's divine love in the sacrament of marriage, that it may last till one's last breath.

8–9

9. Pope Benedict XVI, far from despising *eros*, evaluates it positively, noting that "there is a certain relationship between love and the Divine: love promises infinity, eternity—a reality far greater and totally other than our everyday existence. Yet we have also seen that the way to attain this goal is not simply by submitting to instinct. Purification and growth in maturity are called for; and these also pass through the path of renunciation. Far from rejecting or 'poisoning' *eros*, they heal it and restore its true grandeur" (*Deus Caritas Est*, §5).

It is important to distinguish between delightful love and sacrificial love. Both are from God. Although other forms of love know delight at times, and can even inspire sacrifice, *agapē* is a unique combination of the two. If it knows delight, this is more than an emotion or feeling, since it comes from the mind and the will, as it rejoices with the truth (1 Cor 13:6), which may or may not overflow to the emotions. But it is also sacrificial, as we see Jesus' laying down his life out of love: He "has loved me and given himself up for me" (Gal 2:20). And "he loved them to the end" (John 13:1). But even sacrificial love can be a delight. It was what enabled Marianist martyr Blessed Jakob Gapp, just before the Nazis beheaded him for his defense of the Catholic faith, to write his family: "This is the happiest day of my life."

Although Paul considers **prophecies** the charism most to be sought (14:1), he lists them as the first to be **brought to nothing**. That is because they will no longer be needed. They belong to the bits and pieces of insight given in this life; but in the presence of the sun such star lights will vanish. **Tongues**, too, **will cease** for the same reason. Here they are, as it were, the lisping of souls who touch the †mystery but fall short of comprehending it. All **knowledge** of God in this life is fragmentary—not false but fragmentary—as if one were looking at a map or a satellite image of a city but not living in it.

10   The **perfect**, that is, the total, will banish **the partial**. The beatific vision will encompass all that the partial arrived at stumblingly, and offer infinitely more. What is revealed to us in this life is an icon of the realities that await us (Heb 10:1).

11   Paul now introduces two examples of the partial and the perfect. The first is the image of the **child** and the adult. He had used this earlier to contrast the immature Corinthians, who needed milk, and mature Christians, who could be given solid food (3:2). Here he uses it to contrast the present life with the future blessedness. As children learn bit by bit, so in this life Christians learn to know God piecemeal, as it were, through prophecy, meditation on the Word of God, and teaching. Adults reach an integrated understanding that enables them to drop the training wheels of childhood. So the charisms belong to the earthly stage and will no longer be needed in the kingdom.

12   **At present we see indistinctly, as in a mirror**. In the first century a mirror was a polished disk made of an alloy of copper and tin, sometimes silver or even gold, with a handle of metal or ivory, sometimes enameled.[10] Far from having the perfection of today's mirrors, they were usually concave or convex, thus giving some distortion and never giving an exact representation of the

---

10. Spicq, *Theological Lexicon*, 2:73.

object. Insight into the mysteries of God, whether through the charismatic gifts of prophecy or knowledge or through vision or mystical experience, is inescapably partial, imperfect, obscure. It contrasts with the knowledge **then**, in the next life, **face to face**. This is the earliest intimation of what theologians later would call the beatific vision. To be face-to-face is not simply to be in the presence of the other but also to look directly at each other, in the kind of communion that lovers experience while looking into each other's eyes. Since the Holy Trinity is pure spirit, the vision would be via the soul, the mind filled with the divine light, and the will with the embrace of perfect, divine love.[11] Notice that the difference between this life and the next is not love (although love will be perfected beyond imagining) but in the manner of knowing—here by faith, there by direct vision. The love experienced here is the same love that endures into the beatific vision.

At present I know partially; then I shall know fully, as I am fully known. The last little comparison is remarkable. Although we know God imperfectly in this life, he knows us perfectly, and while our knowledge of him can never be infinite, as is his knowledge of himself, we will know him and ourselves in him as he has known us all along. In this life our knowledge of ourselves is obscure, imperfect; we continue to learn about ourselves every day. The only one who knows us perfectly is the God who made us. In seeing him, we will see ourselves perfectly in the light of his knowledge and his love. Not only will we enter into the inner secret of God's being, the Holy Trinity, but the †mystery of ourselves also will be revealed. In 8:3 Paul said, "If one loves God, one is known by him." That does not mean that God doesn't know us if we don't love him. It means rather that our love of God is a sign of his special elective love for us, which the Bible calls his knowing us (Amos 3:2; †elect). Our loving God means that we have been given to participate in an experiential way in God's knowledge and love of us. It is only in God that we find our true identity. But in this life even this is obscure. Then we will see God as he really is and ourselves as who we really are in him.

Those who hear this verse at a wedding ordinarily find it a beautiful conclusion to this hymn about love, but they rarely notice the problems it creates in light of the entire previous passage. Nearly every word has its exegetical problems. **So** is the NAB's translation of the Greek, which means, literally, "Now then." But is this a logical conclusion ("Thus there **remain** . . .") or a temporal conclusion ("Now, in this life, there remain . . .")? As a logical conclusion, it would make sense if only **love** were mentioned. But how do **faith** and **hope** last

13

---

11. The humanity of Jesus will be viewed with our human eyes after our resurrection.

in eternity, when Paul expressly says that in *this* life "we walk by faith, not by sight" (2 Cor 5:7) and that "hope that sees for itself is not hope" (Rom 8:24)? Both these virtues concern what does not yet appear (Heb 11:1). By Paul's own witness, however important they are, they are partial and temporary. So the temporal meaning makes more sense: "In this life, the three things that last are faith, hope, and love." Obviously other things in this life, like the charisms and the sacraments, also last during this life, so the sense of lasting here must be comparative: faith, hope, and love are more important even than all the other gifts and virtues because they unite us directly with God. Thus they are traditionally called the theological virtues.

On the basis of the *now . . . then* contrasts of the preceding verse, we might expect something like this: "Now (in this life) there abide faith, hope, and love, these three, but *then (in the next life) only love will abide.*" But instead we read, **but the greatest of these is love**. Thus Paul is not concluding with a *now . . . then* contrast. Rather, he is telling the Corinthians that in this life, the charisms they prize so highly are of a lower order than faith, hope, and love. Gifts differ, and not all have every gift. But every Christian should have faith, hope, and love. And love is greater than the other two because it is the goal of faith and hope, and it makes those virtues active in return (see 1 Thess 1:3). The NAB, as we expect, gives the plural verb **remain** for the three subjects, faith, hope, and love, but the Greek has the singular "remains," indicating the closest bond, as if they are all shoots of the same vine. The verse provides a bridge to the next section.

Reflection and Application (13:8–13)

Often when †ministering at weddings where this chapter is proclaimed, I wonder if any of the congregation, even the bride and groom, really know what they just heard. The atmosphere of the celebration is so charged with the charm of romantic, marital love that Paul's full meaning easily gets lost. I wonder if many are not divinizing romance, as the ancient pagans did, instead of hearing God say he wants to transform it, purify it, ennoble it by incorporating it into Jesus' own sacrificial love of the Church. Our culture is intoxicated with recreational sex, which paradoxically deceives in its promises and leads to broken hearts and often unplanned consequences, sometimes tragic. That is certainly a far cry from what Paul is talking about. He is not even talking about the infatuation of emotional love that is often merely the invitation to a more committed relationship. If love does not go beyond emotion, it is not surprising that we hear of people leaving their spouse "because I don't love you anymore." Paul is talking about *agapē*. That is the love of total self-gift, of which the source and paradigm is Jesus crucified for love of his bride, the Church. There is delight in that love, but it is the delight that one experiences when giving oneself away, the joy of Jesus who loved his own "to the end" (John 13:1). It is a delight experienced in the will, even when there is no emotional residue to it. To love one's enemies, to forgive and do good to those who have hurt us, does not mean we will automatically feel a warm fuzzy in our heart for them. It does mean that with the grace of God (for *agapē* is God's gift rather than our own creation) we transcend feelings and experience the peace of Jesus at the deepest level of our soul.

Already in the Old Testament, love of God and neighbor was a command (Lev 19:18; Deut 6:5), a command that Jesus himself repeats (Matt 22:34–40). And commands are addressed to the will rather than to the feelings. But Paul also makes it clear that without the gift of the Holy Spirit, we will never fulfill that command adequately; he even says we will not fulfill it at all (Rom 7:22–25). Why? Because now we are not only to love but also to love *as Jesus has loved us*. That is what is new about the New Testament: "I give you a new commandment: love one another. As I have loved you, so you also should love one another" (John 13:34). Fortunately that kind of love has not only been shown to us outwardly in Jesus' self-gift on the cross. If that is all it was, we would never be able to do it. But it is also available to us from within when we open ourselves to God's grace. *Agapē* is God's love poured into our hearts by the Holy Spirit (Rom 5:5), enabling us to love divinely. Yes, *divinely*—to love as God himself loves (Matt 5:43–48). Surprisingly, however, the infusion of that love, far from destroying the lesser forms—the human forms—of love, purifies and protects and empowers them to become all that God originally meant them to be. That is exactly what we see in Jesus, who is God loving with a human heart.

The Gifts in Practice

1 Corinthians 14

Chapter 12 dealt with the †charisms from a theological viewpoint: how to identify their source; their unity and diversity; and how they are related to the Father, Son, and Holy Spirit and the body of Christ. Chapter 13 then dealt with love, which is what motivates and gives value to the charisms, since it is love that builds up (8:1). Now in this chapter he gives practical directives aimed at restoring and preserving order in the worshiping community, where some have created a chaotic situation because of their unenlightened enthusiasm and insensitivity to good order.

Prophecy Superior to Tongues (14:1–12)

¹Pursue love, but strive eagerly for the spiritual gifts, above all that you may prophesy. ²For one who speaks in a tongue does not speak to human beings but to God, for no one listens; he utters mysteries in spirit. ³On the other hand, one who prophesies does speak to human beings, for their building up, encouragement, and solace. ⁴Whoever speaks in a tongue builds himself up, but whoever prophesies builds up the church. ⁵Now I should like all of you to speak in tongues, but even more to prophesy. One who prophesies is greater than one who speaks in tongues, unless he interprets, so that the church may be built up.

⁶Now, brothers, if I should come to you speaking in tongues, what good will I do you if I do not speak to you by way of revelation, or knowledge, or prophecy, or instruction? ⁷Likewise, if inanimate things that produce sound, such as flute or harp, do not give out the tones distinctly, how will what is being played on flute or harp be recognized? ⁸And if the bugle

Early Christian Worship

What did a gathering of the Corinthians for worship look like? All we can be certain of is that it was a combination of structure and spontaneity. The weekly Eucharist and the †*agapē* demanded a regular meeting time on the Lord's Day. It would probably have been very early in the morning or after the workday, if the Christians had to work on that day. We don't know whether the Eucharist took place before, during, or after the meal. The texts give us no clue as to the time for spontaneous praise and sharing of the word through prophecy and teaching, but a likely place for it would have been after the reading of the Scriptures, which, Justin Martyr (a century later) tells us, took place before the consecration of the elements. Singing of psalms and spiritual songs played a part (Col 3:16). Taking our cue from 1 Tim 2:1–4, we can assume that there were prayers for government leaders; for Paul, the founder of the community; and for those in need in the church. It is also likely that there was an early form of the kiss of peace (mentioned by St. Justin;[a] see 1 Cor 16:20), and of course the narrative of the institution with the consecration of the bread and wine, the Lord's Prayer, and Communion. All these elements form part of the Catholic eucharistic liturgy today, though extended use of spontaneous praise and word charisms is ordinarily left to a prayer meeting.

a. St. Justin, *First Apology* 45.

---

gives an indistinct sound, who will get ready for battle? [9]Similarly, if you, because of speaking in tongues, do not utter intelligible speech, how will anyone know what is being said? For you will be talking to the air. [10]It happens that there are many different languages in the world, and none is meaningless; [11]but if I do not know the meaning of a language, I shall be a foreigner to one who speaks it, and one who speaks it a foreigner to me. [12]So with yourselves: since you strive eagerly for spirits, seek to have an abundance of them for building up the church.

OT: Jer 1:10; Ezek 36:36; Amos 9:11, 14; Zech 1:16; 6:12, 15
NT: 1 Cor 8:1; 1 Thess 5:20

Paul's advice to **pursue love** does more than connect this chapter with the   1
preceding. It indicates that *agapē* is not something that develops automatically; one must work at it or, better, pursue it. The word suggests a footrace, where the runner strains every muscle to attain the goal—the image Paul uses of himself pursuing the goal of his heavenly calling in Phil 3:12–14 and which he used above to urge the Corinthians to "run so as to win" (9:24–26). But his high

evaluation of love over the †charisms does not mean they are useless. On the contrary, they are the hands that charity uses to build the Church. That is why he immediately adds **but strive eagerly for the spiritual gifts** (the *pneumatika*). Since they are gifts freely given, that would mean praying for them and being open to receive them. This exhortation to "strive eagerly" for the charisms seems to fall on deaf ears for most in the Church today, quite unlike what Tertullian expected of the newly baptized in the Church at the end of the second century and St. Hilary in the fourth (see sidebar "Baptism and the Charisms" above). Why does Paul place such an importance on these spiritual gifts? And why does he want everybody to seek them? Because they are needed for the building up of the Church. They are the equipment of all the faithful for living out their mission (Eph 4:12), given them by their baptism.

Since prophecy, a word gift, is especially helpful for building the Church, Paul adds **above all that you may prophesy**. Matthew refers to prophets in his community several times (10:41; 11:9; 23:34, 37), and they frequently appear in Acts (11:27; 13:1; 15:32; 21:9–10). In its broadest sense, prophecy is speech inspired by the Holy Spirit. Although other forms of speech may also be inspired by the Spirit, prophecy seems to differ from the word of wisdom and the word of knowledge described above (1 Cor 12:8) in that it is primarily exhortative, that is, "for . . . building up, encouragement, and solace" (14:3). It is different from teaching in that it is done under the spontaneous inspiration of the Spirit, while teaching presumes some kind of orderly preparation. In the Old Testament to be a prophet was the calling of the few, but on the first Pentecost, Peter says the Holy Spirit has now been poured out on all flesh, so that sons and daughters, young and old, servants and handmaids would prophesy (Acts 2:17–18). Although occasionally prophecy refers to prediction (as in the case of Agabus who predicts a famine, Acts 11:27, and Paul's imprisonment, 21:10–11), it can also refer to a spontaneous composition of a hymn, as was the case with Zechariah at the birth of John the Baptist (Luke 1:67).[1] The book of Revelation is an example of prophecy in the form of vision, which also includes evaluative messages concerning the churches of Asia Minor (1:3; 22:19). It can be a passing gift or, in a person gifted in a more permanent way, it becomes an office, listed next to that of apostle in 1 Cor 12:28; Eph 4:11.

2   Verse 2 affirms prophecy as superior to tongues, but it also tells us something more about the latter gift. Tongues is a prayer language of the individual to God. That appears as its primary function. In saying that the tongue-speaker

---

1. "Spiritual songs" in Eph 5:19, which is distinguished from psalms and hymns and parallel to "singing and playing to the Lord in your hearts," may also refer to spontaneous compositions. See also Col 3:16.

Saint Augustine on Tongues

Although the charismatic gift of prophecy is referred to in Christian literature up to the eighth century, references to tongues disappear early, probably because the later writers thought of them as foreign languages, which they did not experience. But preconceptual prayer and song did survive in what Augustine calls jubilation: "Words cannot express the things that are sung by the heart. Take the case of people singing while harvesting in the fields or in the vineyards or when any other strenuous work is in progress. Although they begin by giving expression to their happiness in sung words, yet shortly there is a change. As if so happy that words can no longer express what they feel, they discard the restricting syllables. They burst into a simple sound of joy, of jubilation. Such a cry of joy is a sound signifying that the heart is bringing to birth what it cannot utter in words. Now what is more worthy of such a cry of jubilation than God himself, whom all words fail to describe? If words will not serve, and yet you must not remain silent, what else can you do but cry out for joy? Your heart must rejoice beyond words, soaring into an immensity of gladness, unrestricted by syllabic bonds."[a] Notice that St. Augustine uses the example of workers singing without words, not as an example of nonverbal prayer, which it is not, but only as an instance in human life where deep emotions go beyond words. Similarly, the prayer of jubilation expresses great joy by casting aside the "restricting syllables" and praising God straight from the heart.

a. Augustine, *Psalm 32, Sermon 1*; in CCSL 38:253–54.

utters mysteries in spirit, Paul is saying that the object of the prayer goes beyond rational speech. It is preconceptual, preverbal prayer, akin to a musical composition prior to words being fitted to it. One could call it nonconceptual, nonverbal prayer, but I prefer the terms "preconceptual, preverbal" because most often it prepares the mind to listen for the "intelligible" (v. 9) word that concretizes the experience of tongues, a bit like electrolysis bringing together a solution's scattered elements into a visible form. Though "tongues" can also mean foreign languages, that does not seem to be the meaning here, as we will show below on interpretation of tongues in 14:12. We would say today that it is prayer of the heart that goes directly to God, bypassing the mind. **No one listens** in the sense of understanding what is being said.

Prophecy, which is addressed **to human beings**, has three purposes: **building up, encouragement, and solace**. "Building up" is a favorite expression of Paul's, appearing six times in this chapter (vv. 3, 4, 5, 12, 17, and 26). It is the

3

figurative meaning of a word that means literally construction of a building. Earlier in the letter, Paul had told the Corinthians that they are God's building (3:9). In Eph 4:7–16, Paul writes:

> But grace was given to each of us according to the measure of Christ's gift. . . . And he gave some as apostles, others as prophets, others as evangelists, others as pastors and teachers, to equip the holy ones for the work of ministry, for building up the body of Christ, until we all attain to the unity of faith and knowledge of the Son of God, to mature manhood, to the extent of the full stature of Christ, . . . from whom the whole body, joined and held together by every supporting ligament, with the proper functioning of each part, brings about the body's growth and builds itself up in love.

This is the Magna Carta for building up the Church. First of all, the grace that Paul is speaking of in Eph 4:7 is not the grace that saves, which is never measured but is poured out in abundance (Rom 5:15, 17, 20; Eph 1:8); here Paul speaks of the grace of the charisms, which Christ measures out to each one according to his purpose. In Eph 4:11 we see certain persons who have been established in offices, one of which is the prophet—and these too are Christ's gift to his Church. But remarkably, the goal of these official †ministers is to engage and direct the church-building ministry latent by divine gift in every Christian. This is no small point. Everyone has a particular grace to build up the body of Christ (1 Cor 12:7; Eph 4:7), and those in leadership need to discover, encourage, and direct this church-building gift in each one and then orchestrate it with the gifts of other members of the community.

As Paul expounds this in Ephesians, the goal of all the building up is to bring the Church to the maturity of Christ, so that the Church will perfectly reflect the holiness of Christ and be the bride without spot or wrinkle for the great wedding feast of heaven (5:27). The process requires the active participation of each member (4:16). One of the figures for each member here is "ligament," a bodily member. But the body image is enriched by that of the building in a word hard to translate into English: *synarmologoumenon* (4:16). It refers to the entire process of quarrying stones, smoothing their edges so they fit snugly, fixing the dowels that would lock them together, and then continuing the process until the building's construction is complete. It is a marvelous image of building up the community in the unity of love.

Love is the building power (1 Cor 8:1). "Let each of us please our neighbor for the good, for building up" (Rom 15:2). But prophecy is outstanding for its ability to do so. Already in Jeremiah one of the functions of prophecy was to build up (Jer

1:10). Although the prophet is also commissioned to tear down, and the book of Revelation describes plenty of tearing down, it seems that Paul sees the gift primarily, if not uniquely, in its positive functions. **Encouragement** is closely related to building up. It suggests an interior strengthening and refreshment. **Solace** is another closely related word meaning comfort, consolation, or encouragement.

The advantage of prayer in tongues for the individual is his own upbuilding, his own facility in prayer and closer union with God. But the rest of the members cannot benefit unless there is an interpretation (vv. 5, 27–28), whereas prophecy, given in intelligible speech, **builds up the church**. Charisms are given for the building up of the Church, and obviously if one member is built up, all members benefit from the grace given to the one. But Paul doesn't want individuals to be communicating publicly in tongues unless there is an interpretation, which then makes it similar to prophecy. Though not all speak in tongues (12:30), Paul says, **I should like all of you to speak in tongues**. Does he mean that seeking the gift is optional? That would hardly correspond to Paul's desire. He knows the value of tongues from his own experience (14:18) and doubtlessly from others' reports. But the gift he urges them to seek more eagerly is prophecy because of its ability to build up the Church.

Again, prophecy is preferable to tongues in the worshiping assembly **unless** the tongue-speaker **interprets**. What does Paul mean by interpreting here? The Greek verb can mean either "translate" or "interpret." For example, Luke tells us that the name Tabitha, translated, means "Dorcas" (Acts 9:36). But when Jesus explains the Scriptures to the two travelers in Luke 24:27, that is not translation but interpretation. Now if the tongue-speaker were to *translate* his prayer, that would mean he really understood the words he was saying, but Paul says he is expressing mysteries. Furthermore, if no one else interprets, the tongue-speaker should *pray* for an interpretation (1 Cor 14:13), which he would certainly not have to do if he knew the language he was speaking. This confirms our understanding of tongues as preconceptual prayer, a prayer of the spirit or heart rather than of the mind (which is inactive, "unproductive"; 14:14). Interpretation, then, is a subsequent gift, putting words to the preconceptual utterance of tongues, which could be done by the speaker or a listener. We are not therefore talking about language translation but Spirit-inspired praise in tongues followed by a suitable rendering of the sounds in communicable words.[2] The parallel with musical composition is helpful: a composer might first create a melody and later he or she or someone else might come up with words that suit it (see sidebar).

2. See George T. Montague, *The Spirit and His Gifts* (New York: Paulist Press, 1974), 34; idem, *The Holy Spirit: Growth of a Biblical Tradition* (1976; repr., Eugene, OR: Wipf & Stock, 2006), 274–83.

6   This verse shows the kind of word-speaking that ministers to the community. Presenting a hypothetical visit in which he would only speak in **tongues**, Paul shows the uselessness of the gift for public worship without some understandable result. We wish Paul had given us an example of a **revelation**, but the only help is his other uses of the word. In Gal 1:12 he speaks of the revelation of the gospel to him; in 2:2 he says that he went up to Jerusalem "in accord with a revelation." And finally he speaks about his own visionary experience as a revelation (2 Cor 12:1, 7). Hence it could refer to any type of heavenly communication, whether in word or vision. **Knowledge**, **prophecy**, and **instruction** (teaching) were listed earlier (1 Cor 12:8–10, 28–30; 13:1–2), and we have already discussed the first two at those points. Teaching differs from the others in that it is more closely linked to apostolic or pastoral authority and supposes a greater knowledge of the faith, which Paul himself would have had. The point here is not the content of each of these gifts but the fact that they can be understood in a way that tongues cannot.

7–12   In 14:7–9 Paul simply uses examples of musical instruments' issuing a nonverbal sound to show that if the worshipers **do not utter intelligible speech, how will anyone know what is being said?** Then he uses the example of someone speaking a language that the hearer does not know: communication simply does not happen. Is this evidence that Paul thought the tongue-speaker was speaking an actual human language? In the light of the other evidence we have shown above, the answer is no. It is simply another example of speaking something the listeners do not understand. Similarly, when Paul says **if the bugle gives an indistinct sound** when urging troops to **get ready for battle**, he is suggesting that tongues indeed produce sound but, unless they are interpreted, the assembly has no idea if the message is a comforting one or a call to arms. Paul concludes this section by urging them to turn their eagerness for spiritual gifts (*pneumata*, **spirits**) to seeking **an abundance of them**, not for their own glory but **for building up the church**. This indicates, once more, that the charisms are not natural talents but gifts one should pray for and then seek to exercise.

Reflection and Application (14:1–12)

What is the gift of tongues? A phenomenon in recent years that has excited charismatics and often troubled others is this gift of tongues. Those who have received and use the gift testify to its effectiveness in prayer and also its opening them to other gifts. But it has sometimes become a defining boundary that has divided rather than united, although it has fared better in the Catholic Church than in some Protestant churches where tongues-speakers were expelled or left their congregations to found charismatic ones. Popes Paul VI, John Paul II, and Benedict XVI have all praised and blessed the Catholic Charismatic Renewal.[3] What can be said about the biblical foundation for this gift, and what can be said for its contemporary relevance for the Church?

First of all, both in Paul and in the Acts of the Apostles, it is clear that tongues is a gift of prayer (see commentary). And prayer is not always verbal. The psalmist says he is weary with his sighing, his groaning, his moaning: "I am wearied with sighing" (Ps 6:7); "I wail with anguish of heart. . . . My groaning is not hidden from you. . . . My heart shudders" (38:9–11); "I lie awake and moan" (102:8). Paul speaks of Christian prayer as a groaning prompted by the Spirit (Rom 8:23, 26). We know too that there are experiences we cannot find words to express, whether moments of ecstatic joy or deep sorrow. When confronted with †mystery, words do not suffice. Thus Paul says that when one prays in tongues, one is expressing "mysteries in spirit" (1 Cor 14:2) and one's conceptual mind is inactive (14:14). This is the kind of prayer of the heart that the Church's long mystical tradition has described. Conceptual, verbal prayer, word prayer, certainly has its role (Jesus taught words in the Lord's Prayer), but no concept, because it is limited, can contain God. The words of revelation and the prayer of faith can touch God, but no human word can wrap itself around him. Prayer in tongues not only accepts that but also testifies to it in a loving, reverential, even awestruck way. It is a nonverbal prayer or song of praise (14:15) and thanksgiving (14:16). When spoken aloud in the assembly, it calls for an interpretation: a rendering of its sense in intelligible words (14:13, 27–28).

Is it a gift of speaking foreign languages? The Greek word *glōssa* can mean "tongue" as the organ of speech, or "language." But the expression in 1 Corinthians is a special case. Although Paul calls for an interpretation of the tongue when spoken aloud publicly, he understands interpretation to be an additional gift given in prayer (14:13) and not therefore a translation by some listener who recognizes the language. The link between an inspired nonverbal message and its inspired verbal interpretation would be analogous to the link a songwriter creates between melody and the words that fit it. This is the best understanding of the phenomenon that Paul describes as praying or speaking in tongues.

But what about the Pentecost experience? "Then there appeared to them tongues as of fire, which parted and came to rest on each one of them. And they were all filled with the holy Spirit and began to speak in different tongues,

---

3. See Oreste Pesare, ed., *"Then Peter Stood Up . . ."*: *Collection of the Popes' Addresses to the Catholic Charismatic Renewal from Its Origin to the Year 2000* (Rome: International Catholic Charismatic Renewal Services, 2000).

as the Spirit enabled them to proclaim" (Acts 2:3–4). At first sight it seems that they were speaking different human languages. But on careful reading of the entire passage, 2:1–13, we note that the text speaks three times about the crowd *hearing* them in their own languages. Thus the phenomenon of their speaking need not have been any different from what we find in Paul's writings, except that the miracle was that of hearing or, we could say, of interpretation.

That being said, there is plenty of anecdotal evidence of people hearing words in a known language when someone spoke in tongues. Father Daniel Gagnon, OMI, was preaching in English to an Iraqi congregation in Detroit in 2004 when he felt inspired to begin speaking in tongues. Afterward an Iraqi came forward and said he heard Father Dan speaking Arabic, and he related the message he heard. Recently an African priest visiting a charismatic parish in Michigan heard the celebrant pray in the native dialect of his village in Nigeria.

My own experience of tongues for nearly forty years confirms the value of this gift. Praying and singing in tongues has been a great gift for me. It has had the effect of calming my spirit like a lake whose stormy waters have been stilled so as to reflect what is real, the truth as God sees it, and it has readied me to receive the word like a pebble dropped into the still waters and creating a ripple to the farthest shore. When used publicly in a prayer meeting, it has stilled the participants into a listening mode and readied them to hear the word of the Lord with a fresh, *now* meaning.

Is the contemporary phenomenon identical with that described by Paul in 1 Corinthians? Of course we have no recordings of those gatherings two thousand years ago, but there does seem to be a good fit with what he describes there. The point to be retained is that with this gift the ordinary faithful can pray in a way that surpasses their understanding, just as the Holy Spirit enables us "to know the love of Christ that surpasses knowledge" (Eph 3:19). Thus it is one of the many charisms that Paul urges the faithful to earnestly seek (1 Cor 14:1).

Tongues Need Interpretation (14:13–19)

---

¹³Therefore, one who speaks in a tongue should pray to be able to interpret. ¹⁴[For] if I pray in a tongue, my spirit is at prayer but my mind is unproductive. ¹⁵So what is to be done? I will pray with the spirit, but I will also pray with the mind. I will sing praise with the spirit, but I will also sing praise with the mind. ¹⁶Otherwise, if you pronounce a blessing [with] the spirit, how shall one who holds the place of the uninstructed say the "Amen" to your thanksgiving, since he does not know what you are

saying? ¹⁷For you may be giving thanks very well, but the other is not built
up. ¹⁸I give thanks to God that I speak in tongues more than any of you,
¹⁹but in the church I would rather speak five words with my mind, so as to
instruct others also, than ten thousand words in a tongue.

OT: 1 Chron 16:36
NT: 1 Cor 12:10; Eph 5:19

It is clear from verses 13–14 that tongues, an activity in the human spirit, is a   **13–15**
kind of contemplative prayer in which the mind is inactive or at rest. Paul does
not say this is a bad thing. Quite the contrary, **my spirit is at prayer**. For the
spirit to be at prayer is a wonderful gift. Jude urges his readers: "Build yourselves
up in your most holy faith; pray in the holy Spirit" (Jude 20), which sounds
very much like Paul telling his faithful that praying in tongues builds them up
(14:4). In the common worship, however, the expression of tongues should
lead to some kind of verbal resolution if it is to be helpful to others. Thus Paul
recommends praying and singing praise with both **the spirit** and **the mind**.
"Singing praise" with one's spirit indicates that tongues were sometimes sung. It
is perhaps to some such songs that Eph 5:19 and Col 3:16 refer when grouping
"spiritual songs" along with psalms and hymns. The reference to **praise** tells
us that such was a primary activity of tongues and that spontaneous creation
of songs, melody, and words took place in the Corinthian assembly. In prayer
groups today the participants often sing chorally in tongues. We don't know
whether the Corinthians did so or not.

The custom in the Jewish synagogues of answering **Amen** to a public prayer   **16–17**
carried over into the Christian assembly and has continued down to our day.
"Amen" derives from the Hebrew verb meaning "to be firm, established," and
is the expression of total agreement and solid commitment to what was proclaimed in prayer. Note that here in verse 16 **blessing** is parallel and equivalent
to **thanksgiving**. For most Catholics today, blessing means praying over a person
or thing, but in Jewish and early Christian tradition, it also meant to bless and
praise God for what he has done, either in creation or in saving his people. The
focus is on God rather than on the person or thing to be blessed. The problem
here is that, if someone prays or sings only in tongues without interpretation,
an amen could not be said by the **uninstructed**. The NRSV renders this term
as "outsider," the JB and NJB as "uninitiated person," and the NIV as "one who
finds himself among those who do not understand." The meaning of the Greek
idiōtēs has to be determined from the context, for it can mean a private individual
as distinct from a public person or official, a layman compared to an expert,

Prophetic Form

LIVING TRADITION

The Old Testament prophets, speaking for the Lord, use the "I" form: they speak for God in the first person. In one of his Easter homilies, Bishop Melito of Sardis switches to this prophetic form:

> I have freed the condemned, brought the dead back to life, raised men from their graves. Who has anything to say against me? I, he said, am the Christ; I have destroyed death, triumphed over the enemy, trampled hell underfoot, bound the strong one, and taken men up to the heights of heaven. I am the Christ.
>
> Come, then, all you nations of men, receive forgiveness for the sins that defile you. I am your forgiveness. I am the Passover that brings salvation. I am the Lamb who was immolated for you. I am your ransom, your life, your resurrection, your light, I am your salvation and your king. I will bring you to the heights of heaven. With my own right hand I will raise you up, and I will show you the eternal Father."[a]

a. Melito of Sardis, in SC 123:60–64, 120–22; trans. International Commission on the English Liturgy. Office of Readings, Monday within the Octave of Easter.

or an outsider compared to a member. In Acts 4:13 it means "ordinary." Here in 1 Cor 14:16 it is properly translated "uninstructed" because it would refer to whoever is not instructed by hearing an interpretation of the message in tongues and even more so to any newcomer unfamiliar with the phenomenon of tongues. The same word is used in 14:23–24 along with "unbeliever," but it is not clear whether the two there are distinguished or whether they are meant to designate the same kind of person. Even the initiated would be unable to say amen to uninterpreted tongues, but, as in 14:23–24, Paul is especially concerned about the effect on the nonbelievers or those inadequately formed neophytes who might be turned off or at least would **not** be **built up**.

18–19   Throughout this instruction, Paul has been careful not to denigrate the gift of tongues when he compares it with prophecy, both because tongues are a gift of the Spirit and also not to offend the Corinthians who prize them so highly. Here then Paul says, **I give thanks to God that I speak in tongues more than any of you**. Notice how he considers such prayer to be a gift for which he thanks God. This is an additional way Paul shows his link with the Twelve and the primitive Jerusalem community. Not only has he too seen the risen Christ (9:1), accrediting him as an apostle, but he also has experienced their initial Pentecostal experience as well. In adding **but in the church** he is distinguishing the use of tongues in the assembly from their use in private prayer, where interpretation is not necessary. In the assembly the Christian, even in the profoundest experience of prayer, should be sensitive of the effect of his prayer on others.

Prophecy Brings Conversion (14:20–25)

²⁰Brothers, stop being childish in your thinking. In respect to evil be like infants, but in your thinking be mature. ²¹It is written in the law:

"By people speaking strange tongues
    and by the lips of foreigners
I will speak to this people,
    and even so they will not listen to me,

says the Lord." ²²Thus, tongues are a sign not for those who believe but for unbelievers, whereas prophecy is not for unbelievers but for those who believe.

²³So if the whole church meets in one place and everyone speaks in tongues, and then uninstructed people or unbelievers should come in, will they not say that you are out of your minds? ²⁴But if everyone is prophesying, and an unbeliever or uninstructed person should come in, he will be convinced by everyone and judged by everyone, ²⁵and the secrets of his heart will be disclosed, and so he will fall down and worship God, declaring, "God is really in your midst."

OT: 1 Kings 18:39; Isa 28:11–12; 45:14; Dan 2:47; Zech 8:23
NT: Matt 5:13–16; 10:16; Acts 2:13; Rom 16:19; 1 Cor 13:11; Eph 4:14

There is a difference between being childlike and being **childish**. Paul plays **20** on that difference here. The value that the Corinthians place on tongues—and here we are dealing with uninterpreted tongues—as a higher, more divine gift than any of the word gifts, shows that their **thinking** is childish, immature, like the thinking of those who create cliques by clinging to one preacher over another (1:10–2:5). In terms of your moral life, Paul says, be innocent **like infants, but in your thinking be mature**. That means to begin to see things in their proper light, and just as with the idol offerings, that means thinking of the effect of their actions on others.

In this section Paul is especially concerned with the effect of uninterpreted **21–22** tongues on those who are not members of the community. The initiated members may not be able to derive fruit from uninterpreted tongues, but the uninitiated are in danger of something much worse: being turned away from the faith. Thus Paul thinks of the words of Isa 28:11–12, which he quotes freely and edits slightly to apply more clearly to the Corinthian situation. Isaiah had repeatedly warned the people of Israel that unless they convert, they will perish at the hands of the Assyrians. Since they would not listen to him, God will now communicate through **people speaking strange tongues** and **the lips of foreigners** (the Assyrians) as a judgment upon their lack of faith. This change will not lead them to faith but only confirm them in their disbelief: **even so they will not listen to me**. The strange tongues of the Assyrians will be God's sign to them, fulfilling the prophecy of Isaiah. But this sign will not lead unbelieving Israel to faith. It is in this sense that **tongues are a sign . . . for unbelievers**.[4] If tongues are not interpreted, they are likely to confirm the visitor in unbelief. But **prophecy is not for unbelievers but for those who believe**. Thus Paul says that tongues are a sign, but he does not say that prophecy is a sign. A sign has an ambiguity about it, which may be misinterpreted, as indeed it was at Pentecost by some in the crowd who scoffed (Acts 2:13). Prophecy, however, is intelligible speech and lacks that ambiguity.

23–25   Here Paul finds a parallel to Isaiah's view in Corinth. The **uninstructed people or unbelievers** who **come in** not only would be surprised but also likely turned off by the phenomenon of uninterpreted tongues. The word "uninstructed" is an indication that some explanation of the phenomenon should be given to visitors, but even more important, interpretation in comprehensible words should be given to any message in tongues.[5] Without it, tongues could become a sign of judgment upon them, but not a judgment that would lead to conversion. It would drive them away. The effect of prophecy is different. **If everyone is prophesying, and an unbeliever or uninstructed person should come in, he will be convinced by everyone and judged by everyone** ("reproved by all and called to account by all"; NRSV). What Paul means by this is not that the community would condemn the unbeliever but that God through the gift of prophecy would convince the person of his sins. The judgment would lead to conversion. Nathan did this to David in revealing his adultery and murder (2 Sam 12:7–12). In the history of the Church, saints and confessors like John Vianney and Padre Pio were able to read hearts, revealing sins that people had

4. We must admit that Paul's perspective here is not quite the same as that in Acts 2:1–11, where the phenomenon of tongues draws the crowds, some of whom hear a message in their own language and others scoff at the phenomenon as the effect of drunkenness. Here in Corinthians he is perceiving only the negative effect that disorderly tongues would have on unbelievers.

5. Paul does not have in view choral singing in tongues as is done today in many charismatic groups. I know of professional musicians who have found the practice to be beautiful and attractive.

hidden. It is conceivable that something similar occurred in Corinth, though it need not have been a prophet's public revelation of the unbeliever's sin. Rather, in the public context of Corinth, as often happens in hearing the word preached today, the individual is cut to the heart and of his own accord confesses his sins. According to Acts 2:37, this is what happened on the day of Pentecost, when those listening to Peter's sermon were "cut to the heart," repented, and sought baptism and the gift of the Holy Spirit. Finally, we should repeat that the disorder here is the pastorally insensitive use of tongues. Paul is aware not only of the interior needs of the community but also of the evangelizing potential of the assembly for visitors. That calls for guidance concerning order, as he will now explain.

Practical Rules of Order (14:26–33a)

[26]So what is to be done, brothers? When you assemble, one has a psalm, another an instruction, a revelation, a tongue, or an interpretation. Everything should be done for building up. [27]If anyone speaks in a tongue, let it be two or at most three, and each in turn, and one should interpret. [28]But if there is no interpreter, the person should keep silent in the church and speak to himself and to God.

[29]Two or three prophets should speak, and the others discern. [30]But if a revelation is given to another person sitting there, the first one should be silent. [31]For you can all prophesy one by one, so that all may learn and all be encouraged. [32]Indeed, the spirits of prophets are under the prophets' control, [33a]since he is not the God of disorder but of peace.

OT: Isa 45:14–15; Zech 8:23
NT: Rom 15:33; 1 Cor 12:7–10; 14:6; Eph 4:12; 1 Thess 5:19–21

As is usual, after teaching on a topic, Paul concludes with **what is to be done**. **26**
The assembly here would be the weekly meeting to celebrate the Eucharist and the †*agapē* meal, with spontaneous prayer preceding or following. The list of activities is not exhaustive, but it gives us some idea of the kinds of sharing done at the assembly. With our Bibles and missalettes, we often read or recite the psalms. But in the Old Testament as well as the New, the word **psalm** refers to a song, whether traditional as in the Psalter, or composed and sung spontaneously by a participant in the worship. **Instruction** ("teaching" or "lesson" in some translations) would be less spontaneous and require some knowledge of Scripture and of the apostolic tradition. It would require some preparation

in order to be effective. A **revelation** would mean some kind of direct divine communication, such as a vision (see 2 Cor 12:1, where visions and revelations are paralleled) or verbal inspiration. Paul himself received a revelation that took him to the third heaven, but its content was incommunicable (2 Cor 12:1–5). Evidently that sort of revelation is not intended here, since it is to be shared with the community. To the Galatians, Paul wrote that he went up to Jerusalem because of a revelation (Gal 2:2). Whether there is much difference between a revelation and a prophecy (which is not listed here) is doubtful, since the book of Revelation is called both a "revelation" and a "prophecy" (Rev 1:1, 3; 22:18). Paul assumes that one person would have a **tongue**, meaning a nonverbal expression of praise or thanksgiving, and another **an interpretation** of it. All these gifts derive their value in the measure that they contribute to **building up** the community.

27–28   Paul indicates that no more than **three** should speak in tongues, and they should do so in order. He is clearly not referring to one's personal prayer here but to a message in the public assembly. This suggests the possibility that the Corinthians indeed were giving messages in tongues out of turn and even all at once, creating a chaotic situation. Was this done in the belief that one had no control over the impulse, or was it part of the competitive spirit that Paul denounced in other situations earlier? From what Paul says in 14:32, it is likely that many thought they had no control over their tongues when they felt moved by the Spirit. Not so. Only **two or at most three** should speak in a tongue, and only if there is someone present who can **interpret**. Since one would have to know ahead of time if an interpreter were present, it seems that certain persons in the assembly were known to have the gift of interpretation, and this could include the speaker himself (14:13).

29   The same rule holds for **prophets**. Since tongues should be followed by interpretation, so prophecy should be followed by the gift of discernment. This is an important principle concerning the gift of prophecy, and it indicates that speech apparently given under divine inspiration may be discerned by **others** to be totally from the Lord, or only partially so, or not at all. The gift of prophecy, after all, operates according to the individual's gifts, faculties, and temperament.[6] On the one hand, in some cases the person could be simply projecting one's own needs or thoughts. On the other hand, persons deeply immersed in prayer can, through the gift of prophecy, share a word that is truly from God and capable of moving hearts. Yet such revelations should never be assumed to

---

6. It is reported that St. Joan of Arc, whose interrogators said her messages were the product of her imagination, replied, "Of course my imagination! How else would God speak to me?"

Control of Religious Experience?

Paul's statement that "the spirits of prophets are under the prophets' control" raises the question of what kind of control he means, particularly when we know that saints and mystics have experienced ecstasy and rapture, and Paul himself says that he was taken to the third heaven and doesn't know whether he was in the body or out of the body (2 Cor 12:1–4). Paul clearly excluded the kind of frenzy identified among the Greeks as marks of the supernatural. When the saints and mystics are overcome by ecstasy and rapture, it is normally in personal prayer rather than in a public context like the liturgy and is marked by deep peace and loving focus upon the Lord. Like Paul's experience (2 Cor 12:4), it is often incommunicable. Far from being a loss of freedom, Christian ecstasy engages freedom to the fullest, for the will is responding to the supreme good in love. Genuine ecstasy or rapture is a gift; it cannot be induced or planned by the subject. If one loses sensible contact with the surrounding world, so as not to sense even a pinprick, the experience, though transformative, is always temporary, after which one returns to normal everyday life. Often one is told, either by the vision or by one's spiritual director, to record the experience as best one can, or one is directed to give a message to someone (as Juan Diego was told to speak to the bishop). Thus, unlike the Greek oracles, the person remembers what was revealed. Now what Paul is saying in 14:32 concerns the *communication* to the assembly of what is received. And thus whether to speak out what one has received, and when to do it, is under the prophet's control. The word "received" may indeed be beyond one's control, for it is unmerited and surprising, but the decision to share it publicly is not. And all prophetic utterances are to be discerned (14:29; 1 Thess 5:19–21).

be infallible. Earlier Paul had said, "Do not quench the Spirit. Do not despise prophetic utterances. Test everything; retain what is good" (1 Thess 5:19–21). Those who **discern** are the entire community, but this will also demand that some authority structure be present to decide in case consensus cannot be reached. Already in the Thessalonian community seven years earlier, Paul had established an authority structure ("those . . . who are over you in the Lord"; 1 Thess 5:12), and it is unthinkable that Paul would not have done so here. On what basis would the community discern? Obviously on how well the prophecy coheres with the confession that Jesus is Lord (12:1–3) and with the apostolic tradition and Paul's teaching. Most prominently, that would include making sure that the word promotes charity (chap. 13). Paul does not say "at most" **three** prophets should speak, as he did with the tongue-speakers, thus softening the rule and suggesting that occasional exceptions might be permissible.

30   **But if a revelation is given to another person sitting there, the first one should be silent.** This verse seems to assume that the first one speaking a prophecy is doing so at length, in which case if another receives "a revelation," he should motion to the speaker to allow him to speak. Mutual respect and love should reign.

31–33a   If **all prophesy one by one**, there will be order and **all may learn and all be encouraged**. In the Greek world various religious groups believed that when a divine spirit possessed one, there was no control over the outcome.[7] Indeed, the Pythia of Delphi and the priestesses of Dodona, who enthralled Greek culture as revealers of the divine, went into an altered, frenzied state of consciousness, and it was taken as a mark of their being possessed by a supernatural power that they could not remember what they said in their ecstatic state.[8] The movement of the Holy Spirit is not like that. **The spirits of prophets are under the prophets' control.** There is a difference between the strong urging of the Spirit and a compulsion that removes the person's freedom. Even when one seems overwhelmed by the Spirit, the Spirit who moves the individual is not other than the Spirit who moves the community in love, order, and peace.

Reflection and Application (14:26–33a)

Prophecy today. Prophecy is speech inspired by the Holy Spirit. It can appear in various forms, such as spontaneous poetry (Luke 1:68–79) or visions such as we find throughout the book of Revelation. In charismatic prayer groups today, it is often verbalized in the "I" form, as God himself speaking. The important point for Paul is that the word should be an intelligible communication for the benefit of all, including visitors to the community. The fact that one feels inspired does not guarantee the authenticity of one's prophecy. Paul had said in his first letter: "Do not despise prophetic utterances. Test everything; retain what is good" (1 Thess 5:19–21). Among the norms of discernment: Does the prophecy give glory to Jesus as Lord (1 Cor 12:1–3)? Does the life of the speaker support the truth of the word?[9] Is it in accord with the apostolic tradition and teaching of the Church? Is the community or the visitor able to say "Amen" to

---

7. Euripides describes one such madness or frenzy in *Bacchanals* 651–770.

8. See John R. Levison, *Filled with the Spirit* (Grand Rapids: Eerdmans, 2009), 154–77.

9. The †Shepherd of Hermas says: "Determine the man who has the divine Spirit by his life" (*Mandate* 11.7). The true prophet is gentle, quiet, humble, while the false is arrogant, shameless, talkative, wanting a seat of honor, acquainted with luxuries, and seeking money (11.11–12).

the prophecy (1 Cor 14:16)? Does it have a salutary effect on the community? For such speech to be truly inspired, a personal prayer life is a prerequisite. Paul's point is that every Christian should seek the gift of the Spirit whereby one will receive a fresh word of the Lord capable also of inspiring others.

Liturgy today. When we compare what we know of the liturgy in Corinth with our liturgies today, we note both similarities and differences. The Eucharist is central to both, though the form of the prayers surrounding the consecration differed from community to community in the early Church. The †*Didache* 9–10, for example, gives a formula of consecration but also says that if a prophet is present, he may celebrate as he sees fit (10:7). There was also a liturgy of the word, which involved reading from the Old Testament and, as the words and deeds of Jesus circulated before the composition of the Gospels, surely they would have been read or remembered in some way.

The spontaneous sharing we see in the Corinthian community has passed into faith-sharing Bible studies and prayer groups today, and a much more formal structure reigns in the liturgy, with only the bishop, priest, or deacon authorized to formally break the bread of the word for the congregation. This evolution to a greater uniformity is understandable as the Church grew and community came to mean not just an extended household but also an international body spread throughout the world. There was also the emergence of splinter groups whose teaching was suspect, among them the †Montanists, who claimed their direct inspiration by the Holy Spirit in insubordination to the bishops.

The beauty of the Catholic liturgy is that wherever one goes in the world, it is the same eucharistic celebration, even though there are differences between the rites and there may be cultural adaptations. That being said, what one brings to the liturgy needs to be fed by other means, especially spontaneous faith sharing and prayer among Christians. This we can learn from our brothers and sisters in Corinth.

How the gifts build the Church. One way to understand the variety of the gifts and offices in Paul's Letters is to see them as expressing and fostering the various elements that are essential to the community's life. The community is essentially one of worship and praise (the function of tongues), in which the Word of God comes alive with a *now* meaning (the gifts of prophecy, interpretation, words of wisdom and knowledge). It needs to integrate these fresh insights with the tradition (via teachers). It is a community that administers wholeness to its members and to others (via healing) and builds up their faith through constantly fresh surprises of the Spirit (via miraculous powers). It also is a human community that needs many services (including administration;

Rom 12:8). It is a community that reaches out to those who have not yet heard the good news (via evangelists; Eph 4:11). Finally, it seeks the unity of the Spirit (Eph 4:3), and that means a continuity not only with the larger community of the Church throughout the world but also with the community of the past, going back to the authentic tradition that stems from the risen Christ and the primitive Jerusalem community. The Apostle fulfills this function: he is the visible link between the community of believers and the risen Christ (1 Cor 9:1; Acts 1:22; compare John 20:29) and the assurer of continuity in the tradition (1 Cor 14:36). Catholics see this role fulfilled today in the bishop.

Practical questions about charisms. Readers of Paul's teaching on the †charisms may have two different reactions. They may think this is something for the early Church but without relevance to Church life today, or if they take it seriously, they will wonder, "Do I have a charism? What am I supposed to do to get one?" and similar questions.

If it is not clear from this section, it certainly is clear from elsewhere in Paul's writings and the New Testament that everyone baptized into Christ has a charism. In Eph 4:7, after describing the gifts we all have in common, Paul turns to the charisms and says: "Grace was given to each of us according to the measure of Christ's gift" (see also 1 Cor 12:7). And 1 Pet 4:10 says: "As each one has received a gift, use it to serve one another." So the answer is yes, you do have a gift. But it does not mean that you have activated that gift or that you are exercising it. Some of the gifts are exercised in worship, such as tongues, prophecy, words of wisdom or knowledge; others in healing; still others in services to the community or evangelizing. The point is that the exercise of any of these gifts, which go beyond natural talents, comes from a movement of the Holy Spirit. And the effects are evident in their impact on others, even if the gift is manifested in the manner in which one performs a simple act of service.

Paul urges his faithful to "strive eagerly for the spiritual gifts" (14:1). This suggests that desiring one or more of the gifts is not only a good thing; desire should also prompt prayer to receive them. Often today, especially in the charismatic movement, people attend a seminar or retreat, which leads to being prayed over for a release of the power of the Holy Spirit in the charisms. You will know you have received a gift when you begin to use it. And then you must continue to use it, as the 1 Peter 4:10 says, because you are now a steward of God's grace.

But each gift in the Church is like a musical instrument in a symphony. It is meant to play its part in a larger performance, at the appropriate time and under the direction of a leader, that is, under authority. Some people use the gifts to become Lone Rangers, but that is not God's plan for their use. When Paul says the gifts are made for building up the body (14:3), this assumes a sense of order—which is exactly what Paul was trying to teach the disorderly Corinthian community. They did not sound like a symphony but more like an orchestra warming up.

Thus a charism is to be discerned by its effect on the community: does it build up, encourage, console (14:3)? "Do not quench the Spirit. Do not despise prophetic utterances. Test everything, retain what is good" (1 Thess 5:19–21).

A Mysterious Intrusion? (14:33b–40)

33b As in all the churches of the holy ones, 34women should keep silent in the churches, for they are not allowed to speak, but should be subordinate, as even the law says. 35But if they want to learn anything, they should ask their husbands at home. For it is improper for a woman to speak in the church. 36Did the word of God go forth from you? Or has it come to you alone?

37If anyone thinks that he is a prophet or a spiritual person, he should recognize that what I am writing to you is a commandment of the Lord. 38If anyone does not acknowledge this, he is not acknowledged. 39So, [my] brothers, strive eagerly to prophesy, and do not forbid speaking in tongues, 40but everything must be done properly and in order.

OT: Gen 3:16
NT: 1 Cor 16:14; Eph 5:22–24; 1 Tim 2:11–15; Titus 2:5; 1 Pet 3:1–2, 5

The attentive reader will experience surprise at this text because it introduces something that not only seems unlike Paul elsewhere but actually seems to contradict what he assumed in 11:4–5—that women prayed and prophesied in the assembly. That is why a number of scholars think this passage was inserted by another hand later than Paul, possibly to conform to more conservative norms, such as might be expected in a Jewish synagogue. They also observe that in some manuscripts verses 34–35 appear after verse 40. As a matter of fact, if verses 33b–36 are omitted (and even more so if 33b–38 are omitted), the thought moves smoothly from verse 33a to the conclusion in verses 39–40. Some think that this later insertion was to combat some kind of disorder such as †Montanism, in which women had a prominent role.

However, a major objection to this hypothesis is that the troublesome passage   33b–35
occurs in all the manuscripts, even in those where it is displaced; and in the

more reliable manuscripts, the order is what we have in the text above. Moreover, the passage is not unlike one in 1 Tim 2:11–15, which forbids women to teach in the assembly.[10] If, then, we accept that Paul himself wrote or dictated this passage, perhaps after receiving a report of the unruly situation in Corinth, we must reconcile his statement **women should keep silent in the churches, for they are not allowed to speak**, with 11:4–5, where they pray and prophesy. Thus here he must be referring to speaking other than praying or prophesying. What kind of speaking would that be? The sequence about asking **their husbands at home** suggests that the speaking is questioning, perhaps even disputing what is said, possibly even publicly expressing disagreement with their husbands. The early communities met in homes, and the woman in her own home may have felt the right to speak out. "Woman" (*gynē*), then, contrasted here with "husband," means "wife." And so the woman who prophesies must respect her role as wife and refrain from the kind of intrusive questions that might cause embarrassment to her husband. Within his encouragement to all to prophesy (14:1, 31), Paul wishes to protect the marital relationship, and this fits the context of his calling for order. So in the end the passage need not be so intrusive as it may seem.

36   Paul ends this little section, as he does in 12:29–30, with two †rhetorical questions. **Did the word of God go forth from you?** In calling the gospel the word of God, the Apostle stresses its divine origin at the same time that he implies its human, geographical origin from the original Jerusalem community. If the Corinthian community had been the base from which the word of God first went forth, it might have some right to authorize the Church's practices. But such was not the case. **Or has** the word of God **come to you alone?** That is, the Corinthians may be *a* church, but they belong to *the* Church, the sum of the network of churches birthed by the word. Paul wants the doctrinal unity of the churches to be reflected in practices common to them all.

37   The last verses of this chapter flow so smoothly from the discussion of prophecy in 14:29–33a that it seems likely either that Paul or a disciple inserted the preceding section about women later, slipping it in along with the other rules of order, or that Paul made a deliberate digression in his dictation, with the clear intention of coming back to prophecy in this verse. **If anyone thinks that he is a prophet** may indicate that someone in the community has prophesied that women should remove their veils. If so, Paul is condemning such teaching as

---

10. Of course, the Pauline authorship of that letter is disputed. See my commentary *First and Second Timothy, Titus*, CCSS (Grand Rapids: Baker Academic, 2008), 16–24.

false. Understanding the return to prophecy at this point is important because of the weight of the Apostle's claim that he is writing **a commandment of the Lord**. Did Jesus give a commandment about women being silent in the assembly? Or were even the specific directives of Paul about prophesying laid down by the Lord? This is hardly imaginable. The commandment must have been of a more basic nature, namely, the command to be at "peace with one another" (Mark 9:50), from which Paul could logically derive his instruction about order in relationships, especially in the assembly.

Playing on the word "acknowledge," Paul says, **If anyone does not acknowledge this, he is not acknowledged**. What does it mean not to be acknowledged? Does it simply mean, "Don't pay any attention to him"? The context of the Lord's commandment surely makes it more serious than that. To be acknowledged by God, to be known by him, is to be in his grace: "If one loves God, one is known by him" (8:3). To be disobedient to the Apostle and to the Lord's command is to show lack of love for God and thus to endanger one's salvation.

38

Lest the Corinthians think Paul is saying that it is safer to avoid using the †charisms, he now returns to the positive note he struck in 14:1: "Strive eagerly for the spiritual gifts, above all that you may prophesy." Here he says **strive eagerly to prophesy, and do not forbid speaking in tongues**. He has taught the same in 1 Thess 5:19–20: "Do not quench the Spirit. Do not despise prophetic utterances." The whole of chapter 14 is summed up in his final words: **Everything must be done properly and in order**.

39–40

Reflection and Application (14:33b–40)

What meaning does this text have for us today? Does divine revelation disapprove of women's expressing their thoughts or disagreeing with men in the church? Are marriages in the twenty-first century protected if only husbands but not wives ask intrusive questions? Is wives' subordination to husbands the order that God ordains? Are women who refrain from speaking their minds in public to be considered more devout than those who do? The modern reader has the right to ask such questions, and they amount to asking what authority this text has for the Church today. I offer the following considerations:

1. We simply do not know the details of the situation Paul is addressing. Was it a particular disorder in the church of Corinth, or was it occurring in other churches too, so that Paul would intend his directive to apply to all his churches? It would seem from verse 33b and verse 36 that he does.

2. The cultural norms of the day must be taken into account. Paul was creative in many ways, certainly encouraging women in roles they did not enjoy in the synagogue, but he also did not want to so upset the social order as to make it impossible to evangelize. The situation here, where women are forbidden to ask intrusive questions, is not quite the same as in 1 Tim 2:12, where women are forbidden to teach, but the cultural context is the same. The distinction between official and unofficial, or domestic, teaching corresponds to the culture of the day, where there is little evidence of women ever serving as professional teachers, although they did have important roles of teaching within the family.[11]

3. The primary concern of this text is to preserve and safeguard the marital bond. Today's understanding of what is appropriate and inappropriate for spouses in a public setting has changed. But in today's setting the question may still be asked: how do husbands and wives respect and protect their own union when one or the other is interacting in a public setting?

4. Just as any biblical text must be judged in the light of the whole canon, this text must be judged in the context of the rest of Paul's writings and especially of his conduct regarding women. Paul's women collaborators were many. We know the names of eight of them: Priscilla (Prisca), Junia, Phoebe, Euodia, Syntyche, Tryphaena, Tryphosa, and Persis. Priscilla, along with her husband (he is usually mentioned second when both names are given), instructed the preacher Apollos (Acts 18:26).

5. The need to read this text in the light of later social situations like those of today illustrates the need for a Church authority to interpret the Scriptures. This the Church has done today in several ways: Pope John Paul II's Apostolic Letter *Mulieris Dignitatem* (*On the Dignity and Vocation of Women*) is a good example of how Church authority reads the scriptural data on women today. And the practice of the Church is even more revealing. In my other book in this series, *First and Second Timothy, Titus*, I wrote:

> What are we to make of the exponential explosion of women in ministry in the Church today, both in teaching and in roles of authority? Women with doctoral degrees are teaching not only in Catholic universities but [also] in seminaries where they participate in the formation of future priests. And women are serving as chancellors in dioceses, where they are the right arm of the bishop, exercising his delegated authority over the diocese. Women are serving as heads of offices in the Church at the national and international (i.e., the Vatican) levels. And what

11. Bruce W. Winter, *Roman Wives, Roman Widows: The Appearance of New Women and the Pauline Communities* (Grand Rapids: Eerdmans, 2003), 116.

are we to make of the honor given by the Church to St. Catherine of Siena, St. Teresa of Avila, and St. Thérèse of Lisieux with the title Doctor, or "Teacher," of the Church, indicating the extremely valuable contribution of women's teaching to the life of the Church? . . . Are we to say that the Holy Spirit who inspired this text has not also been at work in bringing forth the contribution of women we see today to the building of the Church?

The Resurrection

1 Corinthians 15

Death has always been a †mystery to the human race, and world history could be written as a struggle to come to terms with it. Early cave drawings and burial accoutrements attest to humans' desire and belief that they could somehow survive death. Plato gave a philosophical rationale for that survival by his teaching on the immortality of the soul. Modern medicine, however, has made a dent in death's kingdom by prolonging the average span of this life, but its success has only been in delaying the inevitable. Even philosophers who hold that human life ends with the grave struggle to remove the pall of futility cast over life by the specter of certain death.

In his extensive survey of the ancient world's belief in the future life, N. T. Wright writes:

> Who were the dead thought to be, in the ancient pagan world? They were beings that had once been embodied human beings, but were now souls, shades, or *eidōla*. Where were they? Most likely in Hades; possibly in the Isles of the Blessed, or Tartarus; just conceivably, reincarnated into a different body altogether. . . . We cannot stress too strongly that from Homer onwards the language of "resurrection" was not used to denote "life after death" in general, or any of the phenomena supposed to occur within such life. The great majority of the ancients believed in life after death, . . . but, other than within Judaism and Christianity, they did not believe in resurrection.[1]

The Old Testament struggles with the question of the future life and, from the viewpoint of man's natural constitution, comes up with surprisingly negative

1. N. T. Wright, *The Resurrection of the Son of God* (Minneapolis: Fortress, 2003), 82–83.

answers: man will return to the dust from which he comes (Gen 3:19), his end appears no better than that of animals (Eccles 3:18–21), and what abode of the dead there is, Sheol, is a shadowy half-life at best (Job 10:20–21; Pss 94:17; 115:17).

But within its own history, Israel had an experience of *life* that opened up new and unheard of possibilities. Their own existence as a people had come about by the intervention of a God of historical action, who had not only delivered them once from slavery in Egypt but also bound them to himself in covenant, thus making their future his own. A faithful God, he promised fullness of life to those who would remain faithful to him. Though this fullness of life was first understood to mean land and descendants and material blessings (Gen 15:1–7; Deut 28:1–68), it was inevitable that the question of its bearing on personal survival beyond death should ultimately be raised. There were growing doubts about the equity of reward and punishment in this life, best stated by Job and Ecclesiastes. But the covenant theology met its moment of truth when it was confronted by the death of its martyrs—those who died precisely in order to remain faithful to the covenant. Could the covenant union and its promise of the fullness of life be thwarted by the very act of fidelity to it? The problem thus raised in its most acute form prepared for God's clearer revelation in later passages of the Old Testament. The image of resurrection, which earlier texts had used in a purely figurative way for the restoration of the nation after exile (Isa 26:19; Ezek 37), Daniel took literally as a promise of bodily resurrection for those who had died for their faith (Dan 12:1–3). Later texts like 2 Macc 7 graphically depicted the martyr's repossession of the body. But if vindication beyond death was granted to the martyrs, why should not God also vindicate the person whose *life* is an unjust suffering, even though that person may die a natural death?

The common thread in all these texts is the belief in God's vindication of the just, as Habakkuk had already written: "The one who is righteous because of faith shall live" (2:4), and as the psalmist had sung: "I am always with you. . . . With your counsel you guide me, and at the end receive me with honor. . . . None beside you delights me on earth. Though my flesh and my heart fail, God is the rock of my heart, my portion forever" (Ps 73:23–26). This vindication of the just was seen necessarily to encompass the overcoming of death, whether by repossession of the body (2 Macc 7), the glorious transformation of the resurrected body (Dan 12:1–3), or entrance into immortality even in this life (Wis 1:15; 3:2, 6).

As a Pharisee, Paul believed in the resurrection of the just, which was denied by the Sadducees, but he believed that such a wonderful event would only happen at the close of the †age, not that it could happen to anyone before that. But meeting the risen Christ on the road to Damascus shocked him into the new reality that was being proclaimed by the Christians he was going to haul to trial. His conversion locked him solidly into the faith and witness of the first disciples. Jesus, the Righteous One (Acts 3:14; 7:52), had been raised from the dead (4:2), making him Messiah and Lord (2:36). And this brings us to Paul's discussion here at the end of his First Letter to the Corinthians.

Paul began his letter with a powerful proclamation of the Crucified One (1:18–25); now he concludes and climaxes it with a proclamation of the Risen One. But even more important, these pages are a manifesto of the resurrection of all those who are Christ's members. As the Apostle's discourse on the cross was occasioned by the Corinthians' misunderstanding of the sacrificial death of Jesus, so this section is occasioned by the misunderstanding by some of them about the reality and nature of the resurrection. The source of this misunderstanding is probably twofold. First, the Greek mind had no conception of bodily life after death. Plato held the soul to be immortal, but he certainly did not think of the person's reclaiming bodily life. And second, the experience of the Spirit was so strong among the Corinthian Christians that some of them considered that in itself to be the resurrection that Paul proclaimed. These could have found some justification in the Wisdom tradition that spoke of immortality being experienced even now (Wis 6:18; 8:17), and even more immediately in Paul's preaching that, through faith and baptism, Christians have passed from death to life; they have died with Christ and risen with him. It would have been but a small step to conclude with a purely spiritual understanding of the resurrection of the body. Not so, says Paul.[2]

The Apostolic Witness (15:1–11)

[1]Now I am reminding you, brothers, of the gospel I preached to you, which you indeed received and in which you also stand. [2]Through it you are also being saved, if you hold fast to the word I preached to you, unless you believed in vain. [3]For I handed on to you as of first importance what I also received: that Christ died for our sins in accordance with the scriptures; [4]that he was buried; that he was raised on the third day in

2. For a thorough, solid study of ancient beliefs and a vindication of the Church's faith in the resurrection, see ibid. For a short but excellent reflection on the meaning of the resurrection for Christians, see Donald Senior, "The Bones of Jesus: Bodily Resurrection and Christian Faith," *Origins* 37, no. 40 (March 20, 2008): 642–47.

accordance with the scriptures; ⁵that he appeared to Cephas, then to the Twelve. ⁶After that, he appeared to more than five hundred brothers at once, most of whom are still living, though some have fallen asleep. ⁷After that he appeared to James, then to all the apostles. ⁸Last of all, as to one born abnormally, he appeared to me. ⁹For I am the least of the apostles, not fit to be called an apostle, because I persecuted the church of God. ¹⁰But by the grace of God I am what I am, and his grace to me has not been ineffective. Indeed, I have toiled harder than all of them; not I, however, but the grace of God [that is] with me. ¹¹Therefore, whether it be I or they, so we preach and so you believed.

OT: Isa 53:5–12; Hos 6:2

NT: Luke 24:27, 34; Acts 9:1–2; 1 Cor 11:23; 2 Cor 11:5, 23; 1 Thess 4:13–14

Catechism: Christ died, 595–623; was buried, 624–30; is risen, appeared, 638–44; according to the Scriptures, 652

Lectionary: 15:1–8: Sts. Philip and James; Christian Initiation: Presentation of the Creed

Here Paul lays the foundation for all that follows. The Corinthians seem to have forgotten the very heart of his gospel. He reminds them of what happened: he **preached,** they **received,** and now in the gospel they **stand.** The emphasis falls on the last word: holding on to the original proclamation is the only thing that keeps them together and stable. It brings salvation and eternal life, but they should not presume that "once saved, always saved": "Whoever thinks he is standing secure should take care not to fall" (1 Cor 10:12). Salvation is a process (**you are . . . being saved**) in which their ongoing fidelity is decisive. But they must hold it exactly as **the word I preached to you,** that is, in the form in which Paul preached it. Otherwise **you believed in vain.** Salvation is tied to an event—the life, death, and resurrection of Jesus—as formulated by the apostolic tradition. To deviate from it is to imperil one's eternal salvation.

The *form* of verses 3–7 is a series of doctrinal elements that sounds like a creed, a formula already well established before Paul. It is not a formulation of abstract truths but a recitation of God's saving deeds. This creed testifies to what is **of first importance** in Paul's message. The many instructions he gives in this letter all flow from this source. He **handed on** what he **also received,** not merely from his vision of the risen Christ but also from the apostles in Jerusalem and the Christian community. From the verb "handed on" (Greek *paradidōmi,* which was translated into Latin as *tradere*), we get our word "tradition." In Paul's Letters we have mostly his teaching and little of the initial proclamation with which he won converts. But here in a nutshell we have the essence of his message, which meticulously follows the pattern of the Palestinian church (Acts 2:14–36). Christ's death was **for our sins.** How did the early Church know that

1–2

3

the death of the Master was not just the unfortunate execution of a prophet who claimed to be divine but actually the most important event in the history of the world, the redeeming death of the Son of God, by which all humankind could find forgiveness of their sins? It was based on what the Master himself said, that he would shed his blood "for the forgiveness of sins" (Matt 26:28). And they realized, with the Master's help and that of the Holy Spirit after his resurrection, that these events were prefigured and prophesied in the Old Testament (**in accordance with the scriptures**), particularly in the prophecy of the Suffering Servant in Isaiah 52:13–53:12:

> He was pierced for our sins,
>> crushed for our iniquity.
> He bore the punishment that makes us whole,
>> by his wounds we were healed.
> We had all gone astray like sheep,
>> all following our own way;
> But the LORD laid upon him
>> the guilt of us all. . . .
> By making his life as a reparation offering . . .
>> the LORD's will shall be accomplished through him. . . .
> My servant, the just one, shall justify the many,
>> their iniquity shall he bear.

Many other passages also spoke of the sufferings of the just person, especially in the Psalms (see 22; 41; 69; 88).

4   Unlike the simple past tenses[3] used for Jesus' death and burial, **was raised** is actually in the perfect tense, thus meaning "has been raised," indicating his permanent and ongoing presence with the Church. The early Church understood the resurrection to be **in accordance with the scriptures**, probably in light of the Suffering Servant who would "be raised high and greatly exalted" (Isa 52:13). Peter in Acts 2:25–36 quotes Pss 110:1 and 16:8–11. In his sermon to the synagogue in Antioch of Pisidia (Acts 13:33–34), Paul quotes Ps 2:7 and Isa 55:3. The **third day**, referring to the morning of Jesus' resurrection and the discovery of the empty tomb, would soon be referred to as "the Lord's day" (Rev 1:10). Even the "third day" was understood as according to the Scriptures, probably in reference to Hosea (6:2), who speaks of Israel's being chastised by "the LORD," but "on the third day he will raise us up." But there is also a cluster of Old Testament texts that eventually enriched the Church's understanding of

3. Aorist in Greek.

"the third day." In Gen 1:11–13 the third day is the first appearance of life on earth (compare the new creation in Christ: 2 Cor 5:17; Gal 6:15). On the third day Joseph releases his brothers from prison (Gen 42:18), "the LORD" manifests himself in glory on Mount Sinai (Exod 19:11, 16), the Israelites prepare to break camp and cross the Jordan (Josh 3:2), and Jonah was released from the belly of the great fish (Jon 2:1, 11)—a †type of the resurrection of Jesus (Matt 12:40). Thus "the third day" connotes a new life, a new beginning or manifestation of God's activity on earth.

The listing of those to whom the Lord appeared is not exhaustive but official, **5–6** and the order is not necessarily chronological. Although the Gospels tell us that women were the first to witness the resurrection, they are not mentioned here, probably because in the Jewish culture of Paul's day, only men's testimony was accepted as valid. **The Twelve** had become such a technical term for the group appointed by Jesus (Mark 3:13–19) that it could stand for them even in the absence of Judas or Thomas (John 20:24). The appearance to **more than five hundred brothers at once** is mentioned only here in the New Testament, but it seems to have been part of the †*testimonia* that the early evangelists gave as they spread the gospel. As Paul writes this letter, **most** of those witnesses are still alive, **though some have fallen asleep**, a term used in Christian vocabulary for those waiting to be awakened by the resurrection (see John 11:11–14; 1 Cor 11:30). That many are still living means that their witness is still readily available for anyone who wishes to check it out.

Paul mentions **James**, without further identification, as one well known to **7** the community. This James is probably the "†brother of the Lord" who assumed leadership of the Jerusalem community when Peter departed on mission to other locations. In adding that Jesus then appeared **to all the apostles**, Paul is designating a larger group than the Twelve already mentioned above.[4]

Paul speaks of Christ's appearing to him **as to one born abnormally**. This **8** is the NAB's attempt to deal with the puzzling word *ektrōma*, which literally means "aborted" or "stillborn."[5] Some commentators take the expression to refer to Paul's late call, not having been one of the Twelve and probably never having seen Jesus in his earthly life. But in that case we would expect something like "late born" or "born overdue." Another plausible interpretation comes closer to the meaning of the Greek word. As a Jew and a Pharisee persecuting the Church, Paul was like a stillborn infant. He was brought to

4. See Acts 14:4; Rom 16:7; 1 Cor 9:5; 12:28; Gal 1:17, 19.
5. See 1 Cor 15:8 in other translations: "as though I was born when no one expected it" (JB), "as though I was a child born abnormally" (NJB), "one untimely born" (NRSV).

Fig. 13. The Conversion of St. Paul, Acts 9:1–6, illustration from "The Holy Bible," engraved by Ligny, 1866 (engraving), by Gustave Dore (1832–83).

life and sight when Christ appeared to him on the road to Damascus. The NAB translation is a generalizing one that allows for various understandings of "abnormally."

9–10   After adding his own testimony to the creedal recital, Paul is keenly aware of how his calling differed from that of the others mentioned. He had **persecuted the church of God**, and that should have made him unfit to be an apostle. But as the First Letter to Timothy will explain, "I was mercifully treated, so that in me, as the foremost, Christ Jesus might display all his patience as an example for those who would come to believe in him for everlasting life" (1 Tim 1:16). God often calls the most unlikely, as he has done with the Corinthians (1 Cor 1:26–31). Not only did Paul not have good works of which he might have boasted (Phil 3:4–6); he also was the worst of sinners for having persecuted Jesus in his members (1 Tim 1:15). Hence he can say it is only by **the grace of God** that **I am what I am**. And that grace has continued to work in his life. He first says in a self-effacing way, **His grace to me has not been ineffective**, but then in a positive way he says he has **toiled harder than all of them** (the other apostles and evangelists). He is not holding himself above the others, because whatever he has been able to do has been by **the grace of God [that is] with me**.

After this brief expansion on his own ministry, Paul returns to the point   **11** made in 15:1—the one gospel that he handed on to them and they received. The apostolic witness to the resurrection of Jesus is not divided: **whether it be I or they, so we preach and so you believed**.

Reflection and Application (15:1–11)

This earliest creed, the foundation of the Christian faith, is not a list of principles or ideas but a recitation of facts. In this it is not unlike the creed in Deut 26:5–10, which is a recitation of the saving acts of the Lord in the history of Israel. There are those today who maintain that the resurrection of Jesus was only spiritual, not a physical one, or that the resurrection was nothing more than the emergence of Christian faith, not necessarily tied to a real resurrection of Jesus' body—so that they would not be disturbed if his bones were found somewhere. However, this does not square with Paul and the New Testament evidence elsewhere. After all, even Jews who disputed the apostolic witness did not deny that the tomb was empty (Matt 28:11–15). Paul's text is precious because it is the earliest written witness we have of Jesus' resurrection, and it mentions by name witnesses, "most of whom are still living," Paul says.

N. T. Wright has brought together the main arguments for the historicity of Jesus' resurrection. How does one explain this sudden belief of frightened disciples that their Master rose from the dead? An empty tomb would not of itself mean a resurrection, because, as the Jewish leaders claimed, the body could have been stolen. But it was the Lord's appearances, *with* the empty tomb, that convinced the disciples that Jesus was risen. Given the understanding of the day that resurrection meant something bodily, if there was no empty tomb, there would have been no ground for the belief that Jesus had risen. The appearances, however, were not in accord with contemporary understandings of resurrection. Jesus' body was not only risen but also transformed. The disciples were expecting neither. "Something had *happened*, something which was not at all what they expected or hoped for, something around which they had to reconstruct their lives and in relation to which they had to redirect their energies."[6]

All this has much to say about the dignity and destiny of our bodies and a redemption that is as total as our person, body, and soul. The destiny of the resurrection grounds much of Paul's conviction that the body is a member of Christ and a temple of the Holy Spirit (1 Cor 6:15, 19).

No Resurrection of Anyone Else? (15:12–19)

¹²But if Christ is preached as raised from the dead, how can some among you say there is no resurrection of the dead? ¹³If there is no resurrection of the dead, then neither has Christ been raised. ¹⁴And if Christ has not been raised, then empty [too] is our preaching; empty, too, your faith. ¹⁵Then we are also false witnesses to God, because we testified against God that he raised Christ, whom he did not raise if in fact the dead are not raised. ¹⁶For if the dead are not raised, neither has Christ been raised, ¹⁷and if Christ has not been raised, your faith is vain; you are still in your sins. ¹⁸Then those who have fallen asleep in Christ have perished. ¹⁹If for this life only we have hoped in Christ, we are the most pitiable people of all.

OT: 2 Macc 7:14; Isa 26:19; Dan 12:1–2
NT: Matt 22:23–32; Acts 2:22–36; 23:6–8
Catechism: Christ's resurrection, principle of our own, 655, 993–95
Lectionary: Anointing of the Sick

From this point onward to verse 34, Paul will show how the resurrection of Christ necessarily involves the resurrection of his members—or better, perhaps, how the nonresurrection of the members would necessarily imply the nonresurrection of Christ. He does this first by showing the fallacy of those who believe in the resurrection of Christ but not that of Christians (15:12–19), then by showing the solidarity of Christ with his members in the image of the firstfruits (15:20–28), and finally by drawing on some practical arguments (15:29–34).

6. Wright, *Resurrection of the Son of God*, 700. See also his *Surprised by Hope* (San Francisco: HarperOne, 2008).

The false position of **some among you** does not seem to be coherent. How 12–13
could they possibly deny the resurrection of others if they believed that Jesus
had risen from the dead? Perhaps they feel caught in the dilemma that Paul
dealt with in his First Letter to the Thessalonians: When Christ returns, the
living can enjoy eternal bliss because their bodies are not corrupted. But how
can Christians share in the resurrection of the body if they have died and their
bodies are corrupted? Those who held such a view argued that Jesus' body was
an exception to this problem because it was not in the grave long enough to
undergo corruption, but not so for the rest of us who die. Even if this is the
thinking of only a few, it demands vigorous refutation, and it gives Paul the occasion to expound on the meaning of Christ's resurrection for Christians. There
is a simple lack of logic in their position. Their presumed principle, that there is
no resurrection of the dead, is proved false by the very resurrection of Christ.
In the apostolic †kerygma the resurrection of Christ announces the resurrection of the dead. Instead of saying that James and John were "proclaiming that
Jesus had been raised from the dead," Luke records that they were "proclaiming in Jesus the resurrection of the dead" (Acts 4:2). In 1 Thess 4:14 Paul had
written: "If we believe that Jesus died and rose, so too will God, through Jesus,
bring with him those who have fallen asleep." Later in the present letter, Paul
will explain more fully why the two resurrections are inescapably linked. Here
he simply asserts the fact. To deny the resurrection of the dead is to deny the
resurrection of Christ.

But to deny the resurrection of Christ would have disastrous consequences. It 14
would mean that the apostles' preaching is **empty**, or "in vain" (NRSV), "without
substance" (NJB), "useless" (JB, NIV). It not only lacks any historical basis, but
its very object has also vanished. As a result, the Christians' faith is also **empty**.
For to become a Christian is to confess with one's lips that Jesus is Lord and to
believe in one's heart that God raised him from the dead (Rom 10:9).

A further disastrous consequence: the apostles would be liars, perjurers, **false** 15
witnesses not only before men but also before God, for they claim that God
has done something when in fact he has not. If bearing false witness against
another Israelite could bring severe consequences (Deut 19:16–21), even death
to the perjurers (Dan 13:61–62), what might be said of one who bears false
witness against God? Skeptics may claim that the apostles made up the stories
about Jesus' resurrection. Paul here reveals his deep conscientious rejection of
any such deceit.

One cannot claim that **Christ** has **been raised** and at the same time claim 16
that **the dead are not raised**. They are the two sides of the same coin.

17–18   A final disastrous consequence: not only is the apostolic witness "empty," but **your faith is vain**. All losses that Christians have suffered—like the loss of social acceptance because of their rejection of idols (chaps. 8–10)—have been useless, futile. They have been putting their faith in an illusion. Not only that, **you are still in your sins**: you will not be saved from eternal death, the consequence of sin. It is not just the saving death of Christ that has won forgiveness for sins; it is also the resurrection that seals it. Christ "was handed over for our transgressions and raised for our justification" (Rom 4:25). But if there is no resurrection of Christ, there is no forgiveness of sins, nor will there be a resurrection of his followers. They will perish.

19   In this hypothesis, Christians are not only as bad off as they were before they believed; they are *worse* off, because they have invested their lives and their energies in an illusion. In the Greek the word "only" appears at the end of the clause, so it could be translated, "If in this life we have hoped in Christ, and that's all . . ." That is, if our only hope in this life was Christ, and now that hope is dashed, we have certainly proved ourselves to be the most foolish of all, for others have at least limited earthly hopes to live by. But the NIV, JB, NJB, and NRSV take it as in the NAB: **If for this life only we have hoped in Christ**—the idea being that if our hope was only for what we could get out of Christ in this life, then **we are the most pitiable people of all**, for whatever benefits such hope might bring, they are dashed by inevitable death. The overall meaning of Paul is clear enough: the hope by which Christians live is a puff of smoke if Christ is not risen and if the dead are not raised.

Reflection and Application (15:12–19)

If we take seriously Paul's affirmation here, we need to ask ourselves whether faith in the eternal life of the resurrection is *in fact* the dominant magnet of our life. Am I, like Paul, living the kind of life that would be foolish apart from the reality of the resurrection? Am I really betting everything on Christ, or am I hedging my bets, making sure I squeeze everything I can out of this life while hoping not to lose out on the next? Certainly resurrection faith can be lived in any state of life. Married couples can live and form their children in the light of eternity: virtue, for example, is more important than achievement or possessions. Some will embrace celibacy for the kingdom. Others will become missionaries. Others will dedicate their lives to service for the poor and will live simply in order to do so. Aware that our real citizenship is in heaven (Phil 3:20), we can hold our goods and the persons we love with a relaxed grasp (1 Cor 7:29–31) because the fullness of life is not here: it is to come.

The Firstfruits: Christ's Connection with His Members (15:20–28)

> **20But now Christ has been raised from the dead, the firstfruits of those who have fallen asleep. 21For since death came through a human being, the resurrection of the dead came also through a human being. 22For just as in Adam all die, so too in Christ shall all be brought to life, 23but each one in proper order: Christ the firstfruits; then, at his coming, those who belong to Christ; 24then comes the end, when he hands over the kingdom to his God and Father, when he has destroyed every sovereignty and every authority and power. 25For he must reign until he has put all his enemies under his feet. 26The last enemy to be destroyed is death, 27for "he subjected everything under his feet." But when it says that everything has been subjected, it is clear that it excludes the one who subjected everything to him. 28When everything is subjected to him, then the Son himself will [also] be subjected to the one who subjected everything to him, so that God may be all in all.**

OT: Gen 3:17–19; Pss 8:7; 110:1; Isa 26:19; Dan 2:44; 12:1–3
NT: Acts 3:15; 26:23; Rom 5:12, 18; Col 1:18; 1 Thess 4:14
Lectionary: 15:20–23: Funeral for Baptized Children; 15:20–24a, 25–28: Mass for the Deceased; 15:20–27: Assumption of the Blessed Virgin Mary; 15:20–26, 28: Christ the King

After detailing the somber and radical nothingness to which the Christian   **20** faith would be reduced without the resurrection of the faithful, Paul develops a positive theology of the resurrection as a single †mystery of Christ and the faithful combined. The first image he uses is that of the **firstfruits**. The Torah required every Jewish man to bring the first harvest sheaf of grain and a cake from the first batch of new dough to the priest, as a token of gratitude that the entire harvest was really the Lord's gift (Lev 23:10–14). Hence it was a kind of consecration of the entire harvest to the Lord, the part standing for the whole. The day prescribed for this rite was the sixteenth of the month of Nisan, precisely the day on which Jesus rose from the dead. It was probably this providential coincidence that gave Paul the idea of speaking of Jesus' resurrection as the firstfruits. This metaphor will be complemented with that of the "firstborn from the dead" in Col 1:18, Christ's own resurrection being elsewhere described as a birth (Acts 13:33; Heb 1:5) and the risen Christ as "the firstborn among many brothers" (Rom 8:29).

21–22   The second image Paul evokes is that of solidarity—in death with Adam, in life with Christ. **Since death came through a human being, the resurrection of the dead came also through a human being**. All human beings, sharing the same nature as Adam, also share his heritage of sin and death. But Christ is the final Adam, reversing the sin, the curse, and death. The contrast shows how realistically Paul thinks of the union of the faithful with their head, Christ. A renewed human race is in the making! The bodily resurrection is still future, when **in Christ shall all be brought to life**.

23   This will happen **at his coming**. This is the first occurrence in 1 Corinthians of the Greek word †*parousia* for Christ's second coming, which had occupied Paul's major attention in his First Letter to the Thessalonians (2:19; 3:13; 4:15; 5:23). In secular Greek it was used to describe the appearance or arrival of the emperor or king to a city in the kingdom. He would usually be mounted on a white horse, and when his coming was announced in the city, the local officials and many of the populace would go out to meet him, escort him with great pomp into the city, and often bestow divine honors on him. In claiming divine honor for Christ, Paul is implicitly denying it for all emperors and kings. But his main purpose is to affirm the certainty of the resurrection of the faithful by tying divine honor specifically to the final coming of Christ.

24   **Then comes the end**. Some scholars have taken "the end" in the sense of "the rest, the remaining," that is, the resurrection of the non-Christians. But the Greek word *telos* does not mean "the rest," and in the New Testament it means the end of all things (Matt 24:6, 14; Mark 13:7; Luke 21:9). Here Paul is not concerned with non-Christians: that would distract from his argument. Nor does there seem to be any basis for the view that there would be an interval of time between Christ's coming and the resurrection of the dead, as if there would be an earthly reign of Christ, a kind of millennial reign (Rev 20:4–6). There is no evidence in Paul anywhere that he thought of something like that. On the contrary, Christ's reign began with his resurrection and is going on right now (Rom 8:34; Eph 1:20–23), to be climaxed with the conquest of death in the resurrection of the faithful (1 Cor 15:54–55). Having achieved that, his mission has been accomplished, and **he hands over the kingdom to his God and Father**. The resurrection of the dead will only be the last in a series of victories over **every sovereignty and every authority and power**. These doubtlessly refer in the first place to the demonic powers of the spiritual realm, with whom Christians battle in this world: "with the principalities, with the powers, with the world rulers of this present darkness, with the evil spirits in the

heavens" (Eph 6:12). But inasmuch as these demonic spiritual powers at times use earthly authorities (such as Nazism, Stalinism, or terrorism), those earthly sovereignties too will be abolished.

But all this is in process. Christ **must reign until he has put all his enemies** **25**
under his feet. Paul here adapts Ps 110:1, a psalm understood already in his time to refer to the Messiah. Although in the psalm it is God who puts all things under the Messiah's feet, Paul sees Christ here as the one who is winning the battle. This battle is carried on by Christ through his Church, in its struggle against evil and the powers of darkness in this world. But victory is assured by the primordial victory of Christ's own resurrection.

The last enemy to be destroyed is death. Here Paul personifies death as **26**
Christ's mortal enemy that won only an apparent victory in causing Christ's death on the cross, for his death was followed by his rising from the dead and initiating a reign against sin, the cause of death. In 2 Tim 1:10 Paul says that Christ "destroyed death." There the verb translated "destroyed" means, literally, "disabled," which has an interesting nuance, because in the present life we do not see physical death eliminated; but for Christians it is no longer a threat because of Christ's resurrection and the promise of our own. Here "destroyed" in 1 Cor 15:26 refers to the final triumph over death, which comes in the resurrection of the just.

In this verse Paul alludes to Ps 8:7: "You have given him rule over the works **27**
of your hands, put all things at his feet," a psalm originally referring to God's giving humanity dominion over creation. God gave Adam dominion over creation, but Adam betrayed that trust and brought death; yet Christ regained dominion by defeating sin and death and bringing life (1 Cor 15:22). Hence Paul fittingly applies the psalm to Christ, to whom God has given universal dominion: God **subjected everything under his feet**. Everything, that is, but God himself, **the one who subjected everything to him**.

But lest this exaltation of Christ above all things should lead to understand- **28**
ing him as another god separate from God the Father, Paul, concerned for the sake of the truth to preserve the monotheism that was his heritage as a Jew, says that **the Son** (the only place in Paul where the title is used absolutely) **himself** **will [also] be subjected to the one who subjected everything to him**, that is, to the Father. Sent by the Father as man, Jesus completes his mission by raising the dead and bringing them with himself to the Father, **so that God may be** **all in all**. This last expression should not be taken in a pantheistic sense, as if everything *becomes* God. It is rather Paul's way of describing the final consummation, which is really beyond words.

The resurrection of all the faithful will be the ultimate triumph of Jesus, King of kings and Lord of lords (Rev 19:16). Creation itself, which has been groaning to see its ultimate purpose fulfilled, to be restored along with a redeemed and transformed humanity (Rom 8:22), will reach the goal for which God created it. Its Lord and King, the final Adam (1 Cor 15:45), Jesus Christ, will reign in place of the old Adam over a cosmos at peace. In Ephesians and Colossians, Paul will describe this consummation as the *plērōma*, the "fullness," of Christ filling all beings with his transforming glory (Eph 1:23).

Then Christ will be subject to the Father. The image here is of the king's son who goes out to conquer for his father and returns in a triumphant parade. Having wrested the kingdom of the world from all hostile powers, primarily sin and death, Jesus now presents it to his Father, kneeling before him, as it were, in humble obeisance. It is in his humanity, which he has shared with humankind and creation, that Jesus subjects himself to the Father, for as the divine Son he is equal to the Father, proceeding from him by way of generation, as the creeds say.

Thus the promised destiny is not merely the bodily resurrection of each individual faithful person. It will be the heavenly Jerusalem (Rev 21:2), the wedding feast of the Lamb (19:7, 9; 21:9), the banquet of the kingdom (Matt 22:1–14), the new heaven and the new earth (Rev 21:1), the consummation of union not only with God but also with one another, where those once lost have been found—the great homecoming—to the applause of all creation.

Supporting Arguments (15:29–34)

²⁹**Otherwise, what will people accomplish by having themselves baptized for the dead? If the dead are not raised at all, then why are they having themselves baptized for them?**

³⁰**Moreover, why are we endangering ourselves all the time?** ³¹**Every day I face death; I swear it by the pride in you [brothers] that I have in Christ Jesus our Lord.** ³²**If at Ephesus I fought with beasts, so to speak, what benefit was it to me? If the dead are not raised:**

> **"Let us eat and drink,**
> **for tomorrow we die."**

³³**Do not be led astray:**

> **"Bad company corrupts good morals."**

³⁴**Become sober as you ought and stop sinning. For some have no knowledge of God; I say this to your shame.**

OT: 2 Macc 12:43–46; Isa 22:13
NT: Luke 12:19; Rom 8:36; 2 Cor 1:8–9; 4:10–11
Catechism: baptism cannot be repeated, 1272

This section resembles 15:13–19, which drew some of the consequences of not believing in the resurrection of the dead. Here Paul argues from concrete practices: those who practice baptism for the dead and his own risking his life for the sake of the gospel.

This verse has proved to be a very difficult one for the exegetes. Translations **29** differ only slightly: **baptized for the dead** (NAB, NIV, JB), "baptized on behalf of the dead" (NJB, NRSV). But interpretations offered have been diverse. Three of the most significant are the following: The Greek Fathers understood "the dead" to be those who were being baptized: thus Chrysostom[7] holds that Paul is referring to a baptismal formula or part of the baptismal rite, in which "the dead" means the bodies of those being baptized, subject to mortality because of sin and ritually immersed in death by the sacrament. In Rom 8:10 Paul says that "the body is dead because of sin." And Chrysostom continues by quoting Rom 6:3: "We who were baptized into Christ Jesus were baptized into his death." There are two problems with this interpretation, however. Paul speaks of those who practice this baptism as "they," when we would expect "we," since it applies to all Christians. Second, the Greek says that those who are being baptized are doing this for those who have died; the most obvious sense is that it is for others, not for themselves.

The second explanation offered is that the practice was similar to that of the Mormons today: undergoing baptism in proxy for those who died without baptism. In this view, Paul is neither approving nor condemning the practice, merely using it to show that their practice is meaningless if they did not believe in the resurrection of the dead. The problem with this scenario is that such a practice would smack of a kind of magic, without the dead person having any act of faith, nor any prospect of making such an act of faith in the afterlife (unlike infant baptism, where the likelihood of growing into the faith of the parents is present). Is it likely that Paul would take a neutral stance on such a practice?

A third interpretation would take the preposition "for," or "on behalf of," in the sense of receiving baptism with "a view toward the dead." For example, the pagan spouse of a Christian who has died would request and receive baptism in the hope of being rejoined with the beloved in the resurrection of the dead. Such a practice would be understandable, but was it frequent enough for Paul to use it as an example?

7. See also Chrysostom, *Homilies on 1 Corinthians* 40.2; see also 23.3.

Doubtless the Corinthians knew what Paul was referring to, even though we struggle only with probabilities. The bottom line is that Paul is arguing from a practice that makes no sense without a belief in the resurrection of the dead.

30–31   Paul's other practical argument is much easier to understand. Paul's heroic efforts, even risking **death** daily, make no sense if he did not believe in the resurrection. In 2 Cor 11:23–28 he details many of these dangers and struggles, several of which we would not know from Luke's accounts in the Acts of the Apostles:

> . . . far greater labors, far more imprisonments, far worse beatings, and numerous brushes with death. Five times at the hands of the Jews I received forty lashes minus one. Three times I was beaten with rods, once I was stoned, three times I was shipwrecked. I passed a night and a day on the deep; on frequent journeys, in dangers from rivers, dangers from robbers, dangers from my own race, dangers from Gentiles, dangers in the city, dangers in the wilderness, dangers at sea, dangers among false brothers; in toil and hardship, through many sleepless nights, through hunger and thirst, through frequent fastings, through cold and exposure. And apart from these things, there is the daily pressure upon me of my anxiety for all the churches.

Paul is willing to swear, not by God, but by the **pride** he has in the Corinthians **in Christ Jesus our Lord**. This is not a boasting about himself but rather about the grace already operating in the community, despite its many faults.

32   In 2 Cor 1:8–9 we learn of the mortal struggle Paul had in Ephesus, where "we were weighed down beyond our strength, so that we despaired even of life." Here he speaks of it metaphorically as fighting with wild **beasts**, the contest that many Christians would face in reality in the Colosseum. **So to speak** (literally, "according to the human") can also be translated, "for merely human reasons" (NIV), "if my motives were only human ones" (JB), "in a purely human perspective" (NJB), "with merely human hopes" (NRSV). The alternative translations fit the context well, since Paul is contrasting his faith in the resurrection with any futile human motive he could have had. That would have been senseless **if the dead are not raised**. Finally Paul quotes the words of the wicked in Isa 22:13, **Let us eat and drink, for tomorrow we die**, a widespread Epicurean slogan as well, according to which the only response to certain death is to make the goal of your life the pursuit of pleasure.[8]

---

8. Herodotus relates that at richer persons' banquets in Egypt, a man would carry around an image of a corpse in a coffin and proclaim, "Drink and make merry, but look on this: for such shall you be when you are dead" (*Histories* 2.78.1).

Why does Paul quote this other slogan, **Bad company corrupts good morals**? It refers to the corruption of morals rather than to the doctrine that he has been defending. But that is the point: bad doctrine will lead to bad morals. If you don't believe in the resurrection, if your personal survival ends with the tomb, if worms claim the ultimate victory, if there is no judgment or eternal life, then the primary foundation for moral life crumbles. Whether the dissidents believe death is the end, or whether they claim superior knowledge that resurrection is only a metaphor for a spiritually renewed life here on earth—it all amounts to the same. "Resurrection means endless hope, but no resurrection means a hopeless end—and hopelessness breeds dissipation."[9] **Stop sinning** may therefore refer to the moral lapses the Corinthians have fallen into (cliques, idolatry, drunkenness, and rudeness at the Lord's Supper), or it may refer to those who are propagating the idea of a purely spiritual resurrection. In either case they show that they **have no knowledge of God**. For knowledge of God means both knowing the one true God (1 Thess 1:9) and living righteously (Jer 22:16). To deny the resurrection is to attack the heart of the Christian faith and to imperil the holiness to which it calls. Honor and **shame** were categories of supreme importance in the ancient world; to reinforce his teaching, Paul does not hesitate to invoke them as he concludes this section.

Reflection and Application (15:29–34)

Some years ago an ad for a popular American beer ran: "You only go around once, so go for all the gusto you can get," which, of course, meant drinking their beer. Paul believes this life is short (1 Cor 7:29), but instead of being anxious about it and seizing every possible pleasure it offers, he has a deep interior freedom and peace because he is certain he will enjoy the glory of the risen Lord (1 Cor 7:20–31).

How Can It Happen? The Risen Body (15:35–49)

---

[35]But someone may say, "How are the dead raised? With what kind of body will they come back?"

[36]You fool! What you sow is not brought to life unless it dies. [37]And what you sow is not the body that is to be but a bare kernel of wheat, perhaps, or of some other kind; [38]but God gives it a body as he chooses, and

9. David E. Garland, *1 Corinthians*, BECNT (Grand Rapids: Baker Academic, 2003), 721.

to each of the seeds its own body. [39]Not all flesh is the same, but there is one kind for human beings, another kind of flesh for animals, another kind of flesh for birds, and another for fish. [40]There are both heavenly bodies and earthly bodies, but the brightness of the heavenly is one kind and that of the earthly another. [41]The brightness of the sun is one kind, the brightness of the moon another, and the brightness of the stars another. For star differs from star in brightness.

[42]So also is the resurrection of the dead. It is sown corruptible; it is raised incorruptible. [43]It is sown dishonorable; it is raised glorious. It is sown weak; it is raised powerful. [44]It is sown a natural body; it is raised a spiritual body. If there is a natural body, there is also a spiritual one.

[45]So, too, it is written, "The first man, Adam, became a living being," the last Adam a life-giving spirit. [46]But the spiritual was not first; rather the natural and then the spiritual. [47]The first man was from the earth, earthly; the second man, from heaven. [48]As was the earthly one, so also are the earthly, and as is the heavenly one, so also are the heavenly. [49]Just as we have borne the image of the earthly one, we shall also bear the image of the heavenly one.

OT: Gen 2:7
NT: John 12:24; Rom 8:29; Phil 3:20–21; Col 3:4
Catechism: conditions of the risen body, 645–46, 997–1000

35   Having dealt with the fundamental truth of the resurrection, Paul now considers two questions that might still be urged by those who cannot understand a bodily resurrection. The questioner asks Paul to demonstrate how our resurrection can happen. The first question concerns the event of the resurrection: **how** will it take place? The second concerns the nature of a risen body: **what kind of body** will it be? The apostle will reply to them in reverse order.

36–37   Here Paul creates an imaginary dialogue (a †rhetorical technique known as †diatribe), taking on the role of a teacher confronted by an especially dull student. In this way he avoids attacking the Corinthians directly. This imaginary student does not comprehend even the most elemental wonder of nature. A seed must die if it is to bear fruit. What is buried in the earth is far different from what it will one day become.

38   **But God gives it a body.** Instead of saying, as a horticulturalist might, that the seed produces the plant, the flower, and the fruit, Paul stresses that this miracle of nature is the work of God. He is aware that the comparison with the human body falters on one point: the dead human body does not sprout a new life of its own accord. The point is that what God does to the plant in the order of nature, he can and will do to the human body in the

order of grace. As we marvel at the wonder of nature, which is God's work, why should we doubt that he can transform the human body as well? **To each of the seeds its own body**: "body" here probably means the body that the seed will become. The acorn is transformed into an oak and yet retains its own identity, not becoming a maple or a birch; so also through the resurrection, the transformed body will be in essential continuity with the body that constituted the human person in one's earthly existence. My risen body will be my own, not someone else's. One does not lose one's personal identity by resurrection: one finds it in a new way.

But from identity Paul turns to difference. The variety of seeds he has just 39–40
mentioned segues into varieties of flesh: **Not all flesh is the same**. As there is variety among plants, so also among animals. And that segues into the difference between **earthly bodies** and **heavenly bodies**. The sun, the moon, and the stars differ in brightness from earthly bodies. Thus Paul prepares the reader to think of the difference between the glorified body and the earthly body (15:43). Already in Dan 12:1–3 the glory of the risen righteous is compared to the stars of heaven, and Jesus says that "the righteous will shine like the sun in the kingdom of their Father" (Matt 13:43).

Here Paul digresses from his earlier line of thought. In the previous verse 41
he contrasted heavenly bodies with earthly bodies. Here he speaks about the difference of brightness among the heavenly bodies, the stars themselves suggesting, if we follow the metaphor, that each risen body of the faithful will differ in glory from the others. **Star differs from star in brightness**. "Brightness" is the NAB and JB translation of *doxa* in its four uses in this verse; the NIV and NJB have "splendor," while the NRSV goes for the more literal "glory." In fact, there is an exact Greek word for brightness, *lamprotēs*, used in Acts 26:13 for the brightness of the sun. For the stars, instead, Paul here uses "glory," characteristic of the resurrection body (15:43), subliminally hinting at the glory of the risen bodies of the faithful, which will differ from one another just as the stars differ in "glory."

Paul now returns to the contrast in verse 40 between the earthly body and 42
the heavenly, risen body. He draws four contrasts. First, the earthly body **is sown corruptible**. Notice the reprise of the image of sowing, with which Paul began all these comparisons (15:37). There the focus was not on the dying of the seed but on the new "body" it becomes. Here Paul compares the corruptible character of the human body, obvious from decomposition after death, with the **incorruptible** character of the risen body. Like the body of the risen Jesus, the bodies of the risen faithful will never die, will never decompose again.

43   Second contrast: The earthly body **is sown dishonorable**. With death, even the most attractive body becomes "dishonorable" as the processes of decay begin their work. But the bodies of the †elect will be **raised glorious**. This detail indicates that the resurrection is not a resuscitation, a return of the body to its natural, living state, but a transformation, sharing the same kind of glory that the risen Lord has, suggesting the kind of brilliance that the disciples saw in his transfiguration (Matt 17:2).

Third contrast: the **weak** body becomes **powerful**. Weakness here refers to the human condition as prone to accidents, to injury, and ultimately to death brought on by sin. That it is powerful means not only that it is free of those human limitations but also that it is endowed with new capabilities. Paul does not specify what these are. According to the Gospels, Jesus was able to pass through walls (John 20:19, 26), appear in different places without having to walk there (Matt 28:9, 16–17; Luke 24:36), and disappear at will (Luke 24:31).

44   Fourth contrast: the **natural body** becomes a **spiritual body**. "Natural body" translates *sōma psychikon* in the NAB, NIV, and NJB. *Psychikon* (the same word used in 2:14) is, literally, "soulish," the adjective form of soul, which the JB tries to capture by translating "when it is sown it [the body] embodies the soul." The problem with that is that the soul no longer inhabits the dead body. The RSV and NRSV translate it as "physical body," but that does violence to the Greek word, which does not mean physical. It also implies that the spiritual body has nothing physical about it. Paul could have said "fleshly body," but his word choice indicates simply the contrast between human life in this world and the risen life to come, so "natural body" is probably the best approximation of what Paul is saying. The Greek word evokes the LXX version of Gen 2:7, where, as a result of God's inbreathing, man became "a living being" (*psychēn zōsan*, literally, "a living soul"). "Spiritual body" appears to be a contradiction in terms, certainly to the modern mind. For what is material is not spiritual, and vice versa. Some could take the term simply as a euphemism for "pure spirit." Any appearance in bodily form would then indeed be ghostlike. But that is not Paul's understanding of the risen life, for he shares the understanding of Judaism of the time, especially among the Pharisees, who took bodily resurrection quite literally. "Spiritual body," therefore, does not negate physicality. It means rather that the risen body is fully inhabited and transformed by the Holy Spirit. Even in this life the body can become "one spirit" with Christ (1 Cor 6:17), however partial and imperfect that may be. So the contrast is not between the physical and the nonphysical. Resurrection will be a recuperation of all that is God-given in our present physicality, but transformed as Jesus' body is.

The Body of the Resurrection

LIVING TRADITION

Saint Augustine comments: "People are amazed that God, who made all things from nothing, makes a heavenly body from human flesh. When he was in the flesh, did not the Lord make wine from water? Is it anything so much more wonderful if he makes a heavenly body from human flesh? . . . Is he who was able to make you when you did not exist not able to make over what you once were?"[a]

a. Saint Augustine, *Sermons for the Feast of Ascension* 264.6; in FC 38:406.

Paul now cites Gen 2:7 LXX, to which we referred above, contrasting the **first man, Adam**, with Christ, **the last Adam**. Whereas Adam became "a soul having life," Christ became **a life-giving spirit**. This happened at his resurrection. It does not mean that Christ ceased to be body and became pure spirit.[10] That would go completely against Paul's entire thesis in this chapter. It rather means that by the glorification of his body on Easter morning, Jesus possessed the Holy Spirit as the Spirit's supreme and unique source, to be conveyed to all those who join themselves to him in faith. As Luke puts it, the risen Jesus received the Spirit in order to give it to us (Acts 2:33; Eph 4:8–10). In the new creation, Christ, the one who breathes forth the Spirit (see John 20:22), assumes the role of God in the first creation.

45

In saying that **the spiritual was not first; rather the natural and then the spiritual**, Paul could simply be stating that in time Adam came before Christ. But that would be obvious to the Corinthians. It seems rather that Paul is alluding to an idea found in Philo, borrowed from Platonic thought, that God first created an ideal man, a "heavenly man," or spiritual man in God's image, and then from the earth the earthly man called Adam in Gen 2:7.[11] No, Paul says, the earthly man, Adam, came first, and the ideal, heavenly man, the true "image of God" (2 Cor 4:4), came last: Christ. The first man was taken **from the earth, earthly**, as in Gen 2:7. **The second man, from heaven.** Is Paul here referring to the incarnation? Although that is possible (see John 3:13; Eph 4:9–10), it is more likely that he is referring to the risen, glorified Christ, who has been the

46–47

10. In 2 Cor 3:18 *kyrios* ("Lord") and *pneuma* ("spirit") are linked, but the expression *kyriou pneumatos* can grammatically be translated in many different ways: "the Spirit of the Lord," "the Lord of the Spirit," "the Lord who is the Spirit" (NAB, NJB, NIV), "the Lord who is Spirit" (JB), "the Lord, the Spirit" (NRSV). Whatever translation is taken, in the light of the rest of Paul's Letters, the identification of the risen Christ with the Spirit is dynamic rather than ontological: Christ is the source of the Spirit.

11. Philo, *Allegorical Interpretation* 1.12.31.

subject all along. If one presses the meaning *from* heaven, then it could refer
to Christ's second coming. But he may simply be contrasting the two realms
of their existence, earth and heaven.

48–49   From Christ, the heavenly man, Paul now moves, as he did earlier (12:14;
15:12–19), to Christ's members. As human beings have shared the nature of the
earthly man, those who share the life of the heavenly man will bear his likeness.
**As we have borne the image of the earthly one, we shall also bear the image
of the heavenly one**. Paul will repeat this in Rom 8:29: "For those whom he
foreknew he also predestined to be conformed to the image of his Son."

Some important manuscripts present an alternate reading of 1 Cor 15:49,
followed by many of the Fathers of the Church: "*Let us* also bear the image of
the heavenly one." The difference is in only one Greek letter, the big ō replacing
the small *o*, so it is easy to see how a scribe could have made a change invol-
untarily, or perhaps voluntarily, seeing the opportunity for exhortation, as the
Fathers certainly did. But most modern translations follow the future tense of
the NAB, since the statement follows logically from the preceding. Notice that
in verses 45–49, Paul is thinking of human nature as such, whether a person is
living or dead. This is important to counter the Corinthians' possible position
that the living could enjoy the resurrection because they are incorrupt, but the
dead could not. No, there is no way even the living are of themselves fit for the
resurrection, as Paul will say explicitly in the next verse.

Reflection and Application (15:35–49)

"Star differs from star in brightness" (15:41). As star differs from star in
brightness, so the glory of each glorified body will differ. This is of great significance. Each of the faithful will give God a particular glory for all eternity that
no one else will give. I have used this truth many times to encourage youth and
particularly people who are down on themselves or suffering, assuring them
that they will give God a glory that no one else will. Such is the uniqueness of
the vocation of each of us.

The Key Is the Transformation of All (15:50–58)

---

[50]This I declare, brothers: flesh and blood cannot inherit the kingdom
of God, nor does corruption inherit incorruption. [51]Behold, I tell you a
mystery. We shall not all fall asleep, but we will all be changed, [52]in an
instant, in the blink of an eye, at the last trumpet. For the trumpet will

sound, the dead will be raised incorruptible, and we shall be changed. [53]For that which is corruptible must clothe itself with incorruptibility, and that which is mortal must clothe itself with immortality. [54]And when this which is corruptible clothes itself with incorruptibility and this which is mortal clothes itself with immortality, then the word that is written shall come about:

> "Death is swallowed up in victory.
> [55]Where, O death, is your victory?
> Where, O death, is your sting?"

[56]The sting of death is sin, and the power of sin is the law. [57]But thanks be to God who gives us the victory through our Lord Jesus Christ.

[58]Therefore, my beloved brothers, be firm, steadfast, always fully devoted to the work of the Lord, knowing that in the Lord your labor is not in vain.

OT: 2 Chron 15:7; Isa 25:8; Hos 13:14
NT: Matt 24:31; Rom 7:13; 1 Cor 6:9–10; 2 Cor 5:4; 1 Thess 4:15, 17
Catechism: condition of the risen body, 999
Lectionary: 15:51–57: Mass for the Dead; 15:54b–57: Vigil of Assumption of the Blessed Virgin Mary

The solemnity with which Paul begins this verse indicates that he is mov- **50** ing this closely reasoned chapter to its climax. He has just been contrasting the earthly with the heavenly, mere human bodily existence with that of the resurrection. The question then remains: how is it possible for a human body, a decaying human body, to attain this glorious future? The contrast is so absolute that no bridge, no crossing over, seems possible. In this, Paul would agree with those Corinthians who deny the resurrection because of what happens to the body at death: how could a rotting body possibly share in the glory of the kingdom? It cannot, Paul affirms, first by using the Jewish terms for humanity in its weakness, **flesh and blood**, and for the life of glory, **the kingdom of God**. This would apply both to the living and the dead. Then he uses terms more understandable in the Greek world: **corruption** and **incorruption**. Whether the body is corruptible, still living, or in fact already corrupted in the grave, it cannot **inherit** the kingdom or the life of incorruption. Human nature cannot raise itself. But God can. How? The next verse explains.

Behold is frequent biblical language for announcing a revelation, as the **51** angel revealed to Mary the †mystery of the miraculous conception (Luke 1:31). **Mystery**, as we explained in commenting on chapter 2, is God's secret, which is now being revealed. Since God's power is the only thing that can work the resurrection, so only his word can reveal it. **We shall not all fall asleep**. Paul considers that there will be people living at the time of the final resurrection. He could hardly be assuming as certain that he will be alive at the Lord's coming, because he knows that Jesus said that the Father had not revealed the time of it (Matt 24:36), nor was it given to the disciples to know when the kingdom would be established (Acts 1:7). And besides, some in the Corinthian church have already died (11:30). The point is that **we will all be changed**, including the living. A change, a transformation, will be necessary not only for those whose bodies have decayed in the tombs but also for the living. That is the key. If some of the Corinthians believe that only the living would be candidates for the resurrection since they could be taken into the kingdom as they are, without change, they are mistaken. The living have no advantage over those whose bodies are rotting in the grave. They too must be transformed. The key is *the transformation of all* into the likeness of Christ.

52–53   In verse 52 Paul uses familiar biblical images for the last day: suddenness, **the last trumpet**, the resurrection. Augustine interprets the trumpet "as some very clear and prominent sign," which he elsewhere calls the voice of the archangel and the trumpet of God (referring to 1 Thess 4:16).[12] By God's re-creative act, **the dead will be raised incorruptible**. Using the passive tense, "will be raised," is a biblical way of saying, "God will raise them." The important thing is not just that the decayed bodies will be raised, but as verse 53 says, **that which is corruptible must clothe itself with incorruptibility, and that which is mortal must clothe itself with immortality**. Paul uses the image of clothing in 2 Cor 5:1–4 for the completion of the body's destiny in its heavenly habitation. But the point again is that *we all* **shall be changed**, not just the already corrupted but the corruptible as well—that is, the living.

54–55   Paul sees this transformation as the fulfillment of a divine promise hidden in two passages of Scripture. His first citation, **Death is swallowed up in victory**, does not follow exactly the LXX of Isa 25:8 as we have it but may reflect an earlier version. In any case it agrees in thought with the Hebrew: "He will destroy death forever." The second quotation is from Hos 13:14 ("Where are your plagues, O death! where is your sting, Sheol!"), but Paul interprets it quite differently from the Hebrew, which depicts the Lord calling up death with its plagues and the netherworld with its sting to destroy Israel for its sins. However, the LXX, which Paul follows here, reads, "I will deliver them out of the power of Hades, and will redeem them from death: where is thy penalty, O death? O Hades, where is thy sting?" Thus in this †rhetorical climax of the chapter, Paul

---

12. Saint Augustine, *Letter 34*; in FC 20:128.

Saint Augustine: The Twinkling of an Eye

LIVING TRADITION

The glance of our eye does not reach nearer objects more quickly and distant ones more slowly. Rather, it reaches both with equal speed. Similarly when, as the apostle says, the resurrection of the dead is effected in the twinkling of the eye, it is as easy for the omnipotence of God and his awe-inspiring authority to raise the recently dead as those long since fallen into decay. To some minds, these things are hard to accept because they are outside their experience, yet the whole universe is full of wonders which seem to us hardly worth noticing or examining, not because they are easily penetrated by our reason but because we are accustomed to seeing them. But I, and those who join me and are striving to understand the "invisible things of God by the things that are made," wonder neither more nor less at the fact that in one tiny seed all that we praise in the tree lies folded away.[a]

a. St. Augustine, *Letter 102, To Deogratias*; in FC 18:151.

turns to the poetry of the Old Testament, where he sees death and the netherworld as enemies that are themselves put to death by the resurrection of the dead. Noting that the sting must be more powerful than a scorpion's, Garland comments, "It enables death to exercise its dominion over the entire world, but its venom has been absorbed by Christ and drained of its potency so that the victory over death now belongs to God and to God's people."[13]

56   This cryptic sentence, **The sting of death is sin, and the power of sin is the law**, is probably shorthand for something Paul has previously explained to the Corinthians, which he will develop at length in his Letter to the Romans (5:12–14; 7:7–13), written from Corinth. He continues to personify death here as a serpent or a scorpion that stings its victim before devouring it. Sin puts its victim on the path to death (Gen 2:17; 4:7). And the law makes sin more deadly because when one sins, one not only goes against one's †conscience but one also disobeys a positive command. That is why it was not sufficient for Christ to rise from the dead: he must also deal the deathblow to sin, the cause of death (15:4–5, 17).

57   This verse comes like a drumroll and a cymbal clash at the climax of a masterpiece. It is like a banner proclaiming victory in a ticker-tape parade—or, in the experience of the Corinthians, the parade of champion athletes in the Isthmian games. Echoing the word **victory** in verse 54, it bears its banner triumphantly in a procession of thanksgiving for the gift made possible **through our Lord**

13. Garland, *1 Corinthians*, 745–46.

Jesus Christ. In Rom 7:25, after a long description of his struggle with sin and temptation, Paul gives thanks to Jesus Christ for his deliverance. Here he dares to use the present tense, **gives,** or "is giving," us the victory, because although the resurrection of the body is in the future, resurrection power is already at work in us through the indwelling Holy Spirit (Rom 8:11). There is thus a solid assurance that, far from being "the most pitiable people of all" (15:19), we are the most blessed.

A final counsel puts a finishing touch on the chapter. Paul has not been engaged in a polemic. He addresses the Corinthians affectionately, **my beloved brothers** (and sisters), whom he has been teaching rather than reprimanding. And then, in keeping with biblical style, his concluding advice provides an †inclusio for a theme with which the chapter began: **Be firm, steadfast** echoes 15:1–2, where he reminds them that the gospel is something "in which you also stand . . . if you hold fast to the word I preached to you." **Always fully devoted to the work of the Lord** echoes earlier themes about the church as the temple (3:16), in which they each have a building role (8:1; 14:12, 26). Finally, whereas denial of the resurrection of the dead would mean that Paul's preaching would have been in vain and their faith would have been in vain (NAB: "empty"; 15:14), the Apostle wants to reassure them that, faithful to his teaching, their **labor is not in vain.**

Reflection and Application (15:50–58)

In an email to a priest friend of mine, an atheist doctor wrote: "What is the meaning to our existence? I would say: The purposes of all living things are two: (1) to survive and (2) to reproduce—to pass life to the next generation. I think there is nothing beyond death for us as individual people." He goes on to say that he does not consider life to be hopeless, but his hopes are strictly limited to this world. The book of Ecclesiastes, which is part of the canon of Scripture, sounds quite similar in its stress on the value of the present life, as long as one limits one's expectations thereto. But Ecclesiastes is only a dark thread that sets off the brilliant gold displayed in the whole Bible. Beyond the valley of human life lies an Everest that is the ultimate destiny of the human person. The human heart has a capacity that the present world cannot fill. What a cruel joke it would be to be endowed with an appetite that could never be fulfilled! The believer knows better: "Thou hast made us for thyself, O God, and our hearts are restless until they rest in Thee" (St. Augustine). And more than that, even our bodies will share the glory of the risen Christ. Such is the hope that hopes beyond human

Reunion in Glory

The vibrancy of our destiny in God can be seen in the sermon that St. Gregory of Nazianzus gave at the funeral of his dearly beloved brother: "Why am I so earthly in my thoughts? I shall await the voice of the archangel, the last trumpet, the transformation of heaven, the change of earth, the freedom of the elements, the renewal of the universe. Then I shall see my brother Caesarius himself, no longer in exile, no longer being buried, no longer mourned, no longer pitied, but splendid, glorious, sublime, such as you were often seen in a dream, dearest and most loving of brothers."[a]

a. Gregory of Nazianzus, *Funeral Sermon: On His Brother Caesarius* 21; in FC 22:23.

hope (Rom 4:18) and empowers Christians to do things they could never do by their own strength, as the heroic lives of the saints attest. Peter quotes Ps 16 as expressing the words of Jesus: "My heart has been glad and my tongue has exulted . . . because you will not abandon my soul to the netherworld, nor will you suffer your holy one to see corruption" (Acts 2:26–27).

But there is more. All creation will have achieved its goal (Rom 8:19–22). The life of glory and the beatific vision is not like looking at God through opera glasses, unconcerned about other viewers—unfortunately a very common idea among Christians. The New Testament describes it as a banquet (Matt 22:1–14; Luke 14:15–24), a city (Rev 21:1–22:5), the procession of a vast multitude (7:9–17), where every tear of separation will be wiped away (21:4).

Conclusion

1 Corinthians 16

This final chapter is really a long postscript. The teaching portion of the letter climaxed with the preceding chapter. This short chapter deals with certain housekeeping details like the collection for the poor in Jerusalem, Paul's travel plans and those of his collaborators, a final exhortation and greeting. These kinds of details bring us down from the lofty teaching on the resurrection to the details of everyday life—a reminder that behind the letter is the story of a lot of personal interaction.

The Collection (16:1–4)

---

¹Now in regard to the collection for the holy ones, you also should do as I ordered the churches of Galatia. ²On the first day of the week each of you should set aside and save whatever one can afford, so that collections will not be going on when I come. ³And when I arrive, I shall send those whom you have approved with letters of recommendation to take your gracious gift to Jerusalem. ⁴If it seems fitting that I should go also, they will go with me.

NT: Acts 13:1–14:28; 2 Cor 8:1–9:15; Rev 1:10

1–2   If you wonder where our Sunday **collection** originated, here would be a good place to start. Paul speaks of this collection at length in 2 Cor 8–9. Of course, there were collections in the synagogues, especially to take care of the poor and widows who had no other means of sustenance. But here it is a question not merely of a collection in one community but also of a massive fund-raising campaign with all the churches Paul had evangelized. Probably there was no other factor more than this that impressed on these early Christians that there was *one* universal Church. It would not only tie all the Pauline communities together but also tie them in a very concrete way to the Jerusalem church. Teaching the doctrine of the unity of the Church was one thing. Experiencing it in the pocketbook was another. In *The Little Prince*, Antoine de Saint-Exupéry writes that it is the time you spend on your rose that makes your rose so dear. Similarly, investing in the Jerusalem mother church means the †diaspora churches would have an ongoing interest in its life and mission. And the collection would also show the Jerusalem church that Paul was not a loose cannon, starting his own church, but that, on the contrary, he had the mother church at heart. The gift would help mold the churches together. Why would the church in Jerusalem need help? Was it due to the idealistic communal life Luke describes in Acts 2:44–45; 4:32–37? To the famine mentioned in Acts 11:28? Or to persecution from the non-Christian Jews in economic ways? Or to the fact that a large number of the new Christians there were from the poor? Perhaps a combination of all of these.

Now in regard to is the way Paul introduced new topics earlier in the letter (7:1, 25; 8:1; 12:1) in response to questions the Corinthians had proposed. So they apparently already knew about the collection and were asking how they should go about gathering it. He tells them to do it in the same way as he **ordered the churches of Galatia**, whom he evangelized on his first missionary journey (Acts 13–14). **The first day of the week** refers to the day of celebrating the Eucharist, the "Lord's day" (Rev 1:10), so called because it was the day of Jesus' resurrection. Every Sunday was considered Easter Sunday, and that is still the spirit of our celebrating the resurrection on the first day of the week. How long the Jewish Christians continued Sabbath observance is not clear, but Acts 20:7 refers to the first day of the week as an established time for gathering to celebrate the Eucharist. On this day the Corinthians should **set aside and save whatever one can afford**. Was this to be done at home or at a weekly collection? Since Paul mentions the first day of the week as the time to do this, it seems more likely that it would be done when the Christians gathered. Unlike the temple tax, which was levied on all equally (Matt 17:24–27), the contributions were to be according to one's means and entirely voluntary. Paul does not want the collection to be **going on** when he arrives. That would be time-consuming, and it appears that he wants the collection to be sent shortly after his arrival. If winter is approaching, when sea travel is risky, it would be necessary to sail quickly.

3–4   Throughout his ministry Paul took every precaution to avoid suspicion of his motives. Thus instead of expecting support from the community, he worked at his trade while at Corinth (Acts 18:3; 1 Cor 9:6, 18), and here he expects the community to appoint trustworthy persons to carry the gift to Jerusalem. Josephus, the first-century Jewish historian, tells of four Jews living in Rome who converted Fulvia, "a woman of great dignity," to the Jewish faith and then persuaded her to give them purple and gold for the temple in Jerusalem, only to take the gifts and abscond with them. Tiberius Caesar, emperor from AD 14 to 37, was informed of the crime by Fulvia's husband, Saturninus, and therefore he banished all Jews from Rome.[1] Such an outcome with the Corinthians' gift for Jerusalem would have been disastrous for Paul's entire Gentile mission. Though the delegates would represent the community, they would also represent Paul, who, as their founder, would **send** them with **letters of recommendation**. Paul was known to the Jerusalem church, as the delegates would not have been, and the gift would strengthen Paul's reputation with the receivers as well as manifest the unity of the Gentile churches with the mother community. Paul himself would lead the delegation **if it seems fitting**. It is significant that he does not say, "I will go with them," but **they will go with me**, for he assumes his primary authority as the founding apostle and the one who will facilitate their introduction to the Jerusalem church. "If it seems fitting" leaves many conditions unspecified, thus respecting both the Corinthians' preferences but also Paul's intention to spend a longer time with the community (16:6–7).

Reflection and Application (16:1–4)

The collection and unity. Probably no other factor on the practical level sealed the unity of Paul's churches with the mother church in Jerusalem more than the gift of the diaspora churches. At the very beginning of his mission, Paul was distrusted by many of the Jewish Christians in Jerusalem, and there was tension leading up to the Council of Jerusalem (Acts 15). Distance and meager communication no doubt added to the unease felt in Jerusalem about Paul's freedom with the Gentiles. The collection was Paul's way of saying: "There is only one Church; we are all one family. My churches are deeply grateful for the

---

1. Josephus, *Jewish Antiquities* 18.3.5. See Suetonius, *Life of Tiberius* 36. This expulsion was earlier than the one under Claudius in AD 49, which Suetonius (*Life of Claudius* 25.4) says was over a dispute among the Jews about a certain "Chrestus," probably a reference to Christ. Acts 18:2 says this was why the Jewish Christian couple Aquila and Priscilla left Rome for Corinth.

spiritual riches we owe to you, and we want to show our gratitude by sharing our resources in return" (see 2 Cor 8:13–14).

Today the collection at Mass is a similar way of testifying to the unity of the community, to the commitment of each individual to its support and growth. We have a sense of ownership in those enterprises in which we invest. From the very beginning, communion in the Church meant more than spiritual fellowship. It was a visible and joyful sharing of resources (Acts 2:44–45).

Paul's Travel Plans (16:5–12)

⁵I shall come to you after I pass through Macedonia (for I am going to pass through Macedonia), ⁶and perhaps I shall stay or even spend the winter with you, so that you may send me on my way wherever I may go. ⁷For I do not wish to see you now just in passing, but I hope to spend some time with you, if the Lord permits. ⁸I shall stay in Ephesus until Pentecost, ⁹because a door has opened for me wide and productive for work, but there are many opponents.

¹⁰If Timothy comes, see that he is without fear in your company, for he is doing the work of the Lord just as I am. ¹¹Therefore no one should disdain him. Rather, send him on his way in peace that he may come to me, for I am expecting him with the brothers. ¹²Now in regard to our brother Apollos, I urged him strongly to go to you with the brothers, but it was not at all his will that he go now. He will go when he has an opportunity.

At this point it is not easy to piece together a map of Paul's travels because the Second Letter to the Corinthians may be a collection of more than one letter, with various comings and goings and not always in chronological order.[2] Furthermore, the fact that he writes of his intentions does not mean that he was able to carry them out. His plan here may not have materialized as he intended, for in 2 Cor 1:8–2:13; 7:5–13 he speaks of intending to go first to Corinth, then to **Macedonia**, and then back to Corinth, whence he hopes they will send him on to Judea (2 Cor 1:16).

In 1 Cor 5:7–8 Paul uses the Feast of Passover as background for his exhortation to "clean out the old yeast" since "our paschal lamb, Christ, has been sacrificed." Hence it is likely that he wrote this letter on or around the Feast of

5–7

8–9

---

2. But see Thomas Stegman's commentary on 2 Corinthians in this series (*Second Corinthians*, CCSS [Grand Rapids: Baker Academic, 2009]). He follows a number of other recent studies that hold it to be a single letter.

Passover, in the spring. Seven weeks later the Jews celebrated the Feast of Weeks, or **Pentecost** in Greek, considered as the conclusion of the †paschal season. It was also a favorable time for travel. Paul does not plan to leave Ephesus before that date, because **a door has opened for me wide and productive for work**. Such work would include evangelizing new converts, giving further formation to those already in the faith, and preparing leaders for the house churches that were beginning to multiply in and around Ephesus. It was no doubt from there that Paul sent Epaphras to evangelize the latter's hometown of Colossae, over a hundred miles to the east (Col 1:7; 4:12; Philem 23). **But there are many opponents** is a bit of an understatement in the light of Paul's expectation of being killed there (2 Cor 1:8–9).

10–11   Paul had earlier mentioned that he was sending Timothy to the community (1 Cor 4:17). Was he the bearer of this letter? Hardly, since Paul here assumes he is still coming. **If Timothy comes** need not express Paul's indecision on whether to send Timothy but rather the many uncertainties of travel and communication and disruption of plans to which all travelers in those days were exposed. Thus Paul frequently hedges his hopes with conditions like, "if the Lord is willing" (4:19), or "if the Lord permits" (16:7). **See that he is without fear** is taken by some scholars as an indication of Timothy's timid character (2 Tim 1:7). That is probably reading too much psychology into the text. Since Timothy was much younger than Paul and possibly fearful that they would not take his delegated authority seriously, Paul simply wants the Corinthians to know that Timothy does have the Apostle's full authority: **he is doing the work of the Lord just as I am**. We know from the rest of the letter that the Corinthians are a fractious lot, and if they can fight over which leader is more important (1:11–17), they might easily brush Timothy aside as being a second-class leader in comparison with Paul, the original apostle. Hence **no one should disdain him**. He will have a difficult mission, no doubt, if he is to follow up and even enforce the severe corrections Paul has laid out in this letter and to reconcile the discordant groups within the community. Thus the Apostle hopes that Timothy, having accomplished his mission, may return to Paul **in peace** and not burdened by failure and rejection. **The brothers** who would accompany Timothy returning to Paul are no doubt his traveling companions.

12   Calling **Apollos** as **our brother** underlines Paul's conviction that, far from being a threat to Paul, this early, popular preacher was one with Paul in a common mission (3:5–8; 4:6). Paul was not loathe to send him with Timothy's companions; in fact, he **urged him strongly** to do so. **But it was not at all his will that he go now**. The word "his" in "his will" is supplied by most modern translations, although some of the Fathers take the phrase to mean that "it is not God's will that he go now." The next sentence, however, makes it likely that it was Apollos who felt strongly that he should not go now: **He will go when he has an opportunity**. What caused Apollos's reluctance? Was he afraid that he might stir up more party spirit? Did he feel that Paul needed his help in the expanding community in Ephesus, or in the possibility of Paul's imprisonment? We can do no more than guess.

Final Exhortation and Greeting (16:13–24)

> ¹³Be on your guard, stand firm in the faith, be courageous, be strong. ¹⁴Your every act should be done with love.
>
> ¹⁵I urge you, brothers—you know that the household of Stephanas is the firstfruits of Achaia and that they have devoted themselves to the service of the holy ones—¹⁶be subordinate to such people and to everyone who works and toils with them. ¹⁷I rejoice in the arrival of Stephanas, Fortunatus, and Achaicus, because they made up for your absence, ¹⁸for they refreshed my spirit as well as yours. So give recognition to such people.
>
> ¹⁹The churches of Asia send you greetings. Aquila and Prisca together with the church at their house send you many greetings in the Lord. ²⁰All the brothers greet you. Greet one another with a holy kiss.
>
> ²¹I, Paul, write you this greeting in my own hand. ²²If anyone does not love the Lord, let him be accursed. *Marana tha.* ²³The grace of the Lord Jesus be with you. ²⁴My love to all of you in Christ Jesus.

OT: Josh 1:6–7; 2 Sam 10:12; Ps 27:14
NT: Matt 24:42; 25:13; John 13:34; Eph 6:11–13; 1 Thess 5:6; Heb 13:17; Rev 22:20
Catechism: keeping watch, 2849; respect for church leaders, 1269; Marana tha, 451, 671, 1130, 1403

Concluding the letter, Paul first gives a general exhortation (16:13–14), then a specific application in regard to Stephanas, who has arrived in Ephesus with his companions (16:15–18), and finally his own parting greetings.

13–14

Be on your guard ("Be vigilant," NJB; "Be awake to all the dangers," JB; "Keep alert," NRSV) picks up the Master's constant warning to his disciples: "Watch" (RSV: Matt 24:42; 25:13), particularly the warning to his three closest ones in the garden of Gethsemane: "Keep watch" (26:38), where the injunction is equivalent to praying lest they fall in the hour of trial (26:41). "Stay awake" implies that some temptations, whether to embrace erroneous teaching or to yield to immorality, come by surprise. In Christian vocabulary one really sleeps only in death, and until then life is a constant wakefulness, begun at baptism: "Awake, O sleeper, and arise from the dead, and Christ will give you light" (Eph 5:14). Having corrected the Corinthians on their failings and sins, Paul wants them to be alert lest those or other deceptions catch them off guard. This will help them to **stand firm in the faith, be courageous, be strong**. This triple exhortation echoes Paul's favorite image for spiritual growth, both of the individual and the Church. Christian tradition has developed many images for the Christian life: it is a journey, the climbing of a mountain, a spiritual ladder, and so on. But for Paul the Christian life is a *growth* in strength and stability. It may be less dramatic but, like the tree that sinks its roots ever deeper into the soil, growth is measured by stability that enables fruitfulness. Like the acorn that becomes a tree, it means becoming daily more and more what you are in Christ: become what you are! Thus in Eph 3:17 he prays that his readers may be "rooted . . . in love," with God's *agapē* being the life-giving soil in which the tree of faith will draw its nourishment and strength and growth. So here Paul adds: **Your every act should be done with love**. That is no small order, as we will observe below. This statement sums up a major theme of the epistle: "Love builds up" (8:1), and it is the center of all charismatic activity in the Church (chap. 13).

15–16   Suddenly Paul's thoughts turn to **Stephanas**. Paul himself had baptized him and his household (1:16), **the firstfruits of Achaia**. This term, which Paul also uses for Christ as the first to rise from the dead (15:20, 23), not only means that others would follow but also conveys a certain seniority, dignity, or leadership, although the context makes it clear that what they led in was **service of the holy ones**. They **devoted themselves** to that service; the expression suggests that the community became a priority for them, probably even financially, if indeed the mention of "household" indicates that Stephanas was a person of means. Were they given some form of pastoral responsibility in the community? **Be subordinate to such people** certainly suggests that they and other †ministers—**everyone who works and toils with them**—should be listened to. It is sometimes suggested that the Corinthian church community had no local authority but survived and flourished merely by the †charisms of the individuals. Aside from being sociological nonsense,[3] this also goes against evidence in Paul's earliest letter that there were in the community those who "are over you in the Lord" (1 Thess 5:12). Admittedly, authority structure is not an issue in the letter, and the emphasis here is on selfless service, but **be subordinate** does imply following their directives as well as their example (see above on 1:16).

3. In one of his lectures Luke Timothy Johnson points out that if you give a task to ten people in a room without a designated leader, before long a leader will emerge.

Stephanas is quite likely the bearer and the reader of this letter, with authority from Paul to interpret it for the community.

Stephanas, Fortunatus, and Achaicus are probably the ones who brought   **17–18**
Paul the Corinthians' letter, which gave the apostle the occasion to answer many of their questions. They brought great joy to Paul and helped fill the gap he experienced by their absence. They not only **refreshed** Paul's **spirit** but also the spirits of the Corinthians: **yours . . . as well.** How could their visit to Paul refresh the Corinthians' spirit? That probably means that on their return to Corinth, they would refresh the spirit of the community by the happy news of the visit.

In sending **greetings** from **the churches of Asia,** in the plural, Paul suggests   **19**
that by this time there are several house churches not only in the areas around Ephesus but also in the city itself, a further indication of the success of his mission there and the reason why he feels he cannot immediately leave for Corinth. This is confirmed by the mention of **Aquila and Prisca together with the church at their house.** Aquila was a native of Pontus (Acts 18:2) but had lived with his wife in Rome. They were Jewish Christians who belonged to one of the synagogues in Rome, but the preaching about Christ led to such conflict among the Jews that the emperor Claudius expelled all Jews from Rome in AD 49 (Acts 18:2). The couple landed in Corinth, where Paul first met them; he lodged with them and labored in their workshop, making tents (Acts 18:2–3). After some time they moved to Ephesus, where they helped Paul in his evangelizing ministry. It was probably there, where Paul ran into life-threatening dangers (1 Cor 15:32; 2 Cor 1:8–9), that they "risked their necks" on his behalf (Rom 16:4). After Claudius was assassinated in AD 54 and before Paul wrote his Letter to the Romans, they moved back to Rome, perhaps as a vanguard for him, for they are the first ones mentioned in Paul's long list of greetings in Rom 16 (v. 3).

Greet one another with a holy kiss. We can imagine that this letter was read   **20**
by Stephanas to the gathered community in the context of the liturgy, and after its conclusion the community would greet Stephanas and companions who may have arrived with him with the kiss of peace and would exchange that kiss with one another. It would be a sign of their acceptance of Paul's message but also of their acceptance and love of one another, which was not a minor issue throughout the letter.

Paul regularly dictated his letters but frequently would add his own signature   **21–22**
("with what large letters," Gal 6:11; see Col 4:18; 2 Thess 3:17). Paul's invoking a curse on **anyone** who **does not love the Lord** may well come as a shock to today's Christian reader. We may wonder if this is the same Paul who sings so lyrically about love in chapter 13, teaches that love builds up (8:1), that love fulfills the

law (Rom 13:8, 10) and extends to all (1 Thess 3:12). Yes, it is the same Paul, but we need to hear his words in the light of the whole Bible and of this letter in particular. The word *anathema*, **accursed**, is not used as a curse upon all unbelievers. It is a formula for exclusion from the community.[4] In Deut 27:14–26 there is a series of twelve curses upon those Israelites who violate different stipulations of the moral law, concluding with "Cursed be anyone whose actions do not uphold the words of this law!" Paul cites this curse in Gal 3:10. Now we have seen that there are certain things that Paul has clearly said merit excommunication from the community. He gives chief attention to the incestuous union of a man with his father's wife, but he extends it to other forms of immorality (1 Cor 5:1–13). Without using the word "curse," the Apostle warns that the disastrous effects of Israel's infidelity in the desert could be visited upon those members of the community who worship idols or wallow in immorality (10:1–22). Paul's statement could also be a way of showing that those who curse Jesus (12:3) will themselves suffer the curse. This *anathema*, then, is like a thunderclap climaxing the publicly proclaimed letter. Addressed to the community, it echoes Joshua's "Choose today whom you will serve" (Josh 24:15), as if Paul were saying: "I'm not kidding in what I have written. It's a matter of being in or out. Decide!"

Marana tha. Here Paul repeats an Aramaic phrase that by this time has become a catchword in the Christian communities: "Our Lord, come!" (NRSV; see Rev 22:20). It was a prayer for the glorious †parousia of the Lord Jesus.

23–24   Paul had begun his letter by wishing his people **grace** (1:3), and now he concludes it with the same. This is not a mere formality, nor is it accidental. Grace could be called the heart of Paul's gospel. He certainly hammered it home to the Galatians, who were forgetting it in favor of circumcision and the food laws, and it becomes a major theme of his Letter to the Romans. Christian life is a response to the gift of God in Christ Jesus. And finally, Paul sends them his *agapē*: **My love to all of you in Christ Jesus**. If he has said some hard things to his people in this letter, it is only because authentic love is "living the truth in love" (Eph 4:15), and he who devoted an entire chapter (13) of this letter to *agapē* cannot fail to embrace them, even at a distance, with the love of which he himself has been the unworthy recipient.

Reflection and Application (16:13–24)

As we reflect on the entire letter in the light of Paul's concluding lines, we learn much about the Apostle's selection, formation, and work with his collaborators.

4. See note in NAB on 16:22.

First of all, as we have pointed out in the commentary, Paul was not a Lone Ranger. He worked in teams. We can see that teamwork even in his letters, which often introduce others as cosenders: Sosthenes (1 Cor 1:1), Timothy (2 Cor 1:1; Phil 1:1; Col 1:1; 1 Thess 1:1; 2 Thess 1:1; Philem 1), and Silvanus (1 Thess 1:1; 2 Thess 1:1). Those whom he recruited were, on the one hand, persons experienced and mature in the faith, and therefore probably older, like heads of households such as Stephanas and probably Titus (Justus), Silvanus, and Sosthenes (who may have been the synagogue official in Acts 18:17). But he also chose young Timothy, whom he took with him, forming him on the way. He must have seen great promise in this young man, whom he grew to love and entrust with some of his most delicate missions, like the one to Corinth (16:10). We do not know Epaphroditus's previous qualifications, but he proved worthy of the title of Paul's "brother and co-worker and fellow soldier" (Phil 2:25). Paul appointed a number of women to important ministries in his communities, and one married couple, Priscilla (Prisca for short) and Aquila, and they instructed the preacher Apollos in the faith (Acts 18:26). Although Paul, at the beginning of his second journey, had a falling out with Barnabas over John Mark (Acts 15:36–39), we do not detect in the letters any moments of strife between Paul and his collaborators. On the contrary, there is a sense that all are in the same Christ-given mission, and Paul supports them warmly, even affectionately (2 Cor 8:23; Phil 2:19–24). He considers them his brothers and sisters (2 Cor 2:13; Phil 2:25).

All this has much to say about ministry in the Church today. At times Church units have fallen into the secular boss-subordinate model, where those in authority "lord it over them, and their great ones make their authority over them felt" (Mark 10:42). But Jesus said, "It shall not be so among you" (10:43). We sense in Paul and his co-workers not only a servant leadership but also a fraternal loyalty because they are bound together not by a job to get done but by a mission to fulfill—and more important, they are bound by a common brotherhood in Christ.

This attitude should spill over beyond the parish. I have begun to work at a spiritual practice that has helped both me and others. When driving in traffic, I ask myself whether that other driver is my competitor or my brother or sister. It does make a difference.

Suggested Resources

From the Christian Tradition

Bray, Gerald, ed. *1–2 Corinthians*. Vol. 7 of ACCS. Downers Grove, IL: InterVarsity, 1999.

St. John Chrysostom. *Homilies on First Corinthians*. Vol. 12 of NPNF1. Edited by Philip Schaff. Translated by Talbot W. Chambers. Buffalo: Christian Literature Publishing Co., 1889. Available online: http://www.newadvent.org/fathers/2201.htm.

Kovacs, Judith L., trans. and ed. *1 Corinthians: Interpreted by Early Christian Commentators*. The Church's Bible. Grand Rapids: Eerdmans, 2005.

Scholarly Commentaries

Garland, David E. *1 Corinthians*. BECNT. Grand Rapids: Baker Academic, 2003.

Thiselton, Anthony C. *The First Epistle to the Corinthians: A Commentary on the Greek Text*. NIGTC. Grand Rapids: Eerdmans, 2000.

Midlevel Commentaries

Hays, Richard B. *First Corinthians*. Interpretation. Louisville: John Knox, 1997.

Thiselton, Anthony C. *1 Corinthians: A Shorter Exegetical and Pastoral Commentary*. Grand Rapids: Eerdmans, 2006.

Popular Commentaries

Hahn, Scott, Curtis Mitch, and Dennis Walters. *The First and Second Letters of Saint Paul to the Corinthians*. 2nd ed. Ignatius Catholic Study Bible. San Francisco: Ignatius, 2004.

Zanchettin, Leo, ed. *I and II Corinthians: A Devotional Commentary; Meditations on St. Paul's First and Second Letters to the Corinthians*. Ijamsville, MD: Word Among Us, 2003.

Other Resources

Murphy-O'Connor, Jerome. *St. Paul's Corinth: Texts and Archaeology*. Collegeville, MN: Liturgical Press, 1990.

Glossary

agapē **meal**: In connection with the Eucharist, Paul's communities had a love feast, much like our potluck suppers, in which the sharing of food symbolized the *koinōnia*, the community of all in Christ. We do not know whether the Eucharist was celebrated before, during, or after the meal. Though Paul did not use the term *agapē* for this arrangement, it soon became a popular designation for the meal that accompanied the Eucharist.

age: "This age," meaning the present era of the world, is in contrast to "the age to come," the final establishment of the kingdom of God, involving the resurrection of the just. "Rulers of this age" (1 Cor 2:8) may refer to those in political or religious power who despise the message of the gospel, or to the demonic powers who rule over the world (1 John 5:19).

apocalyptic: from the Greek *apokalypsis*, meaning "revelation," referring to dramatic, usually visionary scenarios of the end times.

brother of the Lord: Different from James the son of Zebedee, called with his brother John to follow Jesus (Matt 4:21), another James is referred to as "brother of the Lord" in Gal 1:19 (see 1 Cor 9:5). Other brothers of Jesus are mentioned in the Gospels (Matt 12:46; Mark 6:3; John 2:12). The Hebrew and Aramaic words for "brother" can cover a wide range of relatives, as does the word "brother" in many languages even today. Abraham's nephew is called his brother (Gen 13:8), and in the same Gospel that speaks of the brothers of Jesus (Mark 3:31–34), Philip is called brother of Herod, though he is his half brother (Mark 6:17).

Captivity Epistles: Those Letters of Paul indicating that they were written from prison: Ephesians, Colossians, Philippians, and Philemon. Second

Timothy was also written from prison, but that letter is classified with 1 Timothy and Titus as one of the Pastoral Epistles.

charism: a spiritual gift bestowed on the individual by God primarily for the benefit, the building up, of the Church. Distinct from the grace that saves, which is given to all, charisms differ according to the individual and God's free choice. Paul urges all to seek the "spiritual gifts," or charisms (1 Cor 14:1). The lists in 1 Cor 12 and 14 and Rom 12:6–8 are not meant to be exhaustive, for they do not mention celibacy and marriage, yet these are also considered charisms (1 Cor 7:7).

chiasm, chiastic (from the *x*-shaped Greek letter *chi*): a literary arrangement of words or ideas in a symmetrical pattern, as *A, B, B, A* or *A, B, C, B, A,* or a more extended pattern.

conscience: "a judgment of reason whereby the human person recognizes the moral quality of a concrete act that he is going to perform, is in the process of performing, or has already completed" (Catechism, 1778).

diaspora: literally, "dispersion," referring to Jews living outside of Palestine.

diatribe: a rhetorical technique in which an author or speaker engages in an argument with an imaginary opponent (see, for instance, 1 Cor 15:35–38).

Didache: Greek word (*didachē*) meaning "teaching," short for *The Teaching of the Apostles*, an early handbook of Christian ethical, liturgical, and community instructions, usually dated by scholars to the late first century. It concluded with a chapter warning about the final times.

elect ("chosen"): the faithful who are chosen by God's grace for eternal life. This does not deny the free will of those who choose to reject God's offer of salvation nor the free will of those who accept his call and live accordingly. In the parable of the banquet, which ends, "Many are invited, but few are chosen," that is, "elect" (Matt 22:14), those who are unworthy to enter are those who were invited but refused to come. Those who accepted are "the chosen."

eschatology, eschatological: having to do with the end times (from *eschatos,* "last"). In the biblical view, history is linear—moving from a beginning to a conclusion at some point in the future—as opposed to cyclical. Depending on the context, eschatological language in the New Testament is sometimes used to indicate that the final times are already here with Jesus and the gift of the Holy Spirit ("realized eschatology"); at other times it refers to the end yet to come.

inclusio: a unit of text framed by the repetition at the end of the same word, words, or ideas used at the beginning; an inclusio gives a sense of unity to the enclosed text and provides it with a pleasing conclusion. Very common in ancient oral and written exposition.

kerygma: the apostolic preaching or its content, the heart of which was the saving death and resurrection of Christ and the sending of the Holy Spirit.

minister: often used today for clergy, in the New Testament the term may have the broadest sense of "servant" or, more narrowly, of one officially designated to provide the community some specific service, as, for example, in Acts 6:1–6.

Montanism: a Christian movement begun in Asia Minor in the middle of the second century by Montanus, with two women, Prisca and Maximilla, who claimed direct prophetic revelation from God. It spread to Europe and Africa, eventually winning the Church writer Tertullian to its cause. It collided with Church authorities who condemned it.

mystery: from the Greek verb *myō*, meaning "to be shut or closed," especially of the lips or eyes. In Paul's writings it refers to God's plan of salvation, which was hidden in God but is now revealed in Christ. See "paschal mystery" below.

parousia: the second coming of Christ.

paschal mystery: The life, death, and resurrection of Christ and the sending of the Holy Spirit is, as a whole, called paschal because it is patterned on the Jewish Passover (English "Pasch"; Greek *pascha*; Hebrew *pesakh*), celebrating the Israelites' deliverance from slavery in Egypt, an Old Testament event fulfilled in Christ's passing from death to life and opening for his followers the path to salvation.

paschal, or Passover, meal: The main event of the Jewish celebration of Passover, commemorating the Lord's deliverance of Israel from Egypt. Jesus said he longed to eat "this Passover with you before I suffer" (Luke 22:15), and so the Jewish feast became the Christian Passover and the paschal meal became the Eucharist, which celebrates the Christian exodus from sin and death effected by the death and resurrection of Jesus.

paschal season: in the Jewish calendar, the time between Passover and the Feast of Weeks; in the Christian calendar, the time from Easter to Pentecost.

patron-client relationship: The Mediterranean societies of New Testament times were generally structured in such a way that an individual with fewer means of support (a client) could enter into a relationship with a person of greater means (a patron). The patron would assume a certain degree of responsibility for his client, and the client in turn would render services to the patron.

rhetoric: the art of persuasive discourse. On the one hand, in its positive sense it is obvious that a message delivered in pleasing and persuasive speech is more likely to be effective than one poorly constructed. On the other hand, rhetoric is sometimes used to mean a polished veneer to unsubstantial or deceptive content.

Septuagint (abbreviated as LXX): a Greek translation of the Hebrew Bible dating from the third and second centuries BC, so called because of the tradition that it was the work of seventy(-two) scribes. Often quoted in the New Testament, it was the Bible used by Greek-speaking Jews and Christians.

Shepherd of Hermas: a noncanonical but popular Christian writing of Roman provenance, with parts of the *Mandates* and *Similitudes* and *Visions* ranging from the first to the second century AD. It deals with such issues as postbaptismal sin and repentance, the relationship of rich and poor in the community, and for our purposes here, discernment of true and false prophecy.

sophist: any of a number of Greek teachers of philosophy, rhetoric, or art who flourished in the fifth century BC but whose influence continued in their emphasis on clever, subtle rhetoric over substance, and in their reputation for specious reasoning.

syncretism: the fusion of two or more religious beliefs or practices, as was common in the Hellenistic period and in the history of Hinduism.

testimonia: a Latin term referring to accounts of personal witnesses, especially to the resurrection of Jesus. It can also refer to scriptural texts bearing witness to Christ.

type, antitype: Type refers to a person, an event, or an object in the Old Testament in which the New Testament sees a prefigurement of something that is fulfilled in the New Covenant. The fulfillment is the antitype. For example, the Passover lamb is a type of Christ, who is the antitype, the fulfillment.

Index of Pastoral Topics

This index indicates where 1 Corinthians provides material related to topics that may be useful for evangelization, catechesis, apologetics, or other forms of pastoral ministry.

Index of Sidebars

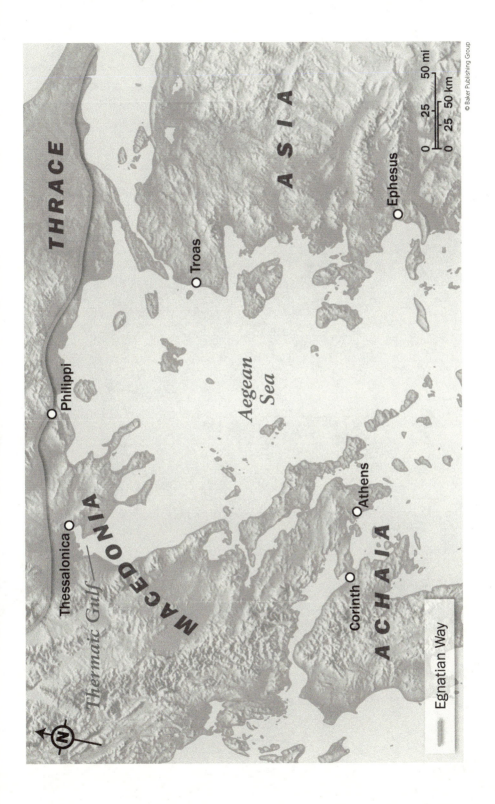

THRACE

MACEDONIA

THessalonica

Thermaic Gulf

Philippi

Troas

*Aegean
Sea*

ASIA

Ephesus

Athens

Corinth

ACHAIA

N

Egnatian Way

0   25   50 mi

0   25   50 km

© Baker Publishing Group